INTEGRATED MARKETING COMMUNICATION

CREATIVE STRATEGY
FROM IDEA TO IMPLEMENTATION

THIRD EDITION

Robyn Blakeman

University of Tennessee, Knoxville

ROWMAN & LITTLEFIELD
Lanham • Boulder • New York • London

Executive Editor: Elizabeth Swayze
Assistant Editor: Carli Hansen
Senior Marketing Manager: Kim Lyons
Interior Designer: Andrea Reider

Credits and acknowledgments for material borrowed from other sources, and reproduced with permission, appear on the appropriate page within the text.

Published by Rowman & Littlefield
A wholly owned subsidiary of The Rowman & Littlefield Publishing Group, Inc.
4501 Forbes Boulevard, Suite 200, Lanham, Maryland 20706
www.rowman.com

Unit A, Whitacre Mews, 26-34 Stannary Street, London SE11 4AB, United Kingdom

British Library Cataloguing in Publication Information Available

Library of Congress Cataloging-in-Publication Data

Names: Blakeman, Robyn, 1958– author.
Title: Integrated marketing communication : creative strategy from idea to
    implementation / Robyn Blakeman, University of Tennessee, Knoxville.
Description: Third edition. | Lanham : Rowman & Littlefield, [2018] |
    Includes bibliographical references and index.
Identifiers: LCCN 2017042452 (print) | LCCN 2017051349 (ebook) | ISBN
    9781538101063 (electronic) | ISBN 9781538101049 (cloth : alk. paper) |
    ISBN 9781538101056 (pbk. : alk. paper)
Subjects: LCSH: Communication in marketing.
Classification: LCC HF5415.123 (ebook) | LCC HF5415.123 .B557 2018 (print) |
    DDC 658.8/02—dc23
LC record available at https://lccn.loc.gov/2017042452

Printed in the United States of America

Contents

Preface

Selling a product or service today requires the creative and strategic use of multiple media options. Understanding how to use those options to best effect requires having a firm handle on how business theory affects the development of the creative message. Professors, instructors, and students in myriad disciplines will appreciate the unique approach of this book—which takes a combined look at both marketing *and* advertising rather than focusing on just one or the other. The goal here is to provide readers with a simple introduction to how the business of marketing can be transformed into a visual/verbal message and how that message can in turn be strategically delivered.

Today's business environment requires students to be well-rounded professionals, understanding not only the business of advertising and marketing but also how to choose and employ the best media options to deliver the message and reach the intended target audience. This book focuses on:

- communicators employing the correct message;
- placing the message in the most appropriate media; and
- using the most advantageous communications approach.

Instructors who can combine both marketing and advertising tactics let students know that marketing and design are no longer separate entities; they are the result of all parts working as a cohesive whole.

In order to achieve this cohesive visual/verbal message, the choice of media vehicles employed depends on several factors, such as a brand's life-cycle stage, copy length, who is to be reached, what objectives need to be strategically accomplished, how the most important attribute will be visually and verbally presented, and the overall tone of voice used to deliver the message throughout the campaign. To ensure effective delivery, the text breaks down the varied media options into individual chapters, allowing instructors to tailor both lecture and projects around how each vehicle can or cannot accomplish the overall marketing and advertising goals.

Instructors teaching courses that focus on finding strategic and creative solutions to business problems will find that this text not only simplifies abstract design and con-cept-building principles but also clearly and simply outlines:

1. how to lay the foundation for the development of a marketing plan, creative strategy, and creative brief;

2. how a creative strategy fits in a business plan and how it is developed and used;
3. how to use a creative brief to develop a brand image and/or concept that is cohesive across multiple media and speaks to the intended target; and
4. how to write and design for multiple media using the strategy developed during the business phase.

To keep up with the ever-changing media environment, I have updated the discussions on newspaper, magazines, out-of-home and transit, electronic media, and mobile to include more interactive options. The discussion on social media has been expanded to include the growing use of video; additional alternative media examples and case studies have also been presented. Although not all visuals used in the text are available in color, the e-edition of the book uses the color images whenever possible. New to the third edition is the inclusion of discussion questions and additional teaching materials.

A complimentary Instructor's Manual and Test Bank are available, as well as an open-access Companion Website for students that includes interactive flashcards and other learning material. Visit http://textbooks.rowman.com/blakeman3e or e-mail textbooks@rowman.com for more information.

Introduction

Have you ever seen an ad and said, "Wow, that's cool?" Or thought it was stupid, or that you could do it better? If you have, you're not alone. Unfortunately, creative teams rarely get to do whatever they want with an ad. They must meet strict prerequisites for an ad to be considered effective or successfully sell a product or service. What ends up in print, online, or on television isn't all about the message; it's also about how the message visually and/or verbally accomplishes a marketer's business plan of action.

There's a lot of really good advertising out there, but if an ad doesn't reach the target audience with a relatable message . . . if it doesn't strategically accomplish a predetermined set of objectives or goals . . . if it doesn't clearly push a single attribute important to the target . . . no matter how cool that ad is, it will fail. Some of the most mundane, seemingly uncreative ads you are exposed to are often more successful at accomplishing these prerequisites than their more entertaining counterparts.

Successful, memorable advertising needs to figure out how to tie the business of advertising to the creative of advertising, part of the foundation of integrated marketing communication (IMC). Creative represents the voice of business and can ultimately determine the success or failure of a product or service in the marketplace. It is important for you to understand that the advertising creative process is not an art—it is a marketing function. To be successful, advertising must seamlessly integrate the business of advertising into a visual/verbal message that not only sells but also can build or maintain image as well as engage the target, all at the same time.

In a nutshell, the goal of advertising is to generate revenue through information and entertainment. To do this, account and creative teams must build an interpretive creative strategy based on a sound business plan. A creative strategy looks at who is most likely to purchase and what it will take to get them to purchase. A business plan that employs IMC expands the creative strategy's voice by using one visual/verbal message throughout multiple media. This consistent visual/verbal message can be more accurately targeted to reach those most likely to purchase or use the product or service by incorporating a message developed with their specific needs, wants, and lifestyle in mind.

The development of an effective IMC campaign requires you to look at the creative side of advertising as a part of the business of advertising rather than seeing the two as separate functions within the advertising process. Although two very distinctive and different mind-sets will need to analyze these areas for advertising to succeed or make a profit, they must work together. A creative idea doesn't work unless the groundwork for that idea is laid down in the marketing process, is tied directly to those most likely to use or purchase the product, and is appropriately placed in media vehicles they are likely to see, hear, and/ or interact with.

The focus of this textbook is to teach you (1) how to interpret a business plan to create an idea and (2) how IMC uses a strategic approach to build and sustain brand-to-target relationships using a coordinated message in diverse media. We'll first cover the differences between traditional advertising and IMC and then delve into the details of marketing plans, creative briefs, copywriting, and campaigns. Handy templates serve as a guide to help you execute your creative ideas. In the latter half of the book, we'll look at specific media—traditional outlets such as newspapers and magazines but also social media, mobile, and new alternatives. Each of these chapters explains the medium, considers the pros and cons of using it in an IMC campaign, and offers hands-on details for crafting creative in that format. Case studies throughout the text are designed to help you see IMC in action.

Integrated Marketing Communication

Here We Go Again

Understanding **advertising** today requires a look at where advertising in the United States began. **Integrated marketing communication (IMC)** can trace its roots to long before the invention of computers and industrialized manufacturing, all the way back to one-on-one trade among friends and neighbors.

Early in the settlement of the United States, most of the population lived and worked in small, tight-knit communities. While word of mouth was probably the first form of communication between sellers and potential buyers, it was personalized selling that built and retained relationships between local consumers and merchants.

Local citizens could rely on area craftsmen for handcrafted items such as furniture and boots and shoes that were custom made to meet a buyer's individual needs. Household goods such as pots, pans, coffee, tea, ammunition, and tobacco were sold by (or could be ordered through) the resident grocer, while local farmers supplied the community with a variety of meats, fruits, vegetables, and dairy products.

The mid-nineteenth century ushered in the Industrial Revolution, and for the first time, mass-produced goods, often manufactured in far-off places, were sold to a wide audience. The custom work of the craftsman was all but replaced with machine-produced products, effectively ending the two-way dialogue between local merchants and residents. Taking its place was a generic one-way statement from an anonymous manufacturer to an unknown, uninvolved consumer. Limited competition and media options made advertising efforts simple and wide-reaching exposure more or less guaranteed—for a while.

Advances in technology eventually expanded media options and encouraged competition. Product categories once dominated—often for generations—by one brand were suddenly inundated with multiple equivalent products. Features once considered unique or cutting edge in one brand could now be easily and economically copied by other brands within a category so that what was once a selling point for a particular brand became a routine product feature within months. Without any distinguishing features or meaningful differences between individual products, brand image erodes—along with consumer brand loyalty. The unqualified number of diverse and often misused or incorrectly used media options contributed to this erosion by splintering consumer attention further—offering too many media options to successfully guarantee reaching a specific target audience—and diluting brand awareness.

Today, IMC has resurrected the relationship between buyer and seller by re-creating an environment of consumer-focused communication efforts. IMC's ability to strategically deliver a consistent message to the right audience through the correct media is crucial to the successful implementation of an IMC creative series. To do this effectively, marketers must develop a creative strategy that not only coordinates advertising efforts, both visually and verbally, but also answers the target market's most important question: *What's in it for me?*

What Is Integrated Marketing Communication?

IMC, also known as **relationship marketing,** works to interactively engage a specific individual, using a specific message through specific media outlets. The goal is to build a long-term relationship between buyer and seller by involving the targeted individual in an interactive or two-way exchange of information. Expertly placed media efforts and the use of computer **databases** play a big role in getting the message to the right target audience, as does the development of a consistent visual/verbal image for the product or service.

It wasn't until the mid-1990s that IMC first began to attract and hold the attention of marketers. Up to this point, most advertising dollars were spent on more traditional mass-media advertising, such as print (newspapers and magazines) and broadcast (radio and television), that sent a more generalized message to a large audience. IMC, in contrast, focuses on the use of alternative or promotional media, such as direct marketing and sales promotion, the Internet, and social media, to name just a few, to reach individual consumers with a personalized message. Consumers in today's marketplace are inundated with thousands of advertising messages daily; they must pick and choose which will be remembered and which will be ignored. IMC attempts to ensure that the message will be remembered by replacing unwanted one-size-fits-all tactics with an individualized message to a much smaller target audience in language consumers can understand and relate to and in media they are sure to see and use.

Messages used in an **IMC campaign** must be tailor made to fit a specific target audience's needs, wants, and lifestyle. The goal is to reach one individual within the target with a specially designed message that will create a lasting relationship and develop a brand-loyal consumer who will continue to purchase that brand without the need for continuing advertising efforts.

Each brand or product must be as individualized as the target. The enormous number of media options and virtual product anonymity in many categories make it necessary for marketers to create an identity for a brand or service that will make it stand out from the competition.

It is important that the product's image match the target's self-image, and the advertised message must get and hold the target's attention among the clutter of competing brands.

If it sounds as though it's more expensive to get a message to individual targets compared to a mass audience, it is. IMC is often more expensive to employ than traditional advertising methods, but the results can be worth the expense.

Communicating with a target that has a known interest in the product or service increases **reach**, or the number of interested people who will see the message, and reduces **frequency**, or number of times an ad or promotion will need to be used. Exposure to the message is essentially guaranteed when the message is placed in a special-interest medium the target is known to use, making purchase more likely.

The initial steps required to attract a brand-loyal consumer are more expensive than those needed to retain a brand-loyal customer. Once the consumer thinks of a brand as her only choice, the need for additional communication efforts can be reduced, minimizing costs.

Traditional advertising, on the other hand, takes longer to build loyalty. Because it is less likely a given target will have repeated exposure to a mass-media vehicle, the amount of time required to educate the target on the features and benefits of the product or service is increased. The result is a target who is often unable to recall the product's name at the time of purchase.

Basic Reasons for the Growth of IMC

Technology has changed the way corporations market their products and services. Customers are now in control of what they buy, when they buy, and where and how they buy. Computerized databases have given a name and personality to the mass audience. Advertised messages can be addressed to an individual and can feature products he or she has a known interest in, based on past purchase behavior. The Internet and other interactive media make it easy to purchase virtually any item without leaving the house, at any time of the day or night, using a toll-free number or Internet site. Consumers are better educated about products and can seek out additional information at their leisure. Marketers realize consumers have many product options from which to choose when making a purchase. Because of this, thinking has gone from being sales oriented to being customer driven in a relatively short period of time.

Before IMC, traditional marketing efforts were simple, aimed at making a sale and increasing profits. This type of tactic, where the seller does no more than deliver a message to a buyer, is known as an **inside-out approach**. IMC, on the other hand, is consumer driven and understands the consumer has many choices available in any single product category.

Marketers are now focusing on an **outside-in approach,** in which products are designed to meet consumers' individual needs and wants.

Successfully employing IMC requires a change in corporate philosophy or a different way of thinking about and planning for strategically effective marketing communications. To be effective, IMC must be looked at as a process for building a relationship with the target and developing a product or offering a service that meets the specific needs of targeted individuals. Product performance and quality are also critical components to success. Each time the target repurchases, the product or service must match her expectations and consistently deliver reliable results (see case study 1).

Why IMC Fails

IMC fails when it is seen as just another communication effort rather than a corporate philosophy expressed both inside and out.

Most people think of IMC as being in parity with advertising, with its one-image/one-tone-of-voice approach. However, unlike traditional advertising, IMC really comprises all aspects and any "interaction points" of planned or unplanned communication between the brand, service, or corporation and the target audience and is affected by both inside and outside influences.

Planned contact is external and includes outside advertising and promotions employed to reach the target. **Unplanned contact** is internal, or corporately focused on employees and vendors, and is the least controllable of the two. Because of this, it must be the most flexible form of contact in order to adjust to changing market, corporate, or consumer conditions. Corporate philosophy plays a major role in unplanned contact, which includes:

- Employee gossip
- Word of mouth
- Governmental or media investigations
- Management performance
- Customer service initiatives
- How sales associates greet clientele
- Product quality and performance
- In-store and out-of-store displays
- Packaging
- Distribution
- Price
- Store locations
- Uniforms
- Deliveries
- Delivery drivers
- Dress codes

- Sales tactics
- Management style and/or philosophy

These all will have a direct impact on how the target views the product or service and will affect both initial and repeat sales.

Any change in corporate philosophy brought about by IMC efforts must be communicated internally as well as externally. Even the smallest details affect the success of IMC, and for it to work, every individual in the company, from the top down, must buy into the message being delivered to the consumer. If this is not the case, the target will receive mixed messages: a disconnect between what he hears in communication efforts and what he experiences when dealing with a company representative. Consider the following example: If the message to the public is "Fly the Friendly Skies," every employee with access to the public must be made aware of and understand this message. Nothing will kill the momentum of this advertising campaign faster than the target's meeting an angry ticket agent or snooty customer service representative.

What Drives IMC

To successfully use IMC, corporations must absorb the message into their corporate philosophy to ensure the target receives a consistent message and a reliable product or service. But this is only one of many initiatives that drive IMC. To be truly consumer driven, IMC planning must also address several issues:

- Research
- Database development
- Use of the Internet
- Employing correct media tactics
- Building brand-loyal consumers
- Creating an interactive relationship
- Brand development
- Projecting a consistent visual/verbal image
- The promotional and media mix
- Evaluation

Research

IMC can't work without an intimate knowledge of the intended target audience—those individuals research has determined are most likely to buy the product or use the service. Research is key to understanding what the target audience wants, how buyers will use the product or service, where and how they live, what media vehicles they use or see, and what they are looking for in a customer-brand relationship. Information gathered in the research phase will be used to determine the best promotional and media mix to reach the intended target audience and the type of message that will motivate purchase.

C	**CASE STUDY 1**

IMC Advertising: NIVEA

Overview

NIVEA is one of the most recognized skin and beauty care brands in the world. NIVEA cream was first introduced in 1911, and the NIVEA brand now extends to fourteen product ranges worldwide, from sun care to facial moisturizers, deodorant, and shower products.

Objectives

The goal was to increase UK market share for NIVEA Men, but the brand also wanted greater market penetration for male skin care products. In other words, it wanted not just a greater share of the existing market, it wanted to *expand* that market. It wanted more men buying skin care products. One key aim was to move men from just considering skin care products to making actual purchases.

NIVEA also wanted to sell more male skin care products to women, who research indicated, were often the initial purchaser of skin care products for men. Another objective was to develop the NIVEA Men brand image. The NIVEA brand has always stood for products that are reliable, user-friendly, and good value for money. The brand's core values are security, trust, closeness, and credibility. These values would be strengthened and expanded on with the relaunch, to get more men and women to think of NIVEA as their first choice for skin care.

Tactics

The NIVEA Men team devised marketing strategies to deliver its objectives. These strategies set out how the objectives would be achieved within the designated budget set by the management team.

This focus on product development combined with an emphasis on consumer needs is a key differentiator for NIVEA Men. It is a major reason the brand is still the market leader in the UK for male facial skin care products.

It is important to get the promotional balance right. NIVEA Men promoted the new launches of its products through a mixture of above-the-line and below-the-line promotion. The use of sport was a key element here. NIVEA Men supported football events at a grass-roots level through its partnership with Powerleague to build positive relationships with men and help create stronger brand affinity. It also allowed the brand to build and maintain a consistent dialogue with men, which helped drive sales.

Above-the-line promotion included television and cinema adverts, which reached a wide audience. By linking its products with sports, NIVEA Men aimed to build a positive male image for them. The brand also benefited from press advertorials in popular men's magazines, making daily use of skin care products more acceptable to men.

Promotions were used to attract new customers. For example, distribution of free samples encouraged trial of NIVEA Men products, which drove purchase. These promotions have helped build brand awareness and consumer familiarity, which reinforce the brand presence. There is a dedicated NIVEA Men website to support its products and educate men on their skin care needs. To enhance the brand, a "Configurator" tool was created on the website to help customers determine their skin type and find the products that best suit their needs.

Results

NIVEA Men adopted a range of key performance indicators to assess the success of the brand's relaunch in the UK. It looked at:

- *Market share.* Did the relaunch accelerate this growth and help achieve its market share objectives? NIVEA Men is a market leader in many countries and is consistently gaining additional market share.
- *Overall sales.* Was this in line with objectives? Internationally, NIVEA Men skin care products grew by almost 20 percent. Its sales in the UK market at retail were nearly £30 million and in line with expectations.
- *Brand image ratings.* NIVEA Men won the FHM Grooming Award for Best Skincare Range for the fifth year running. Voted for by consumers, this award illustrates that NIVEA Men has an extremely positive brand image with consumers compared to other brands.
- *Product innovation.* In response to consumer feedback and following extensive product innovation and development, the NIVEA Men range has been expanded and the existing formulations improved.

These results show that in the UK, the NIVEA Men relaunch met its overall targets—a significant achievement considering the difficult economic climate. The marketing plan for the relaunch used past performance and forecast data to create a new marketing strategy. This built on the brand's and company's strengths to take advantage of the changing male attitudes toward using skin care products.

Source: http://businesscasestudies.co.uk/.

Database Development

The growth of IMC can be traced to the development of **database marketing**. Database marketing uses a computer to store personal information about individuals and their past purchase history. Unlike traditional advertising methods, which focus communication efforts on a large group of targeted members, IMC targets individuals. Every time a consumer makes a credit card or grocery store purchase, visits a website, subscribes to a magazine or trade organization, or fills out a warranty or rebate form, personal information about the consumer is gathered and stored in a database. This information is used to direct future communication to only those individuals known to be interested in a product or service, eliminating advertising waste and allowing for a more personalized appeal.

The ability to talk to a target audience member by name is not all that new. What *is* new is how much is known about the targeted individual and her special interests. Because messages can be designed to specifically address issues of importance to the target, the question *What's in it for me?* can be answered for every target group or niche market. Database information also plays a role in determining the best media and promotional mix, creative strategy, and overall message strategy needed to reach the intended target.

Use of the Internet

The use of computer databases to identify targeted audiences and the growth of the Internet as an information source is behind the initial and ongoing success of IMC. The Internet has personalized communication efforts between buyer and seller, moving from talking *at* the target to talking *with* the target (particularly through social media sites). As an educational and informational tool, the Internet can persuade and motivate consumers to take the next action-oriented step—such as picking up the phone and dialing a toll-free number to speak directly to a customer service representative or to request additional information, make a purchase, give feedback, ask for coupons, request sales promotion materials, or enter a contest or sweepstakes—all on their own time, from their own home or office, and with few distractions. The use of credit cards and the availability of multiple quick and easy contact options have made interaction and purchase immediate and, more importantly, interactive.

Consumer use beyond branded pages includes search, viewing branded and original video content, playing games, and interacting with varied social media sites such as Facebook, Pinterest, and YouTube, to name just a few.

Employing Correct Media Tactics

It's no longer necessary for IMC to depend only upon traditional advertising vehicles such as print and broadcast media to reach the intended target audience. Modern IMC is about using any type of communication vehicle to reach the target audience.

It's impossible to develop a relationship if the target never sees the message. Students of advertising often think only of advertising when deciding what media to use when developing their IMC program. But the options are much more diverse than that. The IMC media grab bag also includes public relations, direct marketing and sales promotion, out-of-home and transit, the Internet and social media, mobile marketing, and alternative media sources such as revolving truck-side billboards, ticket stubs, or toll gates.

The focus in IMC is on getting a coordinated message out to the right target via the best media. The advertised message must appear in the right place at the right time, no matter how unusual that "place" may be. If the target can see it or hear it, it is a potential advertising vehicle. It doesn't matter if it's a shopping bag, a bathroom stall, the sidewalk, a bathroom mirror, an athlete's body, athletic gear, T-shirts, shopping carts, product placement in a television show or movie, pop-ups, or a scrawl on a curb—everything has message potential written all over it. This kind of advertising is known as alternative media. The role alternative media plays is small compared to that of the promotional, traditional mass-media vehicles and digital options, but it is no less important. Although traditional media vehicles are where most advertising is still placed, don't stop there. Times are a-changin', and traditional vehicles might not be the best places to find the target.

If the message doesn't reach the target audience where it is, budgets are wasted; and unless it is utterly unique, the product will not gain enough acceptance to survive in a cluttered product category. The increasing cost of mass-media advertising makes the old hit-or-miss ways of advertising obsolete. Advertising messages must be placed in the media that research has proved to be seen or used by the target market on a regular basis. What media should be used will depend on the target, the objectives that need to be accomplished, and the overall strategy.

Building Brand-Loyal Consumers: The Long Road to Loyalty

For decades the middleman—the retailer—has successfully silenced communication between buyer and seller. IMC removes this barrier by encouraging consumers to actively participate in communication with the seller.

Individually targeted buyers can easily gather information or shop from the comfort of their own homes at times convenient to them. By picking up the phone or visiting a website, they can place an order, ask a question, or request additional information from a knowledgeable customer service or technical representative. In many cases, consumers can order products built to their individual specifications, make suggestions, and give feedback about a product or service or about customer service initiatives. This **two-way dialogue** between buyer and seller solicits brand loyalty by allowing the consumer to receive a product specifically made to his needs and be a major contributor to ongoing product and corporate development. **Brand loyalty** means that the target will not only favor a product or brand over all the others in the category but will do so reliably, building the lasting, long-term relationship needed to build **brand equity** or become the product leader in any one category.

By concentrating communication efforts on a specific group of individuals, you develop an approach that consistently and effectively speaks to the target's needs. Message development based on a target's needs, wants, and special interests sets a product or service apart from competitors, and this is the basis for an effective creative strategy.

Creating an Interactive Relationship

It took a long time for today's product and corporate leaders to understand that it is less expensive to retain old customers than it is to constantly look for new ones. Communication tactics used in an IMC approach shift communication efforts away from the traditional **one-way mass-media monologue** to a two-way dialogue between buyer and seller. This approach builds a relationship by allowing the target to give feedback, discuss ideas, and register complaints as an involved consumer.

Building a relationship between buyer and seller is a necessary precursor to building a brand-loyal consumer, and brand-loyal consumers require less advertising effort, which leads to rising profit margins.

Relationships are built on dialogue. One feature that distinguishes IMC from traditional advertising efforts is that advertising speaks *at* a group of individuals through mass-media vehicles about perceived problems or interests, while IMC speaks *to* (or *with*) a single individual about his known problems or special interests.

Brand Development

Because today's consumers are exposed to hundreds—if not thousands—of diverse advertising messages daily, it is important that a product or service have a personality, or brand image. A **brand** is a product's identity: the name, symbol, image, and use that distinguish one brand from another. A brand's name is something the consumer trusts based on his or her history with the product. If the product tastes the same, works the same, or fits the same every time the consumer buys, she no longer spends time thinking about or looking for a replacement. This is **brand loyalty**.

Brand value is the sum of every experience the consumer has—not only with the product but with the company that makes the product. Are the sales associates courteous every time the target enters the store? Do delivery drivers drive cautiously and make deliveries at times that don't inconvenience consumers? Is the product always as fresh as the advertising says it will be? These are the types of influencers that affect brand image. Every experience between the seller and the target will affect both the brand image and brand equity.

All communication efforts should work to anchor or position the brand's identity and image in the target's mind. If the brand's image mimics that of the consumer, it creates a tie that binds the product to the consumer's lifestyle. A reliable brand offers reliable results and will be the first product the target thinks of and recognizes when purchasing. With all the similar brands available in any one category, the goal is to make the brand a familiar face among a crowd of strangers to the consumer.

Projecting a Consistent Visual/Verbal Image: The Business Strategy behind Creative

Advertising is more than a creative idea: It is the result of months of planning and strategizing. Advertising encapsulates a study of the product or service, the competition, and the target audience into an effective and coordinated business and creative strategy.

The results seen digitally, on television, or in print media are just a small part of the business of advertising. At its most basic, advertising is a process that reacts to the client's or marketer's business needs by finding a creative way to sell a product or promote a service. Remember, a successful IMC campaign talks directly to a specific target about a specific point he is interested in and placed in a medium he will be exposed to often.

Traditional advertising is no longer the most strategically effective way to reach a media-blitzed, often apathetic audience. To reach today's savvy and educated consumer with the right message requires a message that relates to the target's life experiences, reflects the target's image of himself, and is repeated enough to develop an identity or relationship with the target.

An IMC campaign is based on a set of objectives that communication efforts need to accomplish. Each campaign focuses on a single **key consumer benefit** of the product or service that research has found is important to the target. This benefit may be unique to the product, or it may feature a creative solution that sets the product or service apart from the competition. **Strategy** refers to how the key consumer benefit will be creatively delivered to the target. What is collected during target investigations should be used to build an appropriate message strategy that will talk directly to the target about the product, addressing points especially important to the target.

It is important that all pieces in an IMC creative series have a consistent visual identity and send a consistent verbal message that is easily recognized as the tone, or voice, of the product or service. The visual/verbal identity must talk the talk and look the part consistently from media vehicle to media vehicle. This is not to say the ads should be repetitive—that would be boring—but they do need to have something that ties them together visually, such as the layout style or typeface, color, or spokesperson or character representative (see figure 1.1). Verbally, ads can be tied together through the copy or the headline's voice and style.

Figure 1.1. These thumbnail campaign ideas use a consistent headline, tagline, logo, and visual "tone" to create a familiar identity for Art Market Gallery across creative pieces. Images courtesy of Paul Domingo, University of Tennessee.

The bottom line is that every communicated experience should look and sound famil-iar. The ability to strategically direct a cohesive message to the right audience through the correct media is crucial to the successful implementation of an IMC creative series.

The Promotional and Media Mix

The ability to reach the targeted audience using the best promotional and media mix avail-able is another of IMC's many strengths. The **promotional mix** includes public relations, advertising, direct marketing, sales promotion, out-of-home and transit, the Internet and social media, mobile, and alternative media.

Communication efforts are often directed at different audiences, each requiring its own message and promotional mix. Determining which combination of promotional vehicles to use often depends on the target's overall knowledge about the product or service. For example, those who know little about a brand will need a different promotional mix than those who are more regular users.

The **media mix** breaks the promotional mix down to specific media vehicles such as newspaper, magazine, direct mail, Facebook, guerrilla marketing, gaming, and so on. The media mix can be either concentrated or assorted. A **concentrated media mix** places all advertising efforts into one medium. An **assorted media mix** employs more diverse media. Like the promotional mix, the type of media mix employed will depend on budget, overall objectives, and the target audience and its degree of brand knowledge and/or loyalty.

Let's take a brief look at a few of the major players that make up the promotional mix we will be looking at in more detail later in this text.

1. Public relations
2. Advertising, including newspaper, magazine, radio, and television
3. Out-of-home and transit
4. Direct marketing
5. Sales promotion
6. The Internet and social media
7. Mobile
8. Alternative media
9. Personal selling

Public Relations

The job of public relations is to give a product or service news value. The most common form of information distribution is done by issuing a news release, but news conferences and interviews are also useful. Such exposure is often free, but it is not always guaranteed. Information sent to local news outlets is not always picked up and used, and when it is, the news staff often rewrites content. Not all forms of public relations rely on the ability to generate news; others, like event sponsorships and brochures, are paid for, have guaranteed message content, and occur on a predetermined schedule.

Public relations is an effective way to announce events or repair a damaged reputation. Strategically, public relations can be used to inform, tantalize, or build curiosity around a product or service launch, deliver testimonials, or whet the consumer's appetite for upcoming promotional events.

Advertising

"Advertising" is a term often used to generically describe all forms of advertising communication. In reality, it covers only communication appearing in print media, including newspapers and magazines, and in broadcast media, including radio and television. Advertising is known as a mass-media vehicle that can reach a large, less-targeted audience. Advertising must be paid for, so media placement and message content are guaranteed. Traditional vehicles are still the best choice to build brand awareness and develop brand image.

Out-of-Home and Transit

"Out-of-home" is a broad term that describes any advertising seen outside the home. This mass-media vehicle can be simply designed or have digital or three-dimensional components. Most boards use a single dominant but colorful image with a small amount of copy or no verbal elements beyond the logo. The most commonly employed vehicles include outdoor boards, mobile billboards, and wall murals. A board or mural is a great support vehicle that is best suited as a reminder or teaser vehicle when used in an IMC campaign.

Transit advertising is on the move. It can be found on buses, trains, planes, and business vehicles; in and around stations, terminals, and shelters; or on platforms or benches. Most are very creative and colorful and can include three-dimensional images or quick response (QR) codes, be interactive in some meaningful way, or have GPS devices that change based on the vehicle's location. Like out-of-home, transit advertising has little to say, so it is best used as a support vehicle.

Direct Marketing

Direct marketing, also known as direct response, employs such media vehicles as direct mail, catalogs, infomercials, and telemarketing. Because direct marketing uses databases to reach an exclusively targeted audience, it is one of the best ways to talk to the target on an individual level and induce an immediate response. The availability of credit cards, toll-free numbers, order forms, and websites makes purchasing from home convenient, fast, and easy. Both sales promotion and direct marketing are considered promotional vehicles, and both are great ways to build brand awareness and encourage purchase.

Sales Promotion

Sales promotion uses incentives or motivators as an enticement for consumers to buy or use a product or service. Typical incentives might consist of coupons, rebates, samples, contests, sweepstakes, buy-one-get-one-free offers, and premiums such as T-shirts, pens, pencils, and calendars, to name just a few.

Sales promotion incentives can generate interest and are best used for new product launches, "try me" opportunities, or attempts to resurrect an aging brand.

The Internet and Social Media

The Internet allows target audience members the opportunity to gather information or to shop from the comfort of their own homes at a time when they are exposed to fewer distractions. Products can be purchased online, and the target can seek out additional information interactively through chat rooms with other product users or one-on-one talks with customer service or technical representatives.

The goal of social media marketing is to deliver content that social media users will share with friends and family that assists the brand with building brand awareness, gaining feedback, and broadening reach. Social media can help personalize a brand by creating interactive opportunities with its target audience. The opportunity to directly respond to questions, complaints, or rumors keeps brands in touch with their target and gives loyal users a chance to voice their opinions, making them feel a part of the brand's success.

Mobile

Mobile is one of the best ways to reach a busy, distracted consumer, since the device is always on and always with the target. A great reminder vehicle, it can deliver a personalized message to targets wherever they are. Mobile offers brands a diverse array of advertising options, such as search, mobile web, text, and video options, gaming, e-mail, coupon delivery, and other interactive options such as QR codes and augmented reality (AR). Users with GPS capabilities can opt in to be reached via text or e-mail when they are near a brand or be alerted to a sale.

Alternative Media

Alternative media refers to the use of any clean, printable surface that can be utilized to deliver an advertising or promotional message. Appropriate surfaces might include, but are not limited to, sidewalks, exercise equipment, fruits and vegetables, an ATM, or a gas pump nozzle. These unique media vehicles often reach the target audience more effectively than advertisements in print or broadcast media, so advertising efforts and costs are minimized but maximum exposure is achieved. This nontraditional approach looks at the demographic, psychographic, behavioral, and geographic profile of the target audience and determines what surface, vehicle, or type of event will or will not reach it.

Personal Selling

Since this text deals exclusively with consumer promotions and personal selling is usually found in corporate environments, it will not be discussed in detail here. But as a member of the promotional mix, it is worth mentioning. Personal selling is face-to-face selling between a buyer and a seller, the ultimate interactive relationship. However, its one-to-one nature makes it very expensive, relegating its use almost exclusively to the corporate environment.

In choosing the most appropriate media mix to reach the target, it is important to know the targeted consumers: where they are and what they see, hear, or view. Employing the use of alternative media opens a whole range of communication possibilities. The right media mix for the client's product or service might include any of the following: newspaper or magazine articles; remote radio broadcasts; outdoor boards; banners; transit advertising, including both interior and exterior options on buses or taxis; small airplane banners; building signs; caps and cups; a message stuffed in the pocket of a new garment; grocery receipts, packaging, and window or in-store displays; table tents; posters; shopping bags; bill or credit card stuffers; freestanding inserts; text messaging; home pages; and banner and pop-up ads. These are only a few of the alternative media options available for use in an IMC campaign. Which ones are most appropriate for an individual campaign is determined by the target and the brand.

Evaluation

Evaluating the results of traditional advertising efforts is fairly easy: Did the campaign make money or a return on the brand's initial investment? Very basically, **return on investment (ROI)** is determined by how much money was spent on advertising versus how much money was made.

Evaluation determines whether all goals or objectives for the IMC campaign have been met. If they were, great—the message should continue without changes. If not, the advertising team must determine what outside or inside influences got in the way, such as competitors' advertising, whether the correct message was used, whether the target audience saw and understood the message, and so on.

Evaluation can be a rejuvenator or an annoyance. There are many who feel the evaluation techniques used in IMC are inadequate and do not accurately assess results. However, as it stands right now, evaluation is the best indicator of what worked, what should be used again, where additional attention needs to be directed or backed off on temporarily, and what needs to be changed to accomplish the overall objectives.

IMC is designed to make money, but additional ROI or outcomes require more than a strong profit margin to survive in today's competitive market. It is also important to determine such things as brand awareness, how the target views or positions the product or service against leading competitors in the category, and smaller but no less important issues such as how many new contacts were made, the number of responses resulting from direct-mail efforts, and the number of participants in the most recent sales promotion.

Tying It All Together

The Difference between Traditional Advertising Methods and IMC

Traditional or mass-media advertising uses conventional print and broadcast media such as newspapers, magazines, radio, and television to get a message across to a mass audience that may or may not be listening. Because the messages are general rather than personalized in nature, this sort of advertising does not build a relationship with the target audience, and it takes longer to build brand loyalty.

Successful relationships require nurturing, a component missing in traditional advertising efforts. Without dialogue, information can travel only one way, as a monologue from the seller to an often passive and distracted buyer.

That being said, when pure message is all you want to get out, traditional advertising methods are still the best way to build awareness or influence consumer attitudes about a product or service.

Traditionally, advertising has always taken a lead role, with public relations, sales promotion, and direct marketing used as support mediums. IMC, on the other hand, analyzes the various options available and chooses only those that will most effectively and consistently reach the target audience. *Advertising is no longer a marketer's first—or even best—media option, and often it is not used at all.*

The Line That Divides

IMC differs from traditional advertising in the way it chooses media, uses databases to talk to individual members of the target audience, tailors messages to the target's self-interest, and creates consistency between advertising pieces via layout and message delivery.

IMC is everything traditional advertising methods are not. IMC is about communicating the client's message or the key consumer benefit associated with the product or service both consistently and cohesively. It's about developing an image that is recognizable to the target no matter what medium it appears in.

Traditional advertising knows the target audience; IMC knows the targeted individual and uses a message that relates specifically to that audience member's needs or wants. Unlike traditional advertising, IMC vehicles can be personalized to speak to one person within a target group or to other shareholders such as employees, retailers, or tradesmen.

Media choices are based on the target's lifestyle, and IMC messages appear in media vehicles the target is sure to see and use. The brand's overall image should be expressed consistently in the choice of creative strategy, message, and layout style used as well as reflected in the product name, logo design, packaging, price, and overall design layout. No internal or external customer interaction point should be overlooked. These images will further reflect the image and reputation of both the consumer and the store where the product can be purchased or the service can be used. Often, traditional advertising methods do not coordinate these elements, sending multiple or unrelated messages to the target. IMC strategically coordinates these elements, both inside and out, into one consistent brand image targeted to a very specific audience.

Being able to define a product or service for a target requires a communications plan of attack. The business of advertising would go nowhere without a creative solution that can cut through the advertising clutter and not only capture the target audience's attention but also reach out and communicate with its members. To do this effectively, IMC must develop a creative strategy that not only coordinates advertising efforts both visually and verbally but also answers the target audience's most important question: *What's in it for me?*

Defining a Creative Strategy Statement

"Creative" describes a unique and individual idea. "Strategy" is a plan to accomplish that creative idea or concept. Employing an IMC creative strategy is all about sending the right visual/verbal message to the right target audience through the right media in order to achieve the overall communication objectives.

A creative strategy statement is an integral part of the marketing communication process. Once the goals or objectives are set up by the client, the advertising team can begin developing an effective creative strategy that will accomplish them. Effective strategies are the slippery yet essential monsters that define advertising direction. Determining the right strategy requires research. You are not looking at ideas, describing a creative look, or solidifying media outlets at this point; you are looking at solutions to an advertising problem. These solutions assist in the development of a concept or theme that can be consistently executed both visually and verbally within multiple media without losing substance or focus.

A successful creative strategy statement is developed from information found in the client's marketing plan (discussed in chapter 2) and is written from the consumer's point of view. It needs to ask, on behalf of the target, *What's in it for me?* How will it solve my problem or make my life better? The answers should ultimately lead to an idea, unique to the product or service, that will influence the target to act on the message and make the product or service stand out from the competition.

The creative strategy statement will define the IMC campaign's visual/verbal tone of voice and is the foundation for the communication phase of an IMC campaign. The creative strategy affects every aspect of IMC and will ultimately give the product its image and voice and define seller-to-buyer contact.

Who Develops the Creative Strategy Statement and for Whom Is It Intended?

The creative strategy is usually developed by the agency account executive (AE), but it can also be developed jointly with the client. Representing the business side of advertising, the AE acts as the liaison between the client and the agency and the client and the creative team. The creative team includes, at the very least, a copywriter and an art director. This team of "creatives" will use the creative strategy to develop the overall concept or idea. Their interpretation of the creative strategy begins the construction phase of message development.

The Look of a Creative Strategy Statement

Creative strategy statements can take many different forms, depending on the agency and the overall size and scope of the project. The longer, more explanatory form has two main areas. The first looks at the communication objectives; the second dissects the creative strategy statement into four main sections: the target (primary and secondary), the competition, the key consumer benefit, and the proposed promotional mix. Let's take a brief look at each one (see template 1.1).

Communication Objectives

Creative strategies must accommodate a specific set of objectives, or what the client needs communication efforts to achieve. Objectives are determined by problems the target or product category may have and any market opportunities the product must take or create to overcome these problems.

Objectives describe what it is you want the target to think, feel, and do after exposure to the message and should answer the target's number one question: *What's in it for me?* Some of the most common objectives might include creating brand awareness, or what the target should think or know about the product or service after exposure to the advertising message; defining a need the product or service can fulfill, such as how the target will feel

TEMPLATE 1.1

Creative Strategy Statement

1. Communication Objectives

2. Creative Strategy Statement. Each section should be answered with no more than one or two sentences.

   a. Primary and Secondary Target Audience Profiles

   b. Competition

   c. Key Consumer Benefit

   d. Promotional Mix

or how much can be accomplished by using the product or service; and encouraging action on the part of the target, such as making a purchase, visiting a showroom, or calling for more information. Determining how these objectives should be addressed will be the first hurdle the creative team must clear before a creative direction is determined.

Creative Strategy Statement

Each of the following sections should be addressed with no more than one or two sentences. A successful strategy requires the creative team to have a thorough understanding of the target audience, the competition, the product's key consumer benefit, and the media options or promotional mix.

The Target Audience   The **primary target audience** is identified based on research as the most likely prospect to buy the product or use the service. **Secondary target audiences** are often influencers whose opinion the primary target audience member trusts or seeks out for advice. Take, for example, a campaign for the iPod. Advertising efforts may focus on a primary target of fifteen- to twenty-eight-year-olds, with a secondary audience of parents or grandparents of the primary target. Messages targeted to the primary audience may focus on image and features, while advertising targeted to the secondary audience may add information on price or purchasing options.

A thorough understanding of both audiences will help the creative team determine the answers to some important questions: What does the target audience want? Are its members aware of the product or service? What will influence their decision to purchase? How will the product be used in their daily lives? Are they currently using a competitor's product? If so, what do they like or dislike about that product? What will it take to convince them to switch brands? Are there any major influencers or secondary target audience members who must also be reached?

Advertising to a single target audience no longer has the impact it once had to deliver the brand's image and promise. Many purchases require little or no thought; others, especially high-dollar purchases or products that reflect a target's lifestyle, need to fit in, or desire to be the first to own, are influenced by other individuals trusted by the primary target. These individuals are known as **outside influencers**.

In his book *Strategies for Implementing Integrated Marketing Communications*, Larry Percy identifies roles an individual can play that can positively or negatively affect his decision or another's decision to buy:

- Initiator: the individual who originally decides to purchase a product or use a service
- Influencer: an outside person or group of people who recommends or discourages the purchase of a product or use of a service
- Decider: the person who ultimately determines what will be purchased
- Purchaser: the individual who initiates the purchase or use of the product or service
- User: the individual who will use the product or service

It's important to remember that IMC talks not to a target audience but to a single individual within that targeted audience. Every time the target considers a particular purchase, he assumes a mind-set or plays a role. That role will determine the type of message the target receives. Initiators must be made aware of the product or service and the benefits that come with ownership or use. Influencers, such as family and friends, salespeople who may or may not recommend the product or service, and professional influencers such as doctors or financial advisers, must understand the reason a product or service should be recommended or overlooked. The decider must have the answer to the question *What's in it for me?* before deciding whether to purchase. The user must not only use the product but also be willing to recommend and repurchase the product or reuse the service.

The Competition   This is not a list of competitors but rather a look at what competitors are doing and saying in their advertising and a statement regarding what the client's brand must do to compete within the product category, stand out from the competition, and attract the target's attention. Knowing how the product is positioned in the mind of consumers, or what they think about the product or service, will help determine a unique and individualized concept direction. A new product will need to have a brand image and position created for it; an established product will need to have its image and position supported; and a mature or reinvented product may need its position altered in the target's mind or its image rebuilt or reestablished. It's important to know what leaders in the product category are doing so that the new message can address or challenge them with its own unique image and voice, avoiding a me-too approach. It is also important for the target to know why the client's product is better than the competition's.

The Key Consumer Benefit   The key consumer benefit is the answer to the target's question *What's in it for me?* It is the one product or service feature and benefit combination that research has shown to be the most important to the targeted audience. All IMC communication efforts will focus on this feature and its corresponding benefit.

It's important that the creative team know enough about the product or service to be able to understand, define, and highlight the key consumer benefit's inherent drama. The successful translation of this drama into a meaningful benefit tailor made to fit the target's self-image and lifestyle will make the product or service memorable, and it will stand out from the competition.

Advertising must be memorable in order to achieve the stated objectives. Memorable advertising will deliver a key consumer benefit that that will solve a target's problem or reflect a creative concept or idea that resonates with the target's lifestyle or self-image. For an ad to be memorable, it must:

- Tell a visual and verbal story that can hold the target's attention.
- Push one strong idea of special interest to the target—one that is important to the target, fulfills a need or want, and can be delivered both visually and verbally.
- Clearly repeat the product name throughout the copy and represent it visually throughout the ad.
- Use an appeal that matches the key consumer benefit and target audience profile.
- Have a creative element or benefit that makes the ad stand out from other competitors in the brand category.

The Promotional Mix   Once the team has a thorough understanding of what needs to be accomplished, who the target is, and what his motivation is to purchase, it's time to consider the best promotional mix to reach the intended target.

This section should give the creative team an idea of where the message will appear, since media choices often affect the overall message to be delivered. Choices beyond—or even instead of—traditional advertising can make it easier to reach the target audience during each step of the decision-making process.

How will the advertising team know which media within the promotional mix to use? They must ask the following questions:

Public Relations
- Is there something newsworthy about the product or service?
- Is it a new product launch?
- Is the product or service sponsoring any charitable events or opening new production facilities?
- How does the company fit into the local community? Are relations good or bad?

Sales Promotion
- Why is there a need to give something away?
- Does the brand strategically need to increase short-term profits?
- Is this a new product launch, where samples or "try me" opportunities would increase awareness and/or sales?

Direct Marketing
- How well does the company know the target audience?
- Will addressing the target personally increase awareness or induce purchase?
- Is there access to a computer database of target names, interests, and past purchase history to make a personalized message relevant or motivational?
- Is this a product or service that lends itself to creating a long-term relationship?
- Is there a target or prospective target niche that has been overlooked by previous communication efforts that fit the target profile?

Internet
- Do members of the target have a computer? If so, do they use it to seek out additional information and compare products?
- Is this a rational or life-sustaining purchase, such as food or clothing, or is this a purely emotional or fun purchase?
- Is this a product that requires interaction with customer service or technical representatives?
- Does this product offer upgrades? Is there a need to update the consumer on product changes or uses, and can this be done through personalized e-mail notices?
- If dealing with multiple targets, can alternative information be delivered with greater frequency and with less expense electronically?
- The Internet takes a product or service global; is the company able to handle this volume of consumers and keep customer service initiatives high and delivery timely?

Out-of-Home
- Will the target regularly pass by or use any of the available vehicles?
- Does the life-cycle stage, or age of the brand, require reminder messages?
- Does the brand need to reach a large mass audience?
- Can the message easily be tied into the media mix, fortifying and ensuring a consistent message across vehicles?

Mobile
- Will the target reliably respond to mobile notices?
- How many mobile users are reachable?
- Can the product or service show a strong return on investment?
- Is this a type of product or service the target will opt into for information and promotions?

Alternative Media
- Is the target hard to reach?
- Can the overall message be made interactive?
- Why does the brand need to create buzz, or need to awe or use unconventional surfaces to reach the target?
- Is there a valid and relevant reason to offer personalized messages or to interact with the target one-on-one?

When used correctly, IMC should successfully integrate all messages throughout the promotional mix into one unified strategy.

Strategy Statements That Get to the Point

An established client making minor changes to a product's performance or image does not require the same amount of research as a new product or client. Existing knowledge about the target and competition can be easily reexamined and reused to coordinate message and media needs. This type of situation will often require a simpler and more informal type of creative strategy statement that is not more than two to three sentences long and includes:

- The target audience to be reached;
- The key consumer benefit; and
- The objective or purpose of the communication message.

Some creative strategies developed for corporate advertising may not use any of the above options and instead rely solely on the company's mission statement as a place to begin idea generation.

Execution of a creative strategy will be discussed in further detail in the section about creative briefs in chapter 4.

Q DISCUSSION QUESTIONS

1. How is IMC different from traditional advertising?
2. What role does personalized selling have in IMC?
3. What are the benefits of having a two-way dialogue between buyer and seller?
4. How has IMC affected buyer/seller relationships, brand image, brand loyalty, and brand awareness?
5. Why is IMC also known as relationship marketing?
6. An ineffective IMC campaign is caused by what internal and external factors?
7. What is the best "type" of message to reach today's consumer?
8. What are the visual and verbal ways to tie an IMC campaign together?
9. What is a promotional mix, and why is it important?
10. What is the role of the media mix in an IMC campaign?
11. What is the major role of each facet of the promotional mix as discussed in the chapter?
12. What is a creative strategy statement? What are the main areas that make up a creative strategy? Define and explain each section.

IMC Marketing Plans

The Role of the Marketing Plan

The **marketing plan** dissects the overall environment in which the product or service will be used. Before any creative executions can take place, a company must first determine what it wants to do financially, strategically, and competitively.

A marketing plan is the client's business plan; it diagnoses the current market situation by looking at any internal and external factors that could affect a product's success. It is an internal document that outlines the company's strengths and weaknesses as well as the opportunities and threats affecting the product or service. A marketing plan determines marketing objectives, or what is to be accomplished; profiles the marketing strategy, or how objectives will be met; identifies the target audience; compares current competitive strategies; and determines implementation and evaluation tactics.

Without a marketing plan, the client cannot determine overall operating and business decisions or justify advertising spending.

Think of it this way: All advertising begins with a client that has a product or service it needs to promote. To do this effectively and expeditiously, the client first must know a few important facts. To begin with, a thorough knowledge of the product or service is important when comparing its attributes to competing products or services. Next, the client needs to determine the target audience most likely to buy the product or use the service and what product attributes the target likes or dislikes about competing products. Finally, the client must decide what kind of message strategy it will take to set its product apart from the competition.

All the questions and all the answers begin and end with research. Each section of the marketing plan must be carefully researched to determine current trends, attitudes, and both market and target needs. Any problematic areas or favorable trends that need to be addressed or exploited will need to be researched further.

Where to Begin: Research

The organization of research takes place in the marketing plan. Research can be qualitative or quantitative in nature. **Qualitative data** employ the use of open-ended questions that can be distributed and collected through interviews, convenience polling, and focus groups. A **focus group** gathers a representative sample of the target audience, usually ten to twelve people, who will use or try the product in a controlled environment. Information gathered in a session can be used to determine creative development, product design, or the effectiveness of product attributes, to name just a few.

    Quantitative data, on the other hand, are made up of closed-ended or controlled surveys, where participants must choose their answers from a preselected set of responses. There are two types of surveys: formal and informal. **Formal surveys** include closed-ended questions where participants choose from a predetermined set of responses such as strongly agree, agree, disagree, and strongly disagree. **Informal surveys** are open ended, allowing participants to give their opinions.

    Surveys need not be completed in a sterile office environment; they can be conducted at malls and shopping centers, in parking lots, online, over the phone, or through the mail. Researchers should not concentrate their efforts on only one type of research technique but should consider using multiple options. Ultimately, the type of research performed will depend on what needs to be accomplished, the product or service to be advertised, and the target audience for the product or service.

    Client input determines what type and how much information needs to be gathered. Once researchers know the questions that need to be answered, they must determine if the information exists or needs to be gathered. There are two types of information available to researchers: primary and secondary data. **Primary data** do not exist and require that original research be gathered from a variety of sources such as surveys, interviews, focus groups, observations, or experiments.

    Secondary data are already available and can be found from external sources like the public library, websites, trade associations, and the US Census.

    Research is the foundation for the development of a marketing plan. The marketing plan solidifies the client's marketing goals or objectives and serves as the launching pad for creative strategy development and all future communication efforts. See the Goldfish Crackers integrated marketing communication strategic marketing plan (case study 2).

What Does a Marketing Plan Do?

Simply put, a marketing plan is a comprehensive look at a business's place within its product category. Its primary function is to detail a business's strengths and weaknesses as compared to its competition and determine any opportunities or reveal any relevant threats within

CASE STUDY 2

C

IMC: Pepperidge Farm Goldfish Crackers Campaign

Overview

By 2004, Pepperidge Farms Goldfish crackers, introduced in 1962, had evolved into a megabrand available in more than twenty-four individual flavors and varieties, from the original cheddar to peanut butter–filled sandwich crackers and crispy rounds. At the end of that year, Goldfish sales in the United States were $168.5 million, making it the number-two snack-cracker brand, behind Nabisco's Ritz crackers. But despite its ranking, the Goldfish brand was slipping; in 2004 sales of the crackers dipped 8.3 percent from the previous year.

To lift its iconic brand out of the doldrums, Pepperidge Farm, a division of the Campbell Soup Company, looked beyond its agency of record—Young & Rubicam Advertising in New York—for creative help. The company charged BrightHouse Live, a small Atlanta-based agency known for its unique approach to marketing and advertising, with developing a clever new marketing campaign for the Goldfish brand. BrightHouse Live created a television-focused campaign that featured an animated goldfish character named Finn. The campaign, which began in January 2005, also included in-store and online marketing and new packaging for the Goldfish crackers. A budget for the campaign was not announced, but according to TNS Media Intelligence/CMR, a unit of the UK–based market research firm Taylor Nelson Sofres, in 2003 Pepperidge Farm spent $16.3 million on advertising for its Goldfish brand, a figure almost unchanged from its spending in 2002.

The new campaign, as well as its spokescharacter, Finn, seemed to resonate with consumers and helped increase sales of Goldfish crackers by about 5 percent within several months of its launch. Media insiders also praised the campaign, using a variety of adjectives to describe Finn, from lovable and funny to spunky and irreverent. Additionally, the Campbell Soup Company credited the campaign and its spokescharacter with boosting Pepperidge Farm's sales in 2005.

Historical Context

According to its website, Pepperidge Farm's humble beginnings in 1937 were in the kitchen of Margaret Rudkin, the mother of three children. To ease the allergies of one of her children, the industrious mom began baking bread for her family that contained none of the preservatives or artificial ingredients found in commercially baked bread. Her efforts in the kitchen soon evolved into a small business named for the family farm in Connecticut: Pepperidge Farm. The first product, whole-wheat bread, gained in popularity with consumers, and in the 1940s the line was expanded to include oatmeal bread, dinner rolls, and stuffing mix. The peripatetic Rudkin also added to the product line by collecting recipes during her international travels, including European-style cookies that she discovered while traveling in Belgium in the 1950s. In 1961 the Campbell Soup Company acquired Pepperidge Farm. The following year Goldfish crackers were introduced after Rudkin discovered the snack cracker during a trip to Switzerland and returned with the recipe and permission to market it.

Ogilvy & Mather had served as Pepperidge Farm's ad agency for forty years. In 1995 it resigned from the Pepperidge Farm and Goldfish crackers account, reportedly because of a business conflict, and agency Saatchi & Saatchi/New York took over the account. When a smiling face was added to the original goldfish in 1997, "Smiley" the Goldfish icon was born. Saatchi & Saatchi created the accompanying tagline: "The snack that smiles back." In 1998, following a consolidation by the brand's parent company, Campbell Soup, Young & Rubicam Advertising in New York won the Goldfish account. The agency introduced a new campaign for Goldfish crackers in 2003 that included the theme song "Jingle for Goldfish." The campaign, which targeted kids eight to twelve years old, featured two scruffy, longhaired musicians playing acoustic guitars and singing the jingle. Television spots placed the singing duo in a variety of settings, including on a school bus and in a classroom. At the request of Pepperidge Farm, Atlanta-based BrightHouse Live joined the team in 2004, and its Finn the goldfish campaign was released in January 2005.

Target Market

Any parent, babysitter, or other person who had ever quieted a fussy toddler with a cup of Goldfish crackers could appreciate the value of the tasty fish-shaped treat. But with the new campaign featuring Finn, a personable animated goldfish, the goal was to help create an even closer bond between the popular Pepperidge Farm brand and the children who enjoyed Goldfish crackers. As an added benefit, the clever spots connected with the adults who purchased the product. The animated Finn also was designed to continue Goldfish crackers' appeal to tweens—kids eight to twelve years old— and teens who had been given the fish-shaped crackers as toddlers but had perhaps stopped eating them in favor of other snacks. To further reach its target market, Pepperidge Farm introduced a Goldfish website, www.pfgoldfish.com, that enabled older kids to go online and play games featuring Finn. The site also offered a variety of activities that parents or caregivers could play with kids three to five years old, such as determining how many Goldfish crackers tall the child was. In addition, new packaging (the milk carton box was replaced with a bag similar to what was used for other products in the line) added to the appeal of the brand for consumers of all ages.

Objectives

1. Update the brand.
2. Reinforce the bond between target and brand.

Competition

In the snack-cracker wars, flavor, as always, was paramount; but in the early 2000s, part of the battle was about the shape of the cracker. Pepperidge Farm's fish-shaped crackers were near the top of the list, with 98 percent of Americans surveyed saying that they recognized and were familiar with Goldfish crackers.

Nabisco, which claimed one of the top spots in the snack-cracker market with its Ritz brand, went one step too far in its competition with Pepperidge Farm when it introduced its own fish-shaped crackers in 1998. Nabisco's new crackers were planned as a tie-in to the Nickelodeon television network's program *CatDog*. The new crackers resulted in a lawsuit, pitting Nabisco against Pepperidge Farm. The latter alleged that Nabisco's new crackers infringed on its Goldfish brand trademark. In 2000 a federal court upheld Pepperidge Farm's claim and ordered Nabisco to discontinue production of its fish-shaped cracker. Later in 2000 Kraft Foods acquired the Nabisco brand for $18.9 billion.

While Nabisco's Ritz cracker brand claimed the number-one spot in the snack-cracker market at the end of 2004, with $232.6 million in annual US sales, the company was still looking for a niche in the shaped-cracker market. Nabisco introduced dinosaur-shaped puffed crackers under its Ritz brand in 2005. The new Ritz Dinosaur crackers were created in direct response to Pepperidge Farm's Goldfish crackers and targeted the same young consumers and their parents.

In 2005 the Kellogg Company introduced its own character-shaped cracker under its Keebler Sunshine cracker brand, Cheez-It. Rather than a fish or prehistoric creature, however, Keebler Sunshine's new crackers were shaped like the cartoon character SpongeBob SquarePants and directly targeted the kids who munched on Ritz Dinosaur and Pepperidge Farm Goldfish crackers.

Targeting an older audience, in 2004 Kellogg introduced Twisterz, another variation on its Cheez-It crackers. The new shape, a twisted cylinder rather than the traditional square, was launched in time for the end of college basketball season and included combination flavors designed to please college-age consumers: Cheddar & More Cheddar, Hot Wings & Cheesy Blue, and Cool Ranch & Cheddar. The new product launch was supported by a marketing campaign created by Leo Burnett/Chicago and continued the brand's tagline: "Get your own box." With $140.1 million in sales, the Cheez-It cracker brand ranked fourth in the snack-cracker market at the end of 2004.

Marketing Strategy

Although New York–based Young & Rubicam Advertising remained the agency of record for Goldfish crackers and other Pepperidge Farm brands, in 2004, when Pepperidge Farm wanted to put a different spin on advertising for the fish-shaped cracker and update the brand, it partnered with Bright-House Live, an agency based in Atlanta, Georgia. Opening its doors in 2003, BrightHouse Live had quickly earned a reputation for devising unusual advertising campaigns. The creative idea developed by the agency was primarily a television campaign that featured an animated goldfish named Finn. A specific budget for the campaign was unavailable, but according to a report in *Adweek*, in 2004 Pepperidge Farm spent approximately $14 million from January through September on advertising for the Goldfish cracker brand.

Prior to the creation of the campaign, Pepperidge Farm devoted more than one year to conducting market research about Goldfish crackers. Included were interviews with mothers and children to determine what the brand meant to consumers. The company also worked with Character, a leading character-development agency within the film industry, to help establish the personality of the new spokescharacter, Finn.

BrightHouse Live created a series of four thirty-second and three fifteen-second television spots. The initial two thirty-second spots, which were first aired in January 2005, highlighted Goldfish crackers' cheddar-flavored variety. Subsequent spots featured the brand's Flavor Blasted and Sandwich Snackers varieties. Each spot showed Finn interacting with other Goldfish crackers as he made plans to help protect them from being eaten by hungry humans reaching for a snack. Finn warned, "To avoid being eaten, you've got to avoid the bowl, avoid the baggies. Cool?" One spot had Finn's advice being ignored by the other Goldfish crackers. As the crackers laughed and jumped into a bowl on a kitchen counter, a person reached into the bowl and took a handful of the crackers. A voice-over stated: "Tasty Goldfish crackers, baked with real cheddar cheese. It's a wonder they're not extinct." Finn sighed and returned to the package to try again to warn the remaining Goldfish crackers about how to avoid becoming a snack for humans. The spot ended with Finn exclaiming, "So much for fish being brain food."

In addition to television spots, the campaign included in-store advertising and Internet promotions on a new website for the product that featured games and activities for kids to play alone or with their parents. As part of a brand update, the company designed new packaging for the crackers.

In an interview reported in *Business Wire* prior to the release of the campaign, Pepperidge Farm's vice president of youth snacks, Steve White, said that by bringing the familiar goldfish to life as the spokescharacter Finn, "we feel confident that kids of all ages are going to love the character as much as they love the snack."

Outcome

At the time of the new campaign's 2005 launch, Pepperidge Farm's Goldfish crackers were among the world's most popular snack crackers, with American consumers devouring more than 85 billion Goldfish crackers annually. Within six months of the start of the campaign, Pepperidge Farm reported that sales of Goldfish crackers were up more than 5 percent. Parent company Campbell Soup also noted the success of the campaign in its third quarter report for the period that ended May 2005. The report stated, "Sales of 'Pepperidge Farm Goldfish' snack crackers experienced good gains due to continued momentum of the base brand and the favorable impact of new advertising featuring the new animated character, 'Finn.'"

Besides resonating with consumers and spurring sales, the campaign was well received by media insiders. Writing in the *Chicago Sun-Times*, Lewis Lazare described Finn as a lovable advertising icon that was "funny and irreverent" with "spunk and soul."

Source: "Goldfish Crackers Campaign," Marketing Campaign Case Studies, http://marketing-case-studies. blogspot.com/search/label/Campbell%20Soup%20Company.

the marketplace. It also defines marketing or sales objectives and determines the appropriate marketing strategy needed to accomplish those objectives, defines the target to be addressed and the competition, and determines evaluative measures.

Developing a plan that incorporates input from customers is the first step in developing a strong IMC plan. For the plan to be truly integrated, it must ensure all messages use the same tone of voice and are reflected in all internal and external communication. If a client wants to increase sales, profits, and brand equity, it must have a plan that will specifically talk to the right audience, define the product and the competition, and offer a product that is unique and consistently reliable. A typical marketing plan comprises seven sections. For a sample marketing plan, see template 2.1.

Let's take a quick look at the seven basic areas that make up a marketing plan:

- Situation analysis (SWOT)
- Marketing objectives
- Marketing strategy
- Target market analysis
- Competitive strategies
- Implementation tactics
- Evaluation

T

TEMPLATE 2.1

Marketing Plan

Marketing plans differ from organization to organization, and their appearance can vary as widely as their content. This example is only one way of developing a comprehensive marketing plan. The marketing plan should be as long as necessary to understand the competition, the client, the target, and the marketing objectives. All business documents should be double-spaced with at least one-inch margins on all four sides. Use either ten-point Helvetica or eleven-point Times to make reading easier. Be sure to number all pages.

Include the following when completing a marketing plan:

Name:

Date:

Assignment:

Situation Analysis:

Marketing Objectives:

Marketing Strategy:

Target Market:

Competitive Strategies:

Implementation Tactics:

Evaluation:

Situation Analysis

The situation analysis looks at current marketing conditions and their possible effect on marketing efforts and how factors in the marketplace can affect outcome. It is here that the product or service, the competition, the target audience, and any environmental, economic, legal, and political situations are dissected and analyzed.

Each of these factors can be broken down and examined further by developing a situation analysis, or SWOT. A situation analysis looks at a company's strengths (S) and weaknesses (W) as compared to the competition and any opportunities (O) for and threats (T) to the product or service within the marketplace.

Further studies will compare current product features with those of the competition, analyze any previous communication efforts, and determine distribution needs.

A thorough look at the target audience and any competitors' advertising efforts will help determine how the situation analysis can be used, if the objectives can be met, or if any modifications will be needed.

Marketing Objectives

From the data developed in the situation analysis, a set of marketing objectives will be devised to determine what the company wants to accomplish through its marketing activities. Over the next year, client objectives will concentrate on various financial outcomes, such as sales or profit issues.

Marketing Strategy

A marketing strategy determines what steps will need to be undertaken to accomplish the stated objectives. It is here where the **marketing mix** will first be identified.

The Marketing Mix

The marketing mix, traditionally known as the *4-Ps*, is a brand's marketing plan of action and includes product, price, promotion, and distribution, or "place." Each will play a vital role in message development. Because advertising today is so consumer focused, many marketing plans employ a fifth *P*—people—to the marketing mix.

- *Product.* This specifically deals with anything having to do with the product, including quality, features, packaging, servicing arrangements, and warranties.
- *Price.* Any price issues are looked at here, such as payment terms, cash or credit options, and any discounts or sales materials.
- *Promotion.* This deals with the communication or promotional mix, including public relations, advertising, direct marketing and sales promotion, out-of-home and transit, the Internet and social media, mobile media, and alternative media. The promotional mix provides a foundation for examining the best promotional options available to reach the target audience with the right message.
- *Distribution, or "Place."* This deals with where the product will be available for purchase.

- *People and/or Personnel.* This section deals with the targeted consumer as well as any internal contact point who uses or comes in contact with the brand; also, the competency and professionalism shown at any customer contact point.

Target Market Analysis

The more that is known about who will be using the client's product, the easier it will be to target the message directly to them. This section breaks down the intended **target audience**, those people research has determined are most likely to buy the product or use the service, into the following market segments: demographics, psychographics, geographics, and behavioristics. Segmentation can also be based on usage patterns, level of loyalty, and specific benefits.

Good ideas should talk to the target in words the target can understand. To do this effectively, target attributes must be isolated in a more personalized way.

Demographics breaks down personal attributes such as age, sex, income, marital and professional status, occupation, education, and number of children.

Psychographics looks at the target's personal attributes that affect lifestyle, such as cultural, emotional, family, health, and social issues as well as hobbies and overall beliefs. Psychographics affect how the consumer will view the product and advertising.

Geographics defines where the target lives and how that affects who he is, how he thinks, his goals, and his limitations. Geographics can be broken down regionally or by city, state, or zip code. Where a person lives often influences the type of product he will buy and where the product should be advertised. A hard-laboring blue-collar worker might have different goals and limitations from those of a college graduate. They use and are exposed to different media and require different messages.

Behavioristic profiles look at why a person buys: Is it loyalty, social acceptance, brand name, or need?

When determining the correct target market for the client's product or service, any one or combination of the above segmentation practices could be used. Answers found within these segments will determine both message content and media choice.

Demographic and geographic information is used to determine if the target market has sufficient disposable income available to purchase the product.

Psychographics and behavioristic data are used in the creative development stage. Demographic, psychographic, behavioristic, and geographic information can be found by purchasing or using existing databases, surveys, or focus groups.

If IMC is to successfully build a relationship and develop advertising materials that are consumer focused, research needs to take a thorough look into the lives of the target audience. As discussed in chapter 1, it is simply too expensive and wasteful to advertise to anyone who is not interested in buying or using a particular product or service. Because IMC is intended to develop a personal relationship and build a loyal client base, advertising must talk to those most likely to use the product or service.

To personalize a message, the creative team needs to know what media targets are most likely to use and what motivates and interests them. The success or failure of advertising depends on whether the information gathered will help determine what kind of promotional mix will reach the target audience members and what kind of message will solve their problem, address their image or social status issues, or satisfy any specific needs and wants.

Again, there may be times when you will need to divide a larger target audience into smaller market segments or secondary markets. For example, if your client is in jewelry and the primary market is eighteen- to thirty-four-year-old women, a good secondary market might be husbands, significant others, parents, or even grandparents. Each would require a creative approach unique to that market segment.

How Are Certain Target Audiences Chosen?

It is important to find a reason a target audience needs the product or service being promoted. What does the target want that is currently unavailable? How can the client's product or service meet that want? What does the client's product or service offer that the competition doesn't? Who are the people who are in need, how do they live, and where do they live? What do they buy now? What are their purchase and media habits? These questions and more can be answered through target profiling.

In his book *Strategies for Implementing Integrated Marketing Communication*, Larry Percy lists five potential target audience groups that can be further broken down into two categories. Knowing where the target audience falls will decide message development and media choice.

Noncustomer Groups

- New category users—those trying the product for the first time
- Other brand loyals—those loyal to competitors' brands
- Other brand switchers—those who have loyalty to no particular brand and will switch based on a sale or promotion

Customer Groups

- Favorable brand switchers—those who favor the brand but will consider switching
- Brand loyals—those who are using the brand and will never switch

Identifying Ethnic and Other Influential Consumer Groups

When targeting for a new product, creative efforts must reflect both lifestyle and buying habits. Different target segments will look at new product launches differently, some more openly and others more skeptically. Both require an approach that talks to their lifestyle. Knowing how the target audience members think and act, what their needs and wants are, what excites them, and what offends them makes addressing their issues and concerns easier. This knowledge helps in building a loyal customer base and allows the product or service to grow and change as the target changes.

Changes may be based on growth of a specific ethnic group, age or purchasing power, geographical relocation, or a change in interests. No matter what the change may be, issues associated with these changes will affect each ethnic and other influential consumer group differently. In the United States there are three very distinct ethnic groups beyond Caucasian: African Americans, Hispanics, and Asian Americans. Within these groups the target can be further broken down by age affecting purchasing power, life-cycle stage, media usage, message content, and media consumption.

Each group, although often part of a larger target profile, requires a message designed especially for it. Brand loyalty throughout ethnic and other influential groups is higher if communication efforts use members of the target group, are written in the group's native language, and appear in print or on a broadcast media targeted to their specific demographic group. Let's look at how these very different markets break down.

African Americans   According to the US Census, African Americans and other blacks make up just over 14 percent of the population. According to research by the Nielsen Group, African Americans shop the most often but spend less on each trip. They shop more often in smaller establishments such as drugstores and convenience stores. Typical households have an annual median income of just over $43,000. Additional statistics show African-American women to be the leading force behind this group's spending growth. More than 18 percent of African Americans have a bachelor's or advanced degree, and just over 44 percent own their own home. Almost half the black or African-American population is married with no children, allowing for discretionary buying. Brand loyal and preferring private-label brands over nationally distributed ones, their top expenditures include housing, food and clothing, cars, trucks, and health care.

African Americans watch more TV than any other ethnic group and are heavy users of premium cable channels. They tend to use the most voice minutes on their phones and watch the most mobile videos. Mobile devices are heavily used to access the web and e-mail. Social media access is often done from a PC, and they tend to favor Facebook in general over other outlets. Print plays a very small role in their media consumption.

Hispanics   The Hispanic market includes many national-origin groups, the largest being Mexicans, Puerto Ricans, Cubans, and South Americans. The US Census reports the Hispanic population at just over 17.6 percent. They are the second-fastest-growing ethnic group in the United States, according to the 2010 US Census, with a median age of twenty-seven years. More than 47 percent of Hispanic Americans are married, and they have the second-largest households overall, with 3.3 members. The median household income is $47,150, and almost 15 percent are college graduates. Most, just over 75 percent, are bilingual.

Image is important to Hispanic consumers, and many admit to being heavily influenced by peer reviews. They believe quality is an important factor when purchasing. According to research by the Nielsen Group, Hispanics spend more but shop less often than other ethnic or racial groups. Those who primarily speak English shop more frequently in supercenters and drugstores, while those who primarily speak Spanish prefer shopping at dollar and convenience stores and warehouse clubs. The most heavily purchased items include children's products, health and beauty aids, and fashion.

Heaviest media use includes watching Internet videos and using mobile devices for web access, shopping, social media, texting, and e-mail. They enjoy engaging with brands online and are typically early adopters. They are both heavily influenced by and influential on social media. According to the Association of Hispanic Advertising Agencies, "the voice of Hispanic marketing," they spend over seventeen hours a week watching Spanish-language TV and twelve hours listening to Spanish-language radio and just slightly less watching and listening to broadcasts in English. They enjoy reading both newspapers and magazines and are most likely to engage with Internet advertising that uses technology in a creative way.

Asian Americans   The Asian-American population includes people of Chinese, Filipino, Indian, Vietnamese, Korean, and Japanese descent, among others. The US Census places the Asian-American population at almost 6 percent. According to the 2012 US Census, it is the fastest-growing and most affluent ethnic group, with a median income of $72,472. It is also the best educated, with 54 percent having college degrees, and has the largest percentage (27 percent) of multigenerational households.

Asian Americans are brand-conscious consumers and are generally geographically concentrated, making them an easy and cost-effective group to reach.

Asian homes are the most "wired" and represent the greatest online use of all ethnic groups. They also are the most inclined to respond to sales and promotions. Typical purchases include fresh produce, baby items, cars, technology, and health and beauty aids.

These tech-savvy consumers are the most active mobile, tablet, computer, and Internet users among all groups looked at. They are avid Internet video watchers and are most likely to share ads, like ads, or purchase products they have seen from ads. They are more likely than any other ethnic group to do offline research on products seen online before purchase.

Defining the Labels Surrounding Target Segmentation

Demographic groups are often labeled based on events that shaped or defined their formative or childhood through adult years. This can be formulated around cultural, economic, and political influences. For example, "Baby Boomers" got their name based on the large number of babies born immediately following WWII. Generation X, or "Baby Busters," got their labels from two different sources. Baby Buster originated because birth rates dramatically declined following the baby boom generation. Generation X comes from a 1991 book by Douglas Coupland entitled *Generation X: Tales for an Accelerated Culture*. The letter *X*, he explained in a 2014 NPR article entitled "From GIs to Gen Z (Or Is It iGen?) How Generations Get Nicknames" by Samantha Raphelson, "was meant to signify his generation's desire not to be defined." The label "Millennials" reflects a demographic segment that came of age in the new millennium. Finishing off the alphabet segmentations is Generation Z, also known as "Centennials" because they were born nearest the turn of the century. Let's take a quick look at each group.

Baby Boomers   No longer the largest targeted population segment as of 2015, they still hold 70 percent of the nation's discretionary income.

This aging demographic is projected to make up 20 percent of the US population by 2029. Educated decision makers, baby boomers are an affluent demographic segment, with an average income of $60,000. Boomers fifty-five and older control more than three-fourths of America's wealth.

The fifty-plus consumer is living longer and is more physically active, better educated, and more financially secure than previous generations at this age. This market is open to new brands and is willing to try new products. Boomers are the biggest buyers of new technology and cars. Most boomers are married, 80 percent own their own home, and 47 percent are still employed. The majority of boomers are white, with only 12 percent being African American, 4 percent Asian American, and 12 percent Hispanic American.

This target group watches more TV than eighteen- to forty-nine-year-olds and spends more time online than teenagers, spending $7 billion online annually. Baby boomers routinely spend time listening to the radio and are heavy users of all forms of print. They are profuse catalog purchasers, making them a great direct-mail target. Purchases tend to be on home improvement products, home furnishings, large appliances, health and beauty, grandchildren, and casual dining. Seventy percent buy at least one product online a month and are avid texters.

Baby boomers do not see themselves as old and worn out but rather as healthy, independent, active, and successful. Advertising efforts should reflect that lifestyle.

Generation X Gen X, also known as the "Baby Bust" generation, is a relatively small consumer group, making up only 16 percent of the US population. According to American Express, they have the largest spending power of any generation, controlling 29 percent of the country's net worth and 31 percent of the overall income; 82 percent own their own home.

Often overlooked by advertisers and marketers because of their small numbers, this powerful target is more educated and makes more money than their baby boomer parents at similar ages. However, they have less wealth overall, thanks in part to decreased savings, lower interest earnings, and increased student debt.

Sandwiched between the much larger and more vocal baby boomer and millennial generations, the often-underestimated Gen Xers came of age following Watergate, Vietnam, and the stock market crash of 1987 that spurred a recession. Thanks to the economic and political conditions of the day, they were often mislabeled as cynical, angry, insecure slackers who question conventionality.

Born before the birth of the Internet, like their baby boomer parents, they had to quickly adapt to the exploding digital landscape. In a 2016 *Adweek* article entitled "5 Reasons Marketers Have Largely Overlooked Generation X," Robert Klara notes, "Their age leaves them with one foot in the past and one in the future—and that leaves marketers confused about which platforms should be used to reach them."

Digitally savvy, this demographic still finds traditional media relevant, with 48 percent regularly listening to radio, 62 percent routinely reading newspapers, and 85 percent watching favored television programming. Sixty percent own a smartphone, and 75 percent use social media. Their Internet use concentrates on shopping, banking, and researching products. Snail mail and e-mail are also favored media outlets.

Brand loyal, Xers look for authenticity, personalized service, and transparency in their advertised messages. Messages that focus on family values, safety, and security will resonate with this target group.

Generation Y The coveted Generation Y, or "Millennial" generation, makes up 25 percent of the population and has more than $200 billion in spending clout.

Thought to be brash, narcissistic, and entitled, this group saw economic prosperity, as well as the devastation of September 11, 2001, and two economic recessions. Millennials are more ethnically and racially diverse than any previous generation and are viewed as being more optimistic and entrepreneurial than their parents' generation.

Born into a digital world, millennials value technology, especially mobile, and are heavy users of almost all forms of digital media. Technology dominates the lives of these digital natives, both personally and professionally. Media diverse, 75 percent of Gen Yers own a smartphone, 63 percent subscribe to paid TV, 90 percent use some form of social media, 90 percent use digital coupons, 50 percent use coupons delivered via snail mail or found in newspapers and magazines, and 54 percent use retail catalogs. They watch content on multiple screens and are known to binge-watch favored programming.

More skeptical of advertising than previous generations, this diverse target can be marketed to if they get something of value that does not interrupt the user experience. Millennials don't like a hard-sell approach, preferring instead to be engaged. Outbound and traditional advertising with splashy copy is unlikely to induce them to buy; nor are mass advertised messages appearing on television, in pre-roll video ads, and in display formats. Interactive inbound marketing tactics are preferred. They will respond to branded content as long as it doesn't feel like an advertisement. Traditionally, they are more influenced by their social contacts than advertising. Media outlets like social networks that can offer up more personalized content will get their attention.

This very diverse group of consumers prefers to express individuality rather than follow trends when making purchasing decisions. They want convenience, personalized messages, and 24/7 customer service and look for brands with a social conscience. Not known for being overly brand loyal, once they are won over, however, they become devoted long-term followers. When possible, millennials will embrace opportunities to cocreate products with the marketers who develop them.

As consumers, they spend time researching brand options before buying and look for advertising that highlights their personal interests and overall lifestyle. They are thoughtful consumers, looking for interactive options that are delivered in an original way and that introduce diverse types of experiences and opportunities. In-store promotional events where they can interact not only with a brand but also with store personnel and other shoppers will increase loyalty. "Turn[ing] the everyday shopping trip into an event appeal[s] to this experience driven generation," Holly Pavilka says in a 2015 *MediaPost* article entitled "Get Creative with Your Millennial Grocery Shopper."

Generation Z   Generation Z, also known as the "Centennial" generation, makes up another 25 percent of the population.

In a 2015 *New York Times* article by Alex Williams entitled "Move Over Millennials, Here Comes Generation Z," Lucie Green, worldwide director of the Innovation group at J. Walter Thompson, describes them as "millennials on steroids." Gen Zers tend to be self-sufficient, realistic, and practical. They are mature and in control. Value-conscious, experimental, innovative, and risk takers, they don't want to stand out in a crowd. This target segment would rather spend their money on college, experiences, or technology than on luxury goods. When buying, they are willing to put in the time to tenaciously research brands and find the best quality for the best price. They tend to be brand loyal to brands that have earned their trust by living up to expectations, making them excellent brand ambassadors.

This target segment understands economic reality, coming of age after the Great Recession, September 11, and the ongoing war on terror. They are a conscientious, hardworking generation that looks to the future. Unlike the millennials, Generation Zers value their privacy; they spend less time on Facebook and instead favor anonymous social media platforms like Whisper or Snapchat, where images are fleeting. The *New York Times* article goes on to say, "As far as privacy goes, they are aware of their personal brand, and have seen older Y-ers screw up by posting too openly."

They are pessimistic about world affairs and have little confidence in government, politicians, or brands. They tend to follow brands that are consistent in quality and project a sense of realism rather than Madison Avenue's advertised views. They want advertising to reflect diversity not only in race but also in the depiction of body types, economic conditions, and gender persuasions. They see themselves as investors in a brand, not consumers of that brand.

This traditionally advertising-avoidant generation needs advertising that is participatory rather than passive. They typically spend more time watching content online than watching TV. They are best advertised to in quick soundbites and ads with minimal text and large visuals. Social media and their phones are staples in their life. They respond to experience-driven campaigns that use inspirational content marketing that is engaging and can be easily and innovatively shared through social media. They do a great deal of shopping digitally as well as in brick-and-mortar stores. Pop-up stores that focus on the customer experience and mobile e-commerce are a couple of options that deliver creative and innovative ways to interact and engage with Gen Zers.

Generation Alpha   There's not much to say about this group, since they are just being born. One thing everyone agrees on is that they will be the first generation to be wholly born within the twenty-first century. Typically, they will be better educated, immersed in all forms of technology, and wealthy. They will be raised by older parents within smaller family units, be more culturally diverse, and live longer.

When determining campaign direction, the creative team should never lose sight of who the target audience is. It is the one that advertising needs to reach and affect.

Talking to the right audience doesn't guarantee success if the message delivered is in the wrong media, but it does highly increase the chances for success. The bottom line is that the creative team should know the target audience so well after reading the research that it is able to address creative efforts to an old friend.

Further Narrowing the Target

As we have seen, target audiences can be further broken down into small specialty and/or age groups. Some products never reach mainstream popularity but do have a very strong and loyal group of users. Concentrating advertising efforts specifically on winning the attention of a small group of mostly affluent consumers loyal to one specific product is known as **niche marketing.** The limited number of consumers keeps competitors from competing in the market or trying to copy the product because it would not be profitable.

Target audiences can be further classified into six distinct age groups. These groups respond to different kinds of advertising. Since they have social and financial differences, it is important to keep the group classifications in mind. Differentiating one target group of consumers from another is crucial.

- Matures: 1909–1945
- Baby boomers: 1946–1964

- Generation X or baby busters: 1965 to around 1984
- Generation Y or millennials: 1982 to around 2000
- Generation Z or centennials: 1996 to around 2010
- Generation Alpha: 2011–2025

Following the baby boomers, the dates defining generation X, Y, and Z fluctuate. Thanks to the changing characteristics of each target segment over time, it is difficult for experts and researchers alike to definitively determine when one segment ends and another begins.

Figure 2.1. The McClung Museum of Natural History and Culture utilized alternative media—in this case, dinosaur footprints in a sidewalk—to stand out. Robyn Blakeman.

Competitive Strategies

Knowing what competitors are doing with advertising and product development is the difference between being a leader or a follower within a product category. Understanding the similarities and differences between a product and its leading competitors is crucial in order for a product to stand out from the competition in the mind of the targeted consumer.

Implementation Tactics

Implementation tactics determine if everything can come off on schedule and in the right order, with the right materials in place, and with the proper people available to carry off the marketing efforts. Additionally, such items as scheduling, budgetary items, timelines, and information on enacting the marketing mix have to be discussed and developed.

Evaluation

Evaluation takes place before the marketing plan is put into effect and again after implementation to determine whether results in fact reflect corporate goals and whether objectives
were successfully met. Evaluation is critical to a successful IMC campaign.

The Creative Strategy and the Marketing Plan

Once the entire advertising team understands the corporate goals, it is time for agency executives to begin considering a creative strategy to direct results. Remember, a creative strategy
is a synopsis of the product or service and the target audience. It should describe the key
features of the product and service and define the overall benefits to the targeted audience.

The marketing plan should answer the target's main question: *What's in it for me?* There
should be enough information in the marketing plan to identify a unique product feature
or specific target need and to start imagining creative direction.

Q   DISCUSSION QUESTIONS

1. What is a marketing plan, and how is it used to build an IMC campaign?
2. How do researchers know whether to use qualitative or quantitative research techniques? What
   are the pros and cons of each?
3. What are the seven basic areas that make up a marketing plan? What are their roles/purpose?
4. What are the four different market segments? Why is it important to define and understand
   each?
5. Why is it important to understand different target groups?

Branding and Positioning

Defining a Brand, Its Image, and Its Worth

The American Marketing Association defines a **brand** as a "name, term, sign, symbol, or design, or a combination of them, intended to identify the goods and services of one seller or group of sellers and to differentiate them from those of the competition." Quite simply, the brand *is* the product or service. **Branding** is a product's identity and its legacy. By building a strong brand image for a product or service, it gives the product a personality, an image, and the single voice or message for the brand. This ultimately determines how the consumer thinks about the product or service and how it stands out from the competition. The more unique the persona created, the more memorable the brand will be.

Target perception is only one aspect of a brand's image. Another key characteristic is brand and/or corporate reputation, or the ability to deliver a reliable performance from purchase to purchase. Repetitive results create repeat purchases and build brand loyalty and brand equity.

Repetitive results relate directly to product performance. Over time, a product or service that has repeatedly proved itself to the consumer creates trust and goodwill. If a product is inconsistent or cannot deliver on the promise made in the advertising and promotional efforts, it can result in unfavorable reviews or bad word of mouth, one of the most powerful forms of communication. Think about it: How many people do you talk to in a day, a week, or a month? Consumers trust in the unbiased opinion given by friends, colleagues, or professionals over those they hear in advertising claims. Eventually, repetitive negative comments will discourage repeat purchases and affect brand equity. See case study 3 for a take on Dracula's use of integrated marketing communication branding.

C CASE STUDY 3

IMC Branding: Dracula

Tod Browning's 1931 production of Bram Stoker's *Dracula* is one of my favorites of the Universal horror collection. And Bela Lugosi's portrayal of the creepy count from Transylvania continues to inspire moviegoers and enthusiasts as well as inform all other depictions of vampires onstage, on-screen, and in books.

Because of that consistency and memorability, Dracula can actually teach important lessons about branding for small businesses, associations, or entrepreneurs.

Lesson 1: Positioning Dracula

Brand positioning should always be done *relative to* the competition. In Dracula's case, he is positioned *against* other classic monsters of the day: Frankenstein's monster, the Wolfman, the Mummy, the Gill Man of *Creature from the Black Lagoon*, and many others.

But effective positioning defines what makes you unique. The famous vampire is differentiated by his aristocratic alter ego—Count Dracula—and by his ability to morph into a bat on demand. While other movie monsters terrified their victims simply by their presence, Dracula first hypnotized with his gaze and then sucked their blood for a protein-rich midnight snack.

Dracula was different—not the same old robot, alien, or zombie. So he has a clear and consistent position in our minds.

Lesson 2: Defining Brand Dracula

Developing the Dracula brand is pulling together various attributes, such as personality, image, and core competencies. What did Dracula stand for?

Dracula was good at mixing with high society. His personality was sophisticated, and—in later movie evolutions of the character—he's quite the ladies' man. He was mysterious, shrouded in intrigue, and was repelled by wolfsbane, garlic, and a cross.

A mirror could not hold his undead reflection. Those and other characteristics are what make up the memorable and unique brand. Dracula was about something remarkable. That's how he got noticed, got publicity, got word-of-mouth buzz—and, ultimately, got new customers (or victims!).

Lesson 3: Developing Dracula's Identity

This is the fun part. In business, it's stuff like your name, logo, tagline, colors, and other elements that make up your trade dress.

For the count, it's his signature cape. (Lugosi was buried in his Dracula cape; it was that important a part of his persona.) It's also his widow's peak hairdo, eastern European accent, hypnotic eyes, nocturnal feeding habits, and propensity to shape-shift into a bat.

It's important that all *your* identity elements are in place—and used consistently—before spending a penny on marketing, communications, or advertising.

Lesson 4: Going Public with Dracula

Dracula enlisted the assistance of Renfield, the real-estate broker who unwittingly helped the count secure a derelict abbey near London from which to "run his business." This was Dracula's "brand launch."

But that launch started *inside* Dracula's castle, as Lugosi prepared his undead minions and his daytime hangout—his casket—for the public launch. That's because he realized that his staff was critical to building a strong brand.

Your employees and frontliners are your best advocates, your most loyal evangelists, and your best brand ambassadors. Like Dracula, your job is to make sure your staff is engaged, bought in, involved, and communicated to continually in the branding or rebranding process.

Only when safely in Carfax Abbey with his staff—minus the hapless Renfield, who had been admitted to the sanitarium adjoining the abbey—did Dracula make his grand entrance into London society, his "target audience."

Here's how you can be sure that—like the count—you'll effectively stand out in a crowded marketplace:

- **Position your business and stand apart.** Positioning is the process by which your business creates an image or identity in the minds of your core market, giving them a *reason* to choose your offerings. Positioning is always done relative to your competition. Consider what makes your business unique. Why should people support Brand You and not Brand B?
- **Specialize and focus.** The aristocratic vampire drank blood from his victim's necks to stay alive. Like Drac, specialization lets you build your brand around your strengths. And this focus allows you to differentiate your business, offers you presumed expertise and perceived value, and makes it easier for prospects and customers to understand your business. Focus allows you to first *simplify* and then *amplify* your message—because the less information we're given, the more likely we are to remember it.
- **Your business's identity is made up of "outer layers"**—those attributes that prospects and customers see and experience. Make sure you're clear on what makes your offerings unique, and then align that difference with your name, logo, tagline, messaging, and other visual and verbal cues that will allow your target market to "get" what you're all about. Like the count's cape, your trade dress can be the ultimate branding tool.
- **It's critical to engage staff and other stakeholders** in embracing what you stand for. In fact, 86 percent of employees say being engaged in the brand would make them more likely to talk positively about the company they work for with others outside the organization. Your customer's notion of your brand is formed from his or her first experience, or "imprint" (or in Dracula's case, love bite), with your business or service. Every interaction is a chance to enrich your brand. Your staff should be able to answer this question every day: "How am I helping deliver on the company's brand promise today?"

Sure, Dracula eventually had a stake pounded through his heart. But don't let his demise distract you from building a strong brand to help increase your business's awareness, differentiate you from the competition, and drive revenues.

Source: Michael DiFrisco, "Brand Dracula: Four Branding Lessons from the Undead," *MarketingProfs*, October 25, 2013, http://www.marketingprofs.com/articles/2013/11927/brand-dracula-four-branding-lessons-from-the-undead#ixzz2oPYTVyjX.

Brand Equity: What Is Brand Equity?

Brand equity is a company or product's reputation in the marketplace. Over time, a brand must repeatedly deliver reliable results to create trust between the target and the brand. Trust translates into brand loyalty and repeat sales.

From the consumers' perspective, brand equity means they are familiar with the brand and know from experience that it brings positive results and unique brand associations. So, to the consumer, brand equity is made up of two kinds of brand knowledge: **brand awareness** and brand image.

Brand equity is our perception of quality based on experience, often before we buy a product. For example, Campbell is a brand, even though it is not a specific product. We buy Campbell's chicken soup or tomato soup—a product—because we know it's a quality brand and thus favor it over, say, a store brand. Consequently, Campbell has more brand equity in the mind of the consumer than does a grocery store brand.

Once a product or service becomes so well known that its name is no longer its sole brand identity, other aspects of its package design or logo treatment, such as typeface, graphic symbol, or color use, can be just as representative as the brand name. For example, most consumers can conjure up the Coke script, the Nike swoosh, or the Bayer Aspirin yellow in their minds without the product in front of them. This is because those brands have equity or ownership of their product categories.

But being the recognizable face of a product category can have its drawbacks. For instance, a brand's equity can be threatened when its brand name becomes the noun used to describe all products within a category, such as Kleenex for all tissue products, Xerox for all photocopies, or Coke for all soda products. We have all been guilty of using one of the above brand names to represent a generic product. These companies have been almost too successful at building **brand equity**, setting themselves apart from the competition so well that their equity is being eroded away as the brand name becomes the representative for a product category or task.

IMC can be used to identify and turn around this generic use before a product's name becomes mainstream and the brand loses its brand identity, its trademark protection, and its target loyalty. Some well-known examples of brands that have lost their trademark protection include aerobics, aspirin, cellophane, cola, corn flakes, escalator, granola, hoagie, kerosene, linoleum, nylon, raisin bran, shredded wheat, super glue, thermos, touch tone, trampoline, yo-yo, and zipper. To better tackle the problem of generic usage head-on, brands might employ public relations announcements or news or magazine feature articles. Advertising or direct-marketing efforts can create awareness and reinforce not only product differences but also the relationship with the target.

Brands: What's in a Name?

A brand is a product's name. Its image is created through advertising and often over a long period of time, becoming part of that brand's reputation. Brands are identifiers: Some are easy to acquire; others we aspire to obtain because of the status they bring or the success they represent. The more intimate the relationship between the target and a brand, the less likely the target is to switch to a competitive brand based on its advertising claims and/or current promotions.

Brand Awareness: Perception Is the Better Part of Advertising

It may seem obvious that before a brand can succeed, the target needs to be aware of its existence. But what is not always so obvious is that the target also needs to be aware of what the product or service offers, how it is different from competing brands, and how it can address their specific wants or needs. It is important that every product or service, whether new, old, or mainstream, know its own product attributes and perceived image before making any claims against or comparisons to competing brands.

Once the target is aware of the brand, the next logical step is for the target to form an opinion based on the product, service, or corporation's reputation, advertised image, and/or ability to fulfill a specific need or want.

Brand Image

A **brand's image** is its personality and its status as compared with other brands of the same or similar quality in its category. Targets must decide whether they like it or don't like it or whether they care about how influencers, whose opinions are valued, will think of them when they are seen using the product or service.

A brand's image is created and maintained by what we think about a product before and after use. Brand image is built in the media and maintained in the mind of the consumer based on quality or lack thereof. Brand image is based on consistency. Every time the product name is mentioned, the consumer associates an image or specific qualities with it.

A brand's personality must be built around the target's needs and wants. It should become a reliable old friend that does not change with each passing fad but can be trusted to bring home consistent results, purchase after purchase.

Most brands in a given product category are the same; today it is easy for companies to quickly create a product exactly like a successful competitor's, often at a lower cost. But reputation cannot be replicated. Advertising should build on that. By creating a brand image or personality for a client's product, creative teams can successfully make it stand out from the competition. Make it more distinct through creative ideas, packaging, and logo design; make consumers see, hear, and feel the product before they need it by using distinctive typography, color, and slogans. If the client's product is the one they think of first and the one they trust, they will purchase and/or use it because it delivers on its advertised promises.

Image development begins by asking a few questions about the product: Is there anything holding back the brand, such as limited size or color choices? How much does the target already know about the product versus that of the competition? Is there any confusion that deals directly with the product's visual/verbal identity, purchasing options, or life-cycle stage?

The Visual/Verbal Brand

Before a brand can achieve equity or develop or maintain loyalty, its product must first have a consistent brand image that can parallel the target audience members' perceived image of themselves. This consistent identity begins with the development of a logo design that appears in all communication efforts and on all packaging. A product's visual/verbal identity should not only define its personality and/or image but also represent a solution to the target's problem. Its distinctive look should be one of the factors that make the product or service stand out from its competition.

A brand's identifying symbol or logo design can include a representative typeface, color or colors, and graphic symbol that reflect the brand's personality and/or use. Another, simpler option might be nothing more than a black-and-white type treatment. A slogan or tagline representing the corporate or campaign philosophy may also accompany the symbol.

When producing multiple pieces for use in multiple media, such as public relations, advertising, direct marketing and sales promotion, the Internet and social media, out-of-home and transit, or mobile or alternative media, it is imperative that the logo design be visible and consistent. Believe it or not, the target may not remember the name of the product, but he will remember the package, color(s), slogan, or logo and look for that when buying. Obviously, the promotional goal is to encourage name recognition, but color or logo recognition will do just as well (see figure 3.1).

Figure 3.1. A new product launch should incorporate known elements of the existing brand (the Starbucks logo) while also developing a visual/verbal message that matches the target audience's lifestyle (healthy, affordable indulgence). Image courtesy of Jenna Kay Boucher, University of Tennessee.

Once the product or service has an individualized visual/verbal identity, image development must also take into account which **life-cycle phase** the product or service is in: new, mainstream or mature, or reinvention.

New Brand

A new product will need to have an image developed for it that matches the target audience's self-image and reflects its members' lifestyle. New products are a blank canvas that will, over time, need to develop brand equity and earn consumer loyalty. To create a competitive advantage, a new product must immediately distinguish its product advantages from those of the competition.

Determining which product advantage to promote will depend on the target, what the competition is doing, what needs to be accomplished, and the creative strategy used to influence the target. Considering these options, a product's advantages may be implied, found among its features and benefits, or based on price, status, or elitism. Additional advantages might center on the creation of a fad or trend, or they might be based entirely on emotional or rational needs. Creating brand awareness is critical to the success of a new product launch.

Mainstream/Mature Brands

Once a brand has been established, communication efforts must work to consistently maintain awareness, reinforce quality and reliability, and continue building a relationship with the target.

Reinvented Brands

Reinvention can occur when a brand needs a new or updated image, or as a result of a damaged reputation. A product's reinvention means looking past sins in the eye and eliminating outdated approaches that directly affect image and target perception. Products that are reinvented, no matter the reason, will have to prove themselves over time in order to rebuild lost equity and regain brand loyalty.

A product's creative message can focus on any one of or combination of the following options when a product's life-cycle stage will play an important role in advertising and promotional efforts:

- *Brand image.* How does the target audience view the product or service?
- *Word of mouth.* What kind of experience did the target audience have with the brand? Whether good or bad, a target's opinions carry a lot of weight with others within the targeted group.
- *Positioning.* What does the target think about the product or service compared to the competition?
- *Education.* How will the product be used? Is it expensive, professional, or technical?
- *Brand awareness.* What does the target audience know about the product or service?
- *Promotional offers.* Is there a need to create involvement through coupons, contests, or samples?
- *Creating a reaction.* Is there a need to get the target to come into a showroom to try the product or visit a website for more information or to make a purchase?

- *Direct comparison to the competition.* Will the key consumer benefit be stronger if a direct comparison of features is made to those of the competition?
- *Use.* Is the product or service revolutionary? Is it easy or difficult to use?
- *Product introduction.* Where is the target's knowledge? Is the product new, old, or considered a reliable old standard?

The bottom line is that no matter what life-cycle stage the product or service is in, for it to become or stay successful the target must believe the message and relate to the image.

Brand Loyalty

Brand loyalty refers to the relationship between the product and the target. Brand loyalty—the target's dependable repurchase of a brand based on favorable and reliable past experiences—is critical to IMC and brand equity. It is important that all advertising and promotional efforts represent the product as it is, not as an exaggeration of what it is. This is the best way to build and maintain brand loyalty, which in turn leads to brand equity.

Brand loyalty is built on trust and the knowledge that the product will deliver what it promises every time it is purchased or used.

Remember, objectives determine what needs to be accomplished through advertising efforts. The product's position in its life cycle will determine what those objectives are as they relate to brand development, maintenance, or reinvention.

Brand-loyal consumers require less coaxing to repurchase. With the cost of advertising in today's market, it is (or it should be) every client's goal to build brand loyalty by targeting its advertising efforts to the right audience, providing consistency of product, and building a brand image consistent with the product's use and/or personality—and then maintain it. The more intimate the relationship between the target and a brand, the less likely the target is to be affected by competitive promotions.

Positioning

Positioning relates to how the consumer thinks about and rates a product or service against the competition. Positioning requires highlighting target-relevant benefits for the product's features. Benefits must be tied to uses that will enhance the target's lifestyle or image. The position of a brand is sometimes confused with brand image: A brand's position in the mind of the consumer is created via advertising and promotion; brand image is created based on experience.

Positioning is effective only if fully researched. The entire advertising team must *know*— not think it knows—how the consumer thinks and feels about the product or service. Questions needing answers include: Who is most likely to use the product or service? What are the benefits to the target of using the product? How does the product stand up against the competition—what makes it unique; what features are duplicated? What is the perceived value of the product within the marketplace? How will the product be made available to the target? Does it come in different sizes, colors, or price ranges? Is it relevant to the target?

One of the ways to break through the advertising clutter is to find out what makes the client's product or service unique and position the product directly against the competition's image. If communication efforts can prove the client's product is bigger, faster, or longer lasting than the competing brand, it is more likely to be noticed and remembered.

It's important to understand that the client's product is probably not the only product of its kind; it is most likely one of many virtually identical products in the category. To make it stand out from the crowd, the creative team must carve out a **niche** or position for the product. Today, most products are no longer mass advertised; rather, as discussed earlier, clients choose instead to use advertising vehicles that are more selectively targeted to eliminate media waste.

A strong position is a direct result of a strong brand. This position is built up over time based on reliability of performance. Branding gives a product or service an air of exclusivity and a unique identity from its competitors within the product category.

Successful, memorable advertising begins with an established position. Once a product's identity is established and accepted, consumers remember it and use it as a measurement device for all other competitors within the category. Measurement may be based on quality, convenience, reliability, or service, to name just a few factors.

Brand image helps to determine the product's position. This is because positioning deals with who the target audience is, what audience members currently think about the product, who the competition is and what the target thinks about them, and, finally, what features are relevant to the target. Once this is known, the creative team can determine and communicate positioning strategies.

In his article "How to Position Your Product," Luc Dupont outlines the seven ways to position a product or service:

- *Originality*. Being first at anything is a short-lived boast, but if the client's product is, use that factor to set the product up as unique.
- *Low price*. Less expensive does not necessarily mean lesser quality. A low price can be a selling point if the consumer is convinced of the product's value.
- *High price*. More expensive does not necessarily mean high quality; the target must be convinced an expensive product is worth the investment.
- *Sex of the consumer*. Not all products are made for both sexes. There are razors especially designed for women and others designed especially for men; fragrances are also gender oriented.
- *Age of the consumer*. Few products appeal to consumers of all ages, so it is important to consider the age of the target audience. Electric cars, for example, such as Tesla, focus on successful tech-savvy environmentalists; small cars like Fiat are targeted to young, urban consumers; branded T-shirts and jeans are standard in a teenage wardrobe, while upwardly mobile professionals might choose Polo as their branded look.
- *Time of day the product should be used*. Some products are intended for use at specific times of the day, such as cereal for breakfast, soup for lunch, frozen entrees for dinner, or popcorn as a late-night snack.
- *Distribution channels*. This relates to how the consumer will receive the product. Examples include ordering through a website or direct-marketing efforts delivered through the mail versus the need to visit a showroom.

Al Ries and Jack Trout, specialists in product positioning, sum it up this way: "In the communications jungle out there, the only hope to score big is to be selective, to concentrate on narrow targets, [and] practice segmentation. In a word, positioning."

Repositioning

A product needs to be **repositioned** when there is a need to change the way it is viewed in the mind of the target. Changing perception is much more difficult than working with an existing position or creating a new one. Repositioning should work to define a new or special niche in a consumer's mind.

Tweaking the Marketing Plan

Successful campaigns can, and should, run for years, continually striving to build both brand loyalty and brand equity. Change should be considered only when the product or company significantly changes. Today's advertised messages often change with the seasons, leaving little time for awareness or loyalty to emerge. The inconsistent repositioning of brands or repeated challenges to competing brands can affect the target's image of the product or service. Companies that are patient and that work at building product loyalty over time will find competitors' constant change less of a factor in building and maintaining brand equity.

Q DISCUSSION QUESTIONS

1. Why is it important to build a strong brand image?
2. Why can having strong and established brand equity be a drawback for certain brands?
3. What is brand image, and why is it important to a product or service?
4. What attributes make up a brand's visual and verbal identity?
5. What are the three life-cycle phases, and what roles do they play when developing a brand's visual and verbal identity?
6. Why is establishing brand loyalty important?
7. What is the difference between positioning and brand image?
8. Why is understanding positioning important to the entire advertising team? What questions need to be asked, and why?
9. According to Luc Dupont, there are seven different ways to position a brand. Define and explain each.
10. Define repositioning and explain under what circumstances a brand might be repositioned.

Creative Briefs

The Big Influence Inside a Small Document

The **creative brief**, also known as a copy platform, creative work plan, creative plan, or copy strategy, is the next step in the evolution of the creative strategy. Information from the marketing plan is used in the creative brief to outline the communication plan of attack.

A small internal document created by the account executive, the creative brief should dissect the product or service for the creative team. It should redefine the target audience, introduce the key consumer benefit, describe the individual features and consumer benefits, define objectives, address the competition, and outline tactics. It is the encyclopedia the creative team will use to define the integrated marketing communication message that needs to be communicated. Think of it as a set of building blocks, meticulously laying the foundation for the concept or idea that will become the visual/verbal message.

The creative brief is not a document that speculates or generalizes; it needs to be detailed and concise enough that the **creative team** of art directors and copywriters can use it to develop a creative solution for the client's communication problem. A creative brief also ensures that the creative team, the account executive, and the client all have a thorough understanding of exactly what objectives the communication efforts need to accomplish.

First and foremost, the creative brief is a business plan that provides the guidelines for developing the creative message. It is not a creative outlet; the account executive is not writing copy or defining or determining what creative should look like. It is a road map for idea generation and visual/verbal development. See case study 4 about CVS.

There is no exact length for a creative brief. The only absolute is that it must contain all the information the creative team needs to inspire ideas and keep focused on what problems need to be solved.

CASE STUDY 4

IMC Branding: CVS Rebranding Strategy

Background

CVS is the United States' second-largest drug retailer and ranked number 13 in the 2013 Fortune 500 list. Its prescription drug sales account for 70 percent of its total revenue. CVS has brought a new concept to the pharmaceutical industry by creating an online pharmacy.

With more than 7,800 stores across the United States, people can easily find CVS almost anywhere in the country and experience the convenience this one-stop store offers. Customers can also make their purchases, including prescriptions, online through its website, http://www.cvs.com, and have their orders delivered to their door.

CVS had a busy and interesting 2014. First, in February, it decided to cease all tobacco sales by October 1. The response—from investors and in earned media—was overwhelmingly positive.

"While there's never a right time to walk away from $2 billion in revenue, this was the right time," CVS President and Chief Executive Larry Merlo said in an interview. "Eliminating this obstacle will allow our company to grow over the long term."

Here is how Merlo describes his company:

> Our company does a lot of different things, and at first glance it may be difficult to see how they're all related. We run retail stores and pharmacies. We operate retail health clinics. We administer prescription benefit plans. We sponsor and conduct health care research. Yet everything we do is tied together by one important idea: We are committed to reinventing pharmacy for better health. Our unique combination of best-in-class businesses positions us to deliver on this promise in a way that no other company can.

Challenges in Health Care

There are many challenges and opportunities in this market. For example, there's the rising cost of health care and what amounts to a growing traffic jam of people waiting to access the health care system. By 2020 the country will be short an estimated 45,000 physicians.

These are troublesome roadblocks because what quickly gets lost in this scenario is preventive care. If health care becomes more expensive and harder to access, people can be rerouted off their healthy path. And many of these detours have dire consequences.

With these and an array of other challenges facing its customers, CVS realized, it needed to be more than just a place where customers go to pick up their prescriptions.

The Problem

Looking to position itself as a more health-focused drugstore, CVS has a new corporate name and initiative to help its consumers quit smoking. The company is changing its name from CVS Caremark to CVS Health (though the store signage will still read CVS/pharmacy).

"We've changed our company name to CVS Health to reflect our purpose of helping people on their path to better health," officials at the company stated.

CVS Health officials say the rebranding effort helps align the company for an expanded role in providing health-care services beyond the traditional retail pharmacy business model.

The drugstore is banking on an image change. The company hopes that by becoming the first chain to stop selling tobacco products, consumers will be convinced that its 7,700 pharmacies are the go-to for their health and wellness needs.

Eliminating cigarettes and other tobacco products from its shelves represents a radical step forward. This offers a good example of corporate authenticity; CVS is signaling a major shift in its retail operations, from a primarily transactional model to a health-service hybrid focused on its customers' quality of life. And it's taking action to back up the rebranding strategy. In fact, action is the rebranding strategy.

The CVS brand is sending a clear signal about its commitment to help consumers live healthier and better lives. Further, this decision to include wellness as a defining brand attribute will likely appeal to non-consumer stakeholders such as hospitals, health insurers, and physicians, who have become attractive partners in the retail pharmacy value chain.

CVS Rebranding Strategy Alternatives

So, how are they pulling it off?

First and foremost, CVS is displaying great courage with its business practices, and savvy instincts with its rebranding strategy.

Although sales of tobacco products at drugstores such as CVS account for less than 4 percent of all tobacco sales, CVS must clearly follow up this big strategic move with other marketing initiatives to help maintain or increase share of wallet among current CVS customers. Additionally, a demonstrable shift to brand values that reflect customer values could boost customer acquisition for CVS—attracting new customers or those switching from competitors.

Results

It is unclear whether the move has yielded any financial benefits to the pharmacy chain. To date, none of the other national pharmacy chains have followed CVS's lead and dropped cigarettes.

The company stated that the new name reflects "its broader health care commitment and its expertise in driving the innovations needed to shape the future of health," while CEO Larry Merlo told *Forbes*, "Changing the name catches up with what we have been doing."

Reflecting on the big announcement from CVS—the elimination of tobacco products from its stores—here are my observations:

This move by CVS did more for the brand than ten years of promotion could ever do. Through a bonanza of PR and social media buzz, it's receiving a dramatic marketing lift. According to data sourced on Topsy.com, the announcement spawned more than 100,000 tweets; even President Obama weighed in! Most significantly, it's forging meaningful differentiation in the market segment.

Think about it. What did CVS stand for before this shift? Nothing too distinctive, right? Today there's a new thought in the back of everyone's mind: "CVS is a genuine advocate for my health."

An outcome like that is every marketer's dream, and CVS achieved it not by "saying" something, but by "doing" something. This is the new success principle of modern marketing. Actions always speak much louder than words.

Conclusion

So, want to be a new brand hero like CVS?

First, it requires a statement of purpose—one that directs action and choices. The bolder, the better. Then it takes courageous leadership from the top to implement that statement of purpose.

Marketing has never been a departmental activity; instead it is one of two major functions of the firm (the other is innovation). And this type of business decision making is maybe the best marketing of all. Hats off to CVS and its CEO for showing us the way.

Note: In the year following its decision to stop selling tobacco products at all its drugstores, people purchased ninety-five million fewer packs of cigarettes in thirteen states, according to a CVS Health study.

Source: "The CVS Rebranding Strategy: A Case Study," Digital Spark Marketing, http://digitalsparkmarketing.com/cvs-rebranding-strategy/.

What Makes Up a Creative Brief?

Overall length, information content, and format vary by agency, but most creative briefs contain, at minimum, the following:

- Target audience profile
- Communication objectives
- Product features and benefits
- Positioning of the product
- Key consumer benefit
- Creative strategy
- Tone
- Support statement
- Slogan or tagline
- Logo

Target Audience Profile

Redefine the target audience here. Remember, the target audience consists of those consumers determined through research to be the most likely to buy or use the client's product or service. They should be characterized in living detail through demographics, psychographics, geographics, and behavioristics.

The goal of advertising is not only to inform but also to find just the right way to inspire the target to act. When developing a creative direction, it's important that the creative team never lose sight of who the target is. The target audience is the reason for developing communication efforts. The creative team must know how the target will react to the message in order to successfully advertise any product. Just knowing what the target thinks, what he finds important, and how the product or service can fulfill his needs and wants makes creating the right message a lot easier. It is easy to strike out by communicating to the masses with a generalized message or hit the ball out of the park with an individualized, consumer-focused message.

Communication Objectives

Communication objectives, or goals, clearly define what the communication efforts need to accomplish. Objectives should pinpoint what the target should think about the product or service, what the target should feel when using the product or feel toward the product over-all, and what the target should do, such as make a purchase or request additional information.

There is a limit to what can be accomplished with one ad or even a campaign. On aver-age, no product or service should have more than one to three obtainable objectives. Each objective needs to focus on communication-related issues. Communication-based objectives give consumers usable, personalized information as opposed to marketing-based objectives, which are sales related. Primarily, creative efforts will focus on positioning objectives that inform and educate the consumer about the product or service compared to competing brands. It is important when determining objectives to know the target's level of knowledge about the product or service. A look at the product or service's life-cycle stage will also be beneficial when determining what needs to be said or shown; what needs to be introduced, maintained, or expanded; and what needs to be overhauled completely. This will affect whether objectives can be accomplished over the short or long term.

Think of it this way: If you have a new product launch or are reinventing a brand, a relationship must be built first on image and then on trust. The first thing objectives need to accomplish is to position the brand in the mind of the consumer while working to build brand awareness. Over time, the objective is to achieve loyalty and, eventually, brand equity. This type of traditionally based or mass-media advertising is known as brand image adver-tising. To be successful, all objectives must translate to results.

Product Features and Benefits

The features and benefits section looks at product attributes and attaches them to target needs and wants. One mistake young account executives or designers often make is to sell a product's features and not its benefits. A **feature** is a product attribute; a **benefit** answers the question *What's in it for me?* Let's use a toaster as an example.

Features are lovely but have no point. The point that needs to be hammered home is what the feature can offer the consumer. Determining a benefit for each of the product's features helps break down the product information into smaller, more manageable bundles, giving concept development a visual/verbal starting point.

See template 4.1 for an example of features and benefits for a toaster. If the product comes in five colors (feature), the creative brief should inform the creative team by listing all five colors. Research gathered on the target audience might suggest to the creative team that the target is upwardly mobile and might have just bought a new home, is on a budget and will be remodeling, or is trendy and just likes to keep up with the most current look in decorating. A benefit that informs the target there's a color that matches any decorating scheme or considers family size by featuring two-, four-, or six-slice models talks to the consumer's current needs.

TEMPLATE 4.1

T

Creative Brief

The purpose of the creative brief is to provide a blueprint for creating an effective ad or campaign. Preparing a brief forces the creative team to learn essential information about the client's brand and its situation and can inspire creativity. A brief can be presented in any number of ways; this example brief is set in two columns: one for headings, the second for information or instructions. See the format below. Place one inch of space between columns, with one-inch margins on all four sides. The creative brief should be double-spaced. Information about the product, target audience, competitors, and so on, must be gathered before an informative, helpful brief can be prepared. If the necessary information is not collected, the brief is useless and the campaign unlikely to be successful.

Target Audience Profile:	Define the target audience in terms of

- Demographics
- Psychographics
- Geographics
- Behavioristics

Identify common key internal and external factors in the target audience's frame of reference. Profile a typical target audience member.

Communication Objectives:	Describe what the ad is supposed to accomplish in terms of what the consumer should

- Think
- Feel
- Do

Is the ad intended to build brand awareness (think)? Is the goal to change consumers' attitudes toward the brand (feel)? What should the consumer do after exposure to the ad: Seek additional information by calling a toll-free number or visiting a website or make a purchase (do)?

These are communication-based objectives. Explain choices made.

Product Features: and Benefits:	List every attribute of the product (feature) and the benefit that results from each. Attributes can be inherent in the product (e.g., ingredients) or be aspects of the image of the brand (e.g., Rolex). List as many features and benefits as are needed to educate the creative team about the product or service. Set up each benefit and feature within this section in the following way:

- Feature: In one sentence, explain what the feature is.
- Benefit: In one sentence, explain what the benefit of the feature is to the target audience.

Repeat this format for each feature and benefit.

Positioning of the Product:	Briefly compare the client's product to its major competitors. Describe any advertising messages used currently or recently for competing brands.
Key Consumer Benefit:	From the features and benefits section above, choose one USP (unique selling proposition) or "big idea" feature/benefit combination that will dominate all ads and be sure to grab the target's attention. Choose either a USP or big idea. Justify choices based on everything stated above. This section should be no more than one to two sentences in length.
Creative Strategy:	Explain how the ad will convince the target to select the client's brand over others. Spell out how the objectives will be met. Select a strategy appeal or appeals and one or more approach(es) and explain choices made.
Tone:	How will the strategy be executed? What execution technique will be used? Will it be humor, fantasy, news? It is not unusual for a campaign to use a combination of tones to deliver the message. Explain direction based on what is presented in USP/big idea and Creative Strategy sections.
Support Statement:	Again, from the features and benefits section, choose a feature/benefit combination that directly supports the key consumer benefit.
Slogan or Tagline:	Include the brand's slogan or tagline here. It represents the company's or the brand's image and/or philosophy. Knowing it can help with creative direction.
Logo:	Place the name of the client, product, or service here.

Benefits can deal with either product feature/benefits or consumer feature/benefits. Features can be inherent in the product (e.g., ingredients) or imply that the status or image of the brand (e.g., Rolex) can affect the consumer's personal image or lifestyle.

Everything the creative team needs to know in order to write and design the visual/verbal message needs to be included in this section. That includes pricing issues and any **detail copy,** such as address, phone, fax, e-mail, hours, or credit card information. This is also where any specific information covering coupons or order forms should be included.

Positioning of the Product

Next, the creative brief should briefly discuss the brands that represent direct competition to the client's brand. Compare each product's similarities and differences to the client's brand, and explain how the target audience sees each brand. Rate the client's brand against its direct competitors based on brand image, positioning, and so on. Describe any advertising messages used currently or recently by competing brands.

This section will help keep the creative team from duplicating what competitors are saying and doing with their promotional efforts. To choose a key consumer benefit and determine the best way to make a product stand out from the competition, it is important to know what competitors are doing (see box 4.1).

BOX 4.1. Features/Benefits of a Toaster

Feature   Comes in five different colors: red, green, blue, yellow, and orange.
Benefit   Makes coordination with your kitchen color theme easier.
Feature   Comes in two-, four-, or six-slice models.
Benefit   No matter what size family you have to feed, there is a toaster size that makes it faster and easier.

Key Consumer Benefit

The key consumer benefit is the one feature/benefit combination that either is unique to the client's product or can be positioned as big or important. The key consumer benefit will be the point that screams from every ad, visually and/or verbally, positioning the product as the one that meets the target's internal and external needs. It will become the one voice of the IMC message and should be chosen because research has determined that it is important to the target audience and will speak directly to its members' interests and lifestyle, encouraging some sort of desired action.

There are two types of key consumer benefits: the **unique selling proposition (USP)** and the **big idea**. The big idea or USP is determined by analyzing the target audience and determining which feature and benefit combination can best accomplish the stated objectives. It will be the tie that binds all advertising and promotional efforts together. Along with the strategy, the USP or big idea will help determine the visual/verbal direction the communication efforts will take.

A Unique but Big Selling Idea

Determining whether to use a USP or a big idea depends on what the product or service has to say about itself compared to the competition and whether the target audience members think its benefits will enhance their lives. If the product or service speaks of individualism or uniqueness or is the first to introduce a product or feature, the best key consumer benefit to use would be a USP. A product that has no outstanding or unique characteristics to differentiate it from the competition will need a big idea. A big idea takes the feature/benefit combination and turns it into a memorable and creative idea that sells.

A USP has a feature/benefit combination that is unique or exclusive to the client's product or service. USPs are also used in promoting a commonplace feature as unique. If competitors have products with an identical feature but are not advertising it, make the feature unique by making it important to the target, and use it to stand out from the competition. For example, all microwaves may have a plug, but no one has found a unique way to make their product's plug a creative symbol. Differentiation can come from a creative idea touching a known interest with the target, fulfilling a need, or creating a status symbol.

Figure 4.1. In this ad, three key benefits are emphasized: Ju-Ju-Be bags are fashionable, well organized, and machine washable. Image courtesy of Leah Thompson, University of Tennessee.

The Big Idea

A big idea is a creative solution that sets the client's product apart from the competition while at the same time solving the client's advertising problem. This does not mean the competition does not have the identical feature, only that it is not pushing it in its advertising. Big ideas that are consumer focused or based on lifestyle will have more longevity than product-oriented ideas. This is because concepts based on lifestyle are more difficult for the competition to duplicate. When using a big idea, creativity is the key to success.

Finding inspiration for a big idea is a little more difficult than determining a USP. The big idea most often must create something unique and interesting out of nothing in order to attract attention and create a relationship with the target. But by focusing on the consumer and her lifestyle, even a generic product feature can alter a target's existing view of a product.

The key is to shape it into an unusual, different, or interesting benefit that will catch the target's attention. There are several places to look for a big idea:

- Life (your imagination)
- Creative strategy
- Product name
- Product use
- Product appearance
- Product features
- Product comparison
- The news
- Pop culture (books, movies)
- Historical reference

A product or service will never stand out from the competition or build brand loyalty if the USP or big idea has a "me-too" message or a "been there, done that" creative. A product must have an identity and offer personalized benefits the target can relate to and a creative approach that offers the target a reason to try it.

In the next step, the creative team will combine the big idea or USP and the strategy to get an idea of what needs to be accomplished creatively in order to create a consistent, memorable, informative, and beneficial idea that touches the target and can transfer easily between media vehicles.

Creative Strategy

The creative strategy is the foundation for the creative direction or concept. Strategy tells the creative team how it will talk to the target and accomplish the stated objectives and the best way to feature the key consumer benefit. The strategy's main objective is to explain how advertising and promotional efforts will position the brand and how it will compete against other products in the same category. The client's product must be made to step up and away from the competition in a way that is important to the target. If research, media, and creative efforts reflect the strategy, a successful outcome is within reach.

The strategy employed by communication efforts is critical to accomplishing brand differentiation. Brand position engenders brand awareness by creating a brand image that is important to the target. Only through research can we determine what these influencers or specific factors are. Advertising clutter can influence these factors.

One of the best ways to make a brand stand out from competing products is to employ a positioning strategy. This is, quite simply, how the product is looked at compared to its competition. To favorably position the product in the mind of the consumer, the creative team must determine what factors or benefits are important to the target and build a message around that. Another option is to use a brand strategy. Branding develops a personality for a product or service that creates a favorable relationship between product value and target need. Building brand loyalty through quality or reliability ensures the product is the only purchase option in the mind of the consumer, leading to repeat purchase.

Several decisions need to be made before deciding on a strategy direction. The first is what approach will be used to determine how the product or service will be positioned, the second is what kind of appeal will be used to reach the target, and the third is the execution technique or tone that will be used to make the appeal.

Many factors can affect the creative strategy. One of the most important is the life-cycle stage of the product or service. Many communication obstacles can be overcome and opportunities exploited by considering and using this information. During a product launch, building brand awareness is one of the most important steps; as interest in the brand grows, building awareness plays less of a role.

The next phase outlines the product's benefits over the competition. As the product's status and/or reputation solidifies, building brand equity or owning a large share of the product category is important. It is also important to keep the target up to date on any product or technological changes associated with the brand. Finally, ensuring brand loyalty takes repeated efforts to deliver a high-quality and reliable product.

The creative team uses the creative strategy section to determine the approach and the appeal combination that will be used to determine the look and overall tone the creative message will take. The approach chosen can focus on the product, the consumer, or the objectives, while the appeal looks at whether the product or service will fulfill an emotional or rational need. Every concept will be built around the choice of approach, appeal, and tone or execution technique.

Let's first take a look at two different types of strategic approaches. The first concentrates on using either a consumer- or product-oriented approach. The second uses the think/feel/do model to define objectives.

Product- or Consumer-Oriented Strategic Approaches

Once the decision is made on whether to focus on the product, the consumer, or the desired consumer reaction, the creative team can begin to flesh out the concept direction. There are several different ways an ad's message can be approached; most can be categorized as having either a product- or consumer-oriented focus. The appeal used will be based on the approach that will be stressed:

- A product-oriented approach focuses on one or more feature(s)/benefit(s) of the product.
- A consumer-oriented approach focuses on shaping consumer attitudes about new and existing products and demonstrating how the product can solve a problem.

Product-Oriented Strategy A product-oriented approach can focus on one of four different areas: generic claim, product feature, USP, or positioning.

- *Generic claim.* Pushes a product category rather than a specific product.
- *Product feature.* Pushes one specific feature of the product—ideally one unique to the product—in all advertising and promotional efforts.
- *Unique selling proposition (USP).* Pushes a unique product benefit important to the target audience.

- *Positioning*. Focuses on how the target thinks about the product or service compared to the competition.

Consumer-Oriented Strategy   A consumer-oriented approach can focus on three major areas: brand image, lifestyle, and attitude.

- *Brand image*. Creates an image or builds a personality for the product.
- *Lifestyle*. Affiliates the product with the lifestyle of the target.
- *Attitude*. Affiliates the product with feelings, attitudes, and overall benefits of use. Strategies under each approach can be used individually or combined.

Think, Feel, Do, Strategic Approaches

Another way to define the strategic direction is to work directly off the desired consumer reaction defined in the objectives.

Think Message Strategies   Think message strategies are used to evoke identity, image, or message and can focus on three different areas: brand identity, generic, and positioning.

- *Brand identity*. A product or service is so established and well known that it can be identified by its logo treatment or package alone.
- *Generic*. If the product or service has no unique characteristics to set it apart from those of the competition, it is important to take a feature/benefit combination not being promoted by competitors and make it appear unique to the product and important to the target.
- *Positioning*. Deals with how the target currently views the product or service compared to the competition. These views may need to be created, enhanced, maintained, or reinvented, depending on the product's life cycle.

Feel Message Strategies   Feel message strategies are used to create emotional or fact-based responses and can focus on six different areas: brand image, association, lifestyle, attitude, respectability, and significance.

- *Brand image*. What should the target think about the product?
- *Association*. What association does using this product or service create between the product's image and the target's self-image?
- *Lifestyle*. What can this product do for the target?
- *Attitude*. What feelings can be created through use of the product to create an emotional tie with the target?
- *Respectability*. What do users of the product have to say about it? Testimonials are a great way to highlight the quality of new products, alleviate fears about products with potential risks, or repair a bruised or damaged image.
- *Significance*. What features and benefits are relevant to the target? This approach is useful for brands that are unique from the competition or that offer features and benefits not inherent in the competition. Creative solutions are the key here. This is

a great way to build status or give importance to previously ignored features. Creative solutions could be used to build status or introduce uses for features never before seen as relevant.

Do Message Strategies   Do message strategies are used to incite action and can focus on four different areas: promotional response, memorable reaction, incentive programs, and interaction.

- *Promotional response.* The competition has one-upped the client. To bring the target's attention back to the client's product, this would be a good time to offer an incentive to create immediate purchase, offsetting the competition's position of power.
- *Memorable reaction.* Used to remind the target audience of its history with a mature brand.
- *Incentive programs.* Offer a reward to the consumer with repeat purchase. Incentive programs are great for building brand loyalty.
- *Interactive.* Create dialogue between the manufacturer and the target. The target can get additional information, give feedback, or make a purchase directly from the seller.

The strategic approach employed will depend on the product or service, the target audience, the key consumer benefit, the overall objectives, and the appeal and execution package employed.

The Appeal of the Message

Once the team has determined whether they will be using a consumer-, product-, or objective-oriented approach, the next step is to determine the appeal or feel.

An ad's job is to persuade. Whether it is successful or not depends on the type of appeal used. There are two types of appeals: emotional and rational. Consumer response depends upon whether the product fills an emotional need or a rational need. Many advertising efforts will employ the use of both appeals.

Emotional needs include lifestyle enhancers such as cars, iPads, jewelry, and fashion. Emotional appeals target image and are used on status-related products. These ads appeal to the target's need to fit in, be a trendsetter, or stand out from the crowd.

Rational needs are life sustaining, like food and clothing. Rational appeals are information based, using facts, charts, or expert opinions to back up claims. These ads are meant to educate the consumer on the product's use, quality, and value.

Appeals are used to attract consumer attention and influence the perception of need for a product. The focus is most often placed on the consumer's need for or use of the product and/or how it will affect the consumer's lifestyle. Message content reflects on the features and benefits of a product or service. Often emotional appeals will work better on brands that have little or no differentiation from competing brands, since communication efforts are more creative and memorable and build image based on the target's psychological and/or social needs.

Since emotional appeals deal with how the target views self-image compared with the product or service's image, both the strategy and message content can be more creative and less rational or functional, focusing on personal pleasure. If the message will focus on lifestyle or feelings, consider the following options: achievement, affection, ambition, comfort, excitement, fear, happiness, joy, love, nostalgia, pleasure, pride, safety, security, self-esteem, sentimentality, or sadness. Strategies focusing on social or image-based emotions might focus on acceptance, approval, belonging, embarrassment, involvement, recognition, rejection, respect, or social status or class.

Rational appeals can take several different forms: feature, competitive, price, news, and image appeals. Feature appeals focus on the most important trait of the product or service. Competitive appeals make comparisons to other brands to point out important or differentiating features. Price appeals use a product's price as a differentiating feature. News appeals give some kind of news about the product, perhaps a new and improved version or a technological advancement or upgrade. Image appeals stress a brand's status or popularity within its category or among other users. Some of the most common informational or rational motives for purchase include comfort, convenience, dependability, durability, economy, efficiency, health, performance, and quality.

If the product or service doesn't fit snugly into either the rational or emotional appeal category, there are alternative appeals to consider. Reminder advertising is used to maintain brand awareness for more mature products. Teaser advertising is used mostly for new product launches to increase curiosity and build interest in a new product before launch. Information is used to tease consumers about the product without showing it.

Tone

An extension of the creative strategy section, the tone or execution technique defines the personality and overall voice or style the advertising message will portray. The only rule is that it should reflect the key consumer benefit.

Once the approach and the appeal have been solidified, it's important to determine how the information will be delivered. The execution style or technique is the development of the visual and verbal tone, what it will look and sound like, or the overall way the ad will be presented to the target.

The tone should be outlined in a couple of sentences that describe the product's personality and the attitude, mood, or spirit of the ad or campaign as presented in the key consumer benefit and strategy sections. This personality can be either stated or visualized in the advertised message. It is important to remember that the style of language uses flags or attracts consumer attention based on quality, fun, or status, as much as any visual can.

Questions to consider when determining tone include: Will the overall visual/verbal message be conceptually emotional or rational in tone? Will the focus be on the product or the consumer? What role, if any, should the competition play? Where is the product or service in its life cycle? Should the tone of the message be hard sell, soft sell, or more visually enticing in nature?

The visual/verbal tone used to address the target audience must be very effective because if the target audience does not connect with the product, there is a good chance the target will not buy it. By now the creative team should be able to determine how that connection can be developed and how the target will respond to humor, facts, or testimonials. Is the product or service newsworthy, can it teach the target something, or will consumers be more interested in a demonstration? Whatever the tone used, it should work toward creating or supporting the brand's image, promoting the key consumer benefit, and advancing the strategy.

The technique chosen should be the tie that binds the approach and appeal together (see box 4.2). It's important to note that the appeal and execution technique may change, depending on whether communication efforts are talking to the primary or secondary targets or influencers. The key is that they must consistently focus on the key consumer benefit each time the specific audience sees the communicated message.

BOX 4.2. Tones/Execution Techniques for Visually and Verbally Presenting the Key Consumer Benefit

To set a rational tone, try using:

• Straight sell or factual message	Reminder
• Technical or scientific	Teaser
• Demonstration	Instructional
• Comparison	Talking head
• Testimonial	Dialogue
• News event or educational	Lifestyle and narrative
• Authoritative	

To set an emotional tone, opt for:

• Humor	Fear
• Fantasy	Sex
• Animation	Scarcity
• Slice of life	

Combination tones can be conveyed by:

☐ Character representative or personality symbol
☐ Product feature or product as the star
☐ Inherent drama
☐ Music

Support Statement

The **support statement** is one feature/benefit combination that can be used to directly support or advance the key consumer benefit. Consider the toaster example used in box 4.1 regarding color and kitchen decor. If this becomes the key consumer benefit, then the support statement for the two-, four-, or six-slice toaster could address how much counter space is required for use or how its stylish design is contemporary enough to complement any decorating scheme.

Slogan or Tagline

Often used interchangeably, the slogan and the tagline are associated with the logo and appear either above it or below it. A **slogan** deals with the company or corporate philosophy; a **tagline** defines the campaign or ad philosophy.

Logo

The logo is the product or corporate symbol. It could be a simple graphic, a line of text, simple initials, or a combination of both a graphic and text. Always be sure to put the logo on the creative brief. It is helpful for the creative team to know for whom they are working.

When all is said and done, the job of the creative brief is to summarize goals, facts, features and benefits, and strategic direction for the creative team. No creative direction should be offered, but the facts will help define creative direction. The next step is conceptual development, or the idea stage. How will the information presented be used to meet the stated objectives? What will be said, how will it be said, how will it be shown, and how will it be laid out on the page? The creative brief is a blueprint; it is the creative team's job to build the house and organize the details.

Q DISCUSSION QUESTIONS

1. Define what a creative brief is and how it is developed and used.
2. Define and describe in detail the ten sections that make up a creative brief.
3. What is the difference between a unique selling proposition (USP) and a big idea? When should each be used?

The Creative Process

Let's take a break from all this business and strategizing and take a detailed look at the creative process.

The Creative Brief Is the Inspiration behind a Good Idea

There is no document that outlines the creative concept or idea development stage. The documents we have looked at—the marketing plan and creative brief—concentrate on marketing assessments and an overall communication profile.

Creative, its interpretation, and its ultimate ability to produce a sale are the driving forces behind any integrated marketing communication ad or campaign. If creative efforts fail, it is because the marketing plan failed. The fate of an ad or campaign is sealed during the development of the creative brief.

Every piece of creative—copy and layout—begins and ends with the creative brief. Before any brainstorming takes place, before any copy is written or any concept laid out, the creative team needs to thoroughly study the creative brief.

The creative brief lays an informational foundation for the creative team to build upon. It outlines what the IMC creative efforts need to accomplish and is the rationale behind creative direction. The creative team will use the knowledge about the target to define the audience the team is talking to. Objectives will determine what the creative efforts will need to accomplish; the strategy and positioning will help determine how the message will be delivered and the image and position needed to stand out from the competition. The key consumer benefit will become the voice of the IMC promotion and must dominate all creative executions, both visually and verbally.

A great idea can usually be stated in one sentence: the key consumer benefit. It is what is done with that sentence that brings an idea to life and creates memorable ideas.

The Soccer Game of Idea Teamwork

Once the creative team has decided on a creative direction, the next step is determining a visual/verbal solution that will bring the idea to life. Coming up with that extraordinary idea is not as easy as most people think it is.

An active imagination is commendable, but it is fallible, and not every idea will be a good idea. However, believing your ideas are the best ideas is the only way to approach the creative process. Fortunately—or unfortunately, depending on how you look at it—there are always other people around to deny or confirm our brilliance. An idea needs to bounce around in your head, and once you've got it under control, it needs to be bounced off a colleague before it can be molded into a good idea. This may seem a little like a soccer match, with balls hitting everyone in the head a few times. You need a partner to play the idea game; this is why creatives often work in teams.

The creative team is made up of an art director and one or more copywriters. This team is responsible for developing the big idea, writing the ad copy, and designing ads that bring the key consumer benefit to life. The creative team takes these ideas and designs them to each media vehicle's strengths and limitations. When copywriters and art directors work together, visual and verbal communication becomes a powerful problem-solving combination.

Who Are the Creatives?

"Creative" as used in this text is a broad term for the conceptual process. A **creative** is a person who is involved in creative activity, especially, in this context, involved in the creation of advertisements. The creative team comprises some very eclectic personalities. Job titles, which are as diverse as the personalities that fill them, depend on where you are in the country and the size of the agency. The following discussion profiles only the most common and generally accepted titles.

- *Creative director.* This title probably varies most across the country, but basically this person is the boss or team leader. He or she handles administrative and/or management functions and is most often involved with television and other high-profile projects.
- *Art director.* Job titles range from junior through senior levels. This person is the workhorse of the advertising agency, with his or her hands in everything. On any given day, the art director could be working on newspaper, magazine, point-of-purchase (POP) advertising, direct mail, multiple digital options, alternative media projects, or television for any number of clients. The person in this position needs to know a lot about the creative process, from conceptual development to photo shoots to production.

- *Copywriter.* These team members write copy and, like art directors, may have a range of titles. Copywriters can find themselves writing copy for multiple media vehicles and even more diverse types of products.

The art director is the visual idea person. The copywriter is the verbal idea person. These two diverse minds sit down together with the creative brief in what are known as **brainstorming** sessions. These sessions are used to generate multiple ideas that will solve the client's advertising problem. Hundreds of good and bad ideas are presented for discussion; most will be discarded, but many will be worked on and developed further.

Anyone associated with a creative team must be open minded and well versed in social behaviors, current issues, politics, movies, music, and the classics. Creatives should be able to use anything from historical references to present-day slang to sell or represent a product or service. These brainstorming sessions are critical to getting boring "been there, done that" ideas out of their heads and getting down to the new, the unusual, and the eventually successful ones. New ideas set a product apart from its competitors and can be the catalyst to building lasting brand images and an ultimate and essential position in the minds of the consumer.

The key to a good brainstorming session is to never be afraid to look and feel stupid and to come up with a really, really bad idea. It's humbling but necessary in order to ignite the ideas of others in the session. One really bad thought voiced aloud can spark another— hopefully better—idea in another.

Stale advertising begins and ends with stale ideas. Most young creatives believe their first idea is their best idea, but it's only their best idea because it's their *only* idea. Test the waters and stretch your legs; you will be surprised where you end up.

The creative cylinders that must be firing to be a successful copywriter or art director include the following:

- Be able to see what is not there. If a product comes in six colors, what does that represent: a canvas, an oil spill, a sunset?
- Never linger in one place too long. A creative solution is often elusive and must be chased down through the clutter of one's own mind. Staring off into space, acting out, or borrowing the actions from the guy on the subway might evoke new ideas.
- Know the profession. What is old can be made new again, but it should not be copied if it is already associated with another product. Using nostalgia in a message can make a point; copying a competitor can be confusing.
- Be a student of media. Watch TV; go to mainstream and independent movies; pick up a book, newspaper, or magazine and read up on current and historical events; watch for fads and trends; watch the fashion wheel of fortune; listen to the radio, surf the web. Knowing and interpreting what's going on in society helps set new trends rather than having to follow them.
- Watch the human species. We're interesting, we're unique, and we can relate to one another's mannerisms, body language, style or lack thereof, eye movement, and hand gestures, or how different personalities and age groups move, eat, sit, stare, and read.
- Know the product. If you haven't used the product, do so. If you are unfamiliar with competing products, use them and compare. You can only successfully sell a product

you are intimate with. Knowledge is power, so empower yourself and you will be able to ignite action and interest in the target audience.

- Understand that advertising is a business. Creative is based on a business plan; it must be on strategy and on target to meet the stated objectives, and it must be on budget. Creatives never get to do exactly what they want. Accept that great ideas are not hindered by limitations but challenged by them.

- Excellence should come with the territory. If you can't spell or you lack grammatical skills, copywriting may not be in your future. If you are visually impaired and have never had an interesting or unique thought, art direction may not be the profession to pursue. Clients pay out large sums of money for the expertise advertising brings to the table. Because of this the competition is fierce, the life span short, and the stress high. It's what makes the profession a compelling one.

- Cry a little; laugh a lot. The creative process is a tough one. The chances of anyone liking any ideas in their original form are slim to none. Changes are a fact of life; rejection of ideas is right up there with death and taxes. Get over it. When an idea does take form and fly, it's like exercising: Initially you don't want to do it again, but once you see the results, you can't wait to start all over again.

It is important to understand that creative doesn't happen in a vacuum. It takes long hours and a lot of reworking before an idea can be presented, first internally to the team and then eventually to the client. Because the creative process takes place toward the end of the advertising process, time is limited. Brilliance may have as little as a few hours to as much as three to four weeks to show itself. Any creative team member must be able to turn on the creative juices at a moment's notice and for long hours at a time. Creatives must be willing to fight for what they believe in but also be able to let those ideas that just don't measure up go—and live to fight another day. Stress should be considered a creative catalyst, not a paralyzing force.

Because of these unique challenges, creatives are pretty well left alone to come and go as they please and to work in as creative and individualistic an environment as possible. If staring out the window or shooting baskets in your office motivates you, more power to you. Whatever gets the creative juices percolating can be found in any creative department.

Is the Idea on Target and on Strategy?

An effective IMC creative series must be **on target** and **on strategy** both visually and verbally throughout the promotional mix. The creative team members must ask themselves throughout the creative development stages whether the creative is still on target with the stated objectives. Is the creative strategy effectively reflecting those objectives? Does the tone, approach, and appeal decided upon for copy and visual images used reflect the strategy? Has the creative brief successfully dissected the product or service in order to understand its features and benefits? Is the visual/verbal message screaming out the key consumer benefit? Does the concept position the product or service away from the competition? Are consumers being reached in a language they can understand and with an image they can relate to? Is the key consumer benefit clearly apparent across all media? Does the promotional mix reflect media the target is sure to see? If the answer is yes to all the above questions, the creative efforts are on target and on strategy. If the visual look and the verbal message are inconsistent and the key consumer benefit is not apparent on all pieces, the creative is off target and/or off strategy. Advertising that is both off target and off strategy can be very entertaining, often even brilliant, but if it doesn't reach the intended target, create sales, and raise awareness, it's useless.

Where Does a Good Idea Originate?

The creative brief begins the idea generation stage. All great ads begin with a good idea. A good idea can come from an overactive imagination, pain, observation, experience, or just plain luck. It is the thing that drives concept. All good designers need to be culturally diverse and open minded and have an overactive imagination. This realm of endless possibilities, this dream state, is the place to define and build ideas. Go beyond the social media and YouTube culture, and look at the world as it once was and as it is. What *was* is very important in defining what *is*.

Go outside immediate likes and dislikes. Start with music, and experience new sounds like those from the archives of rock, jazz, blues, or country. Music is a powerful weapon; everyone relates to it in one way or another. Music makes listeners active participants, whether they're reminiscing or singing along.

Next, go to museums and art galleries to see how art, like advertising, marks history and defines cultures and attitudes. Attend independent film festivals, another cultural marker; note how your peers speak and represent culture, both past and present. Go to the park or the mall and people-watch; play with a child; talk to the elderly. Don't define or label anything you see; just experience it. After all, if we want advertising to touch readers', viewers', or listeners' taste buds or fashion consciousness, we need to understand their world.

Readers and viewers alike respond to stimulants, whether they're reminded of something from their childhood or college days or something they haven't yet experienced but wish to. If the thought is strategically planted, the consumer will decide whether to buy into the idea.

The team's imaginative thoughts will eventually lay the groundwork for an idea. That idea will need to be developed into a concept direction for the client's product or service. All great ads begin by developing, producing, and then eliminating hundreds of ideas that just didn't measure up. Open your conservative mind, and your liberal imagination will follow.

Daydreaming and role-playing are a designer's first line of defense when struggling to solve a client's advertising problem and are an important part of the design process. Those carefree dreams acted out in the backyard—when you imagined yourself a pilot, astronaut, explorer, princess, clown, or juggler—are just waiting to be resurrected. Feel free to act up and act out. Jump aboard that broomstick horse; rebuild that impenetrable fort made of boxes, sticks, and whatever was left over from Mom and Dad's last home-improvement idea. Or run outside or look out the window and excavate that passing cloud for a recognizable image. As an adult, you'll find these are the kinds of thoughts and acts that inspire award-winning ads and memorable slogans.

It's time to reacquaint yourself with your inner child. Instead of feeling ridiculous acting out your innermost creative thoughts, feel inspired.

The Creative Concept

Creative concept is an idea that imaginatively solves the client's advertising problem. Coming up with a brilliant and effective idea takes a lot of hard work. Before a great idea can be isolated, the creative team must pursue many mediocre ones. Conceptual development, or "brainstorming," is a process that starts when an idle imagination is kicked into overdrive and exposes the "unthought of."

Brainstorming is your imagination at work. In the process, good ideas, partial ideas, and bad ideas are considered, developed further, or thrown out.

Brainstorming is still done the old-fashioned way—from gray cells to mouth to paper. Brainstorming sessions may comprise a creative team of copywriters and art directors, or they may involve a solitary session in which you allow your thoughts to mature. Nothing is set in stone, apart from the product's features, so as not to limit the number of ideas the session may generate.

There is no set way that creatives brainstorm ideas; the main goal is to discuss the creative brief and imagine a way to solve a problem. Within the key consumer benefit lies the product's **inherent drama**. What makes it tick? What aspects are interesting or unusual? How will it benefit the target audience? Brainstorming isolates that benefit and places it within various scenarios that have meaning to the target audience. The result should cause the target to think. People don't pay attention to abstract ideas; they pay attention to realism, and they want to know *What's in it for me?*—how the product or service can solve their personal problem or need.

Word Lists

One of the best ways for the creative team to begin visually and verbally solving problems, answering questions, and defining a brand's personality, uses, and features and benefits is to develop a **word list**. A word list is the first step in the brainstorming process. Copy heavy, a classic word list is composed of three columns or parts.

The first column represents the facts or more common words used to describe the product or service. Here, we'll use an orange as the product:

Facts	*Descriptive/Visual*	*Scenario: who, what, when, where, why, and how*
Orange		
Round		
Sour		
Slice		

In the second or middle column, choose a descriptive or visual word to represent each product/service fact listed in column one. (A thesaurus works great for assistance and can be a big help with column two.) This column should lead to previously "unthought-of" directions. Here is where "been there, done that" or old ideas go to die.

Facts	Descriptive/Visual	Scenario: who, what, when, where, why, and how
Orange	Sunshine	
Round	Navel	
Sour	Face contortion	
Slice	Saw	
	Knife	
	Teeth	

The third column puts elements of the first two columns together, describing how they might be visually and verbally used in an ad. Ask yourself questions. Consider the five *Ws*—who, what, when, where, why—and don't forget how. Create a scenario for use either visually or verbally.

Facts	Descriptive/Visual	Scenario: who, what, when, where, why, and how
Orange	Sunshine	HOT, HOT, HOT, Taste
Round	Navel	Show a human navel, talk about the connection to Mother Earth
Sour	Face contortion	Show varied people's reaction to their first bite of an orange
Slice	Saw	No matter how you slice it…
	Knife	Show the options being used
	Teeth	on an orange.

This column should create something the target can feel, taste, or just genuinely experience. Set up the word list so that the words are aligned across the page from left to right; one or more ideas can be expressed in any column for any word.

Are Word Lists Really Useful?

Why do a word list? It opens the door to imaginative thoughts and teaches you to think visually and relate verbally. Word lists help to spark an often-dormant imagination while at the same time building word power. A good word list should include twenty to twenty-five words and visual representations.

The goal of all creative is to develop an image or express an idea that is unique to the client. "Been there, done that" creative is eliminated when some of the infinite options are explored. That means conservative views must sometimes step aside and let the liberal ideas step up. For instance, would you have chosen a duck to sell insurance or used Frankenstein's monster to sell joint cream? Would you have chosen instead to use a pitchman talking about protecting your family or show a bunch of athletes sitting around talking about pain?

Exercising the infinite creative options available really puts a new spin on "never been there, never done that," doesn't it?

Breaking concept ideas down to one or two words helps you to focus on the point you're trying to make. One way to break out of "been there, done that"—the conservative approach to advertising syndrome—is to create and live a little inside the word list.

You will recognize a good idea when it comes along, basically, because it doesn't stink as much as the rest. It's also dead on target and on strategy, it features the key consumer benefit, and it meets the goals laid out in the objectives.

With word list in hand, the next step in a traditional brainstorming session may have a copywriter throwing out a **headline** to promote the key consumer benefit while the art director, with drawing pad and marker in hand, quickly roughs out a **visual** that supports the headline. On average, a creative team can come up with anywhere from fifty to one hundred ideas per session. Of course, not all these ideas will be brilliant. Some ideas are weak, some too complicated, others just plain stupid—but each one inspires another direction or even the possible combination of ideas.

The final step is to search for quality in the quantity. Ideas with potential will eventually be reworked and narrowed down to three to five ideas or concepts that are presented to the client.

Visual/Verbal Relationships

By working with a descriptive word list, you will learn to hone your imagination and gain an understanding of just how much thought needs to go into bringing a product to life both visually and verbally.

In a nutshell, visual/verbal relationships answer the question *Does what is being shown in the ad have anything to do with what is being said in the ad?* If it does, the target will respond to the message and act upon it by calling a toll-free number, stopping by a brick-and-mortar store, or visiting a social media or website and ultimately making a purchase. If it doesn't, the ad is not speaking in the IMC model of one voice used both visually and verbally.

Visual Cues versus Verbal Cues

Words by themselves or visuals without direction cannot sell anything. To understand the message and ultimately act upon it, the target needs to be hit by the one-two punch of a cohesive visual/verbal message. Especially if there is little or no copy on the page, the logo, slogan, or tagline must speak volumes. Once the product's key consumer benefit is determined—what will be stressed in the ad—and what the strategy will be, a headline must be written that creatively presents that idea. The visual chosen for the ad must represent that idea. It is the visual/verbal unit that will powerfully and successfully knock out the competition. The key consumer benefit strategically represented by a cohesive visual/verbal message will become the advertising concept.

It is also important to consider what part of its life cycle the product is in when deciding on the most appropriate visual/verbal message. Is it a new product launch, a current product favorite, or a struggling wannabe? Is it a mature or well-known old friend, or does it need to be repositioned in the consumer's mind because of product inconsistencies or consumer bias that it is old-fashioned?

Constructing Visual/Verbal Cues

The construction of a visual cue rests with one very important design principle: eye flow. Where do you want the target's eye to land within the ad, and where do you want it to go next? This requires knowing what you want the target to focus on in the first place and what kind of relationship you want the visual to have with what is being said in the ad. Let's take a look at some possible visual cues.

- *Key consumer benefit.* The key consumer benefit is the one product feature and target benefit that will be stressed throughout the IMC campaign.
- *Framing.* The visual cue can be highlighted by placing it within horizontal and vertical lines, such as a doorway or window. The frame need not be traditional; any kind of line—curved, wiggly, or angular—will work, so long as it can enclose or pinpoint the image.
- *Placement.* Placement deals with where the product is in relationship to the camera. Is a close-up required to show detail or a long shot to show scope? Will a profile work, or will a head-on shot tell the consumer more? Placement defines how much the consumer needs to see to understand what is being shown.
- *Arrangement.* Arrangement deals with composition, or where the product is placed in relationship to other items or other people in the ad. There are three levels to all images: the foreground, the middle ground, and the background. Making use of these areas can help to place a product in a setting, physically tie the image to the copy, or create ambience. The key is to use what you have and create what you need to produce the required environment to help project an image, feeling, or use.
- *Lighting.* Light reflects emotion. Sunlight is happy, sunsets are romantic, and a dimly lit room is relaxing. Pools or streaks of light create natural eye flow and can be used to draw the eye to some important point, like the copy, product, or logo.
- *Color.* Color also reflects emotion. Soft colors relax; bright colors energize. Red is hot, green is earthy, and black is elegant. Strategically placed color can draw the eye to an important spot, such as the product or logo. When black-and-white photographs feature a spot of color, the result is referred to as **spot color**. This is an excellent way to highlight the product by making it stand out in contrast to the rest of the photograph. Spot color can give a visual the illusion of three-dimensionality. The lack of color can also draw the eye, such as with a black-and-white photo used in a medium heavily saturated with color visuals, which creates a striking contrast.

Now that we have discussed the visual cues, what can be done to tie them to the verbal message?

- *Logo.* One verbal message that crosses the boundary into the visual arena is the product or company logo. A logo is the symbol (visual) that represents a product or company name.
- *Slogans or taglines.* The logo can also have an accompanying slogan or tagline (verbal) that represents the company's philosophy (slogan) or the campaign's key consumer benefit (tagline).

- *Headline.* What the visual shows, the headline needs to explain. The headline is the largest piece of copy on the page. It needs to grab the target's attention by screaming out the key consumer benefit. It should talk directly to the target audience and should play a huge role in tying the strategy together.
- *Body copy.* The **body copy** will continue the story begun in the headline. If you can keep your target's eye moving through the ad to the body copy, the ad has done its job: It has grabbed the attention of those most likely to buy or use the product or service. Body copy is ultimately where the sale will be made.

The visual chosen should radiate the concept and product personality. The type of visual presentation that is used, such as an illustration, graphic, color or black-and-white photograph, or line art will further develop the concept.

The headline's visual punch should relate the message in its entirety, with the details left to the copy. At a glance, the target should know *What's in it for me?*—what the product or service offers her personally.

The visual approach will depend on the target audience. Visuals that show the product alone, in a setting, or in use will get the job done without a lot of creative flair. Use visuals that interest the target, and look to the psychographic and demographic profiles to find ones that will both grab her attention and support the headline. Keeping the target audience in mind will keep the visual/verbal message on target.

All creative efforts must be written and designed specifically for the targeted audience in a vernacular or language targets can understand about problems or situations they can relate to and appear in a medium they frequently see.

There is a lot of bad advertising out there, with no direction, no strong brand identity, and no defined target audience. This kind of advertising usually carries what I call a "been there, done that" creative label. This means the idea has been used before—sometimes many, many times. How many times must consumers see creative teams blow up or animate the Statue of Liberty—or, worse yet, make Mona Lisa smile—for yet another product? When you've seen something once, it's interesting; when you've seen it two or three times, it's boring. Once consumers are bored, they stop paying attention to the message.

Today's consumer is bombarded with thousands of advertising messages each day. A good creative team recognizes this and looks for an innovative way to make its product stand out among the clutter. GEICO did it with the "Gecko" campaign; Aflac did it with the "Duck" campaign.

Enemies of Creativity

The biggest enemy of creativity is the lack of exploration. Believe it or not, anyone's brain is capable of generating multiple ideas, but they must graduate from mere thoughts before they can be shared and acted upon. Successful visual/verbal solutions require the creative team to systematically dissect a brand and exhaustively evaluate all creative possibilities. The team must talk about it, think about it, question it, position it, brand it, place it in a relevant setting (or even an irrelevant one), let it stand alone, compare it to the competition, show before-and-after pictures, and twist it or bend it in as many ways as possible.

Finally, if you take shortcuts by failing to fully research both the client and the competition, ideas will lack focus and be unimaginative. Great ideas take a lot of work, and once you think you've found a direction that will solve the client's problem, you'll do a lot of reworking to perfect it.

Elements That Make Up an Ad: What Goes Where?

There is no right or wrong answer to the question of what goes where in an ad. An ad can be nothing more than a visual, or it can be extremely copy heavy. As long as your ad is informative, advances the product's image, and creates interest in the mind of the consumer, you're on the right track.

An ad can be made up of the following five elements in varied order: headline, subhead(s), visual(s), body copy, and logo. Not every element needs to be present in every ad; however, the order is somewhat predetermined.

The order in which elements appear depends on the concept being emphasized. If the headline has a great consumer benefit or is extremely important to the ad's direction, then it must go first; place it at the top of the design. If the visual says more than words can, then place it at the top of the design. This thought process will also help you determine which element should be the dominant element on the page.

Controlling the order of what the target sees and reads aids him in understanding the advertised message. Figure 5.1 shows the different ways visual/verbal elements can be laid out in a print ad.

The Image behind the Layout Style

Once a concept or creative direction has been determined, the next step is to define the ad's visual/verbal persona. One of the easiest ways an ad's personality can be expressed is through the **layout style**, or how its elements are featured in the design. What does the concept say about itself? Will lots of white space be used for an elegant feel? Will a dominant photograph be used to draw the viewer's attention? Will there be multiple small illustrations scattered throughout the copy to instruct the viewer on how to use the product or service? Will the ad be sectioned off to show the viewer multiple benefits?

Think of layout styles as the clothes for the concept. Does it shout sporty, sophisticated, or modern? Does it demand attention through words, or is a visual worth a thousand words? When designing, it's doubly important to consider what the ad needs to project visually to the consumer as well as what it says. Let's look at nine of the most commonly used layout styles.

- Big type
- Circus
- Copy heavy
- Frame
- Mondrian
- Multipanel

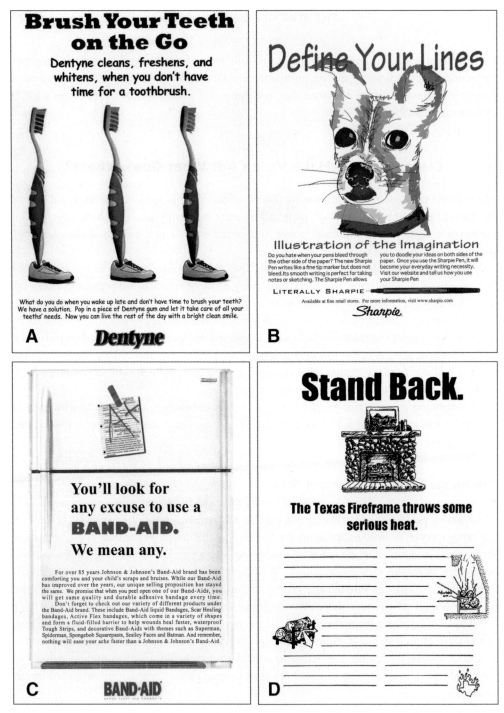

Figure 5.1. The visual/verbal layout of elements in an ad will vary, depending on the concept(s) being emphasized. Sometimes a visual says more than words (B, C); other times, a headline or copy will pack more punch (A, D). Image A courtesy of Natalie Wilt, University of Tennessee; image B courtesy of Alex Crutchfield, University of Tennessee; image C courtesy of Douglas Haas, University of Tennessee; image D courtesy of T. J. Bonner, University of West Virginia.

- Picture window
- Rebus
- Silhouette

Big Type

The big type layout style is used when the headline is the focal point of the ad. If the product or service can boast a definitive consumer benefit, the ad should shout that benefit from the rooftop in very large type. Visuals play a secondary role here. The ad's beauty and appeal are defined by the typeface and what it says. The type size and type weight will often vary, but they should project a distinct pattern. The static appearance of this layout style is very clean and concise. Type works as a graphic, creating mood. If pictures are included, they are small and do not compete with what is being said. If you love the shape, texture, and movement of type, the opportunities to use it as a graphic, verbal element are wide open in this layout style.

Circus

The circus layout style uses everything from the designer's arsenal in the ad. It is not unusual to see multiple type sizes and faces, with assorted **snipes and bursts** (bold, black, often floating callouts) touting grand openings and sale dates in brazenly reversed text. In this layout, there are always too many unrelated visuals to even think about grouping them in an organized fashion. These ads scream chaos; the key to making them work is controlling that chaos. Consider using a grid layout, combining or grouping elements to focus on one dominant image. Try to create as much white space (the white of the page) as is humanly possible. This attempt at structure aids in manipulating the viewer's eye movement in a more controlled fashion, guiding him to move from element to element without missing anything. Structure also alleviates that floating look and grounds the design, giving it more power.

Copy Heavy

Headlines and visuals take a backseat in the copy-heavy layout style. Instead, the focus is on the body copy. A large amount of body copy is used to introduce a product or service. Visuals, if present, are small and are used to show the product or logo.

Frame

Frame layouts are most often featured in newspaper advertising, where it is important to isolate the ad from surrounding text. Frames or borders can be of any weight or design and often define ad size. Frames can be simple, unobtrusive lines, pinstriped, detailed, created via colored backgrounds, or illustrative. Frames can also be used around small photographs or copy points to draw the viewer's eye to them.

Mondrian

Following the style of works by Dutch painter Piet Mondrian, the Mondrian layout style screams sections. Here, multiple geometric blocks of text, graphic shapes, color, and/or shaded areas are used to separate parts of the design and guide the reader through the ad.

Each geometrically or organically shaped section focuses on an element within the ad. This layout style uses bold shapes and color to stand out among the clutter of other ads. By isolating single elements, the designer ensures that each element is viewed independently. Solid geometric shapes, such as circles, squares, rectangles, triangles, and lines, are used to further isolate specific sections but give the ad an almost three-dimensional feel when they are strategically placed near large areas of white space. By placing bright colors within selected shapes or reversing text out of a colored background, you can draw the reader's eye—so show or say something important here.

Multipanel

The multipanel layout style uses pictures with captions to tell a story or feature multiple products in boxes of equal size. These boxes are placed side by side, either butted up against each other or separated by a small amount of white space. Smaller inset photographs can be placed over one large photograph to point out details. Body copy often is replaced with copy captions, located either within the panels or under each picture. This layout style works very well when showing is more important than telling, when comparing one product to another, or when bringing a television **storyboard** to print.

Picture Window

The picture window layout style features one large photograph, often with the headline overprinted. Type can be a solid color, or it can be reversed out of the background. This layout style is best used when you want the reader to participate in the photo, such as when using a headline that helps place the reader in the photograph. For example, you might have a visual of a lake with a sailboat and a headline that asks, "Wish You Were Here?"

Rebus

The rebus layout style is usually crammed full of visuals. Working in tandem with the body copy, visuals are often placed within the text to help illustrate the story. Pictures can also be used as substitutes for words within headlines. This is an elegant layout style and lends itself well to instructional copy, where a picture can be used to demonstrate copy points. Text can be wrapped around images, visually isolating the content from what is being shown. Visuals can be repetitive in size or alternate from small to large in order to create focal points.

Silhouette

The silhouette layout style relies on the grouping of visual elements within an ad. The group of items becomes the dominant element within the ad. A large amount of white space usually surrounds the grouped items, setting them off even more. This layout style works great when multiple products are featured within an ad. By grouping elements in pleasing and even irregular shapes, you give weight to the visuals and create a logical path for the viewer's eye to follow through the ad.

   If the design requires that type accompany each element, consider using callouts. A **callout** is a small amount of copy appearing alongside or below an individual image and connected by a small line. The text is descriptive and might feature price points. This works well when the visual breaks up the headline or the copy or when type is slightly overlaid on a visual or vice versa. White space is at a premium when items are grouped together. At times the silhouette layout style can just be too static; to alter its symmetrical appearance, consider allowing items to touch the edges of the ad in opposing spots.

So Which Layout Style Should Be Used?

There are no rules dictating which layout styles are best suited to a specific media. To decide which style to use, look first to your concept, and then consider how that message will be delivered and perceived. Readability and legibility issues will play a key role in your choice of layout style, typeface, or visual. **Readability** is achieved when a viewer can read an ad at a glance. **Legibility** refers to whether, in that short look, the reader understood the message.

Many of the elements appearing in an ad are of equal importance; it is the art director's job to organize elements into a cohesive package. Elements might include a screaming headline, sale dates, grand openings, new locations, and multiple products—each needing descriptive copy and/or price points. Usually several photographs or illustrations will be needed to show the product. There may also be a need to add detail copy near the logo, ensuring that it will not get lost along the way. These components will help determine which layout style to use.

Organizing elements is the key to success in any medium. Remember that even though an ad might be cluttered, there must be one dominant image. Additional images can be smaller and placed lower in the ad in a grid or as part of the body copy. It is the art director's job to decide what that one dominant element should be, based on information found in the creative brief. A large headline personalizes the message; showing the product alone, in use, or in a setting allows the consumer to interact with the product.

Type Is a Personality Thing

The typeface used in an ad is as important as the message itself. Understanding the visual message of type is critical to building or maintaining a brand's image.

The choice of **typeface** should reflect the personality of the product or the company. Type is not a whimsical or temporary choice. Like layout style, once a typeface is chosen, it should appear in every ad—no matter what the media vehicle. Typefaces chosen for all digital vehicles should match the face used on print vehicles as closely as possible. The typeface should become a representative device for that product or service. Type is an art form of shapes, curves, circles, and lines. Using these elements to define the brand's personality is an extension of the conceptual process. An ad's typeface and style should also reflect the target audience. Bigger type and less-formal layouts work well when attracting younger consumers, whereas cleaner, more-structured layouts work well in attracting older consumers.

Type Styles and Identifiers

There are two distinct varieties of **type styles**, serif and sans serif. A **serif** typeface has feet or delicate appendages that protrude from the edges of the letters, as in the type you're now reading. These appendages can appear at the top and/or bottom of a letterform. **Sans serif** type has no appendages.

Type is categorized by its typeface. Each typeface is assigned a specific name that identifies its distinct set of letterforms. A typeface is part of a larger type family, which includes all the sizes and styles of that typeface. A **font** consists of a complete character set in one typeface and style: for example, all italic upper and lowercase letters, numbers, and punctuation.

Almost every typeface comes in varying weights. Weight represents the thickness or thinness of the typeface's body. These weights include ultra light, light, book, medium, demi/semi bold, bold, ultra bold, and ultra black.

The Language of Type

Different type designs reflect different images, moods, or even genders. Serif typefaces, because of their delicate lines, have a more feminine appeal. Sans serif typefaces boast straight, unadorned lines that give them a more masculine appearance. This masculine/feminine appeal can sometimes be achieved using differing weights of the same typeface. For example, the sans serif typeface Helvetica comes in so many weights that Helvetica Light—a stately, tall, and thin typeface—bears little resemblance to the bulky, stout-looking Helvetica Ultra Bold. Serif typefaces such as Goudy—a round, elegant, yet squat typeface—can represent both masculine and feminine products. The best place to begin when determining which typeface and style to use is to match the likely candidates to the creative strategy, the product's personality, or the tone of the ad, and experiment from there. See figure 5.2 for a few examples of how altering the weight of a single typeface can change its overall voice and personality.

Powerful
Practical
Imaginative

Elegant
Graceful
Delicate

Authority
Diplomatic
Casual

Figure 5.2. Fonts, even in the same type family, can have distinct personalities. Fonts used here, from top to bottom, are Arial Black (Regular), Arial Narrow (Regular), Arial Rounded MT Bold (Regular); Baskerville (Bold), Baskerville (SemiBold Italic), Baskerville (Regular); and Rockwell Extra Bold (Regular), Rockwell (Bold Italic), Rockwell (Regular).

Type Design Rules of Thumb

When designing, the number of typefaces used in an ad should be controlled. The basic rule of thumb is two typefaces per design. The headline, subhead(s), announcement devices, and any prices are usually set in the same typeface; the body copy and detail copy are set in another.

As a rule, smaller copy blocks such as body or detail copy are set in a serif typeface for ease of reading. There is no limit on the different weights that can be used within a design, but common sense should rule the day.

Although there are no hard-and-fast rules about mixing serif and sans serif typefaces within an ad, it is best to use one style throughout the design. The number of point sizes in an ad should also be controlled. An ad with multiple faces in various styles and sizes takes on a circus feel and is perceived as junky or low end. However, any device, if used consistently and/or repetitively, avoids the need to play by the rules.

Logos are a graphic element and are not considered a typeface; they do not need to necessarily match the style of the advertised message.

Type Alignment

Type alignment, or the way type is aligned on the page, can also affect brand image. There are several ways that type can be laid out in an ad. The first is center on center, where type is set with one line centered above another. Alternating the length of lines can create more white space within the ad.

The next most common alignment is flush left, ragged right. This is where all lines of text begin in the same place—along the left margin of the ad. The right side of each line is varied. Type can also be set flush right, ragged left. This alignment is most often used when working with two columns of type that wrap around a centrally placed visual.

The last type alignment option is justified. This is where each line of text begins in the same place along the left margin and ends in the same place on the right margin. This option is not used often in advertising design because type must be designed to fit within this type of format. Justified type often leaves large gaps between words, stretches out long words, or creates multiple hyphens at the ends of lines. Justified type is great for newspaper articles, but it does not look good and is difficult to read in advertising copy.

Type size directly affects readability. Catch consumers' eyes with large text, whet their appetites with medium-size text, sell the product with smaller text, and tell them what they need to know about where and how to shop with the smallest text. If using any secondary subheads or **banners**, they should be slightly smaller than the main subhead.

Look out for widows and orphans. A **widow** is a single word or short line that appears at the top of a page or at the top of a new column of copy. An **orphan** is a short line that appears at the bottom of a page or a word (or part of a word) on a line by itself at the end of a paragraph. The first line in a paragraph should never end up at the bottom of the page or in a column all alone.

Type Faux Pas

Readability and legibility can be adversely affected by several design faux pas. Let's look at a few of the most common.

All Caps

The use of all capital letters anywhere in an ad should be avoided. Consider it for a headline only when it is no more than one to three words long. Most people are not familiar with an all-caps format and as a result must read more slowly.

Reverse Copy

Traditionally, type is set with black letters on a white background. Reverse text uses white or light-colored text on a black or dark-colored background. The use of reversed text in large blocks of copy should be avoided. Readability is minimized because the format is unfamiliar. Reverse text works best for banner announcements, like those advertising grand openings or sale hours.

Italics

Italics should also be avoided because of readability issues. Use italics sparingly; their best use is for emphasis or to set off a special word or phrase, a quotation, or a foreign word.

Decorative Faces

Fancy or froufrou typefaces have no place in advertising. Their elaborate flourishes and decorative appearances make readability and legibility at a glance almost impossible.

Type as a Graphic Element

If you look at type—*really* look—you will see its beauty beyond content. Its form alone is a graphic device. Each typeface portrays a personality, an individualism that takes shape via content. The very randomness of the letterforms creates a uniform message with character and flair. Whether it's childish, traditional, expensive, or shabby chic, each typeface awaits the shape and expression given it by the designer.

A typeface's personality should match the image projected by the product or service and that of the target audience. However you decide to manipulate type—whether you alter the face by condensing or expanding it or by increasing or decreasing **letter spacing**, or kerning on the computer, word spacing, and/or **line spacing**, or **leading** on the computer, type size, or line length—readability and legibility should take precedence over design.

Readability and legibility are also affected by the color and direction of type. Type does not have to be black. It can be any dark color—for example, brown, navy, forest green, or maroon. Light or pastel-colored type lacks contrast against the stark white of the printed or digital page, making it difficult to see and slowing readers down, forcing them to reread in order to understand the message.

Type as a Design Element

Beyond defining a brand's personality, the typeface chosen, if appropriate, should also reflect the ambience of the service or store in which the product can be purchased. The openness or tightness of line and letter spacing can promote this look and feel further, creating a signature look for the product or service. Work with type; make it the client's and, in time, the product's.

Putting Ideas on Paper: The Stages of Design

In this section we'll look at the four stages of the design process:

- Concept
- Thumbnails
- Roughs
- Super comprehensives

Concept

The first stage in the design process is brainstorming or concept development. As discussed earlier, concept refers to your thoughts and ideas about how to creatively solve the client's advertising problem. Concept sets the tone and direction for a single ad or a combination of ads. This is where bad ideas come to die, and good ideas get a second look and perhaps an overhaul and facelift. It's also where daydreams begin to see the light of day. Here the creative team hammers out sometimes hundreds of ideas, only 10 percent of which will bear further development.

All those daydreams come out as ideas, many of which will be rejected. Others may stand the test of development; all are worth sharing. Remember, it is important when you have an idea to present it to others, whether they're other professionals or your classmates. Don't worry about whether the ideas are stupid. I guarantee that you will excel in the realm of the ridiculous, you will be teased, and you may never live it down—but you will inspire ideas in others by sharing those not-so-fabulous thoughts as well as those brilliant ones.

Thumbnails

Thumbnails, or thumbs, are the second stage in the design process. Word lists, as previously discussed, play an important role in thumbnail development. Ideas generated there become a reality at this stage.

Thumbnails are small, proportionate drawings, ranging in size from 2 × 3½ inches up to 3 × 5 inches, that are used to place concept ideas down on paper. Each thumbnail should reflect a different concept direction, headline, subhead, and visual; no two should be alike. Try to use a different layout style for each concept. Further development should inspire alternative concept approaches.

The word "doodle" best describes what a thumbnail should look like. Random headlines, visuals, and layout styles should offer varied solutions to further develop the concept.

Thumbnails can have any number of combinations and components but usually will consist of one or more of the following: a readable headline and possible subhead(s), a recognizable visual or visuals, body copy indication, and a logo. Each thumb should be enclosed in a box representing the final size and shape of the ad and should be tightly drawn and consistent in size (see figure 5.3).

Thumbs should be done in black marker. Color may be added when working within a color medium. Right off the bat, get into the habit of working in marker. Avoid pencils. Markers allow you to work and rework without the benefit of an eraser. When you can

Figure 5.3. Thumbnail example. Image courtesy of Brian Starmer, University of Tennessee.

erase, you can obsess on one thumbnail idea. If you make a mistake or just don't like the way the idea is going, cross it out and move on; that's erasing, designer style.

Thumbnails are an internal design process, rarely, if ever, seen by the client. Headlines, subheads, slogans or taglines, and logos should be written out cleanly and placed in position on the thumb. It is important that other members of the creative team be able to read your thumbs; this helps them understand the concept direction. Visuals should be quickly sketched or traced into position. Body copy should be indicated with parallel lines. These lines represent the placement and the amount of room the copy might take up.

There will rarely be a single thumb that ends up as the final design choice. It is more likely that two or more will be combined to create the overall look of the final ad. The point is to have multiple options for the creative team to discuss.

Thumbnails allow you to work anywhere; it is difficult for even professional designers to be creative on demand a few hours before a deadline. Think about what you need to accomplish and let it perculate a few hours or even a few days if time allows.

Being able to work fast is critical in design. Developing a thought and then quickly sketching a thumbnail wipes out the pressure and anxiety associated with a blank page. Get all your ideas down on paper; thinking ahead makes the creative process a bit easier.

Roughs

Roughs, or **layouts**, are the third stage in the design process, and they are chosen from the best thumbnail ideas. Professionals usually use roughs as their idea-generation stage. Roughs are often presented to the client, especially an established client. Roughs are done at full size, or the size of the final piece, and are done in color if relevant.

If concepts are being presented to a new client who has no representative typeface or wishes to change the image of a product or service, offer alternative type choices on each rough. This allows the client to see the typeface on the page, within the design, and with any visuals or the logo. The image or personality each typeface projects for the target, company, service, or product plays an important visual role in the development of an identity or brand image. If the client already has a signature typeface, continue to use that typeface on the roughs.

Each rough should include a different headline, using the key consumer benefit for guidance and with a supporting subhead if required, as well as visual(s) and layout style if presenting multiple concepts. If creating a campaign series, each series should include at least three pieces, and the concept based on the strategy and the key consumer benefit should be evident in the headline, concept, character representative, repetitive layout style, and/or typeface.

Because clients see roughs and review all ideas, the roughs should be tight, clean, and accurate. It is important that they be checked against the creative brief to be sure they are on target and on strategy before they are presented to the client. Professional-looking layout and conceptual skills should shine here. The account executive (AE) will present the client with three to five design options at this stage. However, it is rare for any ad to make it past the client in its original form; most likely it will be sent back to creative for minor tweaks— or worse, a major overhaul. Final client-approved ads will be reproduced on the computer.

Super Comprehensives

The fourth stage or option in the design process is known as **super comprehensives**, or super comps. Instead of presenting hand-drawn roughs, as the next step, super comps are prepared on the computer and are often used to present work to new clients or to show a new campaign direction to existing clients. With each element in place, a super comp simulates exactly how the finished design will look and read. All visuals, including the logo, are sized and in position, and any readable copy is set in the proper typeface. Body copy, however, is often presented to the client separately, so greeking is used as a stand-in until final copy approval is obtained. **Greeking** is a jumbled arrangement of letters, numbers, punctuation, and paragraph breaks used to temporarily represent body copy, helping give the ad a finished appearance.

Visuals, Options, and Decisions

The visual chosen for any creative piece is important. It should take into consideration the medium to be used as well as the product or service to be advertised. The visual the target eventually sees is a representation of the client's product or service. As the designer, you can decide how to present that image—perhaps through the reality of photography or with the artistic expression of an illustration or graphic design. A more simplistic approach can be achieved with black-and-white line art, or budget constraints might call for clip or stock art. Whatever image becomes the visual voice of the client's product, it should support the strategy, headline, and concept and reflect both the target's and the product's image.

An ad's visual options are diverse. There are five possible visual options the art director might consider using:

- Photographs
- Line art
- Illustrations
- Clip or stock art
- Graphic images

Photographs

Believability is one reason to use photographs. Unfortunately, photography can be expensive, especially color photography. The decision to include a photograph instead of an illustration or line art depends on the concept being used, the image of the product or service, the medium, and of course the overall budget.

Photographs offer an exclusive viewing opportunity. Paper quality, printing issues, and screen resolution will affect how clearly the consumer can see what the product looks like and/or how it is used.

The visual reality offered by photographs allows viewers to see patterns, textures, quality, and color as if the product were sitting before them. The idea of visual variety offers designers the option to showcase the product alone or in use, placed in a relevant setting, or being compared to a similar product. Size is also a visual variable; images can be enlarged to dominate the page or reduced to show multiple views or options.

What's in a Photograph?

The photograph should be of something the target is interested in. If it is, any visual will work, but just in case, here are some guaranteed attention getters:

- Brides
- Infants
- Animals, especially young animals
- Celebrities
- Outrageous costumes
- Outrageous situations
- Romance
- Scenes of tragedy
- Current events
- Slice of life

Gender plays a small role in the choice of visual images. For example, men are attracted to animals, whereas women are attracted to images of infants or children. But no matter the sex of the target, in the end the visual must be relevant.

There is no better way to create a mood or conjure up emotions than with photographs, especially those with people in them. Although photographs take time to set up and shoot, consumers prefer them in ads promoting services such as banking and investing or products such as food. Photographs can more easily show the product being used, and they allow consumers to envision themselves using the product or service.

Using a photograph gives credibility to the product, as do the models chosen for them. Don't use anyone who appears unlikely to use the product or service. Be sure models are suitably dressed and are the right age, ethnicity, and sex.

The Pop of Black-and-White Photographs

Why use black-and-white photos when you can use color? One reason is price. It is much less expensive to use a black-and-white photograph than a color photograph. Another reason is that a black-and-white photograph stands out against a lot of color. This independence in appearance attracts readers' attention.

Black-and-white photographs are also excellent mood or attitude setters. Issues such as drinking and driving and the results from such behavior are often difficult to take in color. Sadness or isolation, even the passing of time, can be represented best in black and white—especially with all the bright colors on adjacent pages or in other locations.

Some organizations, especially charities, do not wish to look too affluent or wasteful when soliciting donations. They might prefer black-and-white photography to color. Fashion ads in black and white are certainly a surprise. They stop readers, making them spend just a minute longer on this anomaly.

Spot Color

An excellent alternative to full-color photographs is a black-and-white photograph featuring one element in color. This is referred to as **spot color**. This is an excellent way to highlight the product, making it stand out in stark contrast to the rest of the photograph. Spot color can give a visual the illusion of three-dimensionality. By adding a spot of color to the photograph, the designer can control eye flow, drawing the viewer's eye directly to the product.

The use of photographs, especially color photographs, requires a large budget. However, color photography at any level, such as spot color, is often worth the price. It brings an ad to life and helps create interest in and involvement by the consumer.

Line Art

Black-and-white line art consists of a line drawing that has no tonal qualities. A drawing is a great choice when an ad is spotlighting a product with small details, such as a lace tablecloth or a delicate china pattern. Drawings simplify a design and create a strong black-and-white contrast on the page.

Products presented as line art can be grouped and still retain their individuality through the strategic use of contrast, shadows, highlights and details, and varying textures. A strong black-and-white drawing retains details without muting quality.

Illustrations

Illustrations, unlike line art, have tonal qualities, so they are more like a photograph. But unlike photographs, illustrations are created rather than reproduced. With illustrations, advertisers can take a more analytical approach by presenting charts and graphs or a lighter approach by creating characters to represent the product.

The choice between using an illustration or a photograph is an interpretive one. Photographers capture reality, but if you want something more imaginative, an illustration also can create reality. If you are looking for a nostalgic, homey look, you might choose an illustrator with a Norman Rockwell style. If the concept calls for a more modern approach, you may look for someone who uses a Peter Max or Andy Warhol style.

Illustrations can create a mood or trend as easily as a photograph does. Depending on the style and color usage, they can represent a laid-back or upbeat approach.

The choice between an illustration or a photograph also depends on the product or service. For an ad that features customer services, emotional appeals, or a food product, consider photographs. To create personality, think illustration. For ambience, it's a toss-up. One thing is for sure: Illustrations and graphics are less-expensive design options than a four-color photograph.

Clip or Stock Art

Using either clip art or stock art is a great option when money is tight. **Clip art** is existing line art drawings. **Stock art** is existing photographs of all varieties that can be purchased and used. These terms are often used interchangeably. The only problem with using clip or stock art is the small chance it may have been used in another ad. To make the clip or stock art unique, try combining one or more items and removing or **cropping** unwanted areas.

Graphics

Graphics have great potential when color is an option. If the client's product is youthful or modern, consider using a more upbeat or graphic approach. Graphic design looks at life and situations abstractly. Bright colors, often chosen for their symbolic meaning, are combined with both geometric and organic shapes to create modern and bold designs. When used together, these shapes are often disjointed, and they are used to create an alternative view of life. When set off by a lot of white space, this design style screams new, bold, or eclectic, especially if the other advertising surrounding it uses a more traditional approach.

If you need something simpler, a graphic can also be nothing more than a single divider line between columns of copy, a graphic box used to highlight copy points, or a logo.

Color's Representational Role

The Mood of Color

Effective color choices can be used as design elements. Certain colors evoke specific emotions and can be used to set a mood or attract the eye. In the unfortunate event that the target should forget the product name, often the use of unique color combinations on packaging can help with recall when determining which product to purchase.

The Meaning of Color

Color can make us feel warm, cold, stressed, or lethargic. We know the sun should be yellow and the sky blue. The elegance, reassurance, or casualness of a color comes from life's experiences; we see life in color and use it to describe an event, an emotion, the passage of time, or life and death.

When using color, be sure it does not compete with other colors on the page but instead complements the mood you are trying to create. Elegance is portrayed with more white than color; red and yellow are hot; blue, cool; and green, life. Be careful not to use too much color, or the ad can become stressful or look gaudy to readers.

Color and Its Emotion

Red

Red is a dynamic and dangerous color with great strength. It can signify passion, lust, and heat as well as blood, fire, and revolution. Whether reflecting positive or negative emotions, it is full of action and reaction. Red is great for men's products or any product requiring a warning label. It also works well for impulse products such as candies.

Orange

Orange reflects the autumn harvest, fire, and the heat of the sun. Orange is a weighty color, suggesting depth and volume. It evokes intense feeling, energy, and inspiration. Products that work well with orange include pasta, precooked entrees, and insect repellants.

Yellow

Yellow is welcoming, open, and vivacious. Yellow is a light, warm or comforting, upbeat color suggesting laughter. Yellow takes on more weight and stands out when combined with a dark color. Most products will work with yellow or yellow highlights, but some of the obvious include vegetables, fruits, sun products, hair products, and paper products.

Green

Green is a relaxing color. It is the color of nature, cleanliness, good health, and money. Green is a good choice for products such as vegetables, garden equipment, tobacco products, pickles, and pasta.

Blue

Blue is an earthy color, signifying water, the sky, and ice. Blue, depending on its hue, can be light or depressing. Blue is a relaxing and refreshing, youthful color that supports make-believe ideas and intelligence. Blue can represent such products as soups, cold beverages, travel, or frozen-food products.

Black

Black symbolizes sadness, isolation, and death or the need to set something apart or end something. Black can also denote elegance, honor, and dignity. It is often used for expensive products such as jewelry, cars, perfumes, or liquors. Black can also be used as an accent color to pop lighter, more vibrant colors off the page.

So where does creative fit with what we know so far? Let's review:
Phase one includes:

1. Research.
2. From the research, the marketing plan is developed.
3. From the marketing plan, the creative strategy statement is developed.
4. From the marketing plan and creative strategy statement, the creative brief is developed.

Phase two includes:

1. From the creative brief, the brainstorming phase can begin. Here is where the theme, creative concept, or big idea is given a visual and verbal voice.
2. Ensuring the concept is on strategy and on target with the creative brief.
3. Preparation of copy and layout.

Phase three includes:

1. Adapting the creative approach for use in each of the media that make up the IMC or promotional mix: public relations, advertising (print, broadcast), direct marketing and sales promotion, out-of-home and transit, the Internet and social media, mobile, and alternative media.

Q DISCUSSION QUESTIONS

1. How does the creative team use the creative brief? Explain in detail.
2. Define the "creative team" members. What is their job?
3. Explain why the visual approach depends on the target audience.
4. What are the five elements that make up an ad? Define each.
5. What determines an ad's visual and verbal persona?
6. How many typefaces should be used in an ad? Why?
7. What are the five visual options available to art directors? How is each suited to varied mediums?
8. What are the emotions associated with color? How can they be used to advertise varied products or services?

Copywriting

Writing copy is one of the first steps taken when moving from business thinking to actual creative brainstorming and eventual execution. In a perfect world, the copy would be written first and would be the inspiration for an ad's design. However, advertising is not a perfect world. It is most likely that copywriting and design will be happening at the same time. Because of this, it is critical that the copywriter and the art director be on the same page creatively.

A copywriter deals with both the imagination and development processes of brainstorming and writing headlines, subheads, body copy, slogans, and/or taglines. Copywriters must use what they learn during the brainstorming process to produce copy that attracts and motivates members of the target audience to not only read the entire ad but to act on what they have read.

Every piece of copy, no matter what medium it appears in, must relate to and complement the visual message, attract the target's attention, build a relationship with the target, and inspire the target to act.

Successful, memorable advertising is a consequence of a little luck, some good interpretive powers, a few great ideas, and the target audience's ultimate capacity to reflect, digest, and connect to the visual/verbal message.

The Components of Copy

The copy's voice is the direct result of the creative brief. Once a creative direction or concept has been decided upon, the copywriter must determine what needs to be said, how much copy it will take to say it, the tone and style appropriate to project the concept, and how to adapt that copy to a particular media vehicle. Copy for print and many digital options can be broken down into four main areas:

- Headlines
- Subheads
- Body Copy
- Slogans and Taglines

The headline, subhead, and body copy all need to function as a unit to build, present, and explain a single message.

Headlines

Headlines That Steal the Show

A headline is the largest piece of copy on the page and is most often the first piece of copy the viewer will notice. A headline's job is to grab attention, stand out on a crowded page or screen, and be unforgettable by either shouting out the key consumer benefit or supporting the visual. Whether it is a single statement or one or more complete sentences, a headline must answer the target's question: *What's in it for me?* This not only helps differentiate the product or service from the competition but also becomes an excellent tool for creating brand awareness or defining a brand's identity for the target.

A headline needs to seduce. It should create enough interest to make the target stay with the ad instead of turning or closing the page. An advertised sales message is not a chosen read; it's what I refer to as an enticed read. The target audience is enticed into the ad because the key consumer benefit is informative, instructional, thought provoking, imaginative, or even suggestive. It lets the target know how the product or service can benefit daily life.

Sometimes headlines are not the best choice for promoting the key consumer benefit. Sometimes it is easier to show the key consumer benefit in action, placing the headline in a supporting role. No matter how the key consumer benefit is disclosed or shown, it is important that the headline relate to the visual. There is no visual/verbal relationship if the headline and the visual deliver separate messages. W. Keith Hafer and Gordon E. White put it best in their book *Writing Advertising*: "The visual and headline are indivisible."

If the headline can communicate both visually and verbally, you may not even need body copy. "Tear. Wipe. Done. Cleaning Is So Labor Intensive." It doesn't get more visual/verbal than that.

Writing effective headlines requires writing and rewriting so that the key consumer benefit says just the right thing, in just the right tone, to the target audience. The key is to be original, and to do this, all the "been there, done that" ideas must be exhausted before the headline can assume the product's identity.

Brainstorming sessions exile a lot of copy ideas to a computer's trash can. But before you decide to empty the trash, consider holding on to some of these refugee headlines. Many can be reevaluated for possible use as slogans, subheads, and opening body copy paragraphs.

Headlines That Talk the Key Consumer Benefit Talk

Most consumers don't get past the headline, so it's important that the headline can be read and understood at a glance. If there is a lot to say, the key consumer benefit needs to be pushed in the headline and any supporting information placed in a subhead. Often, a headline's length is directly related to a product's life cycle. New products and reinvented products require a longer headline to introduce the key consumer benefit and establish or reestablish a brand image. Mainstream products that already have an established brand identity will continue building on or maintaining an existing campaign theme.

Powerful headlines catch and keep the target's attention and pull him into the ad. To guarantee that the target pays attention to the message, consider some of the tried-and-true "benefit" words or phrases listed in box 6.1.

BOX 6.1. Suggestive Words and Phrases That Help Create Attention-Grabbing Headlines

1. You	7. Product name	13. How to	19. Guarantee
2. Free	8. Love	14. Why	20. Results
3. Discover	9. Offer guidance	15. Sale	21. Proven
4. Last chance	10. Introducing	16. Bargain	22. Save
5. New	11. Now	17. Quick	23. Health
6. Announcing	12. Just arrived	18. Easy	24. Safety

Selecting the right words is as important as the tone of voice and style the headline uses to express the strategy. The tone of voice deals with how the message is expressed. Style deals with how the headline portrays the message. The following list of styles is suggested only as a place to start. The way a headline is delivered should not fit a prefabricated mold but should adapt to reflect the brand's image and/or concept and message direction. Consider the following headline styles as another way of brainstorming ideas.

- *Direct.* A direct headline delivers the key consumer benefit with little or no creative flair.
- *Indirect or curiosity.* Indirect or curiosity headlines tantalize with just enough information to make the target curious for more information. One great way to do this is to ask questions or test existing knowledge.
- *Major benefit promise.* A major benefit headline is best used when the key consumer benefit is a USP.
- *Play on words.* If copy is going to mess with the English language, it is important that there be a point. A play on words manipulates words, often giving special meaning to words to match a campaign theme. This headline type can attract a reader's attention and give an ad a personality all its own. But, as with all messages, be sure the word play advances the key consumer benefit.

- *Question.* A question headline style asks the target a question. This headline style requires the audience to think and thus participate. Be sure the question is thought provoking and cannot be answered with a simple yes or no, so the more open ended and less specific the question, the better. Questions can help tie the headline to the visual by showing an immediate benefit through problem solving.
- *Metaphors, similes, and analogies.* Metaphors, similes, and analogies compare the client's product to something else. A metaphor looks at two dissimilar objects to make a point of comparison; for example, "He is a snake in the grass." A simile uses the word "like" or "as" to make a comparison; for example, "sick as a dog." An analogy compares two characteristics that are perceived as similar; for example, comparing dry skin with sandpaper.
- *News or announcement.* A news or announcement headline tells the reader something newsworthy about the product. Maybe it has received a patent or is new and improved, or perhaps a new use has been found for the product. This style works well for announcements or introductions.
- *The reason-why.* The reason-why headline style gives the target a good reason or list of reasons to use the product or service.
- *How-to.* How-to headlines tell the reader how to do or find out something. These work well when tied to psychographical information; for example, how to save money or lose weight.
- *Product name.* Headlines that feature the product name work best for products with unusually pronounced names, new product launches, or reinvented products. These headlines often do not promote a strong product benefit and so do not build or reinforce the brand image.
- *The testimonial.* If a member of the target audience has had a favorable experience with a product or service, let her do the talking. Her experiences with the product are more believable than the advertised message to the target. Placing quotation marks around a headline highlights the fact that it is an actual quote.
- *The command.* A command headline firmly tells the reader what to do: "Get to the zoo."
- *Practical advice.* The practical advice headline tells the target how to do or achieve something: how to make cleaning easier, how to stay healthy, how to make money on investments. Consumers love practical and/or helpful information.
- *Problem/solution.* Sell the solution, not the problem. Don't waste the target's time discussing the problem. He already knows the problem, so if a solution is offered, the headline will have his attention.
- *Flag.* Talk to a specific group—for example, new mothers or people with bad backs—by calling out to them in the headline to catch their attention.
- *Warning.* As the name implies, the headline acts as a warning to the target audience: If you don't do *X*, *Y* will happen.
- *Personal benefits.* A personal benefits headline promises something to the target, such as beauty, health, quality, adventure, or prestige.

Headline Length

A visual headline may work with one word, whereas a fact-based headline may require more than one sentence. Five to seven words are typically required to promote a consumer benefit. Length also depends on the media vehicle. When working with limited space, such as on a transit sign, poster, or billboard, the key consumer benefit is about all there is room for. The rules are not that different when writing headlines for digital media. Search, online, mobile, tablets, and social media heads are typically twenty to twenty-five characters in length. To ensure readers click on an ad, digital headlines need to be descriptive, feature keywords, use conversational language, and, most importantly, engage readers.

A Subhead's Response

There are two basic types of subheads: overline and underline.

An **overline subhead** is used as a teaser or attention getter and appears above the headline. If the headline appears too long or will have to be reduced in size to accommodate everything that needs to be said, consider using an overline as an announcement device.

An **underline subhead** appears below the headline and explains in more detail what the headline is saying, elaborates on the statement or comment made, or answers the question posed in the headline. Ideally, the main underline subhead should not be another statement, but one or two complete sentences. Remember, the headline's job is to grab attention; once it is attained, the subhead should whet the reader's appetite, enticing him into the body copy.

Because the headline and the subhead work as a unit, no other copy should appear between them. It is acceptable to break up the unit with a visual if it strengthens the bond between the headline and subhead and further promotes the message.

Additional subheads can be used to clarify or explain in further detail what the headline is saying or to break up long blocks of text. Subheads appearing in the body copy should read like bullet listings and need not be complete sentences. A consumer should be able to quickly glance through the subheads and know where the copy is going. Each subhead should relate to the content of the copy below it. Multiple subheads can break long blocks of detailed copy into easily digestible bits of information while adding visual interest.

Subheads should be used like chapter breaks, with each new subhead signaling a new benefit, highlighting copy, and creating interest. Readers can scan the subheads in the same way they might scan the chapter listings in a book. Even if the target can't read the copy now, her interest is piqued and she will read it later.

Body Copy That Informs

The smaller paragraphs of text in an ad are known as **body copy**. The message that body copy conveys is the nuts and bolts, heart and soul, of the overall concept.

The body copy's story begins in the headline. It must speak in the same tone of voice as the headline, explaining and backing up any claims made. If the headline asks a question, the body copy will answer it; if the headline is humorous, the copy will have a humorous tone.

Copy continues the key consumer benefit's story by educating the target on the facts, features and benefits, and any supportive points associated with the product or service.

Body copy is essentially broken down into three areas: an opening paragraph, an interior paragraph(s), and a closing paragraph. The opening paragraph needs to finish the thought introduced in the headline and developed further in the subhead. If the target has gotten this far, those two sections must have gotten his attention.

The interior or body of the copy is where the actual selling will take place. This is where supporting features/benefits will be presented that will enhance the key consumer benefit and overall lifestyle of the target.

The closing paragraph needs to ask the target to do something: come into the store, pick up the phone, or go online for more information. Advertising is about making sales; don't be afraid to tell consumers what they need to do.

It is very easy to bore the target audience by droning on with a continuous list of the product's features and benefits. Entertain readers instead by creating a story, something that is fun or interesting to read and that flows toward a climax. That climax is what you want the target to do. Think of body copy as a novel that has a plot (concept). That plot is advanced by events (features/benefits), and those events affect the characters (the target).

In general, body copy should use short sentences and simple words. It should not offend or use slang. Be sure to include a time element in copy to get the target moving toward the desired action. One way to do this is to offer a guarantee, removing any perceived risks associated with purchase, especially if done over the Internet or through a catalog or direct mail.

Things to remember when writing copy that will reach out to the target audience:

- When writing, talk to just one member of the target audience in his own language or vernacular. A conversational tone allows the copy to speak to the target or ask questions of the reader. It's impossible and inappropriate to address any message to a group. Always talk in the first person; use "you" instead of "them." Do not say things like "people" or "they will," but rather "you will." This personalizes the message for the target and allows him to relate the message to his own lifestyle.
- Appeal to the target's rational and emotional sides. In other words, present the information factually, and tie the facts to how the product or service will make the target feel, change her life, or solve a problem.
- Write about the benefits of the product or service based on its individual features. The client's product is not special because of its features; its competition either already has them or will have them in a couple of months. Carving out a niche that features the product's benefits or solutions ahead of the competition will make consumers identify certain features/benefits with it, which is a great way to propel the consumer away from competitors.
- If the copy is long, use multiple short paragraphs and subheads to break up the copy. If the message is broken up into multiple short paragraphs of no more than three to four sentences each, the target is more likely to read it.
- Be sure the opening paragraph continues the discussion on the key consumer benefit first introduced in the headline and explained further in the subhead. Think about what it takes to keep you reading; it must grab your attention and be important to you.
- Keep it simple, and stay on target. Even the most dynamic body copy will not succeed if it is off target or off strategy.

- When writing, avoid abbreviations and technical jargon unless writing copy for a specific profession.
- Avoid using exclamation points anywhere. If you must use them to make your point, you obviously didn't make your point.
- Get to the point, and avoid exaggerated claims. Bragging is great only if it can be backed up with facts. It is the facts that make a product claim believable and what inspires the target to act.
- Close the sale. Every ad should close by asking the target to do something. If the goal is an immediate purchase, include a toll-free number or information about where to purchase. Supply a web or social media address for those seeking additional information.

Copy Length

How long should body copy be? The answer is simple: long enough to inform and entice the intended target into action. The length of body copy depends on how familiar the target is with the product and whether the advertising or promotional efforts are to change or maintain the position in the mind of the consumer.

Copy length is also affected by:

- *The medium.* Reminder advertising, such as a text message or billboard, requires little more than a headline or statement to promote the key consumer benefit. Direct mail, websites, or e-mail messages, on the other hand, require long copy in order to explain the key consumer benefit and move the target to action.
- *The target audience.* Better-educated older targets will wade through longer copy to find out more about the product or service. Younger readers will respond better to large, colorful visuals, spending less time on copy points.
- *The product or service.* If the product or service falls into the rational category, more information will be needed to position the product away from the competition. Products or services falling into the emotional category have few, if any, distinctive features from those of the competition that will need to be explained in any detail. Products such as clothing, perfumes, liquor, snacks, jewelry, beauty products, or soft drinks will traditionally use less copy and focus more on the visual to tell the story.

When to Use Longer Copy
- New product introductions
- Technical copy
- Repositioning or reinventing a brand's image
- Expensive product purchases

When to Use Shorter Copy
- Mainstream products
- Emotional products
- Reminder advertising
- Inexpensive product purchases

Too much copy can keep the target from getting involved with the copy. This is the best time to insert multiple subheads or visuals demonstrating copy points, within the copy, to break it up into smaller, more readable chunks. Too little copy, on the other hand, may not set the product apart from the competition or strengthen or build the product or service's image.

Expressing the Copy's Tone

As we have already learned, every concept has an individual approach, appeal, and tone or execution technique that defines its personality or image. How it is expressed depends on the execution technique or tone of voice employed to communicate the key consumer benefit. It is important that the copywriter thoroughly understand what kind of image the product or service should project. Can that image be developed with a sexual, fantasy, or humor-based tone? Is it newsworthy, or should a specific feature be promoted? Should the target be reminded or teased about the brand, or will a demonstration or instructional tone do the trick? Whichever tone is used to express the key consumer benefit, it should work toward building up the brand's image and successfully promoting the key consumer benefit.

Formats for Expressing a Message's Tone of Voice

A message's tone can take either a rational or emotional direction, or it can be a combination of any of the following from either category.

Emotional Tone of Voice   Emotional tone of voice messages might use one or a combination of the following:

Fear. Since fear can often scare us and trigger an emotional response, it is memorable and a guaranteed attention getter. There are no rules about how much fear the consumer can take before being turned off, so common sense in relationship to product benefits or problem/solution should be taken into consideration.

Humor. A humorous tone looks at the product and the target and places all in an unusual or outrageous situation in which the product solves a problem.

Sex. Sex is another proven way to attract the consumer's attention. It is still possible to intentionally shock viewers with the blatant and often controversial use of sex in advertising. However, for it to be successful at any level, it must have a point, not just sex for sex's sake or shock value.

Music. Music elicits emotion. Use it to set the scene for use or lifestyle enhancement or to create product association with a certain mood-setting song. If what needs to be said is boring, consider setting it to a catchy tune known as a jingle: another way to make an unimaginable, unremarkable, indistinguishable feature stand out from the competitive pack.

Scarcity. If it's hard to get, it will attract certain types of consumers. Scarcity encourages action, and want increases the need for, or the value of, a product. The need to be first or to be one of the few to own something creates status.

Slice of life. Slice of life is the ultimate problem/solution appeal in which the ad presents a problem only this product can solve. There are four stages to a slice-of-life approach: problem, introduction, trial, and solution.

Fantasy. Fantasy takes the consumer on an imaginary adventure. It takes the reality out of an otherwise predictable product and makes it fun—and usually memorable. Many fantasy ads are foolish and fantastic and deal with predictable themes such as food, sex, vacation getaways, and love and romance.

Animation. Animated characters are used to tell the product's story. The characters and the situations they find themselves in are usually very sophisticated and created by computer-generated means.

Rational Tone of Voice Rational tone of voice messages might use one or a combination of any of the following:

Authoritative. Use an expert such as a doctor, scientist, dentist, or engineer to point out product attributes. Other official devices that might be employed to back up claims include scientific studies or survey results.

Factual message or straight-sell. A factual or straightforward approach works on a consumer's needs and wants as well, but instead of selling to the emotions or imagination, the sale is made based on the facts associated with the product. This approach relies heavily on the key consumer benefit and any relevant supporting benefits and features associated with the product or service.

News event or educational. News event or educational tones are used when the product is in the news. Perhaps the client or the product has won an award for quality or service. Being first at anything is not only newsworthy but also a great sales device.

Product feature or star. A feature-based approach concentrates on the key consumer benefit associated with the product. It is nice if the feature is unique to the product, but even an appliance's plug can be made unique if the competition is not pushing plugs and the concept is unique and memorable.

Reminder. The reminder tone keeps well-known products such as table salt or seasonal products in the mind of the consumer.

Teaser. A teaser approach is used to create interest in a product that is not yet on the market. This approach should build curiosity and entice the consumer by talking about a product but not showing it.

Demonstration. A demonstration tone of voice compares the product to the competition; each product's strengths and weaknesses are compared.

Instructional. An instructional tone, as its name implies, teaches the consumer how to do something or explains how the product or service can solve a problem.

Inherent drama. Inherent drama differentiates a product or service from the competition by creating interest or drama around the key consumer benefit. This works well for products that have few, if any, unique characteristics.

Talking head. A character, spokesperson, or consumer tells the product's story or his personal experiences with the product.

Dialogue. Dialogue copy focuses on a conversation between two people, a group of people, or characters.

Lifestyle or narrative. Focus is placed on the target and the role the product plays in her lifestyle rather than on the product itself.

Additional strategic message approaches might compare the client's product to the competition or create a spokesperson or animated personality, creating a personalized approach to the ad. You never can go wrong with a testimonial or endorsement. In a **testimonial**, a celebrity or an average consumer endorses the product by telling his personal experiences with it. **Endorsements** are a little different; the announcer or celebrity often does not personally use the product and is being paid for his time.

These execution techniques are just a starting place for conceptual development. They are meant not as a template but as a jumping-off point. Consider combining one or more ideas, or envision an entirely new and different way to say something about the product or service.

The Detail of Copy

When writing copy, don't forget the detail copy. Detail copy is the small copy placed near the logo or the bottom of the ad to inform the target about locations, phone or fax numbers, web and/or social media addresses, or maps if applicable. Other items to include might be store hours, parking, and credit card information, as well as layaway options and gift certificates. Not all may be applicable for all ads.

Summing Up a Philosophy or Concept in a Few Words

Slogans

A **slogan** represents a company's philosophy or a product's image. It is usually placed either above or below the logo. The two are a unit and should always be used together. A slogan is usually three to seven words in length and can be either a statement or a complete sentence.

The slogan must aid in positioning the product. It must clearly say what the target needs to know about a company or product. Good slogans have longevity and add to a product's brand image, thus building brand equity.

One of the ways to make a product memorable is to tie the slogan to a product or service's image. It should make an association through visual/verbal cues. Consider how a product works or when the product is used; some kind of word association, pun, or rhyming scheme may be memorable and representative. By using visual/verbal cues, the slogan represents a product's image and message.

Tagline

A tagline is not the same as a slogan, although the two labels are often interchanged. A **tagline** generally represents a current strategy or concept. Like a slogan, a tagline is three to seven words in length and can be either a statement or a complete sentence. Taglines do not have the longevity associated with slogans and often change to match the brand's life-cycle stage or current campaign efforts.

Visuals: Tying the Verbal to the Visual

Creating a visual/verbal message is critical. What is talked about in the copy must have a corresponding visual. The product's key consumer benefit should be screamed out in the headline, developed in more detail in the copy, and represented visually through a photograph, an illustration, or a graphic element. By creating a strong visual/verbal relationship, the creative team can stimulate targets' imaginations to envision themselves wearing the product or picking a particular size or color, as well as see and understand safety instructions and/or warranties. Other considerations include the headline itself. If the headline copy creates a visual/verbal relationship—for example, "Is This You?"—and the visual shows a tired, worn-out working mother, then a direct relationship is formed between what is being said and what is being shown.

It is important that copywriters have coordinating visual images in their head when writing copy. Everyone who reads the copy must be able to understand what it is saying and how the visual(s) chosen reflects what is being said. A story line that reflects the target's lifestyle will help her see and experience what is written. It is just as important that the copy create a visual image for the art director. A strong visual/verbal tie also ensures that the client understands the campaign's direction.

It isn't hard to create confusion. If copy is trying to sell the nutrition associated with a brand of dog food and the visual shows a baby, it is difficult to understand the point without the headline's explanation. No one will understand what in the world dog food and babies have in common unless the connection is created both visually and verbally. Consider this connection: If the concept is nutritional value, the ad should show and tell dog owners they need to give their puppy a good start, just as they would a human baby. For the consumer to understand the analogy, the visual and verbal messages need to work together.

The layout style used also plays a role in copy. These visual directions or cues will be worked out during the brainstorming sessions or concept development stage. For example, a picture-window layout style requires a headline that draws the reader into the photograph, a rebus works great for copy that tells a story or gives the reader directions, and a Mondrian layout has a youthful feel and works well with copy that is upbeat or energizing.

The Logo as a Symbol

A discussion about visual/verbal relationships would be incomplete without a discussion of logos. A **logo** is the symbol—and ultimately the image—of a company or product, and it should be prominently displayed on any creative piece. A logo can consist of nothing more than the company or product name represented typographically; it can also be a graphic symbol or a combination of type and graphic. A logo needs to close every ad, even if it's used in the headline. It needs to be the last thing the viewer sees. A logo's graphic means nothing until meaning is given it through positioning.

Visual/Verbal Parts

The purpose and aim of the visual/verbal parts of an ad can be summed up by what each part (feature) needs to accomplish (benefit) and by recognizing a problem and offering the solution. Every ad needs to accomplish the following:

| Problem or feature | → | Benefit or solution |
| Attract attention | → | Headlines and visuals |

Create interest	→	Subheads and opening copy paragraphs
Generate excitement	→	Interior body copy
Induce action	→	Closing paragraphs or detail copy, logos, slogans/taglines

Once the key consumer benefit is determined, copywriters give it both entertainment and informational value. Headlines promote it, subheads defend it, and the body copy develops and highlights its many virtues. Copy is the product's tone of voice. If the copywriter can't write copy that visually and verbally tells the product's story, then it cannot solve the target's problem and successfully compete against the competition.

Writing beyond the Ad: Promotional Devices

Many ads have a promotional device, such as coupons or order forms, attached to them. The copywriter is also responsible for preparing promotional copy.

Coupons

All consumers like to get a break, and coupons are a way to offer something in return for their patronage or loyalty or as an introduction to a product or service. A coupon is an effective, temporary sales device. Coupons should be easy to remove from the ad and should clearly point out the offer.

The design of multiple coupons must be consistent. Headlines need to be the same size, as do percentages or cents-off claims on every coupon. Alternatives can be used when heads are not of the same length, structure, or consistency. For example, if you are working with three coupons—two with fairly long headlines that will break into three lines and a third that is only two lines in length—consider placing the two longer coupons first and third in the lineup, with the shorter coupon in the middle. This maintains continuity without altering type size. All headlines, price points, visuals, expiration dates, and logos should appear in the same place and be the same size on each coupon. Consider placing a dashed line around the coupon to visually encourage the consumer to cut or tear out the coupon.

Finally, it is imperative that the overall appearance be carried through with a repetitive element such as logo, slogan or tagline, color, consistent visual, or spokesperson or animated character. Tie the message, whether verbal or implied, to the visual appearance; make sure the timing works so that one supports the other, and make the placement match the image.

There are several elements to consider when designing a coupon (see figure 6.1):

- Size can vary, but it usually depends on how many coupons will be appearing in the ad.
- The headline should clearly state the offer: "Buy One Taco Burrito Platter and Get a Second Free."
- If the offer is a cents-off or a percentage-off deal, use a larger typeface and point size to make it stand out.
- If the offer can be redeemed at the grocery store, a small amount of body copy is needed to tell the grocer how to redeem the used coupons.

- Grocery coupons also need to have a UPC code so that they can be scanned at the checkout stand.
- Don't forget the product or store logo. Once the consumer tears the coupon out of the ad, she needs to know where to redeem it and on what brand it can be used.
- Most coupons have an expiration date. This time limit should be prominently displayed at the top of the coupon or in bold or italicized type within the body of the coupon.
- If the product comes in more than one size, flavor, or any other variation that might cause confusion for the consumer, add a picture of the product to make it easier to find the correct item.
- Coupons may also include a marketing code. This code tells the retailer where the coupon came from, assisting with future media placement.

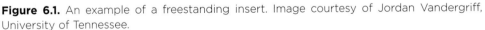

Figure 6.1. An example of a freestanding insert. Image courtesy of Jordan Vandergriff, University of Tennessee.

Freestanding Inserts

Freestanding inserts (FSIs) are one-page, full-color coupon ads that are inserted into the newspaper. These inserts are often double sided and usually feature coupons or announce a special sale or promotion. These nationally distributed inserts are also known as supplemental advertising.

Order Forms

An order form requires the target to do something, perhaps place an order, express an opinion, or relate an experience with the product or service. Additional uses might include an opportunity to ask for a free sample or additional information. If the advertising or promotional goal is to get consumers to ask for additional information or to conveniently place an order directly from the ad, an order form will need to be written and designed for them to use. Order forms are used most often in advertising, direct marketing, or Internet purchases. They are often attached to or found in magazines, in direct-mail pieces, or on web pages. However the target comes in contact with them, they must be well written and well designed.

Information gathered from an order form will be used to develop a database of current and past users and to keep track of anyone who requests additional information. This data will be used in future advertising or promotional efforts, mailings, or sales promotions.

The order form closes the sale. No matter how creatively the key consumer benefit was delivered, if the order form confuses or angers the consumer, everything else was a waste of time. It should not only be an order form but a decorative and creative sales device. As a sales device, it is a call to action, the last step the target takes when purchasing. Make it an easy step (see box 6.2).

Guarantees

Guarantees and trial offers are interactive devices that all but eliminate buyer skepticism and ensure consumer satisfaction. The guarantee is important, so accentuate it in the copy. If the product or service does not offer a guarantee, be sure to stress the return policy or customer service options. A brand-loyal customer is a repeat purchaser and a word-of-mouth warrior concerning all positive and negative contact points.

Good guarantees remove any risk for the consumer and place responsibility for consumer happiness squarely on the client's shoulders. Consumers will gravitate toward those products that have guarantees and away from those that don't.

A guarantee is one of the "little things" the client can do for the target. It is expected, appreciated, and remembered. A guarantee can replace, substitute, or fully reimburse the consumer if not fully satisfied, and hopefully with no questions asked. It should be easy for the consumer, not time intensive or embarrassing.

Copy Sheets

Copywriters submit completed copy on a copy sheet. Every piece of copy that appears in an ad, such as the headline, subhead(s), body copy, slogan or tagline, logo, and any guarantees, coupons, or order form information, will appear on a copy sheet. If it does not appear there, it will not appear anywhere. Each piece of copy should be appropriately labeled and placed in the proper order in which it will be seen in the ad. The client, account executive, art director, and computer artist use the copy sheet as both a visual and verbal guide.

BOX 6.2. Elements of an Order Form

An order form should include the following:

- Step-by-step instructions on how to order at the top of the form.
- A headline to call attention to what is being offered.
- A reintroduction of the offer/benefit. Even if mentioned in the body copy (and it should have been), sum it up here again and briefly tell the target what he or she needs to do. This should be no longer than one to three sentences. Restate it creatively; this is no time to bore the target.
- Blanks for name, address, apartment number, city, state, zip code, phone, fax, e-mail, date of birth, and intended use for the product.
- A request to "Please Print"—consumers don't always have the most legible handwriting.
- A box for appropriate titles such as Mr., Mrs., Miss, Ms., and instructions for what to do next (Circle One).
- If the product comes in sizes or colors or requires a monogram, provide blanks or boxes the target can check off. Make it easy, and make it clear enough that the target will be sure to get what was offered.
- If the consumer is asking for more information, additional questions are needed to ensure appropriate information is sent out. For example, a form for more information about life insurance might include questions about current coverage and dependents.
- Any relevant guarantee information. Tell how the product can be returned, any steps that need to be taken or applicable conditions, and how long it will take for a refund to arrive.
- Prices.
- Ordering options such as toll-free numbers, fax numbers, and website addresses.
- Payment options, such as credit cards accepted, money orders, or checks. State how long it will take for the product or information to arrive. List any shipping and handling costs, and be sure to tell how the product will be shipped.
- If there is a self-addressed envelope attached, instructions to place the form in the envelope. If not, the address the target will need to mail in the form. If a self-addressed envelope will be included, separate copy needs to be written for it (usually after the order form copy on the copy sheet), and it needs to be labeled appropriately.
- Repeat the logo and include the slogan or tagline.

There is no standard format for a copy sheet; most often this is determined by the agency. The example presented in template 6.1 is only one of many options for presenting copy.

Set the copy up in two columns, double spaced, with all labels placed in the left column and all copy confined to the right column. Use ten- or eleven-point Times or Helvetica. There should be approximately one inch of space between columns and one-inch margins on all four sides. Do not run columns together. Be sure to tab over so that all copy remains in the right column.

Coupon or order form copy appears below the logo on the copy sheet. Slogans or taglines can appear above or below the logo, depending on the logo design.

T **TEMPLATE 6.1**

Copy Sheet

Your Name:

Assignment Number and/or Product Name Here:

Headline:	The headline should appear here.
Main Subhead:	The main subhead should appear here if applicable.
Body Copy A:	Tell the product or service's story here.
Subhead:	Multiple subheads are great when making a transition or breaking up a copy-heavy page.
Body Copy B:	Continue the copy here.
Subhead:	You need not use multiple subheads if the copy is short.
Body Copy C:	Continue the copy here.
Tagline:	This could also be a slogan and can either appear above or below the logo.
Logo:	The full logo should appear here.
Body Copy D:	Consider placing detail copy here.
Coupon Copy:	Write all copy for coupon(s), including the need for the logo etc., here.
Coupon 1:	If more than one coupon, place copy for the first coupon here.
Coupon 2:	Place the copy for the second coupon here, and so on.
Order Form:	Place all copy for order form here.

Selling the Client on the Creative Idea

It would be remiss to close this discussion of copy and layout without discussing what happens next. Once copy and layout are done, the entire concept will have to be sold to the client.

The account executive may present anywhere from three to five ideas for the client to consider. Ideas are usually pitched to the client by the account executive in charge of the account. A new product pitch will be done with super comps and pitches to existing clients, often with roughs. There may or may not be a member of the creative team present.

The first step is for the creative team to ensure that the account executive understands the idea, where it came from, and how it relates to the client's communication goals. It's also helpful if the idea can be backed up with research. It is especially important to be able to back up how the idea addresses the objectives, reaches the target, and reflects the key consumer benefit; how the product will be positioned in the marketplace; and what brand image the creative team is trying to build.

Once an ad is accepted, the client needs to sign off on it. Once the client signs off, the ad is ready to go to production with this copy and/or this layout.

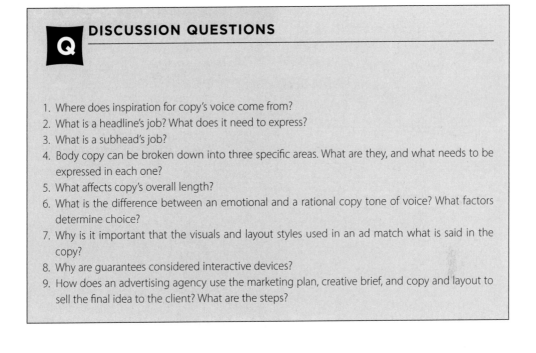

DISCUSSION QUESTIONS

1. Where does inspiration for copy's voice come from?
2. What is a headline's job? What does it need to express?
3. What is a subhead's job?
4. Body copy can be broken down into three specific areas. What are they, and what needs to be expressed in each one?
5. What affects copy's overall length?
6. What is the difference between an emotional and a rational copy tone of voice? What factors determine choice?
7. Why is it important that the visuals and layout styles used in an ad match what is said in the copy?
8. Why are guarantees considered interactive devices?
9. How does an advertising agency use the marketing plan, creative brief, and copy and layout to sell the final idea to the client? What are the steps?

Campaigns

The IMC Campaign

Integrated marketing communication campaigns differ from traditional campaigns in the way they are managed and in terms of overall outcomes. Like a traditional campaign, an IMC campaign has one unifying message and image and talks to a specific target audience. Here is where the similarity ends. Unlike most traditional advertising campaigns, an effective IMC campaign focuses on long-term results that build brand image and brand equity and works toward building a brand-loyal consumer (see case study 5 for a sample campaign). An IMC campaign talks to an individual via a two-way dialogue, creating interactive opportunities to connect directly with the targeted individual. IMC campaigns employ more diverse media vehicles than traditional efforts and choose media based on the target's lifestyle and media usage. Conversely, traditional advertising campaigns talk at a mass target audience in a **one-way monologue** and use fewer media outlets. Finally, in an IMC campaign all members of the promotional mix, beyond advertising, are working together to strategically accomplish the same objectives rather than working as individual contractors.

An IMC campaign can be defined as one that uses diverse media to deliver a strategic, cohesive, centralized collection of planned messages that focus on a single idea or concept. Campaign development can be broken down into four distinct steps:

- Planning the campaign
- Isolating a single idea or key consumer benefit
- Developing a cohesive visual/verbal message
- Selecting the promotional mix

Planning the Campaign

The planning, construction, and launch of a campaign doesn't happen overnight or in a vacuum. It takes a team of dedicated individuals working across many disciplines to bring each phase together on time, on budget, with the right message, placed in the correct media, and addressed to the right target.

In the planning stage, the account executive and the client will look at the marketing plan and review several key areas, including the target audience, the features and benefits of the product or service, the competition, and the marketing objectives.

Target Audience

Knowing what the target needs and wants from this product category and how the client's product fits into or addresses those needs is critical. In order to develop a consumer-focused approach, it is important to know as much about the targets as about the product or service. Their experiences, thoughts, ideas, and uses for the product are what will assist with message direction and positioning.

Features and Benefits

It is important to know more about the product or service than just the key consumer benefit. Knowing the product's attributes, capabilities, and limitations makes it easier to find a creative direction.

Questions to be asked include: How is the brand currently perceived? How does its current image affect what needs to be accomplished? Does the brand need to be strengthened or corrected? How many features does the product have? How is it manufactured? Is it the same, similar to, or completely unique when compared with competing brands? What is the quality of materials used, and how is it reflected in the price, packaging, store layout, and so on?

Today's educated consumer is armed with enough product knowledge to compare brands and make purchasing decisions based on more than just price. The product must offer a tangible benefit either not offered or not recognized by the competition. It is important to know the answers to the questions people in the target audience will ask before they compare products. Targets are not attracted by a great idea alone; they are looking for concrete answers that offer a relevant benefit or solve a real problem. They want to know *What's in it for me?* Why do I need it? What problem can it solve? What are the benefits of ownership? How does it work? Where can I buy it? What does it cost? Is it easy to use? By answering the questions before they are asked, the product or service will appear more relevant than the competition's product or service.

Competitors

As with target and product knowledge, the account and creative team cannot know enough about the competition. How does the client's product measure up? Does the competition have studies or professionals backing up its claims or recommending the product? Do you? What is the competing image, slogan, concept, or theme, and is it different enough from the

CASE STUDY 5

C

IMC Campaign: Ecco's Catwalk

Challenge

Shoe brand Ecco had gone from strength to strength in its homeland of Denmark. In Australia, however, Ecco had just 3.7 percent unaided brand awareness. Those who were aware of the brand thought the shoes were comfortable, but only 9 percent saw Ecco footwear as stylish. And that was a challenge area, as style always came first for Australian women. They were choosing to sacrifice comfort for that pair of heels they simply couldn't live without—and resorting to a range of tactics to help take the edge off the pain. Eighty-eight percent of women admitted to lining their shoes with bandages or tape to protect their toes and heels. A small number even admitted to shoving toilet paper in their shoes during a night out. Ecco set out to prove to women that Ecco footwear could solve their shoe-related problems.

The key objectives were to make women see Ecco shoes as both comfortable and stylish, increasing the style perception from 9 percent to 15 percent; turn Australian women into Ecco advocates, increasing the volume of online conversations by 50 percent and positivity by 5 percent; and, finally, drive a 10 percent year-over-year (YOY) increase in sales.

Insight

Australian women had been conditioned by fashion brands to believe that comfort and style could not coexist. To make it even tougher, experts were regularly inundating women with fashion and beauty claims that did not translate in the real world. This led to the consumer insight: Australian women wanted to believe that style and comfort were both possible in a shoe but needed to hear it from "women like them" before they would trust the claim.

The strategy was to use real women to change the conversation by providing undeniable proof that style doesn't have to be sacrificed for comfort.

Solution

The idea was to host a chic catwalk in one of Sydney's most iconic locations, a catwalk so long that no one would be able to fake comfort. Ecco's catwalk event had two notable differences from a regular fashion show. The first was that the end of the catwalk couldn't be seen; the second was that there was not a model pout in sight. Ecco's real models smiled for the entire 2.812 kilometers (1.75 miles) as they experienced firsthand the comfort and style of Ecco shoes. Ecco then amplified their smiles to the masses through magazine and online executions plus its audience's Facebook, Instagram, and Twitter feeds.

In the weeks leading up to the catwalk, Ecco built excitement by publicly recruiting an unusual type of model: one with absolutely no experience. Ecco's model-for-the-day competition allowed real Australian women to vie for a spot on the record-breaking catwalk through their social media assets. The competition winners were accompanied by other, better-known, everyday women—bloggers, stylists, and fashion writers. These women were invited to walk and then talk. Each brought attention to Ecco and the world's longest catwalk editorially. They let their readers, clients, and friends know that comfort and style can coexist—in the form of Ecco shoes.

Exclusive coverage of the record-setting event was sold to one of Australia's top-rated morning TV programs. In a four-minute segment, *The Morning Show* brought the catwalk to a broader group of Australian women, further validating Ecco's promise of comfort and style.

Results

Ecco's 2.812-kilometer catwalk smashed the world record and grabbed media attention. Ecco secured a 263 percent return on investment through the coverage alone. Thirty-five percent of women thought Ecco shoes were stylish. The catwalk sparked a 117 percent increase in online Ecco conversations. The most common talking points were the record-breaking catwalk and Ecco's latest range of shoes. Positivity of the conversations increased by 8 percent as women shared the good news of a shoe that is both comfortable and stylish. Ecco saw a 16 percent YOY increase in sales during the campaign period.

Media Channels

Ambient, experiential, digital, events, online, out-of-home, public relations, print, television

Source: "Ecco: World's Longest Catwalk," Cream—The Innovation Exchange, http://www.creamglobal. com/17798/31599/ecco-world's-longest-catwalk.

client's? Does the competition offer accessories to go with the product? How long has the competition been in business? What is its reputation? How well does its product perform compared with the client's product?

Knowledge is endless when used to support a concept. Use this knowledge to build the product's image, develop a strategy and concept, and determine how the product should be positioned.

Communication Objectives

Once the target, the product, and the competition have been reviewed, the next step requires another look at the communication objectives, or what the client wants to accomplish with its communication efforts. As discussed in chapter 2, most marketing objectives deal with sales. The conversion to communication-based objectives concentrates on what the target needs to think, feel, or do after exposure to the message. These objectives should be clearly stated, be measurable, be defined as long- or short-term in nature, and relate to the product's position in the product category.

Isolating the Key Consumer Benefit

Determining the key consumer benefit is easier once you know the product, the target, and the competition. With product knowledge, the team can determine how the product or service—as opposed to the competition's product—can affect the target's lifestyle. The decision about which feature/benefit will be used as the key consumer benefit will define the campaign.

The key consumer benefit is the target's motivation to buy. It should fulfill a want or need, create excitement, or make the target feel better or more relaxed. In an IMC campaign, the key consumer benefit becomes the voice of the entire campaign. How it is delivered will depend on the strategy and the choice of tone, approach, and appeal used to define the visual/verbal message. Together, each will lay the foundation for how the brand will be positioned and the development of the brand's image. And of course it should answer the target's million-dollar question: *What's in it for me?*

Developing a Cohesive Visual/Verbal Message

IMC campaigns must appear and speak with one cohesive and consistent tone of voice across the promotional mix. The visual/verbal message is the common thread that will bind all the communication efforts together. A key consumer benefit alone, if clearly stated and properly targeted, should be enough to bind a campaign together—but does not create a lasting visual/verbal identity on its own. The ability to create a visual/verbal relationship between pieces not only assists with brand-name recognition and image development but also is more memorable. The diverse choice of visual/verbal ties should reflect both the strategy and the brand's image and may include typeface and style, layout style, headline and body copy style, color usage, spokesperson or character representative, jingle, package design, logo, and slogan or tagline.

Whatever is used to bind the ads together, it must become synonymous with the product or service—the first thing that comes to mind when the product is mentioned. If a product or service is associated with a catchy statement or phrase that becomes a part of mainstream conversation or a catchy jingle the target can't get out of his head, it raises awareness and gives lasting impact to a campaign.

Why Multiple Pieces?

By this point, you may be wondering why it is important to use a series of ads: Why won't just one or two do? Repetitive visual/verbal ties are what differentiates a campaign from a single-view message. Single-view means the message is seen one time and is not associated with any other advertising used currently or previously. One ad with one message, or even a once-in-a-while message, is not a campaign and does not offer a synchronized message. Individualized message delivery has no repetitive identity reinforcement and does not build or strengthen an existing brand image.

Because consumers are exposed to so many messages, a single-view ad does not create a memorable identity. It takes consistent visual cues and a repetitive message for the reader or viewer to give an ad more than a passing glance. Without repetitive consistency, the experience goes into short-term memory and is quickly forgotten. For a message to be stored in the target's long-term memory, it must be repeatedly seen or heard.

So why do single-view ads at all? There are several reasons an ad may only be seen once, but the two most common reasons are poor planning and overstock or sales-related opportunities. Poor planning is a problem that can and often does affect brand loyalty and brand equity. If the consumer does not receive the correct information, stock is not available, or the message is placed in the wrong media, both the target and the product are affected. Overstocks, on the other hand, provide a great incentive to purchase. Additional stock usually means that lower prices are passed on to a motivated consumer.

No matter the reason, the goal is to use the same campaign-uniting devices that were used in previous advertising and promotional efforts to make a single-view ad fit seamlessly within the campaign pattern.

The Promotional Mix

Once it is known who is being talked to, and why, and what needs to be said, determining the correct promotional mix will be much easier. What media mix will reach the target? Will a more personalized, interactive media mix, such as social media, mobile, direct mail, or website be needed? Does the target need to be wooed back, or is the goal to get her to try the product with some type of sales promotion? Or will mass advertising in print or broadcast do the trick? Remember, to get the target to act, she must first be made aware of the product or service and see the product positioned as different or unique from the competition.

It is also important that campaign ideas translate well from medium to medium. Once the concept is solidified, the final promotional and media mix will be critical to the visual/verbal message. The concept may have the benefit of being expressed in hundreds of words or in only a few, or it may be heard and not seen. Knowing each medium's strengths and limitations will keep the concept from losing its visual and verbal integrity. IMC is not cohesive if the visual or verbal message cannot stand alone.

An IMC promotional mix includes any combination of the following: public relations, newspaper, magazine, radio and television, direct marketing and sales promotion, out-of-home and transit, Internet and social media, mobile or alternative media options. We will look at each one of these individually in chapters 8–18. In whatever medium a piece appears, it must consistently use the same tone of voice and repetitive appearance used to represent the key consumer benefit throughout the campaign.

Synergizing the Promotional Mix Message

Synergistic visual/verbal development is the backbone of IMC. Synergy happens when all messages to the target speak with one tone of voice and project a common image, giving the message more impact than any single message could by itself. Without the synergistic coordination of messages, a cohesive, consistent message to the target that repeatedly reinforces the key consumer benefit cannot be delivered. Multiple uncoordinated messages appearing in multiple media not only create confusion about what the product stands for but also keep the consumer from retaining the message. For example, if public relations works independently of advertising, PR is not privy to the strategy being employed to deliver the key consumer benefit, and coordination of efforts may not be possible. Public relations may mistakenly announce a new product, highlighting one feature/benefit, months before advertising is ready to launch a campaign focusing on a completely different feature/benefit. Inconsistent messages can effectively erode a product's competitive edge. Consequently, brand image and brand loyalty are affected when sales personnel or customer service representatives are flooded with questions for which they have no answers.

Types of Campaigns

Campaigns typically fall into one of four distinct varieties: national, service, corporate, or retail. Let's take a look at each one.

National Campaigns

National campaigns use a diverse promotional mix and can be seen or heard across the country. Campaigns of this size are very expensive and are most often undertaken by the corporate giants. Established brands, large budgets, and a diverse promotional mix drive national campaigns.

Students of advertising often mistake large budgets as the key to making a campaign stand out, while assuming those with smaller budgets will languish or even fail. Nothing could be further from the truth. A big budget does not make a great idea, but it can sure help one along. Memorable advertising is idea driven and target focused on the key consumer benefit.

Service Campaigns

Service campaigns are no different from product-based advertising. Although everyone needs and uses services such as health care, banking, or insurance, the goal is to make the client's service stand out from the competition as the one everyone needs and wants. One of the best ways to do this is to talk about service issues, such as customer service, no health screenings, easy claim service, or no waiting. The key is to offer the same service as the competition but to make it seem more important to the client's service organization. Then, when the target searches for a representative or location nearby, he will see the ad and remember the same visual/verbal message from television or newspaper—and a bond will be created. The advertised message may directly offer a solution to a problem he is having.

Service is about comfort. You cannot touch customer service, but you can experience it every time you enter the bank or need compassionate health care. Giving ads a similar appearance and tone of voice reminds the target of who the client is and what it has to offer every time the target sees an ad. Service campaigns need to emit "warm fuzzies" such as security, trust, and reliability. The very word "service" means more than one thing, so be sure to tie the key consumer benefit to the overall philosophy of the service provider.

Corporate Campaigns

Corporate advertising is basically a company tooting its own horn. Here a corporation takes the opportunity to let its target know what it has been up to, such as cleaning up the environment with new product developments or building homes for hurricane victims. Service to the community creates goodwill, contributes to a brand's equity, and tells environmentally or socially minded targets that this company is helping society or the environment in some meaningful way—an excellent key consumer benefit source. Corporate advertising can raise employee morale as well, because it talks about the company's community and national contributions or involvement, which ultimately affects its employees.

When repositioning is needed to address target needs or to compete with competitors, it is important that the direction the campaign is taking be communicated not only externally but internally as well. Internally, other shareholders such as employees, retailers, and tradesmen often will be asked to adjust or adapt to corporate changes. Internal communication is important to how successful the external advertising efforts will be. For example, if the message to the public is "Hertz: We Try Harder," employees with access to the public must understand this message. Nothing kills advertising momentum faster than retailers or customer service representatives who don't know—and thus can't act upon—the corporate message.

The worst kind of corporate advertising results from bad publicity, where a company must repair its image in the mind of the consumer. This is a very costly and time-intensive process. To build back consumer loyalty, the corporation must prove itself to the target all over again. Politics also plays a big role in corporate advertising when corporations use advertising to influence political leaders on upcoming legislation.

Retail Campaigns

Often referred to as the ultimate real-estate sale, retail campaigns can push individual products but more frequently promote a store or business over individual products. The campaign is usually based on price but can also be based on reputation. A business's reputation foretells price and quality, whether the target is dealing with Tiffany & Co., Zales, or Billy Bob's Jewelry Emporium. Each will approach advertising differently; some will push price, while others exist on image and reputation alone.

Retail campaigns rarely stand out creatively, since price is generally the name of the game. However, uniformity is still critical to memorability and status versus product relationships (figure 7.1). Because price plays such an important role and constant change is a fact of life, a sense of urgency is always present. Whether the sale lasts a weekend, a week, or a month, the goal is to get consumers into the store.

Unlike the other campaigns we have looked at, retail campaigns have a lot to do. They must initiate attention, create interest, announce prices, direct buyers throughout the store, demonstrate or showcase products, and encourage purchase through price or quality. A retail campaign never stops selling, from the signage outside to the shopping bags that purchases are placed in.

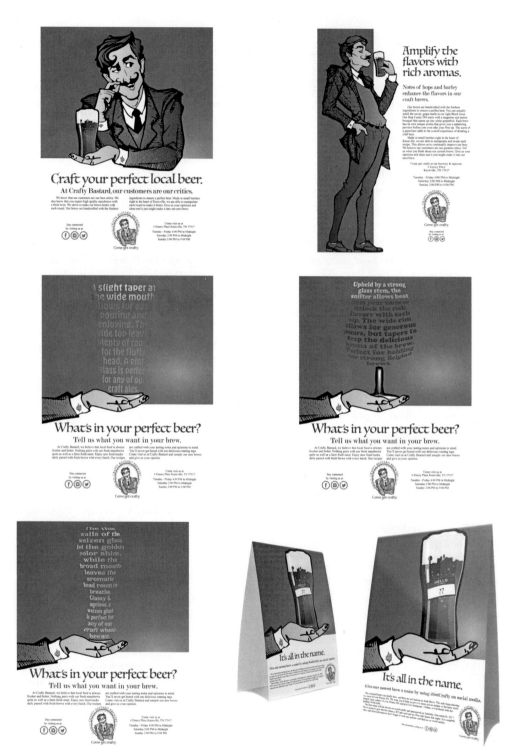

Figure 7.1. These campaign examples use graphics and copy to promote and educate as well as include engagement aspects. Images courtesy of Jordan Vandergriff, University of Tennessee.

All points of contact during the target's shopping experience should reflect the campaign's tone of voice and overall appearance. Here are some of the ways a retail-based IMC campaign can sell the key consumer benefit throughout the entire shopping experience:

- Presale advertising or direct-mail announcements, with or without coupons
- Window displays
- Window signage
- Interior displays or kiosks
- Shelf and rack announcements
- In-store credit card promotions
- In-store signage
- In-store announced promotions
- Promotional buttons or T-shirts for sales personnel
- Unique, attractive, or colorful wrapping tissue and coordinated shopping bags or boxes
- Table tent promotions for restaurants
- Receipt coupons
- Credit card stuffers

These are just a few of the techniques an IMC effort can successfully employ to build image through its communication efforts. However, image is more than advertising or promotional efforts; internal changes that deal with sales personnel and decor should be adapted to match communication efforts. Even a discount department store can deliver discounts without looking or acting like it. Well-stocked store shelves, a clean environment, friendly, nicely dressed salespeople, and attractively displayed merchandise can project quality at a bargain price.

Taking dry research and seemingly unrelated objectives and turning them into a message that speaks directly to the target across multiple media is not an easy task. The success of the creative effort will depend on how well it mimics and delivers the research found in the creative brief. Since the creative brief is limited to statistical information, it is up to the creative team to turn that information into a viable creative solution that is on target and on strategy.

Staying on target requires finding an appropriate creative direction. For a good place to start, look at the brand name, the packaging, and the product's uses. It is the creative team's job to develop connections to the product or service. Consider doing the opposite of what the target expects—like a surprise ending in a movie, lead the target in one direction only to land somewhere else. Consider using plays on words; although advertisers are often criticized for exploiting the English language for their own creative purposes, it is a memorable way to present a message. The only limits to setting the product off from the crowd is to be off target or off strategy by deviating from the brief, reach the wrong audience, or talk to target consumers about something they don't care about.

The message cannot be implied or it will not accomplish the stated objectives or receive the needed recognition and sales throughout all media. Consumers do not want to work at understanding the message; if the message is not clear, they will choose a competing brand whose information is clear and whose benefit is immediately apparent.

Successful campaigns can, and should, run for years, continually striving to build both brand loyalty and brand equity. Change should be considered only when the product or company significantly changes. Today's advertised messages often change with the seasons, leaving little time for awareness or loyalty to emerge. Inconsistent repositioning of brands or repeated challenges to competing brands can affect the target's image of the product or service. Companies that are patient and work at building product loyalty over time will find competitors' constant change less of a factor in building and maintaining brand equity.

Concept Components

IMC campaigns consist of three interrelated components that affect concept development and overall appearance: campaign uniformity and visual and verbal uniformity.

Campaign uniformity means that the overall look and message are consistent no matter the media outlet used or the final appearance of any creative piece. **Visual uniformity** means that all creative materials have a unique appearance or look. This happens when layouts, representative characters, slogans/taglines, or even representative color combinations are found on all pieces. **Verbal uniformity** takes place when all creative pieces promote one idea or key consumer benefit. For the campaign to be successful, it must strategically accomplish the objectives developed in the creative brief and spotlight the key consumer benefit. A diverse promotional mix using the same verbal tone of voice and visual appearance increases the likelihood the target will see and remember the message, positioning the client's product away from the competition.

The components affecting campaign development emerge from the creative brief to form the campaign's overall creative foundation. Before any concept direction can be successful, it must be able to address and accomplish each of the following:

- Every campaign is driven by a key consumer benefit in the form of either a big idea or USP.
- Strategically, all ads work to accomplish the stated objectives.
- The campaign's message must speak directly to the target audience's needs and wants.
- Overall appearance may be based on a specific message or idea, layout or headline style, character or spokesperson, typeface and style, visual element, or color combinations.
- The campaign has a visual/verbal identity that is clearly recognizable in all advertising and promotional devices.
- The concept direction creates a unique brand identity to set the product off from the competition.

Know what needs to be accomplished before beginning the design phase, exhaust the brainstorming and word list stages, and find the unique and discard the "been there, done that" ideas. It is key that any campaign include cohesiveness, consistency, and repetition. Does the campaign idea have *all* these key elements throughout the promotional mix? If it doesn't, what component(s) need to be adjusted to create the uniformity needed?

The Concept Develops the Visual/Verbal Ties

A campaign's unifying nature brings a constant and reliable performance to each campaign piece. For a campaign to stand out from the competitive crowd and attract attention, it must have a visual/verbal look, tone, personality, and appearance all its own. The verbal elements include headlines, subheads, body copy, slogans or taglines, and jingles. Each element has a distinct job in telling the product or service's story. Sound can also unify a campaign through jingles or music or the distinctive voice of a spokesperson. To define the brand's image, it will need a distinct, coordinated tone of voice that can express and identify the brand's personality.

Verbal elements should create a cohesive and consistent tone of voice throughout the campaign and across all media. A campaign's message should be so intertwined that the consumer feels the continuity of thought from one ad to the next.

Verbal elements include:

- *Headlines.* Headlines are most often used to announce the key consumer benefit. Each headline's tone of voice should match the tone, approach, and appeal determined in the strategy and should give the brand an identity. The choice of headline style should complement the brand's image and bring the concept to life. For example, if the target is asked a question in the newspaper, also ask one in the magazine, outdoor, radio, television, and other media.
- *Subheads.* A subhead should continue the thought concerning the key consumer benefit begun in the headline. The subhead's job is to keep the reader moving through the ad by offering tantalizing bits of information.
- *Body copy.* The length and overall voice of the body copy is also a great way to tie ads together. Body copy tells the product's story through its features and benefits, primary uses, and any additional or secondary uses that will help to demonstrate the product's importance in the target's life. The first paragraph should continue the discussion on the key consumer benefit, the middle section should make the sale, and the closing paragraph needs to move the target to action.
- *Slogan or tagline.* A slogan identifies a corporate or product philosophy; a tagline reflects the concept and key consumer benefit used in a campaign. No matter which one is used, it should always appear above or below the logo. If a slogan is spoken on radio and/or television, be sure it appears to be spoken in print by the character representative or spokesperson.
- *Jingle.* If the message can be sung in a catchy way, why bore the target by saying it? Jingles can get in a target's head and stay there; that's why jingles are described as "catchy."

Visual elements speak to the target in a different way; they help the target see or experience the product or service and the benefit it will bring to his life. Visual images can show the product in use or place the product in the hands of the target. The types of images chosen, as well as layout and typeface, can suggest the visual/verbal tone of voice to be used. Color choices can set a mood, and the purposeful placement of elements within an ad can help define the overall product image. Consistency and repetitiveness are key to binding campaign pieces together; remember, nothing can be said or shown just once in any IMC campaign series.

Visual elements include:

- *Layout style*. Layout style, or the overall way each component is laid out or placed within the ad, creates a consistent visual appearance across media. Use the same layout style for each printed piece. Layout styles can transfer to radio and television through tone of voice, with the character or spokesperson delivering the message.
- *Visual images*. The choice of images depends on the concept. If using a nostalgia theme, think about using black-and-white photographs or a Norman Rockwell–style illustration that complements the concept. If the concept deals with making what is old new again, the use of spot color on a black-and-white photograph can highlight the product or logo by creating eye flow. Graphic images give a modern, stylish, or trendy feel to a product; color photographs bring the product alive with rich colors, textures, and detail.
- *Typeface*. The same typeface, type style, and weight should be used in all ads in the campaign. Whenever possible, headlines, subheads, and body copy should be the same point size and length, as size creates a visual unity between ads.
- *Character or spokesperson*. A representative, either animated or human, who can speak for and represent a product gives a personality or face to the product and should appear in all pieces. If possible, the image should be approximately the same size; at the very least, the same amount of image should appear in every ad. A repetitive head-and-shoulders shot, for example, can be used at different sizes.
- *Repetitive border treatments* can create a mood. Use of a decorative border, whether elaborate or simplistic, can isolate both the ad and the elements within the ad by pulling the viewer in, creating an air of exclusivity and elegance. Depending on the graphic images used, borders with images within them or as an extension of them can create an illusion of playfulness or homeyness or give the ad seasonal appeal.
- *Color*. Color, or the lack thereof, can make an ad unique in the same way a particular illustrative, graphic, or photographic style can. The choice of color should support the overall key consumer benefit and strategy. Color choices can be used as design elements to create specific emotions or to set a mood or attract the eye. Color is also easier to remember than product names.
- *Logos, slogans, or taglines*. The logo, slogan, or tagline should appear in basically the same location on all pieces and should be the same size whenever possible.

To help determine whether a campaign is consistent across all media and has all the required elements, see the campaign checklist in box 7.1.

It is important to be familiar with the promotional mix before finalizing concept direction. Knowing where the ads will be seen or heard will help determine the best way to show or tell the concept. For example, should the concept rely on a lengthy verbal message to get its point across, or will media restrictions allow only a few words to make the same point? Will visuals that show the product in use, in a setting, or through a demonstration deliver the key consumer benefit better?

BOX 7.1. Campaign Checklist

1. ____ Does each ad clearly state the key consumer benefit?
2. ____ Does the campaign's message talk to targets in their language and in a way that holds their attention?
3. ____ Does the campaign's message address and answer each stated objective?
4. ____ Is the relationship clear between the key consumer benefit, the headline, the body copy, and the visuals?
5. ____ Is this relationship reflected in the strategy?
6. ____ Does each ad or promotion's overall image match the tone, approach, and appeal stated in the strategy?
7. ____ Does the chosen layout style reflect the strategy?
8. ____ If a jingle was created, do the music and words reflect the strategy?
9. ____ Is the concept as strong visually as it is verbally, no matter what medium it appears in?
10. ____ Is the concept unique to the product, and does it position itself away from the competition?
11. ____ Does the copy's tone of voice match that stated in the strategy?
12. ____ Does the first paragraph of the body copy continue the key consumer benefit discussion begun in the headline?
13. ____ Does the middle paragraph of the body copy give enough information about the product to understand what it is, what it does, and how it will affect the target's lifestyle?
14. ____ Does the copy close with a call to action?
15. ____ Is detail copy included in all ads to make shopping or ordering easier?
16. ____ Is the message clearly consumer focused?
17. ____ Do the visual components match the strategy?
18. ____ Do the visuals match the image created in the headline and copy?
19. ____ Is the logo clearly seen in every message?
20. ____ Does the slogan or tagline appear in every message?
21. ____ If specific color combinations were used in the ads, do they appear in every message, and do they match the tone, approach, and appeal used in the strategy?
22. ____ Is the typeface and style consistent in every ad?
23. ____ Is the layout style evident and the tone apparent in every ad?
24. ____ Is the headline size and body copy length as consistent as possible in every ad?
25. ____ If using a spokesperson or character representative, is he or she seen or heard in every ad?
26. ____ Is the cropping and image size as consistent as possible in every ad?
27. ____ Does the package's design match the brand's image?
28. ____ Does the campaign reflect a long-term focus, with enough time built in to build consumer loyalty?
29. ____ Are there interactive components built into the campaign?
30. ____ Does the promotional mix reflect the target's lifestyle and interests?
31. ____ Is the visual/verbal relationship so strong that if the campaign were thrown into a vat with a thousand other campaigns, the target would be able to pick out the brand's specific series of ads?
32. ____ Does the IMC campaign have one clear benefit, a distinct appearance, and one tone of voice that is apparent across all media?

Spokespersons and Character Representatives

When you want to say something visually, consider using a visual voice in the form of a spokesperson or animated character representative.

The spokesperson for a product is important. He or she must be likable, with an appearance that fits the campaign's overall visual/verbal concept. To determine an appropriate spokesperson, the creative team members must ask themselves: Who does this product remind me of? Remember, it's the product's personality that sets it off from the competition, especially if there are no major differences between brands in the same category.

There are four basic types of spokespersons:

1. Celebrities
2. Specialists
3. Corporate heads or CEOs
4. Common man

Celebrities

A celebrity's popularity with younger target audiences can be transferred to a product, and this popularity can actually build a product's brand equity. It is important that the celebrity's professional image be tied to the product's key consumer benefit. This image translates to the product, so any character flaws that arise in a celebrity over time will reflect upon the product. Celebrity endorsements can be broken down into five different areas:

Unpaid On-Screen Spokesperson Charities supported by a celebrity are the most common benefactors of an unpaid on-screen spokesperson.

Paid On-Screen Spokesperson Paid on-screen spokespersons are one of the most common types of spokesperson. This is where a celebrity is paid to tie her image to a product and physically represent it in all advertising efforts.

Celebrity Voice-Over This type of spokesperson is used for radio and television. Voice-overs are less expensive spokespersons because they deliver the message off-screen and the celebrity is not identified or seen. Celebrity voice-overs are not a great choice for use in an IMC campaign, since a voice-over cannot be used on all media vehicles.

Dead-Person Endorsement A dead person can't speak, but his image can. The use of old interviews or movie clips can associate personality traits, political activism, and even nostalgia with a product. The use of this type of spokesperson is very controversial and often considered in bad taste.

Animated Character Spokesperson Believe it or not, the Keebler Elves and the Pillsbury Doughboy are celebrities. We like them, we trust them, and they have been around so long, we consider them friends. They might make us feel a little nostalgic, and we may even associate their image with a specific event.

Specialists and CEOs

If something needs to be proved, use a specialist in the field, like a doctor, scientist, or engineer. If the goal is to develop a philosophy, create a friendship, or instill trust, use a CEO or owner of a small company or business.

Common-Man Spokesperson

The common man can be someone who uses the product and can talk about his or her experiences or a paid actor representing the common man based on feedback from real consumers. Why use an actor when you can use a real common man? It has nothing to do with trying to deceive the public and everything to do with how the message is delivered. A trained actor will be able to deliver the message with less effort and more believability. Anytime a substitution is made, it must be stated in the ad. That being said, common-man endorsements are becoming more common. It is thought that celebrities, with all their power and faults, have saturated the market and are becoming less believable. They also limit the length of time a campaign can run; star power rarely lasts as long as a product's does.

Personality Traits for an Effective Spokesperson

To reach out and touch the target, the character or spokesperson must resonate with the target. If consumers don't like or respect the image or person delivering the message, they will tune out. We search for people like us, so personality traits should reflect the target's self-image and lifestyle. When developing a character or hiring a spokesperson, consider the following traits:

- Appearance
- Likability
- Trustworthiness
- Expertise
- Credibility

Character representatives begin in an art director's imagination, much like a live spokesperson does. The choice to use a live person or create a character spokesman will have a lot to do with concept and a little to do with budget.

There are times when a live actor simply cannot be found who fits the client's direction or the art director's conceived personality for the product. So, when it can't be found, create it. Budget can also affect whether a spokesperson will be local talent or a celebrity. But at any level, live talent is more expensive to maintain than a character on a page or computer screen.

Character reps may come from word association, folklore, historical characters or events, or even an art director's past experiences. Character reps are easy to work with; they have no demands, are never late, and never grow old. Their images can and often do last longer than a live representative spokesperson. Here are a few character representatives you may recognize:

- MetLife Snoopy
- The GEICO Gecko
- The Energizer Bunny
- The Michelin Man
- Chester the Cheetah
- The Aflac Duck
- Mr. Clean
- The Pillsbury Doughboy

- Mr. Peanut
- Dow Scrubbing Bubbles
- Tony the Tiger

It is important to remember that campaigns are meant to run for a long period of time, perhaps decades. If you keep in mind how the concept can grow and mature over time, you can almost guarantee the campaign will have staying power. This is one of the reasons to stay away from trends and current celebrities and create your own trends and your own celebrities through spokespersons or character representatives.

Stand Up and Stand Out: It Pays to Be Different

Product categories with little or no product differentiation need a unique creative approach to set the product apart—not by features but by status, image, or imagination. This is where the right strategic appeal creates difference among the masses. Targets will buy a created and creative image over the status quo; it just needs to fit their image and their needs. What will be the tie that binds—a character or spokesperson, a jingle, or a theme-related headline treatment, slogan, tagline, or layout style? The key to creative individualism lies in the research and brainstorming stages. Create a trend, tie it to an existing trend, resurrect a trend, or create a voice or a statement that can be reinforced visually through photographs, illustrations, or graphic devices.

Campaigns and their creative imagery and messages allow the creative team to continually remind targets what the client's product or service brings to them over that of the competition.

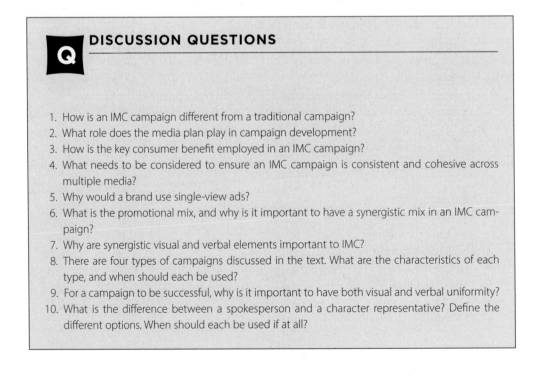

Q DISCUSSION QUESTIONS

1. How is an IMC campaign different from a traditional campaign?
2. What role does the media plan play in campaign development?
3. How is the key consumer benefit employed in an IMC campaign?
4. What needs to be considered to ensure an IMC campaign is consistent and cohesive across multiple media?
5. Why would a brand use single-view ads?
6. What is the promotional mix, and why is it important to have a synergistic mix in an IMC campaign?
7. Why are synergistic visual and verbal elements important to IMC?
8. There are four types of campaigns discussed in the text. What are the characteristics of each type, and when should each be used?
9. For a campaign to be successful, why is it important to have both visual and verbal uniformity?
10. What is the difference between a spokesperson and a character representative? Define the different options. When should each be used if at all?

Public Relations

The Strategic Use of Public Relations in IMC

Public relations is a mostly nonpaid form of communication that builds relationships with both internal and external audiences through communication efforts that reinforce, defend, or rebuild a corporation's or product's image. External audiences are a company or organization's "publics," or target audience. Internal audiences are referred to as stakeholders, or those who have a stake or vested interest in the company's success and reputation.

Marketing Public Relations

When IMC uses public relations to promote a brand, it's known as **marketing public relations (MPR)**. MPR uses nonpaid media vehicles in either print or broadcast to inform the public about a product, service, or corporation. (See case study 6 about Dawn's MPR.)

MPR deals with the "selling" of a corporate or brand image to a specifically defined target audience. Traditional corporate public relations deals with many different publics, both internal, such as shareholders and employees, and external, such as consumers and organizations. This is different from traditional public relations, which is most often utilized as a promotional or informational outlet. Public relations in the past has been relegated to a support role, responding more to what the client wanted than what the advertising message required. This disconnect frequently generated unplanned, mistimed, and incompatible messages that often confused the target and eroded a brand's identity.

BOX 8.1. MPR Tactics

Tactics used in marketing public relations might include:

- Print news releases
- Media kits
- Video news releases (VNRs)
- News conferences
- Celebrity spokesperson interviews or personal appearances
- Sponsored events

Today, timing is controlled, and all communication efforts coming from public relations representatives use the same tone of voice and appearance as other IMC messages. It is not unusual for public relations to be called upon from time to time to create or promote media events to strengthen or maintain interest in the product or service. Because of its access to the press and the press's ability to reach the target, and because of its credible reputation, public relations is able to grease the way for the rest of the promotional mix, both internally and externally.

Reinforcement
Public relations comes into the IMC process with experience in creating opportunities for two-way communication between the company, product or service, and the target, making it a vital player in determining and managing the relationship between buyer and seller. Because of this, public relations is excellent at initiating communication efforts through interactive exchanges between the consumer or technical assistance representatives and the consumer. This dissemination of information gives symmetrical information to all interested parties, bridging the communication gap between word-of-mouth gossip and valid information.

Defense
Ideally, public relations practitioners will find themselves in an offensive position when introducing or maintaining image; but if any kind of negative publicity does arise, they will need to take a defensive position. These actions can play a huge role in creating and maintaining brand equity and brand loyalty. In a crisis or negative situation, the way in which the corporation's view or position is proactively handled can eliminate any lingering negative effects concerning the corporation, product, or service.

Rebuilding
If the public is not given the satisfaction of hearing from the corporation or organization, word of mouth takes over and affects equity and loyalty. Once consumer confidence is lost, it is very time-consuming and costly to gain back. Continual informative messages, often delivered through social media and public forums such as news conferences, can success-

fully deflect countering opinions, hearsay, or investigative inquiries to ensure a product or service's continued success.

The Diversity of the Public Relations Voice

Public relations defines action. Its job is to get the word out about what a corporation or organization is doing locally, nationally, or internationally; how it affects the organization's product or service; and/or what the organization's relationship is with the target. This action becomes usable information to the public. Externally, its most traditional action-oriented tactics include news articles; televised events or interviews with company spokespersons, executives, or CEOs; news releases to local or national newspapers or radio and television stations; news conferences; and social media management.

Communication inside a corporation is just as important as the message sent to the consumer. Devices such as newsletters deliver information on company events, insurance, investments, promotions, and retirements. Additionally, public relations representatives may act as go-betweens for the corporation and the media, setting up interviews, writing speeches, and arranging sponsorships to arouse public interest or attract attention.

Additional responsibilities include using social media to interact with consumers, manage viral campaigns and blogs, planning any necessary restructuring for internal adjustments to new company policies or philosophies associated with an IMC message, the development of corporate or community sponsorships, and the development of celebrity endorsements or the arrangement of appearances at an event.

When used as a marketing tool, public relations can launch products, build or enhance images, and inform consumers for very little money. Costs associated with public relations most often deal with salaries and development of printed materials.

A public relations representative's ability to build relationships and interact with consumers creates an interactive dialogue that makes the customer part of the product's success and future development. An ongoing relationship with the press gives public relations media options not available with any of the other communication approaches. This ability to garner media coverage through events, news releases, press conferences, and interviews makes public relations especially suited to:

- Launching a new product and service
- Positioning or repositioning a product or service
- Generating "buzz" about a product or service
- Affecting and reaching specific target groups
- Crisis control, scandals, or negative publicity for a product, service, or corporation
- Building or maintaining the image of a product, service, or brand

New Products
With a new product launch, public relations can create excitement or anticipation with facts rather than through creative execution. Because of its relationship with the press, public relations is considered more reliable than straight advertising.

CASE STUDY 6

C

IMC Public Relations: Dawn Dishes It Out

Overview

Though consumers understood Dawn Dishwashing Liquid's core equity (tough on grease), they were unaware of its value proposition: Just a little Dawn cleans lots of dishes. As a result, consumers were being lured by lower-priced products in larger-size bottles that appeared to offer more value.

Dawn turned to Marina Maher Communications (MMC) with a challenge: Lead an integrated communications campaign that would illustrate—in a unique, dramatic, and breakthrough way—that Dawn's Lift Action formula is the best value (just one twenty-five-ounce bottle cleans more than 10,000 dishes).

Objectives

The campaign would need to meet three critical criteria:

1. Generate national awareness of the value claim.
2. Create relevance for consumers (including the large and growing Hispanic market).
3. Be easily integrated with other marketing disciplines.

Tactics

To allow consumers to "see" and "believe" Dawn's cleaning power, MMC developed a massive event "torture test" concept that told the story: Dawn Goes the Distance (*Dawn Supera la Distancia*). The key visual—providing news/media value, advertising content, and consumer interaction—was to use daredevil Robbie Knievel, son of the legendary Evel Knievel, to attempt to jump over 10,000 dishes—all cleaned with just one twenty-five-ounce bottle of Dawn! Using Knievel allowed MMC to establish the positioning of "It takes a daredevil to attempt to beat what Dawn can accomplish."

The four-pronged integrated marketing effort featured a giant festival and wash-a-thon—staged at California's Irwindale Speedway (a recognized motocross locale)—and provided highly visual footage for a new advertising campaign. Key elements included:

- Credible eating/washing event (where attendees witnessed the 10,000-dishes dishwashing claim)
- Hispanic market location (Los Angeles, home to a large US Hispanic population)
- "Wow" visual for media coverage and advertising shoot (associating the low-interest category of dishwashing with the excitement of a daredevil motocross attempt)
- Celebrity spokespeople (Knievel to communicate brand value message and Hispanic celebrity host to emotionally connect with Hispanic target audience)

Results

More than 5,000 bilingual flyers were distributed in market and an ANR, airing pre-event, garnered attendance of 1,685 consumers. Irwindale Speedway marquee signage was seen by 525,000 LA-area consumers/drivers over five days. In addition, 1,700 product samples were distributed at the event.

The MMC campaign generated sixty-seven million consumer impressions in just one week. More than 575 TV placements spotlighted Dawn in general market and Hispanic outlets, including CNN's *Headline News, American Morning*, and *Airport; ESPN Sportscenter; Fox News Live*; Univision's *Despierta America*, and Telemundo's *Al Rojo Vivo* with María Celeste. Coverage saturated all top-ten ADI markets in the United States.

Radio coverage included 484 stories, while Dawn's photo ran on the AP wire service, and the *Los Angeles Times* featured the Dawn story and brand name—highly unusual for a low-interest category in the nation's third-largest newspaper.

TV advertising launched on January 12, 2004, and Dawn's brand manager reported: "The Dawn Mileage program creates a permanent impression in consumers' minds about Dawn's long-lasting performance in a way that no competitor can challenge or match. . . . The program generated results well beyond our expectations."

Source: Dawn with Marina Maher, "Dawn Dishes It Out: Changing Consumers' Perceptions on Value," Council of Public Relations Firms, http://prfirms.org/resources/dawn-dishes-it-out-changing-consumers-perceptions-on-value.

Positioning

The way a brand is positioned or repositioned will have everything to do with the target and/or parent company or corporation. If the product is positioned as safe and the corporation that manufactures that product is currently under investigation by a federal agency for safety violations, the product's position will be hurt by corporate actions. Once the consumer loses faith in a product or service, both brand loyalty and brand equity are affected. It can be very expensive and time-consuming to rebuild a product's image. If the consumer dislikes or is distrustful of the corporation, extensive media coverage can enhance these feelings of distrust, effectively dooming any communication efforts.

Generating Buzz

Public relations is a great source for creating a "buzz" or hype for a new product launch. Perfectly timed leaks to the press can create a perceived need for a product or service before it even hits the market. Because the information is coming from a credible source, the news media, a product can hit the market ahead of its competitors based on little information and a lot of excitement. However, the product or service must deliver on what is promised or implied to reinforce credibility and trust. Public relations representatives have many options available to them to create and build brand awareness that have nothing to do with the use of traditional advertising methods. Consider the following options when "buzz" is needed:

- *Sponsorships.* A sponsorship is when a corporation or brand commits its name and money to an event such as a golf tournament, concert, or charity event.

- *Talk shows.* If you can get a talk show host like Ellen or Dr. Oz to talk about a product he or she uses and likes or a company that sponsored an event the host was involved in, the host's popularity and credibility transfers to the product or service.
- *Product placement in movies or television programs.* If you remember the Reese's Pieces trail in the movie *ET*, you understand the importance of product placement. A product's success is usually associated with a character, but it can, if repeated often enough, become associated with a movie or television show. The sheer number of loyal viewers or moviegoers for popular features can boost sales and create or reinvent a brand's image.
- *Celebrity endorsements.* As discussed in chapter 7, celebrities can represent a product based on their success or reputation.
- *On-the-spot promotions.* In an on-the-spot promotion, a corporation takes the product to the people so that they can try or see the product in use. These types of events are often set up on busy street corners, in malls, or anywhere a large number of people will be available to participate.
- *Inadvertent celebrity spokespersons.* An inadvertent celebrity spokesperson happens by accident when a spokesperson's persona is so well liked by the target that he or she becomes something of a celebrity. Often spokespersons appear on talk shows and in the news, creating a nonpaid form of advertising for the product or service.

Reaching Specific Targets

The ability to create a dialogue with both internal and external audiences allows public relations to coordinate messages between its "publics" and shareholders. Public relations works from the inside out to reach targets with a product they trust, from a credible source that has earned a reputation based on a product's repeat performance and quality.

Crisis Control and Scandal

A brand cannot survive if the corporation is under fire or its publics or stakeholders are unhappy or dissatisfied. Positive relationships, built from the inside out, are as important as the message. Public relations representatives orchestrate and maintain much of a brand's, service's, or corporation's image.

Today, a large amount of crisis control takes place via social media. A crisis or scandal can take many forms and vary in size. For example, a handful of disgruntled consumers may be dissatisfied with the level of customer service they recently received, while a larger contingent may respond negatively to environmental issues, contaminated food reports, or recalls associated with the brand. Any level of negative publicity left unaddressed is detrimental to both a brand's image and brand equity. Brands that have a crisis management plan in place can avert scandal and avoid negative public opinion by first acknowledging the problem and then addressing it using both social and news media outlets.

Brands that continually monitor social media outlets can immediately respond to innuendo by dispelling rumors or address a developing crisis by controlling the flow of information. The key to successfully surviving a crisis is to respond to it as quickly and professionally as possible. The slower a company is to respond, the more believable any unsubstantiated information becomes to followers, listeners, or viewers.

Public relations representatives must be careful to avoid causing additional negative word of mouth or viral postings before responding or posting a comment about any crisis. If all the facts are not currently available, they need to let the target know that updates will be posted as soon as they are available. Not all complaints warrant public postings. For personal complaints, questions, and concerns, deal with the individual directly and privately. Use public posting only for issues dealing with a larger segment of the target audience.

In *Advertising Campaign Design: Just the Essentials*, Robyn Blakeman suggests the following steps for managing a crisis:

1. Take immediate action. It doesn't take long for negative publicity to become the hub that negative press revolves around.
2. Be a part of the conversation. Give the facts that are available, and keep consumers updated on changes as they happen.
3. It happened; admit it. Be a part of the solution; let the target know the steps that are being taken to avoid such a mishap in the future. Monitor the ongoing conversation to nip baseless accusations in the bud and clarify points.
4. Do not issue a scripted apology. Social networks are not press conferences and need personal interaction.
5. Ask for a solution. Find out what it will take to make amends. This proactive approach lets consumers know the brand or corporation takes responsibility and cares about what the target thinks. It is also a great way to maneuver the discussion from a negative one to a more positive one.
6. Solve it.
7. Build on it and move on.

Brands that are active participants in the day-to-day chatter on social media will find it a great place to monitor public opinion, talk directly to brand-loyal but disgruntled consumers, distribute information, and dispel negative allegations.

Building or Maintaining Image

Any negative publicity is damaging to a brand's image. Corporations that do nothing often face intense scrutiny from the media, forcing a corporation to face up to and act on the charges or allegations. Corporations that respond immediately to damaging allegations can kill the momentum of any kind of investigation quickly, often with little or no damage to image or equity.

Public relations brings a reputation built on trust and credibility with both the media and the target to the IMC promotional mix. As longtime practitioners of consumer-focused information, public relations representatives are used to building and retaining rapport between a corporation, brand, or service and its publics and other stakeholders.

How Does Public Relations Help IMC Be Consumer Focused?

The emergence of public relations from a supportive role to becoming an essential member of the promotional mix is the result of its compatibility with IMC tactics such as:

- *Relationship building.* IMC concentrates on tightly defining a specific target audience. Products and messages are developed with this target audience and their specific needs in mind. Public relations can take this definition a step further by including internal stakeholders in the planning and execution of the IMC message. By segmenting these various targets into smaller, more manageable groups, a key consumer benefit can be adapted to address each consumer or stakeholder's needs and wants more specifically. Consumer-focused marketing, or relationship marketing, has always been a priority for public relations. The move from traditional sales-based advertising to relationship marketing, or the building of long-term relationships with the target or other stakeholders, is critical to building brand loyalty and creating a dialogue, or two-way communication, between buyer and seller.
- *Tone of voice.* IMC focuses on messages delivered with one tone of voice and one image. Public relations can reflect the key consumer benefit, the strategy, and the visual/verbal message on all communication, both internal and external. This consistent and repetitive use helps maintain that voice and image not only with the press but also through contact with customer service representatives, operators, sales personnel, delivery drivers, and consumers. This coordination of ideals and attitude is as important to brand loyalty as it is to a brand's image.
- *Databases.* IMC employs the use of databases to personally reach individuals within the target audience. Public relations uses databases as informational and educational devices to develop a relationship by interacting one on one with the target.
- *Brand management.* IMC focuses on creating and maintaining the image of a product, service, brand, or corporation and developing brand-loyal consumers. Disgruntled employees, negative word of mouth, government investigations, and recalls can affect a brand's image. The job of public relations is to manage this image from the inside out before it can affect a target's attitude or mind-set toward a product or service.
- *Two-way communication.* IMC focuses on ways to develop an interactive dialogue between the buyer and the seller. Public relations is the first to understand that what happens inside a company affects the product and the consumer. Interactive opportunities allow the consumer to be an internal stakeholder by offering feedback on products and/or customer or technical services.

Incentives and Deterrents of Public Relations

In order to decide whether public relations is right for an IMC campaign, let's look at some of the incentives and deterrents associated with it.

What Makes Public Relations So Great?

The more notable incentives associated with public relations include:

- *Elevated corporate or brand image.* Public relations determines what the target thinks about a product or service or the corporation that produces the product by maintaining its positive position in the consumer's mind through customer service contact or the proper and swift handling of any negative publicity.
- *A well-developed interactive relationship with the target.* Public relations can reach, talk, or bring the product or service directly to members of the target or target groups through such outlets as social media, news conferences, sponsored events, infomercials, or public service announcements.
- *More communication outlets.* Able to communicate at length with both internal and external targets, public relations can tailor a message to an external targeted individual or on a larger scale to internal groups such as union workers.
- *Low cost.* Public relations can get the message out through free media sources such as social media, newspapers, magazine feature articles, or broadcast news sources.
- *The ability to present believable technical or scientific evidence through a credible news source.* Because of public relations' association with the press, both print and broadcast news departments choose to report on studies presented through public relations sources because the information can be, and most often is, backed up by research.

Is There Anything Wrong with Public Relations?

The more notable deterrents associated with public relations include:

- *Short shelf life of news items.* Nothing presented in newspapers or through broadcast channels lasts longer than twenty-four hours.
- *Difficult to modify behavior.* To build loyalty and equity, the target needs to be repeatedly reminded about the product and its benefits. Public relations cannot get this done without the help of other media sources.
- *Inability to measure results.* Determining if the objectives were successful requires a way to measure results, such as how many units were sold or the number of people who attended an event or saw a news conference. Since public relations rarely asks the target to do something like purchase a product or service and is often paired with other mass media or promotional vehicles that do, there is no immediate way to tell if the message reached the intended audience.

Putting Public Relations to Work

Before implementing the public relations portion of an IMC campaign, several decisions must be made, such as:

- What tools need to be used: news releases, news conferences, social media announcements, brochures, and so on?

- What public relations tactics and/or approaches will be used to execute the key consumer benefit and strategy determined in the creative brief?
- What additional media will be used to deliver the message, and when will the message be delivered?

Public relations and advertising are two opposing forces both trying to get the right message out to the right people. Each uses slightly different techniques to achieve the same results; the only major difference is that one is free and the other is not.

Public Relations and Advertising

The tension between advertising and public relations has always been about timing. The question of who should lead and who should follow should be based on the objectives outlined in the creative brief. If the objective is to build brand awareness or maintain a brand's image, then advertising is the best communications approach and should lead the way via print or broadcast. Anytime a product or service has news value, is reinventing its image, is launching a new product, or makes claims that need to be substantiated to give them credibility, public relations should lead with news articles, news conferences, social media announcements, or even exclusive press events.

Why should public relations and advertising be part of the promotional mix? Advertising focuses on the consumers in the form of a monologue, or one-way communication. Public relations turns the communication into a dialogue, or two-way communication.

- Advertising and marketing concentrate on one product for one consumer group. Public relations concentrates on building relationships with many groups to accomplish varied objectives on many levels.
- Public relations and advertising make an excellent team for creating brand awareness, building brand equity, and maintaining brand loyalty.

The Strategy behind Public Relations

The strategy behind using public relations has everything to do with the key consumer benefit, the right target audience to be reached, the message, and the best promotional mix to accomplish the stated objectives.

When you talk about strategy, the first thing that needs to be determined is who will be at the planning table. What role will advertising, public relations, social media, the Internet, sales promotion, or direct marketing play? Or will some other, less-traditional form of promotion be used to reach the target? The answers will depend on what the IMC campaign needs to accomplish and the best way to reach the target.

Planning looks at the target, the objectives that need to be met, the strategy that will be employed to accomplish the objectives, timing, and the assembly of media vehicles that can be used to strategically accomplish the objectives.

IMC planning is not just about message development but also the development of a holistic message for change throughout an organization. Change must take place everywhere for an IMC campaign to be successful. Strategically, IMC must execute an internal plan that reflects the external message. This **inside–out** examination of the varied target groups helps coordinate communication between these very specialized groups. Whether the promotional message is talking to the consumer, the media, retailers, or other quantifiable targets, each audience must receive the message behind the key consumer benefit in its own language and with its specific benefit clearly defined. The ability to define each group and its needs is exclusive to public relations and invaluable when defining the best member of the promotional mix to meet those needs.

Objectives need to be examined to determine the best promotional vehicle to strategically accomplish the stated objectives. Public relations is in a perfect position to manage word of mouth, maintain customer service, manage social media and brand issues, and oversee any unplanned events such as media inquiries or recalls, all of which affect image and strategy.

An effective IMC message can be delivered through press relations, sponsored events, internal and external communication, and reaction to both internal and external feedback to make the message stronger. Its credibility and virtually no-cost way of doing business makes public relations a critical mouthpiece to get and keep the word out about a product, service, or corporation through varied media vehicles.

Strategically, any approach, appeal, or tone can be adapted to public relations' tone of voice. Choices made will ultimately depend on the makeup of the campaign's promotional and media mix. For public relations to hold its own at the planning table, its practitioners will have to see the product or service through the eyes of the marketer and understand that sales and customer relations are intertwined. In order to accomplish the stated objectives, public relations needs to be able to speak the language of marketers, initiate the strategy, and understand the diversity of the promotional mix. This will require adopting an attitude of planned action based on research as opposed to reaction to events and information from corporate executives.

Today, public relations practitioners need to be more than media liaisons, relationship managers, and designated watchdogs for a brand or service's image; they need to be strategic market planners.

On the downside, public relations does not offer the power of the other communication approaches to effectively remind the target about the message. Because of this, it is difficult to change consumer attitudes using public relations alone. Being able to evaluate the effectiveness of each communication effort is a priority for any IMC campaign. The implementation of an IMC campaign requires each member of the promotional mix team to understand what marketers need and want to accomplish and be able to define how public relations can strategically be used to accomplish objectives and determine the estimated **return on investment (ROI)**.

When public relations is attached to marketing and sales, in order to receive its share of the marketing budget, it must be able to show measurable and quantifiable results associated with its efforts. ROI very simply refers to the amount of profit left after advertising and other costs have been deducted. Many believe public relations, as a member of the marketing team, cannot show a measurable ROI unless it is the sole member of the marketing team, as might be found in business-to-business marketing. Others believe it is measurable or quantifiable based only on the amount of media placement predicted during planning as opposed to the actual placement earned. The question that must be answered is: Do certain media outlets carry more weight than others? The answer is yes. Just like the other parts of the promotional mix, the final media mix should be determined based on whether the target is exposed to the media vehicle in order to see the article, hear the interview, or interact with a brand representative.

How do public relations representatives communicate with the media and/or their publics? Let's look at some of the techniques involved. Remember, public relations will also be working from the creative brief, so the message will be coordinated with all other IMC messages.

The Many Documents That Make Up Public Relations

There are many ways public relations talks to its publics and/or stakeholders. Most creative executed by public relations consists of large, copy-heavy pieces such as annual reports, educational materials, infomercials, press conference copy, or public service announcements. The choice of vehicle does not depend on length but rather on who is being spoken to, the promotional mix employed, the message to be communicated, and the desired outcome. Following are some of the more commonly used message vehicles:

- News releases
- Fact sheets
- Media advisories
- Pitch letters
- Press kits
- Newsletters
- Brochures

News Releases

A news release contains the latest news and information about the product or service in the form of a finished news article. It is sent unsolicited to an editor and, if published, will be a form of nonpaid advertising.

News releases need to be both well written and newsworthy enough for editors from print or broadcast media to consider them for publication or broadcast. Writing should be clear, concise, and factual. Leave the creative writing to the advertising creative team; news releases are meant to inform, not entertain.

The ultimate goal of all news releases is to be noticed. An editor may receive hundreds of releases on any given day. Finally, assuming the information is interesting and valuable to readers, listeners, or viewers, it must also appear in the proper format.

The Look of a News Release

A typical news release should follow a very specific format. Template 8.1 shows an approximation of this format.

TEMPLATE 8.1

News Release

Your Name
Your Client's Company Name
Client's Address
Your Phone Number (Day)
Your Phone Number (Evening)
Your E-mail Address

FOR IMMEDIATE RELEASE

Knoxville, TN. June 24—Three-time mountain biking world champion Tinker Juerez will be signing cartons of Kroger yogurt on Friday, June 28, 2014, at the Kingston Pike Kroger.

Tinker Juerez, the new spokesperson for Kroger yogurt, will be arriving at the Kingston Pike Kroger at approximately 10:00 a.m. and will be signing autographs and discussing the importance of a well-balanced diet until 1:00 p.m. Following the autograph session, Tinker will perform an assortment of mountain bike maneuvers.

Tinker will be making appearances around the country to promote Kroger yogurt's "Fit for Life" campaign. "I feel Kroger yogurt should be an essential part of every person's diet. Not only is Kroger yogurt healthy, it's delicious," Juerez said. "With the variety of flavors Kroger yogurt is offering, there is a flavor for everyone. If you're not eating Kroger yogurt, you're missing out."

"We feel Tinker Juerez is the perfect spokesperson for the job," stated Barber Williamson, executive vice president of sales. "The purpose of this campaign is to show the public all the health benefits Kroger yogurt offers. Choosing a well-conditioned athlete fits the image of Kroger yogurt. We feel this new campaign will draw much attention to our product."

-more-

The goal is to have Kroger yogurt stand out from the rest of the yogurts on the market.

Kroger will be releasing its new yogurt design at the beginning of next month. This design will be an entirely new look for the company, one that top executives at Kroger feel will give the company the edge it needs in the yogurt market.

Kroger yogurt will also begin handing out many new promotional items. These items will include free cartons of Kroger yogurt, water bottles, and coupons.

Kroger wants to stress not only how important it is to eat its yogurt but also the importance of a well-balanced diet. If all goes well this summer, Kroger yogurt will truly stand alone in the high-profile yogurt industry.

-###-

It should be typed, double spaced, on an 8½ × 11 sheet of paper, with one-inch margins on all four sides.

The preparer's information should appear in the upper left corner:

- The preparer's name or contact name
- The corporation or organization's name
- The corporation or organization's address
- The preparer's daytime phone number
- The preparer's evening phone or cell phone number
- The preparer's fax (optional) or e-mail address

Beneath the preparer's information and to the far right, type in all caps and underline FOR IMMEDIATE RELEASE. If this is an advance release, state the time and date to be released; for example, FOR RELEASE ON SEPT. 26 EST AT 8:00 AM. Advance releases are known as **embargoes**. The media is under no obligation to honor the requested release date of embargoed material, but the release date is generally observed as a courtesy.

Open the first paragraph with the city and state from which the release or news originated or where the event will be taking place. Next to that, add the month and day of the release or event. The opening paragraph will deal with the key consumer benefit; the body of the release should ideally use at least two quotes from a reliable, relevant source.

Most news releases should not be longer than one page; if you do have more to say, you can break an article into two pages by adding the word "-more-" centered at the bottom of the first page. This signals that there is more than one page and is useful should a page be misplaced.

On the second page in the upper right, place the page number and then an identifier or **slug**. This can be the preparer's last name or the name of the product or service. The copy should continue on the next line. When finished, add the symbol "-###-" to the bottom of the last page, centered, to signify that no pages follow.

Be sure to edit the release before sending it out. Were all names spelled correctly? How is the grammar? Were facts double-checked? Now is the time to proof the release; don't wait for any errors to become public.

What Should Be Said

Here are a few crucial guidelines for writing a news release:

1. *Headline.* Announce the key consumer benefit. It is just as important in a news or magazine article as it is on any creative piece. This is also a great way to tie any communication efforts to come to existing efforts.
2. *Opening.* The opening paragraph should list the most important facts. MPR, as used in an IMC campaign, focuses attention on the key consumer benefit and answers the questions who, what, when, where, why, and how. Do not make the opening paragraph longer than three to five lines.
3. *Facts.* The second paragraph should back up any important facts, perhaps with a quotation or a scientific study.

4. *Get to the point.* Don't waste words. Give the facts in a concise and relevant way.
5. *Avoid hype.* Hype does not lend itself well to a news format. Leave the superlatives to the advertising creative team.
6. *Avoid jargon.* If the release is for the general public, use language it can understand. News is no different from advertising copy when it comes to boredom or confusion; if the text is boring or confusing, the target stops reading or listening.
7. *Action.* The final paragraph should close with what the target should do or know about: any locations, informational websites, dates, or times.

As with any copy, it is a good idea to have the client read over and sign off on the release before it is sent to the press.

Because the competition to be noticed is so fierce, be sure to address any release to the appropriate editor. We all like to be called by name rather than "Sir" or "To Whom It May Concern." This small courtesy can help build rapport with the arrival of the e-mail or fax.

A news release doesn't just happen. Extensive research has defined the target and determined the key consumer benefit to push and the objectives to be accomplished. This type of valuable information helps a release capture the target's attention and create interest.

Fact Sheets

A fact sheet is basically an outline of the news release. It highlights the strategic information gained from addressing the six basic questions—who, what, when, where, why, and how—in essence, creating a cheat sheet for the media.

Media Advisories

A media advisory, or media alert, is sent to the media to entice coverage. It briefly lists the specifics about an event as well as information about interviews, news conferences, or photo opportunities.

Pitch Letters

The purpose of a pitch letter is to entice media coverage. The difference between a pitch letter and a news release is that pitch letters are just that—letters. A pitch letter is addressed to a specific editor, and for the first time, should be creatively written; its role is to get attention. This is a good time to get some feedback from the advertising creative team to make sure the letter can be written in the same tone of voice that is used in other communication pieces in the IMC campaign.

Press Kits

Press kits are most often used to promote special events or announce new product launches. The purpose of a press kit is to inform and educate the media as well as entice a little media coverage.

The press kit consists of a large, pocketed folder, usually attractively designed. Again, the appearance should match that of other advertising and promotional pieces that make up the IMC campaign. Inside the folder is a news release, a fact sheet, backgrounders or background articles, black-and-white publicity photographs, and a promotional item or two. Online kits might also include audio and video files of radio or television interviews, speeches, or any other media-covered event. Press kits tell the story of the event.

Newsletters

Newsletters are an informal way to reach the target. Once sent only through the mail, most newsletters today arrive via e-mail. Their job is to educate, entertain, and inform both internal and external audiences about a product, service, or corporation.

The standard newsletter is four to six pages in length and is printed on 11 × 17-inch sheets, folded and stapled to 8½ × 11. Although they are often informal in style and appearance, newsletters should continue the tone and appearance of the IMC campaigns with which they are associated. By adjusting type size, placing important points in boxes, and double-dosing the use of white space, a newsletter can be attractively designed and easy to read. If the campaign uses unique graphics or a spokesperson or character representative in the campaign, include them along with logos or slogans or taglines and representative corporate or product typefaces on the newsletter. Informal does not mean unattractive or poorly written. The image developed for the other advertising and promotional pieces must carry through in the newsletter.

BOX 8.2. Newsletter Topics of the Day

No matter who the newsletter is intended to reach, the goal is to provide information of interest to their job, their membership, or their association with the organization and any internal or external factors that could affect them or the business or organization. Use this forum to preview upcoming events and new product launches, solicit donations, or announce new hires, promotions, and retirements.

Stories of a more complicated or serious nature should not be tackled here. However, information should be supplied to tell the reader where to go, write, or call for more information.

A newsletter should be an eclectic grab bag of surprises and human-interest quips varied enough to reach a diverse audience. Copy should feature short sentences and multiple paragraphs to enhance white space. Do not waste words; a newsletter is not something the reader will linger over.

Brochures

Brochures are informational documents the public wants to read and will spend time reading. They are frequently technical in nature, explaining detailed procedures, so the writing style must get to the point, avoiding any hype or jargon and aiming instead for clarity.

As a part of the IMC campaign, brochures should maintain the corporate or product image delivered in the advertising and other promotional efforts. Color and good-quality images make a brochure an attractive communication device. (See figure 8.1 for two examples of brochures.)

Figure 8.1. Two very different public service brochure examples. Robyn Blakeman.

Even the simplest brochures are fairly expensive to produce. Appearance can range anywhere from a simple fold to multiple folds; a brochure may also include inserts or have holes or shapes, known as **die cuts**, cut out of them.

As style pieces in an IMC campaign, brochures are attractive and informative. Best of all, the target is interested in and will spend time reading the brochure. Here are some simple writing and design tips to keep in mind:

- Photographs, graphics, diagrams, and charts are essential for a brochure to tell its story.
- Multiple subheads will help move the reader from important point to important point.
- Short sentences and multiple paragraphs make reading easier.
- Type size should be a little larger here, ten to twelve points, to tell the story or to explain technical information. Charts and graphs can go as small as eight points; anything smaller affects readability and legibility.
- Vary the weight of the text to visually break up the page.
- Brochures consist of multiple folded panels. The size of these panels varies, but they are most often 3½ to 3¾ inches wide by 8 inches tall. A standard brochure has six total panels, front and back, when opened flat.
- Headlines can be used on the outside or inside of the brochure. Inside headlines can be confined to a folded panel or cross over multiple panels.
- The front cover should cover the key consumer benefit, either visually or verbally. It is not as important to hit the target over the head with the key consumer benefit in a brochure, since the reader elects to read the piece.

- Copy inside the brochure can elaborate on the key consumer benefit.
- The back cover should feature the logo, slogan or tagline, and contact information. Additional items might include a map or decision- or action-oriented information such as seating charts or price lists.

More elaborate brochures may have pockets to hold additional information such as business cards or free passes. Elaborate or diverse folds are also an option, as are large foldout brochures measuring 11 × 17 inches flat, 8½ × 11 inches folded, that may show a detailed map or a floor plan. If the budget exists, brochures are a creative open door.

Publicity

Publicity is the strategic use of public relations. It is through publicity that a product is made newsworthy to the media. Articles placed in the newspaper, if possible in the section most likely to be read by the target, provide the target with information about the product. Other media options might include social media, web pages, magazine feature stories, radio or television talk shows, and even advertising during programming.

In an article appearing in the *Public Relations Journal*, Joan Aho Ryan and George H. Lemmond sum up the need for product publicity this way: "Cynical consumers, zapping commercials and ignoring print ads, are more receptive to the editorial message. The third-party endorsement allows advertisers to sell a new product while enveloping the commercial message in a creative environment." That is the essence of marketing public relations.

The first stage of the campaign was the public relations news release and internal and external management of information and image; the next step determines how the other possible members of the promotional mix will be used, if at all. These will be discussed in the chapters that follow.

Q DISCUSSION QUESTIONS

1. What is public relations, and how is it used in an IMC campaign?
2. How is marketing public relations different from traditional public relations?
3. What are the external vehicles employed by public relations?
4. What are the internal vehicles employed by public relations?
5. What strengths does public relations have when used as a marketing tool?
6. How does public relations employ a two-way dialogue with consumers? Why is this so important?
7. How is public relations best used in an IMC campaign?
8. Define and explain the difference between these terms: publics, shareholders, and target audiences.

9. How does public relations help IMC be consumer focused?

10. What are some of the pros and cons associated with using public relations in an IMC campaign?

11. What is the strategy behind using public relations in an IMC campaign?

12. What are the documents that can be and often are used in an IMC campaign?

13. Before implementing the public relations portion of an IMC campaign, several decisions must be made. What are they, and what is their importance?

14. When is it best to use public relations versus advertising? Why should public relations be included in the promotional mix?

15. What is the strategy behind using public relations in an IMC campaign?

16. What is the difference between public relations and publicity?

CHAPTER

9

Newspaper Advertising

The Strategic Use of Newspaper in IMC

Advertising is a paid form of nonpersonal mass media in which the sponsor of the advertised message is clearly identified. Advertising uses persuasion to sell, inform, educate, remind, and/or entertain the target about a product or service.

Considered a mass medium because it can reach large numbers of consumers, advertising is most often considered a media option for new product launches or more homogenized and inexpensive products such as ketchup, toilet tissue, and cleaning products, to name a few. Mass-advertised products appeal to large numbers of indistinct consumers and can be purchased across the United States.

Probably the best-known member of the promotional mix, the term "advertising" is often used to describe all forms of marketing-based communication. Although that is not technically incorrect, advertising refers to the media mix that makes up mass-media advertising, including print (newspaper and magazine) and broadcast (radio and television). Each of these mass-media vehicles will be examined separately over the next several chapters. Let's begin the discussion with a look at newspaper advertising. See case study 7 for an integrated marketing communication newspaper case study.

What Is Newspaper Advertising?

Newspaper advertising, also known as **retail advertising,** must accomplish two things. The first is to sell a product or service; the second is to entice the reader into a response. This is

CASE STUDY 7

IMC Newspaper: Nissan Altima

Overview

- International automaker Nissan launched a massive interactive print campaign across twelve Canadian newspapers.
- Scanning a front-page cover-wrap ad allowed readers to view exclusive videos highlighting the innovative features of the 2013 Altima.
- The award-winning campaign drove 6,500 page views with a 42 percent click-through rate, including a 65 percent rise in test drive requests in one day.

The Client

Nissan, founded in 1933 and headquartered in Japan, is one of the world's largest international automakers. The company has a long tradition of innovation within its marketing and advertising departments, and its interactive print campaign with Layar (an app that creates an interactive augmented reality experience) was no exception.

Situation

To promote the innovative technologies available in the 2013 Nissan Altima in the Canadian market, the automaker turned to Postmedia, Canada's largest newspaper publisher, to help create an ad campaign as innovative as the car. For Postmedia Project Manager Maggie Greyson, Layar was the perfect match to provide an innovative experience: "Layar was far above and beyond what the competition was offering. It turned out to be the big, shiny, innovative tool that Nissan was attracted to."

Solution

Together with Layar, Postmedia, creative agency TBWA, and buying agency OMD, Nissan launched a huge interactive print advertising campaign across a dozen Canadian newspapers as part of a larger campaign showcasing its innovation. Several sizes and styles of ads were created, but the centerpiece was a full-spread ad that was wrapped over the front pages of each newspaper.

The ad invited readers to download Layar and scan the car to view exclusive videos about its innovative features. Readers could request a test drive of the 2013 Altima and share their experience across social media.

Results: Test Drives +65 Percent

The campaign was a huge success for Nissan; usage and conversions from the interactive print ads far surpassed company expectations.

More than eight million readers were exposed to the campaign in one day, which led to more than 6,500 page views at an impressive 42 percent click-through rate. But perhaps the most astonishing result of this campaign was that requests for test drives increased by 65 percent as a direct result of the interactive print advertisements.

Based on the results, the campaign was entered in the Canadian Media Innovation Awards and came away a big winner and crowd favorite. Along with three other victories, Nissan's campaign was awarded the top prize of Best in Show.

Source: "Layar Case Study: Nissan," Layar.com, https://www.layar.com/features/inspiration/case-studies/.

a tough job. The reader must wade through an enormous amount of written information before noticing a client's ad amid the mass of indistinguishable gray that characteristically makes up an average newspaper page.

The colorful ads appearing in digital subscriptions must fight just as hard to be noticed as their print counterparts. But they have one advantage print ads do not have: They are interactive. Although smaller in stature, these engaging little ads can transport interested viewers to a web page for more information, locations, or even a coupon. Once the link is clicked on, advertising no longer competes to be noticed amid the array of varied color blocks; it now singularly dominates the viewer's screen and attention.

Newspaper advertising must engage the reader with new and improved claims and juicy got-to-have sales by using bold headlines. Action-oriented claims such as "Buy Now," "50% Off," or "While Quantities Last" are commonly used attention getters in retail advertising.

Advertising appearing in newspaper falls into two distinct categories: local (including classified and display) and national.

Local Advertising
The term "local advertising" has two meanings. The first is that the advertising is of a local nature and tells readers where in their area they can find the product; the second is that the advertising was initiated locally.

Classified Advertising
Local newspapers do classified advertising, dealing with consumers buying and selling, in-house. Categories include garage sales, auctions, job opportunities, and real-estate opportunities. Classified advertising has steadily declined over the years as the bulk of personal buying and selling has moved online.

Display Ads
Display ads can be either local or national. The term "display" refers to the complete list of components appearing within an ad, such as headlines, visuals, body copy, and logos.

National or Brand-Name Advertising
National advertising features brand-name products that can be found at local establishments or acquired through toll-free phone numbers or on the Internet. Carried in newspapers throughout the country, national advertising requires few modifications from city to city outside of personalizing phone numbers and/or addresses.

The Diversity of the Newspaper Voice

Newspaper advertising reaches a lot of people, is effective, offers flexible deadlines, and is relatively inexpensive. Since both digital and print versions of ads normally arrive at the newspaper complete, deadlines of twenty-four hours or less can still make the next day's edition.

Newspapers are read not only for news value but also for the news of advertising; it's where people look for information about sales. It should inspire the consumer to want and/or need the product or service being advertised right now. To do this, price and product description play a prominent role. Retail advertising's primary job is to make a sale. One way to accomplish this is by instilling a sense of urgency through such devices as limited-time offers, limited quantities, two-for-one offers, special sale hours, preferred customer sales, and coupons.

Sales

Newspapers are the place consumers go for sales. Everybody loves a sale. They are abundant in retail, and they promote predictable themes. The key is to decide how a client's sale will be unique and then grab the reader—preferably by the throat. To do this, the creative team must first do a little brainstorming. What is unique, fun, or unusual about the sale that can have some type of added interactive component? How will the strategy promote the key consumer benefit? Headlines, subheads, visuals, and typeface choices all need to reflect the IMC concept or strategy.

Sales should not seem routine. The personality of the sale should reflect that of the target, key consumer benefit, strategy, and product or store. Sales create traffic within a store, and traffic promotes additional purchases. Most sales events are associated with holidays, special events, and overstocks, but why limit yourself? Take an approach the competition would never think of and be creative with a sale. Why not have a sale called "It's Tuesday—Let's Shop till We Drop Together"?

Coupons

Coupons are the IMC bridge between newspaper advertising and sales promotion. Coupons offer the target an incentive to buy.

All consumers like to get a break, and coupons are a way to offer something in return for their patronage or loyalty or as an introduction to the product or service. A coupon is an effective temporary sales device. It should be easy to remove from the ad or upload to a mobile device, should clearly point out the offer, and should be easy to redeem. Incentives often include two-for-one offers or percentage- or cents-off deals.

One of the more attractively designed coupons is known as a **freestanding insert** (FSI). FSIs are one-page, full-color coupon ads that are nationally produced and inserted into weekend newspapers.

BOX 9.1. How Much Does It Cost?

Every consumer wants to know how much something costs before making a final buying decision. This not only determines value but also facilitates brand comparison. However, ads for known high-dollar products often eliminate price and entice the reader through copy promoting benefits, image, and a special sale or financing to make purchasing easier.

As a rule, creative teams should not shy away from displaying price. Make it big, make it bold, and give it class. Let it stand alone or tie it to a copy point. It doesn't matter where it appears, as long as it's there.

BOX 9.2. Where Should the Coupons Go?

Deciding where coupons should go is another one of those great questions. Although there's no rule, it's important to consider how easily the coupon can be removed. Coupons can appear aligned at the top of an ad, vertically down either side, or, most often, at the bottom of the ad.

How Does Newspaper Advertising Help IMC Be Consumer Focused?

One thing newspaper *isn't* is consumer focused. It does not build a relationship with the target, and it isn't interactive in any significant way. So why use it at all in an IMC campaign?

The answer lies in newspaper's relationship with the other members of the promotional mix and the advertising media mix. Newspaper is a great follow-up to news releases, press conferences, or interviews, helping raise awareness and encourage purchase of an existing product or launch a new product. Other options supporting public relations might include the promotion of a corporate cause by asking the target to bring in a canned good or donate clothing to receive free movie passes or a free entree.

By including a coupon, newspaper can work with sales promotion, direct marketing, or alternative media by promoting "try me" offers. T-shirts, cups, toy characters, and even watches promoting a current movie might be given out in local fast-food restaurants when the consumer gives the correct password or repeats a slogan printed in the newspaper.

When a website address is featured, newspaper advertising can refer the target to the Internet to request additional information, or it can feature a toll-free number to call to speak to a customer service representative and/or place an order.

Including a QR code is another way newspaper can get readers to interact with an ad, holding their attention longer, as well as deliver more detailed information about the product or service to interested readers and viewers. To strengthen engagement and purchase, codes found in ads might offer values available nowhere else, or perhaps introduce the first clue to a value-added scavenger hunt. An additional inducement might include the opportunity for winners to offer influencer insights into future brand upgrades or new product launches.

Including information on social media options gives the target additional chances to discuss his experiences with other users, get additional coupons, enter a contest or sweepstakes, or sign up to receive a free product sample.

Some newspapers are even engaging consumers during purchase. The *Sacramento Bee*, for example, is talking to consumers at the newsstand with a fifteen-second ad every time a newspaper is purchased. When it's not dispensing papers, pedestrians can also view messages via the scrolling lighted display featured on the outside of the newsstand. Not limited to just audio or newspapers, these New Age newsstands can show video and dispense samples. Highly customizable, these audio and/or video messages can feature advertising, promotions, or breaking news.

Newspapers are fighting to stay relevant as younger generations turn to the Internet and twenty-four-hour news channels for news of the day. Finding ways to engage readers and offering something they cannot find anywhere else are crucial to sustainability.

Incentives and Deterrents of Newspaper Advertising

To decide whether newspaper is right for an IMC campaign, let's look at some of the incentives and deterrents associated with it.

What Makes Newspaper Advertising So Great?

The more notable incentives associated with newspaper advertising include:

- *Getting it there*. Newspapers have very short deadlines. This allows for last-minute ads or a second chance to make changes to an existing ad, up until twenty-four hours prior to printing.
- *Sized to fit*. Because of the low cost of newspaper advertising, ads can be sized up or down to accommodate both budget and/or information needs.
- *Believability*. Advertising takes on more credibility because it appears alongside editorial material. The difference here from public relations is that public relations *is* the editorial material.
- *Loyal readers*. Consumers buy a newspaper because they want to read the news of the day and see the sales of the week.
- *Cost*. The uncoated paper stock, or newsprint, newspaper is printed on is inexpensive. It can be bought in large quantities, used, and then thrown out. Because of this, newspaper space can be purchased fairly inexpensively. It can reach a mass audience on a daily basis, making it a very attractive medium.
- *Geographically concentrated*. Newspaper ads are seen only by those in the same geographic location as the product or service, minimizing media waste.
- *Frequency*. The number of times an ad can be viewed is affected by how often the newspaper is printed. A newspaper can be published weekly in smaller markets or daily in larger ones. An ad appearing in a daily for one week is six times more likely to be seen than one appearing just one time in a weekly.

- *Coupons.* The use of coupons in newspaper advertising creates an interactive opportunity by giving the target more than information. Coupons must be torn from the ad and carried to the product location to be redeemed.

Is There Anything Wrong with Newspaper Advertising?

The more notable deterrents associated with newspaper advertising include:

- *Mass media.* It is difficult to ensure that an ad will reach the intended target. Newspaper advertising is the least targetable of all the media vehicles we will look at.
- *Creative disadvantage.* The worst problem is the paper stock. The uncoated, inexpensive newsprint causes the ink to bleed, affecting type quality and causing poor photo reproduction. The limited amount of color use can also affect both visual and verbal stimulation.
- *Clutter.* The gray page of a newspaper has a lot going on. An ad could be missed if it is not designed to stand up and stand out.
- *Life span.* Newspapers and the advertising within them are old news within twenty-four hours.
- *Declining readership.* Readership by younger adults is steadily declining, as they rely on news television such as CNN or Fox News for up-to-date information.
- *Limited viewing.* Special sections, such as the sports or financial pages and the comics, allow readers to bypass the rest of the newspaper.
- *Passive medium.* Newspaper advertising does little to involve the reader in the message.
- *Price based.* Newspaper advertising announces sales. Unfortunately, there is nothing classy or image-oriented about pushing price.

The Strategy behind Newspaper Advertising

Understanding the capabilities and limitations of print advertising as opposed to other media options, such as broadcast, the Internet, or social media, is crucial for the success of an IMC strategy. Not all ideas can transfer between media. Knowing this in advance will save the identity of the campaign and ensure the message will reach the target. Strategically, the key consumer benefit must be able to be delivered both visually and verbally in the combined media outlets most used by the target.

Mass-media advertising alone does not look to build a relationship with individual consumers or create dialogue but instead works to inform and build awareness. Newspaper advertising cannot guarantee the target will see the message. However, by placing the ad in a newspaper section of particular interest to the target, it is possible to increase the odds the target will be exposed to the message.

Like all other components of the media mix, advertising selection depends on the target and the overall objectives. If the target is eighteen- to twenty-five-year-olds, newspaper advertising would be a poor choice, unless interactive properties are added, since few people in this age group read the paper on a regular basis, and few, if any, read the paper from front to back.

Objectives that might benefit from newspaper advertising include creating brand aware-ness, maintaining or retaining brand loyalty, creating sales or generating interest, announcing any product changes or additions, and increasing store traffic. Key consumer benefits that lend themselves to the use of newspaper advertising include a USP giving the product or service a competitive advantage over the competition, a unique price, a strong key consumer benefit, or incentive-based coupons.

Don't lose the strategy laid out in the creative brief. Newspaper advertising features the same key consumer benefit, layout style, approach, tone of voice, and images as other pieces within the IMC campaign.

Strategically, newspaper is better suited to a product-based approach such as generic or product feature. Newspaper's relatively poor reproduction capabilities make a consum-er-based approach or use of an emotional appeal difficult to adequately portray both visually and verbally. Rational appeals such as straight fact, testimonial, or news can best hammer home a product's features and benefits.

Before making any final strategic decisions, it is important to look at the incentives and deterrents associated with the product or service and the media mix to be employed, as well as the overall objectives to be accomplished.

The Look of Newspaper Advertising

It is up to the client to decide whether to use an advertising agency or the corporation's own in-house art department to fulfill its communication needs. **In-house** design is most often used for small jobs that need to be done right away or that don't happen on a regular basis. Most clients working with IMC have large advertising budgets and choose to employ an advertising agency's expertise to develop and retain a consistent visual/verbal message.

The overall look of newspaper advertising often reveals whether it was produced in-house or done by an outside advertising agency. Most large in-house advertising depart-ments are staffed with good creative teams, but ads originating from small in-house art departments (usually composed of one or two people) often lack the necessary components to build and maintain a brand image and create memorable advertising that is cohesive with other advertising materials. Most often, ads lack a compatible key consumer benefit headline and a subhead that further educates and entices the target to read on. Prices are often too small to be a viable selling point. Price should always be a benefit in newspaper advertising. It doesn't matter if the price does not reflect the key consumer benefit; it is an important consumer benefit. Finally, the layout is often chaotic. The lack of eye flow and white space causes a junky, cheap look. Agency ads are clean and have a distinct movement from top to bottom and left to right. Everything is seen and read in the exact order the designer intended.

A good ad exploits the page, using one dominant image (visual or verbal) on the page to create a solid, black-looking area that stands out from the gray clutter of the page. Strong contrasts in newspaper attract attention. Line art drawings are very effective because of the strong black-and-white contrasts. Alternatively, lots of white space also can make an ad stand out and can create an aura of elegance.

A successful newspaper strategy requires the creative team to put itself in the consumer's place. What catches your eye? What do you need to know? How do you use it? Where can you find it? Why can't you live without it? The answers can be found through meticulous message construction and the use of a few simple layout techniques.

Advertising is basically a relationship between words and imagery. Design should seek to create a match between what is said and what is shown. The key elements of print are divided between copy and art. As previously discussed, the copy or verbal elements include headlines, subheads, body copy, and slogans/taglines. Art or visual elements include illustrations, photography, charts/graphs, or graphic design as well as logos, type style, and the overall layout.

Advertising is also about interaction and engaging encounters with a brand. Including interactive components in newspaper is an additional way to immerse the target not only in the medium but also in the brand experience. For example, consider adding an augmented reality (AR) component where readers can point their phones at a code to unlock additional content. Adding virtual reality (VR) components to an ad is another interactive way to enhance reader experience and brand interaction. Ads that include viewable glasses could immediately unlock a broad range of possible brand interactions. The *New York Times* included Google cardboard VR viewers in its papers when it introduced NYTVR. Gannett, owner of *USA Today*, has included VR in dozens of editorial pieces over the past several years. Honda, in its first foray into **branded content**, focused on allowing viewers to experience what it would be like to drive the fast Honda-powered Dallara Indy car. *USA Today* offers VR content through its app, as well as through its VR Stories app and on YouTube via the VRtually There channel.

Immersion experiences in any medium will always attract more attention than simple words and pictures. **Experiential marketing** like AR and VR, although still in its infancy for brands, is a great way to create a memorable experience between the target and a brand.

Designing for newspaper isn't difficult but does take strategy, and a good design plan needs specific tactics. It is important that each ad have a strong concept developed from the strategy and a headline that informs the target about the key consumer benefit. The ad must feature the product and promote its price. Each layout should develop or maintain a visual/verbal identity that reflects both the brand and the target and is consistent with the other visual/verbal messages in the IMC campaign. Be sure to create strong black-and-white contrasts, feature one dominant element, promote price or availability, and use white space effectively. Body copy should develop the key consumer benefit and include a call to action. Type should be easy to read and be brand-image specific. The ad should flow easily from element to element, closing with the logo, slogan or tagline, and detail copy to make shopping easier (figure 9.1). The simple, inexpensive, yet informative nature of newspaper advertising makes it one of the leading advertising vehicles.

Clutter

Retail ads have a lot to say and show in a small space. Clutter and chaos are not the designer's ultimate goal. A good newspaper ad organizes elements to control the structure of the ad. To create elegance and order and to stress quality over price, white space should be used

Figure 9.1. This example of newspaper advertising uses bold colors and creatively written copy to drive home the key consumer benefit. Image courtesy of Kaylyn Harris, Jordan Vandergriff, Alex Tombul, Lauren Huguenard, Liz Williams, Maggie Matson, Mara Robinette, and Timmy Strini, University of Tennessee.

liberally. Stay away from bold or bulky typefaces. Consider using serif typefaces, which are more sophisticated. For a more disciplined look, consider lightweight sans serif typefaces.

Size Specifications

Newspaper space is measured from side to side in column inches, or the width of a column of typeset copy plus the gutter. Column width is measured in $2\frac{1}{16}$-inch increments from $2\frac{1}{16}$ inches to 13 inches. The depth of an ad is measured in quarter-inch increments up to 21 inches. While the newspaper works within predetermined widths, the depth of an ad is determined by design and budget constraints. A full-page ad measures 13 column inches wide by 21 inches deep.

The Effect of Newsprint on Design

Newsprint is not an optimal printing surface. The coarse, uncoated, highly bleedable stock affects print quality and color reproduction. Photographs can look flat, and delicate illustrations and typefaces can literally disappear off the newsprint's surface during printing. Good design choices can help alleviate these problems. Make sure the type is not too dainty; keep it big and sturdy. Large type creates large, rectangular blocks of black on the page. Just the opposite happens when headlines and subheads are smaller; they create an excess of white space. Either option can produce positive results.

Body copy should be kept to a minimum. Highlight only what the target needs to do, and include enough about the product to seduce the reader into action. Remember, the goal is to get the target to act, to get up and visit the store, visit a web or social media site, or make a toll-free call and place an order. Newspaper advertising is not meant to educate with large blocks of copy; instead, it entices.

Co-op Advertising

Co-op or **cooperative advertising** means that two individual but compatible clients have paired up to share the cost of the advertising and encourage consumers to use their products together. It is not unusual, however, for there to be more than two members of the advertising media or promotional mix to participate in co-op opportunities. There are two types of co-op advertising: vertical and horizontal. **Vertical cooperatives** are where one sponsor pays more and plays a larger or more prominent role in the ad. **Horizontal cooperatives** have budgets that are equally distributed, giving each sponsor equal exposure.

These highly successful partnerships might team an airline with a hotel chain to promote air and hotel packages to a destination accessed by both. Other co-op ventures might include name-brand coffees served at national restaurant chains or computers that feature "Intel Inside."

Evaluation

Evaluating results is critical to determining the success of any IMC campaign. Success or failure is determined by whether the objectives were met or not. Advertising will rely on other media within the promotional mix to determine if brand awareness and increased sales were achieved, the two most important objectives associated with both print and broadcast advertising.

Newspaper advertising is believable, simple to design, inexpensive to place, and informative. Although it is not highly targetable, loyal readers seek out newspaper advertising for unbelievably low price points, to-die-for sales, limited-time offers, and coupons. Consider making it a part of the media mix for a campaign to localize a national product, create traffic within a store, or announce a new product launch.

Q DISCUSSION QUESTIONS

1. When is the best time to use newspaper?
2. What are the differences/similarities between mass media and niche or alternative media?
3. What is retail advertising and how is it used in an IMC campaign?
4. What other media could also be defined as retail advertising?
5. Why is displaying prices so important in newspaper advertising?
6. To make a sale, newspaper advertising must instill a sense of urgency. In what ways can this be accomplished?
7. How are coupons used to bridge the gap between newspaper and sales promotion? What are the strengths of their use?
8. How does newspaper advertising help IMC be more consumer focused?
9. There are numerous pros and cons to using newspaper advertising. Define and explain each.
10. Explain the strategy behind using newspaper in an IMC campaign.
11. What is cooperative advertising? How can it help move or highlight a brand?
12. How can newspaper be made more interactive and engaging?
13. Why is it important to evaluate the results of an IMC campaign?

CHAPTER

10

Magazine Advertising

The Strategic Use of Magazines in IMC

Magazine advertising concentrates on the creation of an image or mood through visual and verbal relationships. To entice the reader into the ad, magazine ads need to create a conceptual environment that the reader can both relate to and experience through the words and visuals. The show-and-tell nature of magazine advertising allows products to speak for themselves and demonstrate results. Although diverse in nature, many products appearing in magazines are often exclusive or unique and expensive to own. Other products are more mainstream, and their features may be indiscernible from the features of their competitors' products.

Products boasting higher price tags are less likely to be purchased on impulse. Before buying, discerning consumers will research a product's benefits and features, identify where the product fits into their own lives, and determine which problems it can solve. Integrated marketing communication magazine advertising should make information readily available to assist the consumer in making an informed buying decision.

The opposite of the discerning consumer is the trendy shopper who uses magazine advertising to look at all the competing products within a category. With little to differentiate one brand of sneakers from another, product features take a backseat to how consumers are affected by the advertised message and are convinced to purchase by how they will look, feel, or be perceived by wearing the sneakers.

When image and product features are prominent, price plays a more subordinate role in the design; the focus is placed instead on the benefits of owning or using a product or service. Because of this, visuals tend to play a more dominant role, as does lengthy, fact-based copy. Creating a strong visual/verbal relationship allows consumers to see the product being

CASE STUDY 8

IMC Magazine: Max Factor

Background

For more than one hundred years, Max Factor has been developing some of the most creative and iconic market-leading makeup products. Having built a legacy in glamour, Max Factor wanted to define what glamour is and how this has changed decade to decade.

Idea

Max Factor set out to illustrate one hundred years of glamour and define it for the future, using its ambassadors, Gwyneth Paltrow and Marilyn Monroe, as well as bloggers and other industry experts. A partnership with three of Time Inc.'s biggest women's brands, *Marie Claire*, *Look*, and *InStyle*, gave Max Factor an authoritative voice throughout the campaign.

Execution

A highly targeted, expertly crafted twelve-month multiplatform campaign allowed Max Factor to showcase its market-leading credentials in the beauty category and really stand apart from the competition.

The campaign included:

- A glossy twelve-page insert in *Marie Claire* curated by the magazine's specialist team.
- A pop-up glamour studio at Westfield (a New York City mall, located in the World Trade Center), where women could "ask the expert" and receive a makeover by a professional makeup artist.
- An immersive cinema experience with a special screening of *Breakfast at Tiffany's* hosted by Max Factor.
- Behind-the-scenes photo shoot with blogger "Hello October," aka Suzie Bonaldi.
- Interactive web and social activity, as well as targeted newsletter mailings.
- Interviews with top beauty professionals from *Marie Claire*, *Look*, and *InStyle*, exploring their definitions of glamour.

Results

The success of the campaign and delivery of its objectives is reflected in the results. The campaign wove a strong brand story, promoting brand perceptions of expertise, heritage, and inspiration.

Pre-, mid- and post-campaign analysis showed a strong positive shift in perceptions following the magazine media campaign. Max Factor was strongly perceived as an expert in cosmetics, having a rich heritage inspiring women to try new looks.

The campaign promoted brand perception. Max Factor was strongly perceived as a high-quality brand and a better value for the money than its closest competitors. The campaign also decreased the brand's image as old-fashioned and improved its credentials as an expert, glamorous, and stylish brand.

Overall, the campaign delivered differentiation for this long-established makeup brand, providing a unique perspective on beauty today in a dynamic and engaging way for its target audience.

Source: "Magazine Media Brands Deliver Differentiation for Max Factor, Women's Titles Give Authoritative Voice to Legacy Brand Max Factor," https://www.magnetic.media/case-studies/search?sortBy=&sortDirection=&page=35.

worn or used, learn what colors and sizes are available, and review safety information and warranties. See case study 8 for a look at Max Factor's use of magazine advertising.

The Diversity of the Magazine Advertising Voice

Unlike publicity and newspapers, a magazine's message has a long life span. Because of the highly individualized content of magazines, consumers tend to hold on to them longer, often trading with other enthusiasts or friends. This gives advertising a second chance to make a first impression and reach out to a larger portion of the target audience.

A magazine's editorial content plays an important role in the advertising that appears between its covers. For example, advertising found in a home decorating magazine will promote products such as barbecue grills, paint and wallpaper products, and furniture and carpeting as well as patio and pool items.

The Variety of Magazines

There are three basic categories of magazines: consumer, business or trade, and farming. Each of these three categories is broken down significantly further into special interests such as fashion, sports, cars, hobbies, advertising, marketing, public relations, and so forth.

Consumer Magazines

Consumer magazines are an eclectic group of publications comprising articles and advertising either loosely targeted to a broad audience or specifically targeted based on the target's special interests or hobbies. Let's take a closer look at each category by breaking it down further into two distinct types: general interest, including local and regional editions, and special-interest publications.

General Interest Magazines   General interest magazines such as *People*, *Time*, and *TV Guide* enjoy national coverage and large, indistinct target audiences. This type of magazine supports advertising with a more generalized appeal, such as cars, food and beverages, and cold and flu medications, that can be sold across geographic and demographic boundaries.

Metropolitan editions of magazines such as *Texas Monthly*, *Los Angeles Confidential*, and *Atlanta Magazine* are published for consumers in a particular city. Titles most often reference the city in which they are published, and editorial content reflects topics and advertising of local interest. This type of magazine allows local advertisers to reach those targeted consumers in the local community only, eliminating advertising waste.

International editions of national magazines such as *Time* and *Vogue* publish in Europe, Asia, and South America. Geographical or regional editions such as *Southern Living, Midwest Living, TV Guide*, and trade magazine *Adweek*, for example, publish for specific regions of the country or for individual states or cities rather than nationally. This allows clients to appear in a national magazine for a regional price, again narrowing the target and eliminating advertising waste.

Special-Interest Magazines Special-interest magazines feature editorial material directed specifically to a targeted group having a specific interest in the magazine's featured topic. Advertising that appears in these publications generally matches the editorial content, guaranteeing to reach those members of the target most likely to use the product or service.

The more specialized the magazine, the more the advertising creative team knows about the consumer who will see the client's advertising. Dog lovers read dog magazines, car lovers read car magazines, and clothing lovers read fashion magazines. This kind of specialized readership challenges the creative team to create an environment that allows readers to participate in the advertising based on personal experience; this specialized interest produces readers who are loyal and who regularly subscribe to or pick up these magazines at the local newsstand.

The target's special interest in the magazine's editorial material allows for advertising with longer, more fact-based copy that can educate and encourage product trial. Full-color photographs and informative copy can be intimately tied to the self-image of the target audience, creating need and inducing loyalty.

Many special-interest magazines such as *PC World* and *Computer World* have suspended their print versions in favor of an all-digital format; others such as *Newsweek, Southern Living, Car and Driver*, and *Eating Well* are produced in both print and digital versions. These popular digital formats come in basically two forms: (1) those that replicate the content found in their print versions and (2) those that offer original content with enhanced or bonus features.

A digital replica allows readers to flip through pages and click on links to more easily navigate between articles, editorial content, and advertisements. The majority offer access to archived issues, searchable content, downloading capabilities, highlighting and annotations on articles, and social media and e-mail sharing. Additionally, if you prefer your digital subscription to mimic the look of the original print version, all you need to do is turn your tablet and use the landscape option.

Versions with enhanced features and bonus content also afford access to exclusive audio and video content, slideshows, animation, and extra photo galleries. Advertising found on digital versions can incorporate the same rich media options and special placement as well. Virtual bellybands, or animated cover ads that must be clicked on and removed by the viewer to access the rest of the magazine, and cover wraps are great for both advertising and regional versions.

Business or Trade Magazines

When selling products to businesses, the best way to reach this market, other than expensive personal-selling tactics, is to advertise in business-specific or trade publications. Those in charge of purchasing actively seek out both editorial content and advertising for the newest innovations in their specialization, making advertising in business publications advantageous. Business consumers not only need to buy but want to buy the newest product or business-related equipment that will increase productivity and profit. The relatively small size of almost all business markets makes targeting easier than in consumer magazines.

To more precisely determine which business magazine(s) will reach the targeted audience, these publications can be broken down into two distinct types: general business and specialized business.

General Business If you are trying to reach upper-level managers or those in executive positions, business magazines such as *Forbes, Businessweek,* or *Fortune* are some of the best bets. Editorial material as well as advertising content in these publications covers industry on a broad and generic scale.

Specialized Business Magazines Just like special-interest consumer magazines, specialized business publications deal with specific industries, such as manufacturing; research and development; trade, including retail or wholesaling and advertising; and professional, including medical, engineering, and computers.

Farming Magazines

This very diverse and highly targeted type of magazine deals with both consumer and business issues. Most are technically based and deal with the newest innovations in farming, and they are often published regionally in order to deal with the diverse planting, soil, and weather conditions across the country.

How Does Magazine Advertising Help IMC Be Consumer Focused?

Magazine advertising does a little better than newspaper advertising at being consumer focused. Because of their highly targetable nature, it could be argued that magazines are both interactive and educational. Advertising efforts can talk directly to the target's special interests by tapping into the target's self-image. The ability of magazine advertising to build a relationship and thus brand loyalty with the target is the result of the product image transferring to the target's self-image, creating a bond.

What advertising cannot do is develop a dialogue with the consumer. The advertised message is a one-way monologue with an often passive and distracted audience. To create a two-way dialogue, advertising must be used to move the target to the next step: to actively seek out more information by calling a toll-free number or visiting a web or social media site to order or obtain additional information. A small degree of interactivity can be introduced through coupons, quick response (QR) codes, samples, folds, pop-ups, and website and social media addresses by involving the target in the reading or viewing of the ad. As technology advances, however, brands are upping the engagement level by offering AR ads that can be interacted with using the reader's cell phone, introducing mobile apps, using VR, and even making some ads edible.

If the goal is to selectively target and there is a substantial budget, the best media mix might include magazines, mobile, e-mail, cable television, and radio. Mainstream or major television networks such as ABC, CBS, NBC, and Fox, along with magazine advertising, provide a good combination for more generalized products or services that need to look attractive or be demonstrated. Because magazines are printed so infrequently, it is important to consider transferring the brand's image to television, where identity can be frequently reinforced.

Magazines are a good choice if the goal is to inform with long copy or dazzle with color. They are also great at promoting trial by associating the product or service with an activity the target enjoys or by developing image or brand identity. Magazines bring elegance, prestige, and beauty to the product—and thus, the target's image.

Image-based products are often referred to as high-involvement products. The target's wallet and self-image are tied to the brand's identity. If magazine advertising is used for a new product launch, introducing any type of sales promotion at this early stage could adversely affect a brand's perceived exclusivity in the mind of the target. However, sales promotion in conjunction with social media might be used to promote trial, encourage feedback, or create initial interest in a contest or sweepstakes.

Direct marketing can utilize magazine advertising by offering an order form within the ad that the consumer can use to place an order or request additional information. Other direct-marketing devices used for ordering or making inquiries might include a bound-in postal reply card or a freestanding postal insert, also known as a blow-in.

By placing a web address or hashtag within the magazine copy, consumers can be directed to use social media or the Internet to provide feedback or acquire additional information or for advance purchase, another way of making the sale personal, interactive, and exclusive.

Alternative and social media choices are making ads not only interactive but also unique. More readers are using tablets and mobile activation apps to view magazine content. Ads that offer some type of interactive device are more likely to hold the reader's attention in order to open or interact with the advertising. Video options, QR codes, and digital watermarks (invisible digital copyright information) are common devices seen in many magazine ads, as is image recognition technology introduced through augmented reality apps. In an August 22, 2011, *Adweek* article by Lucia Moses entitled "Death of a Salesman? Consumer Marketing Execs Gain Ground in Print World," Condé Nast president Bob Sauerberg sums it up this way: "There's technology wind at our back, and we have the best brands. What we're interested in doing is utilizing technology and content to create new experiences that provide value to consumers in ways they haven't before."

Because of limited printing schedules and long lead times associated with publication, magazines are a bad choice for use with any type of current publicity, unless it is planned or manufactured. New, old, and reinvented products with messages based on image or innovation are ideal for magazine advertising. However, unlike a new or reinvented product, the image of a more mature product will not be affected by the sale mentality of pairing newspaper with magazine advertising in the promotional mix.

Design for magazine advertising, like the other members of the promotional and media mix, will work with the same objectives: strategy, key consumer benefit, and visual/verbal message. It will speak with the same tone of voice and use the same imagery as other communication efforts used in the IMC campaign, such as type, color, spokesperson, and/or layout style, for ease of recognition by the target.

Incentives and Deterrents of Magazine Advertising

To decide whether magazine advertising is right for an IMC campaign, let's look at some of the incentives and deterrents associated with it.

What Makes Magazine Advertising So Great?

The more notable incentives associated with magazine advertising include:

- *Select target market.* The highly targeted and specialized nature of magazines allows copy to talk directly to the person most likely to purchase the product or use the service.
- *Printing capabilities.* Better paper, better print quality, the addition of color, and detailed visuals allow targets to imagine themselves using the product. Printing capabilities allow for both large and small photographs to hold detail.
- *Life span.* Due to the highly individualized content of magazines, consumers tend to hold on to them longer, often trading with other enthusiasts or friends, extending the life of the advertising.
- *Image.* Since magazines reflect readers' lifestyle and interests directly, visuals and concepts that address lifestyle directly address image. Full-color visuals and detailed copy work in tandem to build or retain a product's image.
- *Informative copy.* Copy can be longer, since readers selectively spend more time reading a magazine.
- *Creative options.* About the only creative restrictions in magazine design are the ability to actively demonstrate a product or service—and budget.
- *Geographic selectivity.* Local or regional advertising efforts can reach those most likely to use the product or service without waste.

Is There Anything Wrong with Magazine Advertising?

The more notable deterrents associated with magazine advertising include:

- *Lengthy deadlines.* Advance deadlines often require designers to work months ahead of a publication date. These advance deadlines need to be watched closely to ensure they coincide with other IMC publication or print dates.
- *Cost.* Magazine advertising is indeed more expensive to produce than most other forms of print advertising. The better paper stock and printing capabilities do, however, improve quality and influence design.
- *Clutter.* Unlike newspaper advertising, which must deal with clutter on the page, magazine advertising must compete with the enormous clutter of ads that appear in any one magazine.

- *Publication deadlines*. Magazines have fewer publication dates—ranging from weekly to quarterly—making timely material almost impossible.

The Strategy behind Magazine Advertising

Magazines are a time capsule, capturing lifestyle and values and immortalizing trends. Magazines can offer up the key consumer benefit in brilliant color and, if necessary, with detailed copy points. The more that is known about the target audience's interests, lifestyles, and general demographics, the better. Strategy development designed to meet the special interests of the reader makes isolating a key consumer benefit more individualistic and can accomplish the stated objectives more precisely (figure 10.1).

Figure 10.1. This magazine cover has hidden magazine content under the die-cut steering wheel. Magazine covers that are interactive even in small ways help capture attention and engage the reader. Robyn Blakeman.

Strategically, magazine is not a good choice if the product or service is not image based or if the budget is tight. Other options in these cases might include sales promotion, direct-marketing techniques, or websites, where the target can be addressed as an individual.

The strategy behind creative determines the tone of voice and images that will represent the product or service's message and identity. The decision to use magazines as a part of the media mix will depend on the objectives. Magazines are best used for consumer-based strategies where brand image, lifestyle, or brand attitude can be specifically addressed through the visual/verbal message.

Product-based strategies should not be entirely ruled out if a new product needs to be positioned in the mind of the consumer or if the product or service truly has a unique selling proposition; in these cases, magazines are an ideal media vehicle.

Before determining whether magazine advertising is right for an IMC campaign, here are some additional questions the creative team needs to consider: Is color necessary? Is the use of magazines in the budget? Is the objective to sell image to a specific target audience that can be reached through magazines? Where is the relationship being developed? How will advertising in magazines help reach the target audience? Will magazines be used as a part of the campaign launch or as a support vehicle? What is the life-cycle stage of the product or service? Is there a need to create a dialogue or just to reinforce image? How will interactivity and engagement be created? Is it important to direct the target to customer service or a web or social media site? Do all IMC communication efforts work toward building both loyalty and equity?

BOX 10.1. Transforming Monologue to Dialogue

How can passive, one-way communication be developed into a two-way dialogue? As previously discussed, interactivity begins by asking the target to do something: Call, log on, sign up for a contest or sweepstakes, visit a social media site, come into the showroom, call for an appointment, or take a test drive. Readers viewing ads on tablets or mobile devices might be asked to shake or turn the device, view Instagram images, or view a video. Interactivity engages the target and helps build a relationship that will develop loyal consumers and build equity.

Objectives that benefit from magazine advertising might include generating interest in a new or reinvented product or reinforcing the decision to purchase an expensive product or service by showing benefits of ownership. Additional objectives might include creating awareness, positioning, or building or maintaining a brand attitude.

Key consumer benefits that lend themselves to magazine advertising include the promotion of a unique selling feature, exclusivity, image, prestige, or elegance.

Carrying the strategy through each of the media or promotional mix options in an IMC campaign will require a strong sense of how the target thinks. Strategically, the objectives, key consumer benefit, and visual/verbal message will dominate each media vehicle. A strong tone of voice and equally strong visual imagery must resonate with the target's self-image.

What to Avoid and What to Include in Magazine Advertising

Since magazines sell an idea or an image of affluence, beauty, and even intellect, prices should not be prominent in magazine advertising. Often these ads show no price at all, and they generally include little copy; they let the image sell the product. Consumers should be able to experience the benefits associated with the product or service through the visual/ verbal message and be encouraged to call, engage a mobile app, log on to a web or social media site, or visit their nearest retailer for more information.

Depending on the product, this is also an opportunity to develop a storyline or plot that ties the benefits and image of the product or service to the target's needs and lifestyle. When creatively written, longer copy can sustain a reader's interest long enough to educate and inform. However, the printing surface of magazines is ideal for detailed photographs to show the product's benefits and/or attributes without the need for lengthy copy. The ability to use a broad range of color to set a mood or re-create a time period is second only to the use of visual discussions through photographs, illustrations, or graphics that can show a product in use, assist with image development, and create a trend or an air of exclusivity or fun.

The highly targeted and educated nature of magazine readers allows copy to talk directly to the person most likely to purchase the product, the person who clearly understands its benefits. This is one of the few instances in which "been there, done that" works, as consumers relate their experiences to those the product can solve.

Magazines should be avoided if message frequency is required or if deadlines are an issue. Where most newspapers are printed daily, magazines have fewer publication dates—ranging from weekly to biweekly, from monthly to bimonthly or even quarterly—making the publication of timely material almost impossible. Unlike the twenty-four-hour turn-around of most newspapers, magazine deadlines or submission dates range anywhere from a few weeks to a couple of months before the magazine appears on the newsstands.

The Look of Magazine Design

Everything about designing for magazines is sexier and more exciting than designing for almost any other medium except perhaps alternative media. Elite products allow the designer's fantasy world to come alive. The numerous products without independent identities present a design challenge. Product individualism, or what sets the client's product apart from that of the competition, is achieved through strategy development, layout styles, and/ or type choices.

Magazines reflect personal image. Image portrayal means that it's the creative team's job to make targets see themselves driving this car or using this perfume, or understand the envy friends will feel when they're seen wearing this piece of Tiffany jewelry. It is the goal of magazine advertising to assist consumers with their buying decision by making them feel, see, taste, and imagine the product in their lives.

Before designing, take the time to study the special-interest direction of the magazines the ads will appear in. Look at competitors' ads and do the opposite—or do something similar, but with more individualistic, engaging, or targeted appeal.

Advertising that appears in the pages of a magazine should provide a visually stimulating and informative experience for readers. Visual images should develop an identity and create a visual personality for the product or service. Copy should take the reader on a fact-finding adventure. Product image and user image should be woven throughout this personalized visual/verbal relationship. The magazine's relationship with the consumer allows the advertising to talk directly to the people who will be buying and using the product.

Concepts that address lifestyle directly address image. Full-color visuals and dynamite copy work in tandem to create the appropriate consumer response.

Photographs bring the product or service alive with enhanced details by offering an exclusive viewing opportunity. Textures are magnified, emotions are highlighted, and colors pop off the page. Copy can be longer, since readers selectively spend more time reading a magazine than they do a newspaper. Storylines or plots can be developed to promote uses, scientific studies, demonstrations, purchase options, and trends.

Graphic designs or colorful illustrations attract attention by showcasing interesting shapes and brilliant color variations. Design styles and color usage can re-create time periods and suggest liberal or conservative views. Bold, colorful graphics suggest youth and energy, while subdued colors reflect relaxation and stability.

Interactive options create novelty and support content. *The New Yorker*'s Innovators issue, for example, uses AR to bring its front and back covers to virtual life. Using the AR app Uncovr, the covers infuse both a New York City subway car and the city skyline with interactive reality. To encourage additional interaction, readers can move and tilt their device to find hidden surprises within the skyline.

Target used Shazam to bring interactivity to its ads in *Vogue*. All readers had to do was hold their phone over the ads. The app would then whisk them away to an interactive display on Vogue.com, highlighting scenes from the ads' shoot and purchasing options. Chevrolet uniquely used magazine ads to promote its digital videos. Running in *Esquire* and *Popular Mechanics*, the ad for the Colorado included a video player that was embedded inside the ad. Readers could watch one of three videos about the truck.

Virtual reality is still inventing itself within the covers of magazines. Condé Nast is developing a scripted series, the *New York Times* magazine is using VR to highlight its issues on travel, and *Sports Illustrated* is providing a virtual experience tied to its swimsuit issue.

Interactive magazine advertising doesn't have to go digital. Carlsberg beer educated target consumers on how to fold and use an ad as a bottle opener. Volkswagen South Africa produced an ad featuring its road-eating prowess that the target could actually eat after digesting the content. To show rather than tell how safe the 408 was, Peugeot created an ad the target could punch to inflate the airbag embedded in the visual. These are just a few of the innovative ways brands have used the pages of magazines. Although expensive, they are never dull.

The Importance of Headlines and Subheads

Headlines highlighting strong consumer benefits seduce the target by relating product benefits to image. By touching an emotional chord in the target, advertising can suggest uses and promote New Age fads or Renaissance revivals.

Unlike those in newspaper ads, magazine headlines should not overpower the ad but should be designed into the product's personality or around the ambience created within the design. Garish is always out; structure and informative class are always in. Sizes for headlines vary in magazine ads; however, they are never so loud as to diminish the brand's image or insult the educational or social level of the reader.

In magazines, a reader's attention can be held for a longer period, so headlines as well as body copy can be longer and more informative or instructive. Because of this, subheads are often not needed. However, if there is a great deal of body copy, consider using multiple subheads to break the ad into more pleasing and readable blocks. Like headlines, subheads should not overpower but should blend within the copy block.

The Story of Body Copy

Copy should let the consumer know what the experience will be like when using or interacting with the product or service. Be descriptive; write to the senses and the emotions. In magazines, there is no "buy now while supplies last" mentality or the need to push price, as there is in newspaper advertising. Magazine advertising makes you feel, taste, and smell the product.

Body copy can be virtually nonexistent, short, medium, or long, depending on the message being explained or introduced. The average ad has copy of medium length, just enough to continue the discussion about the key consumer benefit and describe any additional yet relevant attributes. Good descriptive copy should spell out how the product works, what it sounds like, what it feels or smells like, and how much it weighs; it should include a complete examination of benefits and uses. The consumer should experience the product through the copy.

The Image of Photographs

Magazines often use visuals to do the talking. Photographs offer an exclusive viewing opportunity. Because of the coated or shiny paper stock and the high-quality printing used in magazines, the consumer can very clearly see what the product looks like and/or how it is used.

Photographs bring reality home. As readers, we can see patterns, textures, quality, and color as if the product were sitting before us. The idea of visual variety offers designers the option to include background or to isolate the product or image by eliminating background clutter.

Photographs can be small or large; they can show the product alone or in use, placed in a relevant setting, or being compared to a similar product.

The main thing to avoid in magazine design is clutter. The blending of type and photographs should create an elegant or classy, informative, playful, or imaginative appearance. Abundant white space or even black-and-white photographs will set an ad apart from most others in the magazine.

The Appeal of Illustrations

Illustrations create an image of youth and vibrancy, as well as a clean way to display charted information. The colorful interpretations of the product in use or in a setting can reveal a product's personality.

It's All in the Size

Ad sizes depend on the overall size of the magazine. The most common full-size ad is around 8½ × 11. Ad sizes range from one-third of a page to a full page. Available sizes vary by magazine, and they can be found by consulting the Standard Rate and Data Service (SRDS), which lists specific size guidelines for individual magazines as well as closing dates and print-related specifications.

Visually and Verbally Involving the Target

The varied concept approaches used in magazines must accomplish an action or promote the quest for additional research on the part of the consumer. Good interactive or educational devices might include encouraging test drives, using some novel design option such as folds, or interactive options such as samples or order forms. Alternative options might include 3-D pop-ups, interactive mobile phone demonstrations, QR codes, or even the ability to fold and use the ad to complete a specific task, such as open a bottle.

Testimonials also successfully create consumer involvement by evoking curiosity. Informational ads are great educational vehicles, as are recipes accompanying a food product. Emotional appeals, how-to ads, and product demonstrations all work well in magazine advertising.

Cooperative Advertising and Magazines

As with newspaper advertising, it is not unusual for magazines to participate in co-op opportunities with other members of the advertising media mix or promotional mix to sell compatible products or support a special event.

The benefit co-op advertising brings to the target is the ability to combine two viable products into a package savings deal. Product pairing, when done consistently, makes the target think package rather than separate products when considering repurchase.

Magazines may be used to support public relations, direct mail, sales promotion, newspaper, or social media in promoting special events such as the Special Olympics, breast cancer awareness runs, or AIDS-related events. Since magazines influence image and promote prestige, the visual/verbal message will influence all other design associated with the event, from publicity to the design of the direct-mail packages, any accompanying outdoor boards, donation and/or thank-you cards, posters, and banners, to name just a few. Sales promotion items such as T-shirts and cups or water bottles will also project the same image and overall design.

The choice to use the visually stimulating pages of a magazine to bring prestige to a product and reflect the target's interests, self-image, and lifestyle is a design journey into the study of human nature. Magazine advertising can be fun, interactive, serious, colorful, imaginative, and visually/verbally informative. It is perfect for developing a new product's image, maintaining an established image, or rebuilding or repairing the image of a reinvented product.

DISCUSSION QUESTIONS

1. Define magazine advertising.
2. Why should prices be avoided in magazine advertising?
3. There are several categories of magazines. Define each.
4. How does magazine advertising help IMC be more consumer focused? Define importance.
5. Why are magazines considered highly targetable?
6. How does magazine advertising build brand loyalty?
7. Why is it difficult for advertising to develop a dialogue with the target audience?
8. What brands are best suited to use magazine advertising and why?
9. When should brands consider using magazine advertising?
10. What are some of the ways to make magazine ads interactive?
11. When is using magazine advertising a bad choice?
12. What are the pros and cons of using magazine advertising in an IMC campaign?
13. What is the strategy behind using magazine advertising?
14. What should be avoided and what should be included in magazine advertising?
15. What are some of the ways to turn a one-way monologue with the target into a two-way dialogue?
16. What components should be included and avoided in magazine advertising?
17. What copy and design elements should be included in magazine advertising? Explain how to involve the target.
18. How is cooperative advertising used in magazines?

CHAPTER

11

Radio Advertising

The Strategic Use of Radio Advertising in IMC

Radio permeates our world. We are exposed to it everywhere: in the car, at work, while on hold on the phone, in the doctor's office, and while shopping. Because of this, radio has the distinction of being one of the few media vehicles that can be used to reach the targeted audience close to the time of purchase.

As a verbal medium, radio is often considered handicapped when compared to other media vehicles within the promotional mix. Limited by its sound-only format, radio is nonetheless burdened with delivering both the visual and verbal message. Looked at another way, radio could be considered the ultimate integrated marketing communication strategic vehicle. Creative teams that try to make radio advertising conform to the same visual/verbal or show-and-tell standards as print, digital, and television inhibit the target from truly imagining "themselves" without the assistance of a predetermined visual stimulus or using the product or service. Radio is the ultimate strategic use of the target's imagination. (See case study 9, "Post Honey Bunches of Oats.")

Radio ads must create a sense of visual stimulation for the listener. A radio ad should attach the listener's visual imagination with a verbal narration that outlines the features and benefits associated with the key consumer benefit. To make listeners create a personalized visual picture, the verbal message must be colorful, informative, and tied to their personal experiences in order to entice them to place the product in their visual perspective.

Great for building awareness, radio can be used as a primary advertising vehicle for local advertising or as a support or secondary vehicle for regional and national advertisers. As a

CASE STUDY 9

IMC Radio: Post Honey Bunches of Oats

Background

Post Foods' Honey Bunches of Oats began to deepen its reach and commitment to the Hispanic community with a national campaign that aligns the brand's spirit of positivity with the uplifting power of music.

Objectives

1. Align music, national media, digital, shopper marketing, and community relations touch points for greater reach and ROI for Post's Honey Bunches of Oats.
2. Drive strong awareness for the brand and its celebrity connection with Prince Royce.
3. Showcase the brand's positive and uplifting essence.

Solution

The campaign's promotion vehicle was "Honey Bunches of Oats presents: Ring in the New Year with Prince Royce in New York City!"

- Univision Radio used on-air, online, television, and social media platforms to promote an unforgettable campaign that featured A-list Latin artist Prince Royce as he returned home to perform in an exclusive concert; tuning in, logging on, or attending Univision Radio events were the only ways to win tickets.
- In Houston, Los Angeles, Miami, and New York, promotional teams promoted appearances at retail outlets and used customized messaging to encourage listeners to purchase specially marked packages of Honey Bunches of Oats that gave them a chance to win a VIP trip to New York to meet Prince Royce.
- Honey Bunches of Oats became the presenting sponsor of X96.3's annual basketball game in New York, where fans could win Prince Royce concert tickets. More than $15K was raised for the Hispanic Federation and charities to benefit Hurricane Sandy victims.
- Audio and video streaming, e-mail blasts, event listings, and media banners connected users to a custom registration page within Univision.com to register for their chance to win a VIP trip to New York City and meet Prince Royce.
- Participating stations, DJ endorsers, Stage 48 Lounge, and Prince Royce took to their Facebook and Twitter pages to build buzz for the upcoming concert, increase registrations, and create viral conversation that resulted in more than 60,000 social media mentions, likes, comments, and shares.
- To kick off the weekend, on December 30, Stage 48 Lounge in New York City was transformed into a Honey Bunches of Oats experience, with branding inside and outside the venue, signage, premiums, and sampling, including an intimate Prince Royce performance, a meet-and-greet, and a New Year's countdown to prepare guests for 2013.

Univision Radio has always been a critical part to our media plan; however, the latest creativity from the team has taken our partnership to the next level with custom events that have changed the game, delivered value to our Latina consumer, and helped us drive dollar sales.

—Mike Foley
Brand Manager US Hispanic and Export, Post Foods

Results

- 9.5 percent increase in national dollar growth and an even greater increase in New York State of 30 percent.
- The program drove the entire cereal category growth for Post during the period it ran.
- 1,960 on-air announcements
- 1.6 million online impressions, with a 0.10 percent click-through rate (CTR)
- 60,000+ social media interactions
- 2,300 thousand sweepstakes registrations
- 12 retail appearances
- 1,500+ concert attendance

Source: "Radio Case Study: Post Honey Bunches of Oats," Radio Advertising Bureau, http://www.rab.com/public/ncs/caseStudies.cfm.

support vehicle, radio is an effective way to entice the target to action and/or reinforce other communication efforts within the promotional mix.

The Diversity of the Radio Advertising Voice

Delivering simple, low-cost messages to a small but specialized group of consumers is radio's specialty. Radio spots can be written, produced, and aired in as little as a few days. Changes and/or updates to existing spots are easy and relatively inexpensive to make, keeping material timely and making the medium adaptable to changing market conditions.

Radio's very personalized nature builds relationships with the target, especially if a popular radio personality reads the spot on air, giving the product or service credibility and effectively tying the product identity and/or image to that of the DJ.

One way to maximize brand awareness is to tie the product or service to an ongoing sponsorship such as the news, the weather, or a special feature. Sponsorships highlight the product's name and are guaranteed to run at the same time every day, adding extra emphasis to the product's name and image beyond the advertised message.

As one of the most inexpensive media vehicles available, radio allows more advertising to reach the right target. Cost is determined by the length of the spot—fifteen, thirty, or sixty seconds—and the time of day the ad will air. The two most popular and expensive advertising slots, known as "drive times," include mornings from six to ten and afternoons from three to seven. Midday and evening hours are less expensive, as listenership drops off

after listeners begin or end their workday. Other costs associated with radio include produc-
tion-related costs such as hiring talent, including sound effects or music, and the frequency
with which the ad airs.

Since people are often distracted by other things while listening to the radio, spots must
be aired repeatedly to catch the listener's attention. It is also important to remember that
the target will probably not listen to only one station, so multiple media buys on multiple
stations will be required to reach the intended target.

Airtime can be purchased on either AM or FM radio stations. Determining what stations will best reach the targeted audience depends on the stations' programming format.
The two most basic types of radio formatting are talk and music. A station's format defines
the listening audience; because of this, radio advertising can talk directly to the target's special interests.

Satellite and Internet radio, on the other hand, allows radio enthusiasts to either tap
into more than a hundred diverse programming channels or create customized playlists. Sir-
iusXM satellite radio is a subscription-based service, making it a great outlet for marketing
high-end brands to more affluent consumers. Most satellite radio ads are heard on news and
talk radio programming. Listened to mostly in cars, satellite radio is available nationwide and
offers a format for every listener and every advertiser.

Internet contenders such as Pandora and Spotify offer both free and paid versions that
can be customized and downloaded to both laptops and mobile devices. Listeners who use
the free versions sacrifice quality and open the door to advertising. Advertising heard in both
platforms uses both audio and visual ads. Audio ads are woven in between songs; visual ads
are delivered via banners.

Better at collecting demographic and geographic data on its listeners than Spotify,
Pandora seems a better option for local advertisers. Attracted to its large number of users,
marketers can place advertising based on users' registration data such as age, gender, zip code,
musical selection, and time of day and device used.

Because radio is sound only, it's important that what is said or read in other media used
in an IMC campaign be repeated on the radio. This might include a jingle, sound effects, or
the distinct voice of a spokesperson or character representative from television, a slogan or
tagline, or headline style from print.

Radio is not considered interactive or a great image-building option. Although radio is
a one-way monologue from the product or service, it need not be passive. Consider jingles,
especially if they can be turned into participatory sing-alongs in the old-fashioned but well-
loved "Hokey Pokey" style. Remote broadcasts, broadcasts that take place from a location
other than the radio station, are another way to get the target involved and the best way to
use radio to encourage two-way communication between buyer and seller.

In radio, image is created verbally. But radio can be visually stimulating if an ad is written to support the target's self-image. If targets can see themselves using the product, their
image will be much stronger than one manufactured by the creative team. This is especially
true if the image was first introduced elsewhere in the promotional mix and radio is being
used as a support medium.

When radio is part of the media mix, the advertiser will need to decide if the message will run nationally, with the same generic message in all markets, or locally, with the
message adapted for each market, and whether it will be heard on traditional, satellite, and/

or Internet platforms. The generic form of radio advertising is known as national network advertising; more geographically tailored messages are known as local or **spot advertising**.

The national generic message is not used very often. It goes against everything radio is: a highly targetable, highly specialized, and highly personable medium. Local or spot radio is where most advertising is placed. This relatively inexpensive medium offers small local business owners and national advertisers the same opportunity to tailor their message to a specific demographic based on a station's format, psychographically based on lifestyle, and geographically based on location.

How Does Radio Advertising Help IMC Be Consumer Focused?

This very verbal medium must imprint the product's benefits on an inattentive mind, and one of the best ways to do this is to make radio as interactive as possible. Radio ads should give targets an activity—let them sing, hum, or clap along to a catchy jingle, the kind that intrudes upon the unconscious mind whether the ad is airing at the time or not. Radio also offers promotional opportunities through contests or sweepstakes such as trivia games, where a listener calls in with the answer to win a prize, or through giveaways, such as gift certificates or product samples. Remote broadcasts can encourage listeners to stop in at a particular location and take a test drive, pick up freebies like T-shirts or CDs, or meet a celebrity or local DJ. Another method is to take a page out of an old radio script and create an ongoing verbal slice-of-life vignette. If the storyline uses intrigue, humor, or some other curiosity or interactive building device, such as a scavenger hunt, to tell a compelling story, the target will tune in to get the next piece of the puzzle or learn how the next episode turns out.

Radio is often used in public relations to promote events such as blood drives or collection drives or even for new product launches.

Unlike print, where it is easy to ignore advertising by turning the page, the radio audience is captive to the message unless listeners switch stations or turn the radio off. This is less likely when listeners are involved in other activities while listening.

Radio and newspaper advertising can be a powerful combination when adapting to changes in the marketplace, since messages can reach the public quickly and inexpensively.

Like magazines, radio is able to deliver a specialized message to a small niche market. However, unlike magazines, radio is not as useful for big-ticket merchandise or detailed copy. Radio, like newspaper, is meant not to educate but to excite the target to action. If price plays a major role in the communication efforts, radio's fleeting message makes remembering price points difficult.

Radio can also be used to reinforce and localize messages seen on television. The verbal message from television can be used on radio, keeping the cohesive IMC message going. Listeners who have been repeatedly exposed to the televised commercial will be familiar enough with the message that they will be able to replay the visual message or video from the television commercial in their minds.

If the goal is to educate or requires getting the target to act quickly, consider combining radio with newspaper, social media, the Internet, mobile texting, or out-of-home or transit in order to reach a larger portion of the targeted audience.

DJs who use social media in their programming will find it a great way to promote their time slot or encourage the audience to cocreate content or participate in discussions on local, national, or personal day-to-day issues. Social media can also be used to encourage location-based check-ins using services like Foursquare or Facebook at remote broadcast locations such as concerts, bars, or restaurants.

Radio and social media offer not only engagement but also immediacy. Both encourage interaction through stories and events that can be used to elicit immediate feedback from the target.

Incentives and Deterrents of Radio Advertising

To decide whether radio advertising is right for an IMC campaign, let's look at some of the incentives and deterrents associated with it.

What Makes Radio Advertising So Great?
The more notable incentives associated with radio advertising include:

- *Cost.* Radio is very inexpensive to use compared to other media vehicles in the promotional mix.
- *Targetability.* The varied music formats of radio stations make targeting to a specific audience easier.
- *Portability.* Radio can easily be taken by the target anywhere.
- *Quick turnaround.* Messages can be quickly developed and be heard on-air within a matter of days, sometimes even within hours.
- *Interactivity.* Listeners can become involved in the message by calling in to receive a free sample or stopping by a remote broadcast location for free gifts.
- *Imaginative impact.* Radio is an imaginative stimulus. It is a verbal message visualized in the mind of the consumer.
- *Local and national adaptability.* Radio spots can be easily adapted for airing in any location.
- *Frequency.* Radio's relatively low cost allows messages to be aired more often to ensure they reach the targeted audience.

Is There Anything Wrong with Radio Advertising?
The more notable deterrents associated with radio advertising include:

- *Background noise.* Radio gets little direct attention, so advertising must be clever in order to catch and hold the attention of a target who is doing something else while listening.
- *Sound only.* Radio is the imagination of the message. Messages must be written in a visually stimulating way since the target can only hear the message.

- *Fleeting message.* Lengthy informational messages are impossible; the message is gone in fifteen, thirty, or sixty seconds. Listeners cannot spend time going back over the message.
- *Fragmented audiences.* In larger markets, radio ads need to be aired on multiple stations, since the target has many options with the same or similar formats from which to choose.
- *Clutter.* Radio stations run a lot of ads between songs or talk programming. It is a cluttered medium, airing anywhere between fifteen and twenty minutes' worth of advertising in an hour, with the bulk of the advertising being local.

The Strategy behind Radio Advertising

Nobody "listens" to the radio anymore; it has been relegated to background noise that keeps us company while we work, drive, shop, or get our teeth cleaned. For radio to work, it must do one of three specific things: have a catchy tune or jingle associated with the message, include some kind of engagement device, or just be downright intrusive.

Whether radio is strategically right for an IMC campaign will, of course, depend on the target to be reached, the key consumer benefit, the objectives, and the strategic approach. Anything that can be told in story form will work on radio. It is an excellent media vehicle for bringing character representatives or spokespersons to life, and it gives immediacy to the message. Anything that must be spelled out through lengthy copy in order to educate or be demonstrated will not work on radio.

Effective communication objectives might include immediate sales, loyalty programs, increased store traffic, product or service inquiries, encouraging test drives, or developing brand awareness.

Strategically, radio is better suited to a product-based approach, such as generic or product feature. The use of a consumer-based approach requires image to be substantiated in other areas of the promotional mix before it can be discussed on radio. The type of strategy used to deliver the message can be either emotional or rational in nature, but the rational approach does offer more imagination-based options. The best rational-based execution techniques include straight fact, product as the star, testimonials, and news; the best emotional appeals include fear, humor, dramatization, sex, fantasy, and slice of life. The choice of tone, approach, or appeal is affected not only by the stated objectives and target audience but also by a product or service's incentives and deterrents.

Radio is not a good choice if the strategy is based on a unique selling proposition (USP), since this often must be visualized to be understood, especially if it involves some kind of new technology, look, or use.

The Sound of Radio Design

Radio stations can air prerecorded spots or present the material live by an on-air personality. Since DJs are as much a part of the listening pleasure as the music or talk format, the product gets an added boost of credibility. On-air personalities are not provided a script from which to read but instead are given a list of the product's features and benefits to present for thirty to sixty seconds in their own words.

Radio ads need not only employ the use of a spokesperson or on-air personality to deliver the message; they can also use music and sound effects to activate a listener's imagination.

If it's true that nobody's actively listening, then it's the creative team's job to find a way to get the listener "tuned in" to the message—and this must be done within the first three seconds. This can be accomplished using specialized voices or voices that are unique to the ear, sound effects, or music.

Execution Techniques

Several different execution techniques can be used to deliver a radio message:

- Music and jingles
- Narrative drama
- Straight announcement
- Celebrity delivery
- Live donut
- Single voice
- Dialogue
- Multivoice
- Sound effects
- Vignette
- Interview

Music and Jingles

If the message can best be delivered attached to music, then use it. To create ambience or evoke certain emotions, use music from popular culture or a golden oldie. Music, especially an oldie, attracts our attention by dredging up memories and feelings from the back of our minds. These imaginative musings will enhance and enrich the current message.

Jingles are intrusive. They creep up on our unsuspecting consciousness when we least expect it: in the shower, during a meeting, or at a movie. If the concept involves creating a theme song that ties to the slogan or tagline, then develop a jingle. Jingles are interactive, memorable, and a great way to prolong or extend the life of the message.

Narrative Drama

The best way to tell a story is the narrative approach. Narrative dramas take a little slice out of life and deliver it to listeners as dialogue between characters.

Straight Announcement

A straight announcement is just that—an announcement—most often delivered by an on-air personality. This is not a story or an imaginative stroll down memory lane; it's the facts delivered in a straightforward manner. The commercial usually starts out with the key consumer benefit (USP or big idea) and ends with the announcer asking the listener to try the product.

Celebrity Delivery

If the IMC campaign has a character representative or spokesperson, he or she should speak on behalf of the product in the radio spot. If the product has no recognized spokesperson and a celebrity voice is used, be sure the celebrity and the brand's image are a match.

Live Donut

A donut uses a prerecorded opening and closing message. The center, or "donut hole," is filled in live by an on-air personality. This keeps the message moving and does not allow room for the DJ to ad lib.

Single Voice

Use one specific voice when the brand has a recognizable spokesperson or character representative who can deliver the message and is known through use on other IMC pieces.

Dialogue

Dialogue is a good way to let characters talk about the product and its uses, benefits, and features. These characters will be more credible if an announcer is added to the spot to actually make the pitch.

Multivoice

In a multivoice approach, multiple characters carry the message, not by talking to one another but by talking directly to the listener.

Sound Effects

If the ad has a repeatable sound, like the drum-banging Energizer Bunny, use it to bring a visual image to the verbal message. Sounds can also be used to make a point, as with a grumbling stomach to signify that the product can relieve acid indigestion. Music can also be used to set a scene or mood, the same way it might in a movie or television show.

Vignette

A vignette is an ongoing storyline. The varied storylines are tied together by some repeated device such as music, a jingle, a slogan or tagline, or a spokesperson. The first vignette is used to set up the key consumer benefit within the concept, with the following commercials used to expand the storyline or as reminder advertising.

Interview

The interview approach is a good way to use testimonials. In this approach, DJs or product spokespersons solicit interviews with users of the product or service. Often displays are set up at grocery stores, malls, sporting events, or street corners to encourage trial and feedback.

The creative team can use a combination of techniques to get its message across on the radio. The approach chosen should be the best one to reach the target.

What to Consider When Designing for Radio

It is important that radio ads continue the IMC campaign theme. Be sure to carry over music, character representative, or spokesperson from print, digital, or broadcast ads. If any representative sounds, theme music, or a jingle were created, reuse them in radio. This will help with early recognition of the brand name. Be sure to attract the listener's attention within the first three seconds, and then open with the key consumer benefit. Radio advertising must accomplish the following:

- The message must tune the listener in. Get the listener's attention quickly, but be sure to use the tone of voice used throughout the IMC campaign.
- Let the listener know right away the product name and key consumer benefit.
- If the product is hard to spell or pronounce, find a way to help the listener remember it. One way is with a mnemonic, such as a word association or rhyming scheme, to make it easier to remember.
- Write the copy the way a person speaks. Proper grammar is great in print but does not transfer well into broadcast. Use short sentences to make copy points easier to remember.
- If there is a way to control the visual in the listener's mind, do it. If the product's packaging is distinct, perhaps in color or shape, let the listener know.
- Don't be afraid to repeat the product name and its key consumer benefit often; in fact, the more often, the better. As long as the repeated devices are delivered creatively and diversely, a listener will not be annoyed or tune out.
- Talk to the listener in real time. Since the overwhelming majority of radio spots are local, deal with local issues, localities, and personalities.
- Don't lose the listener with a list of facts. Radio is great for building brand awareness, but leave any repositioning or the building of brand image to other media better suited for that task.
- It is important to use the ongoing message of the IMC campaign to bind the campaign together. For radio, consider using the slogan or tagline from print, the personality from television and print, or the music or jingle from television. Radio rarely leads off an IMC campaign, so use the most prominent visual and/or verbal elements available to continue the campaign's tone of voice in radio spots.
- Be careful with sound effects. They are great for getting attention, but they can be annoying and sometimes can even scare a driving listener. It's important to make sure the noises used are easily recognizable to the listener.

The copy sheet used in radio advertising is known as a **script**. The script can be prerecorded by talent hired by the agency or read live by an on-air personality. A radio spot can be of almost any length, but the most common are thirty- or sixty-second spots. The script must be able to be read in its entirety in the time allotted without sounding rushed. A thirty-second spot is approximately sixty to seventy words long; a sixty-second spot is approximately 150 to 180 words long. How many words are used will depend on who is reading the script, how fast he or she must read, and whether the ad contains any complicated word

BOX 11.1. Radio Copy Word Counts

10 seconds	20–25 words
15 seconds	30–35 words
20 seconds	40–45 words
30 seconds	60–70 words
60 seconds	150–180 words

combinations or technical jargon. Two speakers in conversation will take up more time. (See box 11.1 for additional word counts.)

Choosing Talent

The person chosen to speak the dialogue for a spot should represent the product's image and the target demographics. If the product is lawnmowers, a young person speaking the copy can talk about how easy it makes her summer job. But if the message is price or relaxation time at the end of the day, an older speaker will be required. It is also important to be sure every word is spoken clearly so that the message can be understood.

Radio commercials should feel like one person talking to another. Keep the tone of the ad either light and upbeat or laid back and friendly. It is important to make sure the tone is continued throughout the ad to avoid a choppy or disjointed feel.

When deciding whether to use talent or an announcer, look to the IMC concept for the right tone of voice. The choice of announcer should speak with authority, representing the client's voice and personality. Characters should replicate real members of the target audience.

How Should the Message Be Delivered?

Radio spots most often arrive at the radio station in a prerecorded digital format that is ready to be aired. But there are other options available, such as sending a script to be either read live or prerecorded by a member of the station or sending a fact sheet and allowing on-air personalities to ad lib live on the air. How do you know which one will work best for the product or service? First, look to the strategy and the delivery used on other IMC pieces. Additionally, consider the following:

- A script read live on the air works only if no additional sound is required and only one person will be speaking, as with a straight announcement approach.
- Fact sheets allow the on-air personality the opportunity to chat openly about the product or service. If the personality has had an opportunity before the spot airs to test drive, taste, or wear the product, she can add that experience to the discussion. The fact sheet should place the features and accompanying benefits in their order of importance, with the key consumer benefit being first. Often, if the personality is familiar with the product, the brand will get more than the thirty to sixty seconds

of airtime. But there is a danger that the radio personality will go too far and deliver the information in a negative or cynical way. Consider this approach only when the personality is reliable or if last-minute changes are required to an existing ad; for example, with fare changes for airline travel.

- Copy that needs to be routinely updated might benefit from using a live donut. Here, an advertiser prerecords a musical opening and closing. Often the music will fade under or be reduced in volume, creating a musical bridge that ties the opening and closing together. The hole between the opening and closing is then filled in with scripted copy that is read live on the air. The music is the constant that ties the ads together as copy is regularly changed out.

- A commercial that is prerecorded in its entirety is the safest and most professional way to go. If the script requires the use of sound effects, music, or multiple speakers in any combination, it will need the structure, timing, and assurance of a prerecorded commercial.

The Sound We Hear and Its Effects

Sound effects (SFX) are the noises heard in ads: doors slamming, dogs barking, babies crying. They should be used to capture attention and move the copy forward. In other words, they should not be used to create noise alone; they must have a point.

SFX should aid the listener's imagination by creating a visual image in his or her mind. Music can also be used as an attention getter. It is important to note that although music is a sound, it can be used to get attention or to create a mood or set a tone.

A good copywriter tries to paint a picture with words and uses sound to back them up, create excitement, or gain attention. The spoken voice alone is not enough to hold a listener's attention, so SFX are a great way to break up the tedium of the spoken message. A multitude of SFX are available to the creative team. As with all other creative elements, the choice of sounds must be carefully considered. If a sound doesn't move the message forward or have a point, leave it out.

The Creation of a Radio Script

For the copywriter, a script is like an artist's canvas; descriptive words and visually constructed sentences are used like paint to create a picture in the mind of the consumer.

The key to any script is to make the copy flow in a conversational manner and give the talent or person reading the script visual copy cues as to what is coming, such as music or sound effects (figure 11.1). Let's take a look at how to set up a script and what type of visual cues make reading a script easy.

All radio scripts are typed on 8½ × 11 paper and are double spaced. Double-spaced copy adds white space to the page, making it easier to see and read the copy. Use one-inch margins on all four sides, with one inch of space between columns.

A script is broken into two columns. The left side of the script is devoted to labels and the specific audio effects, such as SFX, MUSIC, ANNOUNCER, and TALENT, and should appear in all caps. This makes the instructions stand out from the readable copy.

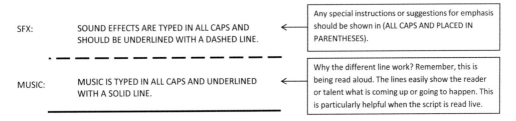

Figure 11.1. Sample radio script showing solid- and dashed-line divisions.

The right column, directly across from the appropriate label, is devoted to the music and/or SFX that will be heard and any spoken dialogue. Any special instructions or suggestions for emphasis should be shown in (ALL CAPS AND PLACED IN PARENTHESES). All spoken copy or dialogue should appear in caps/lowercase and be enclosed in quotation marks.

SFX, or the noises or sounds that will be heard in the ad, are typed in all caps and placed in the right-hand column. Directly under these instructions should appear a dashed line. This is a visual cue to the talent reading the copy that a sound is coming up. It also flags those responsible for the SFX as to when they are coming up and where they belong. SFX may be live but are most often prerecorded to ensure accuracy.

BOX 11.2. How to Tie the Product to Sound

These are ways you can make a product come alive over the radio:

- *Spokesperson.* If the product or service can be tied to a specific region or country, such as teas from the Orient or perfumes from France, then consider the use of a speaker with that accent. Be careful, though; this can become very clichéd.
- *Music.* If the product or service being advertised has little pizzazz, like insurance or investment brokers, then create pizzazz by using music familiar to the target. Musical associations help listeners remember the client's product or service.
- *Authoritative voice.* Authoritative or expert spokespersons attract attention and bring credibility to a product or service.
- *Interviews.* Testimonials by current users of a product or service bring credibility; testimonials delivered from an on-site location bring immediacy.
- *Humor.* Be sure the commercial is funny to the target, or avoid it like the plague. Humor can do more harm than good if it is not done well or is offensive to listeners. When done well, the listener looks forward to the commercial rather than changing stations until it's over.
- *Sound effects.* Use sound effects to make a point and move the message forward. If there is any doubt the sound could be misinterpreted, tell listeners what they are hearing.
- *Diversity.* Alternate commercials regularly. Once a message becomes repetitive, the listener tunes it out. Keep interest high by delivering the key consumer benefit in different ways.
- *Sponsorships.* If the product or service sponsors the news or traffic report, its name will automatically pop into a listener's mind before paid advertising airs.

Music instructions are also placed in the right-hand column and also appear in all caps. Directly under these instructions should appear a solid line. This is another visual cue for those responsible for the music as well as for the talent.

If a recurring character is being introduced, give the character a name and use it in the copy. If no recurring character is being used, use the label ANNOUNCER to indicate the speaker.

Remember, don't be afraid to intersperse the spot with ear-catching sound effects or mood-setting music. It will help to hold the listener's attention.

Be sure to close the spot with the product name, slogan or tagline, and a call to action. Tell listeners where they can find the product, including landmarks, social media hashtags, a phone number, or a website address if it is easy to remember. Be sure to mention the product's name, key consumer benefit, and where it can be purchased at least three times in a sixty-second spot and twice in a thirty-second spot. See figure 11.2 for a sample radio script.

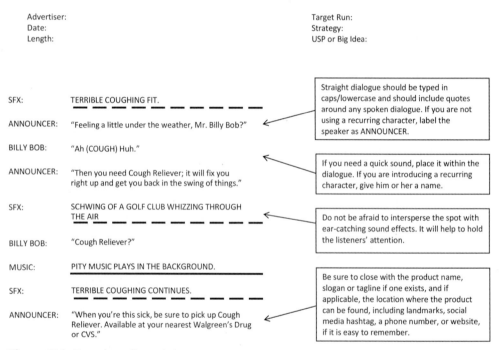

Figure 11.2. Sample radio script.

When using radio, be sure the copy will both visually and verbally stimulate the listener's imagination and incite action. The fact that it is low cost, portable, and highly targetable makes radio advertising an attractive and inexpensive media option. Although most often used as a support vehicle for other media in the IMC promotional mix because it does not build image or promote a two-way dialogue, radio is still a great choice when the goal is to build and maintain brand awareness and localize the product's message.

Q DISCUSSION QUESTIONS

1. What are the strategic uses of radio advertising in an IMC campaign?
2. Why is radio considered handicapped when compared to other media vehicles within the promotional mix?
3. Explain the diversity of radio advertising's voice.
4. How can radio be personalized?
5. To strengthen radio's verbal ties to other ads in the media mix, what elements need to be repeated?
6. Radio is considered a passive medium. How can it be made more interactive?
7. How does radio advertising help IMC be more consumer focused?
8. What are the pros and cons associated with radio advertising?
9. What is the strategy behind using radio in an IMC campaign?
10. What are the execution techniques used in radio advertising? Explain each.
11. To be successful, what must radio advertising accomplish?
12. What are the ways radio can be delivered?
13. What are sound effects?
14. What are the components that make up a radio script?
15. How can a brand come alive over the radio?
16. Why does radio copy need to be both visually and verbally expressed?

Television Advertising

The Strategic Use of Television in IMC

Television advertising influences what we wear, drive, use domestically, and aspire to own. Its show-and-tell style can bring the product or service's story to life, set a mood, demonstrate a use, create a memory, initiate a fad or trend, or define a style.

Despite its cluttered environment and overall expense, television is still one of the best mass-media vehicles available to reach the target audience, build awareness, and develop an image.

Using sight, sound, and motion, television can attract and retain the target's attention, giving the ad the opportunity to entertain and inform. Television's ability to reach the target through very specialized programming allows the product's story to be personalized to match the target's lifestyle, interests, and needs.

When used as a primary media outlet, television is ideally suited for new product launches, reminder advertising for mature products, and repositioning an old product in the mind of the consumer. However, it is too expensive to use if the product or service is not unique in any significant way or does not possess an **inherent drama** that only sight, sound, and motion can dramatize.

Television as a source of entertainment keeps television sets turned on and viewers tuned in. Millions of consumers watch television programming and are exposed to a lot of commercials, but that does not mean they actually watch the commercials. Today's television environment is cluttered with back-to-back commercials, further fractionalizing consumer interest. Getting the attention of any consumer who wields a remote control or owns a fast-forwarding DVD player or DVR requires that advertising be not only entertaining but also useful. (See case study 10 for a look at Aflac's use of television in an IMC campaign.)

Finding ways to avoid commercials is a new American pastime, known as zipping, zapping, and grazing. According to Dean M. Krugman, Leonard N. Reid, S. Watson Dunn, and Arnold M. Barban in their book *Advertising: Its Role in Modern Marketing*, zipping, zapping, and grazing are among the most serious concerns of today's advertisers. The fact that television commercials are considered a nuisance is nothing new; however, it's only recently that viewers can do something about them. Commercials considered uninteresting or irrelevant can be zapped with a channel change. Commercials recorded along with television programs can be zipped over with just a push of the fast-forward button. Viewers who once channel surfed can now lovingly caress their remotes while grazing through channels.

Much newer on the scene than traditional TV viewing is Internet TV. Included under this broad heading are streaming Internet video services such as Hulu and Netflix. As the name implies, **streaming Internet video** is Internet television that digitally distributes television content that can be viewed through your television, computer, or mobile device such as a smartphone or iPad. Both streaming services offer movies, TV shows, and original programming.

Hulu offers two options: Hulu and Hulu Plus. Offering fewer program choices, Hulu is free at Hulu.com, but the viewing experience is modeled after traditional broadcast television that interrupts programming with a substantial amount of advertising. Hulu Plus has a monthly service rate that allows for a larger array of viewing options, but content will still be interrupted with a few ads; no zipping, zapping, or grazing with this service.

The only way to get away from advertising entirely is to use Netflix. Also charging a monthly fee, Netflix offers the better selection of movies and older TV shows, while Hulu Plus offers a greater selection of current-season TV shows and a smaller selection of movies.

So what's an advertiser to do? First, you must get more creative and target the audience with more accuracy than ever before. Second, consider weaving some form of interactive response into the commercial. Television advertising often asks the target to visit a showroom, log on or call for additional information, or make a purchase. Third, consider creating a contest or sweepstakes where the target can be the first to own the product or use the service, or use added-price incentives or free gifts as motivators to order now.

Traditional Advertising versus Interactive Advertising

Research for an integrated marketing communication campaign identifies the target audience members, the programs they are watching, and how they view family, fun, health, and leisure time. IMC works to create an interactive, two-way dialogue between buyer and seller. Traditional advertising methods talk at the target. Creative teams take great pains to ensure their message entertains and informs in the hope of enticing the intended target to read, listen, or view their message. This traditional interaction between buyer and seller is known as a passive monologue.

Interactive television, also known as **direct response**, involves the target in the message process by asking him to call, log in, visit a social media or website, or stop by for further information or to make a purchase. If so inclined, the target can order immediately without the inconvenience of leaving his home or office. Interaction requires contact, so each

C CASE STUDY 10

IMC Television: The "Aflac Duck" Historic Campaign

Overview

Aflac is a major insurance company based in Columbus, Georgia. In 2000 its top product was its cancer-expense coverage, which the company had invented in 1958. Though profitable, Aflac suffered from poor brand recognition; only 12 percent of consumers remembered the company, in part because it had such an unusual name. In response, Aflac wanted to expand its business by improving consumers' awareness of the brand. It also wanted to target thirty-five- to fifty-four-year-old consumers.

In 1999 the company hired a new advertising agency, the Kaplan Thaler Group, to improve its name recognition. The New York–based agency was known for its "Big Bang" approach to advertising: the belief that campaigns succeeded most when they altered consumers' views about the brand advertised. To accomplish this for Aflac, the agency created a new spokescharacter, the Aflac Duck. Voiced by comedian and actor Gilbert Gottfried, the Duck appeared in spots that featured consumers having trouble remembering the company's name. The Duck attempted to remedy this by "quacking" the answer: "Aflac." The lighthearted spots were broadcast on prime-time network TV and during broadcasts of sporting events such as Major League Baseball games.

Aflac spent $35 million on the campaign, and the Duck was a major success. According to *USA Today*'s Ad Track poll, it was one of the most popular spots of 2000. Brand recognition shot up to more than 70 percent and later topped 90 percent. Sales improved 28 percent, in part a result of improved name recognition. The company's accident/disability insurance took off, outselling the company's cancer-expense plans for the first time. The Duck became a cultural icon and continued as the company's advertising focal point through 2004. That year the Duck became one of the first characters to appear on the Advertising Walk of Fame in New York City.

Historical Context

The American Family Life Assurance Company (later called Aflac) was founded as an international holding company in 1955 by brothers John, Paul, and Bill Amos. In 1958 it became one of the first companies in the world to offer insurance against cancer. It expanded its offerings significantly in the 1980s, and by the late 1990s it sold a variety of policies, from dental care to short-term disability to hospital-confinement indemnity and life insurance. In 1990 the company adopted the acronym "AFLAC" as its official name. By 2000 Aflac was insuring more than forty million people. The company excelled at providing policies that helped pay out-of-pocket expenses not covered by someone's primary insurer. This was also known as "supplemental insurance." Aflac was respected in the industry, and in January 2000 *Fortune* included it in its list of the one hundred best companies to work for in the United States. Because of the Fortune 500 company's solid core business and steady growth, in 1999 the National Association of Investors Corporation named Aflac one of its favorite stocks.

Aflac was especially adept at reaching out to small businesses. It tailored certain plans specifically for this market, with a sales force of about 60,000 that helped reach small businesses face to face. It was also the largest provider of guaranteed-renewable insurance in the United States. The company thrived overseas as well, becoming the largest provider of individual insurance policies in

Japan. Aflac's primary business strategy revolved around expanding its product line and focusing on gaining clients through businesses.

Target Market

Aflac was especially eager to connect with consumers in the thirty-five- to fifty-four-year-old age group and to boost sales of accident and disability insurance. While the company's cancer-expense insurance had always been the backbone of its sales, there was not much room for growth in that sector. For Aflac to grow, it needed to expand its other businesses. Because accident/liability insurance was a major part of the industry, Aflac felt that this was the area it most needed to expand. The company also wanted to sell more of its supplemental insurance.

Aflac especially wanted to reach consumers with families. Insurance was a buyer's market. Many companies offered similar coverage policies, and it was important to stand out. Aflac had a good reputation, but its difficult-to-remember name impeded its efforts to attract new customers; only about 12 percent of consumers remembered the brand's name. This limited the company's new sales leads.

Objectives

1. Improve consumer awareness.
2. Expand accident/liability product line.
3. Expand supplemental insurance.

Competition

Aflac's primary competition came from other accident and health-insurance brands, such as Citizens Financial Corp., Conseco, and Amerisafe. All offered services comparable to Aflac's. Several companies were competing in the sector, making Aflac's low brand recognition a serious liability. Aflac issued 98 percent of its coverage on a payroll-deduction basis. This meant that while the company's sales force and its reputation could help it sell its products to cost-conscious corporations, it had a hard time drawing sales leads outside of the corporate sphere. Aflac believed that it needed to change its image with consumers to survive in a tough industry.

Marketing Strategy

Aflac contracted the ad agency Kaplan Thaler Group (KTG), a division of Bcom3 based in New York City, to help the brand break through to consumers. This was the first major campaign conducted by KTG on Aflac's behalf. The company earmarked $35 million for the campaign. KTG cofounders Linda Kaplan Thaler and Robin Koval had developed an approach to advertising they called the "Big Bang." A "Big Bang" campaign altered people's perceptions of a brand or product. Aflac decided this was a good approach for the company.

While trying to develop an idea for the Aflac campaign, some of KTG's personnel had trouble remembering the brand's name themselves. While repeating the name in an effort to memorize it, the ad agency employees noticed that it sounded a little like a duck quacking. That prompted the creation of Aflac's new "spokesman," the Aflac Duck.

The new "Duck" campaign began on December 21, 1999. Gilbert Gottfried, a nasal-voiced comedian known for his work in such films as *Beverly Hills Cop 2*, performed the Duck's voice. One key spot featured two men in a steam room talking about insurance. One man was praising his insurance company, which helped him pay his out-of-pocket expenses following a serious accident. Every time he forgot the company's name, the Aflac Duck popped up to remind him by quacking, "Aflac." As the conversation continued, the Duck grew increasingly impatient with the man, eventually shouting at him. This was the second spot in the campaign, following the Duck's debut in "Park Bench," which featured a similar conversation held on a park bench. Both commercials revolved around people's difficulty in remembering the company's name.

More spots followed. One showed a young couple discussing having their first child. They realized they needed supplemental insurance and were trying to think of the name of a good insurer. Once again, the Duck appeared to remind them: "Aflac." All the initial spots played on the theme of consumers' difficulty in remembering the insurer's name. The commercials turned this weakness into a strength by using it as the source of much of the campaign's humor. The Duck himself was a humorous character, especially in the way he grew increasingly frustrated by consumers' inability to either recall Aflac's name or listen to his prompts.

The spots were mostly aired as a part of what the ad industry called a "prime-time roadblock," a strategy involving running the same commercial on many different stations at about the same time. Aflac ensured a large audience by airing spots during every major network evening news program. The spots were also aired on CNN during *Larry King Live* and *Headline News* and on the financial network CNBC throughout the day. In addition, the spots ran during major sporting events, especially college football, professional baseball, and major tennis tournaments such as Wimbledon. As the campaign took off, the company's advertising spread into prime-time programming across the three major networks: ABC, NBC, and CBS. In July 2001 the Duck made his premiere in Japan, where it was just as successful.

Outcome

The "Duck" campaign was an unqualified success. *USA Today* reported that, based on a poll conducted by the newspaper and market-research firm Harris Interactive, it was one of the most popular campaigns of 2000. The company's name recognition among consumers shot up from 12 percent immediately before the campaign to a resounding 71 percent after the Duck's introduction. As the campaign continued, Aflac's brand recognition soared above 90 percent. The "Duck" spots were a key reason. According to advertising research company Ipsos ASI, the initial "Duck" campaign scored more than double the industry average in brand recall. Aflac also saw sales improve. In the first two weeks of 2000, the company had more sales leads than in all of 1998 and 1999 combined. It also saw annualized premium sales jump 28.5 percent in the second quarter of 2000, giving the company a record $168 million in sales that quarter. For the first time, accident/disability insurance replaced cancer-expense insurance as the company's number-one product. Sales for the year were up a healthy 28 percent, and recruiting was up 22 percent.

The Duck's popularity prompted the company to offer stuffed "talking" Aflac Ducks, which quacked when squeezed, for sale on its website. Proceeds were donated to the Aflac Cancer Center at Children's Healthcare of Atlanta. The company's relationship with the institution dated to 1995, when it funded construction of the cancer unit. Aflac promoted the initiative on CNBC's *Power Lunch*. Company CEO Dan Amos appeared on the program in July with the Duck. The Duck made return appearances on the program throughout the month, promoting the charity effort. By August the company had raised $75,000.

Aflac's reputation thrived. In 2001 *Fortune* named it the fifth most-admired company in the health and life insurance industry. The magazine cited Aflac's "bold approach to advertising" as one reason for the honor. The Aflac Duck became a cultural icon, and the company began to associate itself with the Duck mascot, placing it on the company's website. In 2004 the Duck was named one of the country's favorite advertising figures, besting such characters as Ronald McDonald to become one of the inaugural members of the Advertising Walk of Fame in New York City.

In subsequent years, several celebrities appeared in "Duck" spots, including comedian Chevy Chase, retired baseball star Yogi Berra, and singer Wayne Newton. The Duck was also featured on television shows *The Tonight Show with Jay Leno* and *Saturday Night Live*. The Duck would remain the focus of Aflac's advertising for several years. To explain the company's services better, however, the company began to deemphasize the Duck in some of its advertising in 2004.

Source: "The Aflac Duck (2000) Campaign," Marketing Campaign Case Studies, http://marketing-case-stud ies.blogspot.com/search/label/Aflac%20Inc.

commercial should display a toll-free number, website, or hashtag where the target can find additional information, technical assistance, or help in placing an order. This interaction is active and takes place in the form of a dialogue, or **two-way communication**. The target identifies the message, digests the information, and can get a direct response from the advertised source with just the click of a mouse or push of a few buttons. Advertising clutter is reduced because the target chooses what he wants to see and when he wants to see it.

Traditional advertising delivers an uninvited message to a distracted target and can take weeks or even months to build brand awareness and motivate the target to purchase. **Direct-response advertising** is immediate, allowing the consumer to buy while the commercial is still airing. There is often a bonus offering if the consumer buys in the next few minutes or is one of the first one hundred callers. Active involvement shortens the amount of time needed to build awareness, because consumers pursue additional information on their own time.

Most direct-response products, on the other hand, have little or no competition and thus make the decision to purchase generally easier and faster. Writing for direct response is simple: Grab the listener's attention within the first three to five seconds; make the offer simple, especially ordering information; use experts, testimonials, or studies to validate the product; demonstrate how the product works or what it sounds like; make ordering easy; and repeat the most important information frequently.

Writing a direct-response ad may be simple, but to say it all takes a little longer than traditional advertising, requiring around 90 to 120 seconds. This extra time is needed to lay out the specific selling points and allows the viewer to hear and/or see the product in use. Direct-response commercials are basically a shorter version of the infomercial.

Infomercials and Home Shopping Channels

Most direct-response commercials are found on cable stations, which are less expensive than the networks and have a more specialized programming format. The two most commonly seen forms of direct-response advertising are **infomercials** and home shopping channels.

Infomercials are simply long commercials, usually about thirty to sixty minutes long. This extended commercial message allows time for a demonstration of how the product works; testimonials from satisfied customers; perhaps a professional endorsement or two by an engineer, health professional, or scientist; and finally, the payment and ordering options. The basic premise of these long commercials is no different from that of their shorter fifteen- to thirty-second cousins: Entertain and inform the viewer while making a sale. Infomercials are popular and effective due to their use of toll-free numbers, the acceptance of credit cards, ease of return, and the ability to log on to a website for reviews.

Home shopping channels allow the consumer to purchase anything from jewelry to mattresses from the comfort of their own recliners by dialing a toll-free number, texting, logging on to a website, or using a mobile app. Special prices or payment options are prevalent, and returns are easy. Unlike infomercials, home shopping channels do not concentrate on selling one item from one manufacturer but offer multiple items, often from multiple manufacturers. The channel's designated host most often presents products, but a product representative, designer, or inventor may also present the product's attributes to the viewer. A one-hour program may include anything from pots and pans to hair products, and each product will receive anywhere from ten to fifteen minutes of presentation time.

The Diversity of the Television Advertising Voice

How Television Breaks Down
Television can be categorized into five separate areas: network, spot, cable, syndication, and public.

Network Television
Network television is home to the big four networks: ABC, CBS, Fox, and NBC, with each receiving a sizable share of the available advertising revenue and viewing audience.

Network affiliates, local television stations located across the country, are paid to air network programming at a predetermined time. When network programming is not filling the schedule, local stations fill airtime with local broadcasts or nationally syndicated programs.

Spot Television
Spot television gives advertisers the opportunity to run their ads in individual markets rather than on a national basis. These commercials air between programs, while network advertising airs during programming. Most local advertising revenue is generated from these spots.

Cable Television
Viewers can receive the big four networks in their homes for free, but cable television is a subscription service. Because of this, cable receives income from both subscription rates and advertising revenue. Cable advertising is less expensive than nationally placed advertising, and the highly selective and special-interest programming on many channels makes reaching a specific target audience easier. Unlike network programming that offers a more generic schedule of shows, different cable channels offer very specialized lineups, including news,

movies, documentaries, history, sports, and children's programming, with most running twenty-four hours a day, every day.

Broadcast Syndication

Programs that are in syndication are produced independently and then sold to individual local stations with no consideration being given to any one network affiliation. Syndicated programs can also include reruns of older programs. Local stations are granted some of the commercial airtime, while the syndicate sells its portion to national advertisers.

Original content developed by Netflix and Hulu are popular options and often boast big stars and smaller budgets than programming viewed on traditional television or cable stations. Unlike network programs that are aired at a certain time and day, viewing of original Internet content is determined mostly by the subscriber.

To promote the release of *House of Cards* and *Arrested Development*, Netflix, for example, used TV, print, and online advertising. However, it used very little advertising to promote the show *Orange Is the New Black*. Netflix could do this because it has a lot of data on what its subscribers want to see. Although Netflix's programming may be advertising-free, ads are not absent entirely. A subtler form of advertising used in a vast array of programs is **product placement**, also known as **native advertising**, or advertising placed within programming, eliminating the need for long commercial breaks. Since most characters must eat, drink, drive, use a computer, make a call, or clean up, product placement can be seamlessly and silently woven into the script. Because of the ever-growing number of original-content series being developed for Internet television, it is not unlikely for consumers to subscribe to multiple services if each one offers unique content that is of interest to them.

Sponsor Public Television

Public television is largely noncommercial and supported by individual viewers and in part by nonprofit organizations and state and local governments. Corporate sponsors often underwrite certain programs, but the use of traditional advertising methods on public television is rare. While some sponsored announcements have evolved into a shorter, less-aggressive version of commercial advertising, most sponsorships are understated and use only a logo, slogan or tagline, address, and/or phone number.

How Does Television Advertising Help IMC Be Consumer Focused?

Television involves the viewer through sight, sound sets the tone or mood, and motion allows the target to see the product in action. Used together, sight, sound, and motion place the product in the target's imagination and life. Television is a very expensive mass-media vehicle. It is important when using television to be sure the target is watching. The hit-or-miss mentality of years gone by has been replaced with a high degree of selective targeting. Cable allows advertisers to select specific channels and programming that can reach the intended target in the same way magazines and radio can.

In an IMC campaign, it is important that every time the target is exposed to the message, no matter the vehicle, it reinforces the key consumer benefit and projects the strategy. Look to what visuals are being used in other materials, and be sure the dialogue matches the tone of voice. Beyond that, consider color, spokespersons or character representatives, headline styles, or the execution techniques used elsewhere in the promotional mix to bind the IMC pieces together.

Each of advertising's media vehicles, except for newspaper, takes advantage of audience fragmentation and focuses on reaching the consumer through selective targeting based on special interests, making advertising a great place to build brand awareness or brand image. Public relations can be used to toot a corporation's own horn. Newspaper offers time-sensitive offers and low price. Magazines offer tradition, status, prestige, and class. Radio brings interaction through location-based promotions; and television entertains with sight, sound, and motion and demonstrates the product in use. Social media can help spread the message virally.

When used in conjunction with television, public relations can be used to sponsor or promote local charity events or to acknowledge a corporation's local or national contribution to important ecological or safety issues.

Magazines and television can be a powerful combination if the objective is building or projecting a product's image. Used together, these two vehicles can deliver unique, unusual, and creative solutions to an image-based strategy.

Magazines, cable television, and radio advertising are all great vehicles for selective and specific targeting. Reaching and affecting the target are made easier because special-interest magazines and programming allow advertising to talk directly to the target's interests.

When used as a support vehicle to television or other media within the promotional mix, radio allows listeners to take part in the message by imagining themselves using, wearing, or tasting the product. Purchase can take place quickly by encouraging the target to drop by and test drive, pick up a sample, or set up an appointment.

By including an interactive component, television can draw the target to a web or social media site or to customer service representatives. Information found there can be used to build a relationship between the buyer and seller and contribute to building brand loyalty and equity. Television may be a one-way monologue, but the information presented can encourage interaction through additional research or even trial.

Tying television to social media can create additional interaction. This media marriage is more about integrating a product into television programming than the creation of a traditional advertising commercial. Television advertising used in conjunction with social media is known as social TV. Social TV is not about the hard sell; it's about the overall user experience or the value of the brand placement and interactive experience. In an online August 17, 2012, eMarketer article entitled "USA Network Brings Advertisers into Its Social TV Journey," USA Network digital senior vice president Jessie Redniss tells us: "They are trying to bring brand advertisers into the conversation." For example, movies such as *Pitch Perfect 2* showcased Apple computers, and Dell computers showed up in *Jason Bourne*. Eyewear also plays a major product placement role in movies. A prominent character in *Deadpool* wore a pair of Oxydo glasses throughout the film, Ray-Ban got a lot of screen time in *X-Men: Apocalypse*, and iGreen starred on Melissa McCarthy in *Ghostbusters*. News outlets also get a shout-out: CNN got two and a half minutes of airtime in *Batman v. Superman: Dawn of Justice*.

Television and digital programming are laden with brands. Netflix's *House of Cards* uses product placement regularly. Featured brands include Dell, Coke, iPhone, iPad, and Chevrolet. *American Horror Story* featured Mercedes-Benz, McDonald's found its way into an episode of *The Bachelor*, and Ford shows up in *Angie Tribeca*.

In a March 24, 2011, online MediaPost article entitled "TV Advertising Most Influential," Jack Loechner adds that interaction works: "The survey indicates that the Internet, mobile, and social media channels are enhancing the overall television viewer experience, driving people to watch first-run programs and live events during their initial broadcast." What does this mean? Television viewers are using these various devices to share their thoughts and ideas about programs and advertising they are currently watching, proving that interactive use of social media creates ads that are not only engaging but also a great way to extend the intended message.

Incentives and Deterrents of Television Advertising

To decide whether television advertising is right for an IMC campaign, let's look at some of the incentives and deterrents associated with it.

What Makes Television Advertising So Great?

The more notable incentives associated with television advertising include:

- *Impact.* Television delivers sight, sound, and motion, allowing the target to view the product, see it in action or in the proper setting, and hear the message—all at the same time.
- *Selectivity.* Between the networks and cable, television offers enough diverse programming to selectively choose the exact program the target will be watching, eliminating hit-or-miss placement and cutting down on advertising waste.
- *Audience size.* Television is a mass-media vehicle that reaches a lot of people. Although network television does not reach the numbers of viewers it once did, it is still one of the best ways to reach a target. Network television's national reach allows advertising to introduce, maintain, or reposition a brand's image.
- *Trends and fads.* Television sets trends and influences the way we look and talk; we believe what we see on the screen. We are influenced by what we watch and adapt it to our vernacular or wardrobe. Programming and advertising often rolls over into our personal and work environments as we talk about what we saw on television the night before.

Is There Anything Wrong with Television Advertising?

The more notable deterrents associated with television advertising include:

- *Cost.* Television advertising is expensive. The length of the commercial, the program airing, and the time the commercial will run all determine cost. It is important to

know where the targets will be and what they will be watching when considering
television as a viable media option.

- *Clutter.* There are a lot of commercials running in any given time slot, some running
  back to back. To fight consumer apathy and remote-control rampages, an ad must
  stand out visually and verbally by specifically addressing the target audience and its
  needs.
- *Fleeting message.* Television commercials are fleeting; the creative team has only fifteen
  or possibly thirty seconds to make a point to a group of people who need a sandwich
  or a bathroom break. Develop concepts that repeat major points, and use music to
  flag the target to stop, look, and listen; if she missed the ad the first time around, the
  music can announce a repeat performance.

The Strategy behind Television Advertising

Writing for television is not an easy task. Copywriters must balance their words with the
video portion of the commercial. They must also ensure that the proper information is
included to strategically promote the key consumer benefit and ultimately accomplish the
stated objectives. All copy decisions will be based on strategy decisions stated in the creative
brief.

How can a story be told in only fifteen to thirty seconds and still accomplish the
objectives set up in the creative brief? What will make the key consumer benefit stand out
strategically? Consider some of the following:

- Let the research guide you.
- Make the key consumer benefit relevant to the target.
- Talk to the target audience in words and about situations they can relate to.
- Open with the key consumer benefit.
- Be sure the commercial stays on strategy and on target. Be sure it reflects the same
  visual aspects and tone of voice as other pieces in the IMC campaign.
- Choose a tone or execution technique that complements and highlights the key
  consumer benefit and accomplishes the stated objectives.
- If showing a particular feature or benefit is more powerful than simply talking about
  it, then do so.
- Get to the point and hammer it home, frame after frame.
- Make sure the audio and video work together as a cohesive unit.
- Write to the target. Have the announcer or voice-over talk directly to the target, or
  have the talent deal with situations the target can relate to.
- Mention the product's name and show its packaging repeatedly so that the target
  will remember it.
- Make the key consumer benefit the star of the commercial, and make sure it is clearly
  pointed out to the target.
- Involve the target in the commercial. Show her how she will look in the product or
  how it will keep her kids safe or make her clothes whiter; tell her about the benefits

the product or service delivers. Give the target an interactive activity such as down-loading a mobile app, visiting a web or social media site, or calling a toll-free number for more information.

- Make sure the commercial is the right length. The announcer or talent should be able to speak and move at a natural pace, without rushing. Fill any holes where there is no action taking place.
- Be sure the last frame in the storyboard has either the logo or a final shot of the product with the logo showing. To assist with recall, especially for a new or reinvented product, both are preferred.

It is important to remember that the key consumer benefit must be sold in every frame. It cannot be mentioned or shown only once. Television's short life span, fleeting messages, and inattentive audience require the key consumer benefit to scream out for fifteen or thirty seconds.

Objectives best suited for television advertising include product demonstrations and concepts that entertain, excite, or have a social or personal impact.

Strategically, there is no approach, appeal, or execution technique that does not work for television. The creative team is armed with a toolbox of creative opportunities to show and tell, demonstrate, and activate the target's imagination.

The Sight, Sound, and Motion of Television Design

Television is more than just the random use of sight, sound, and motion. It is about deter-mining the most appropriate setting for the product, the correct choice of talent to deliver the message, the right lighting to set the scene, and the appropriate use of props and music to set the mood or make a point. Finally, the pace or delivery of the message must be in keeping with the overall look and tone of the message. Television is the coordination of sight, sound, and motion.

A television commercial begins as a **storyboard**. This storyboard consists of two parts: the visual aspects, or **scenes**, and the **script**, or what will be said and heard. Television scripts are much more detailed than radio scripts; because television requires a lot more people to produce a spot, the storyboard and accompanying script must talk not only to the client but also to talent, directors, camera operators, lighting and sound people, producers, editors, composers, food stylists, and computer animators, to name just a few.

The Ins and Outs of a Television Shoot

Designing, planning, and shooting a television commercial is a complicated and lengthy process. Very little is done on a whim or at the last minute. Most commercial shoots can take anywhere from several days to several weeks to complete. Before any actual footage is shot, the creative team, along with the director, must walk through the shoot and go over any changes; hold auditions; look at possible locations; gather up the product, props, or cos-tumes; and go over the various technical aspects of the shoot, such as lighting and sound, with the production crew.

Additional decisions, such as whether the television commercial should be produced on film, videotape, or digitally, are made at this point, as are decisions about media placement. Most decisions will be made during the preproduction, production, and postproduction phases. Preproduction includes the development of the script and storyboard, budget, and the hiring of on-air talent, a director, and a production crew. The production stage includes the actual shoot; postproduction includes the editing process.

Big, Small, and Elaborate Productions

How and where a commercial is shot depends on the product, the budget, and the strategy. Commercials can be done relatively inexpensively when shot and produced locally. This type of shoot is relatively simple and contains few bells or whistles. The goal is to get the message out as quickly and effectively as possible.

Nationally produced commercials, on the other hand, use all the bells and whistles necessary to attract the targeted audience. These spots are usually produced and often shot in major advertising markets and then delivered to major affiliates or cable television stations.

Many national spots are produced right in the studio, employing expensive computer graphics. Real or animated talent may be developed to attract attention or to create a specialized atmosphere or a special effect.

Another, often equally expensive option, is to shoot away from a production studio, or "on location," where a remote site is used for the background of the commercial. Locations may be exotic or mundane and are determined by the commercial's overall strategy or concept. Being shot on location gives a sense of reality to the commercial, allowing consumers to see the product in the setting in which it might be used.

Scripts and Storyboards

A television commercial is made up of a script and accompanying storyboard.

Television Scripts

A television script is a very detailed document. Not only does it include everything that will be heard, such as dialogue, music, jingles, and sound effects, but it also contains details; any special instructions to talent, camera, and sound and editing people; and any information concerning scene changes.

Storyboards

Storyboards show the visual portion of the commercial and the timing sequence between what is heard and what is seen, one frame at a time. See figure 12.1 for a sample blank storyboard showing windows for video and boxes for audio.

The visual aspects of a television commercial are known as **scenes**. Each scene is confined in a frame, or the shape of a television screen, on the storyboard. Each individual scene depicts a major piece of action or location change. Any given scene may require additional shots from a variety of angles, but there is no need to show them all. A fifteen- to thirty-second spot usually consists of four to six frames; a longer, less-common, sixty-second spot will need six to eight frames.

Student Name: _____

15   or   30   Second Spot (Circle One)

Name of Television Spot: _____

Grade: _____

Figure 12.1. Sample blank storyboard.

Under each frame appears the accompanying dialogue, sound effects, and music, or the audio portion of the commercial (or the portion of the script that corresponds to that scene). This is an exact reproduction of the script combined with the visual action. A **storyboard** is how the commercial will be presented to the client and any other major production players. The script alone will be used almost exclusively by the talent, although members of the production team may also consult it.

The storyboard lays out the action. Since you cannot realistically show every scene, choose just the most important ones: those that move the commercial forward and that show concept direction. Great artistic skills are not a prerequisite for the visual aspect of the storyboard; the message is more important.

The actual television shoot is exhausting and stressful; two or three seconds of actual footage can take several hours to shoot. It is important to have a detailed script to keep the enormous number of people it takes to shoot one thirty-second spot on the same page. Copies of the script should be distributed to the talent, the director, the client, and the varied production staff, to name just a few. If everybody is on the same page when shooting begins, the commercial will be much more likely to shoot on schedule—and stay on budget.

The cost of shooting and producing a television spot is huge. Television airtime needs to be bought, which is a major chunk of the budget; the spot must be designed, the script written, and the talent and production crew hired. If the plan is to go on location or use a celebrity or computer-generated images, the cost skyrockets even higher. A detailed storyboard is imperative. It must be very tight and very detailed; the schedule and budget can be significantly affected if the storyboard is incomplete or requires changes of any kind once shooting begins. A good storyboard lets the entire production team know in advance where they need to be and what needs to be done.

How to Deliver the Message

Before choosing an execution technique for a commercial, look to the strategy to help determine the best approach or combination of approaches needed to deliver the USP or big idea. Each appeal will be effective, no matter whether an emotional or rational style is used.

Commercial Tones and Execution Techniques

Consider one or a combination of the following execution techniques to deliver the commercial's tone of voice:

- Slice of life
- Spokesperson
- Testimonials
- Demonstration
- Torture tests
- Visual images
- Metaphors

- Creative comparisons
- Vignette
- Expert presenters

Slice of Life

Slice of life refers to the dramatization of a little slice of the target audience's everyday life. This type of approach presents the product as a problem solver. The standard format introduces the viewer to the product, the characters, and the problem. Next it shows the viewer how the product can solve one or more of the problems, perhaps in a series of vignettes, or short stories. The closing tells viewers that the next time they have a similar problem, the product can make their lives better, easier, or healthier.

Spokesperson

The choice of a spokesperson or animated character representative will define the personality and overall image of the product or service. The creative team will have to decide if this visual representative should be real or animated: a celebrity, the CEO or company president, or an unknown person whose image will become synonymous with the product or service. The choice of representative should match the image of the product and the target. Important considerations might include age, gender, and appearance, such as height, weight, and demeanor. How should the character or spokesperson sound? Should his voice be average or distinctive, or perhaps a deep baritone or a Southern drawl is appropriate? All these decisions will affect how the product or service will be viewed—and, hopefully, remembered. The perfect spokesperson should represent, or add to, the product's inherent drama. There is no reason to settle for only one speaker. Whether the spokesperson(s) or character representative(s) appear on-screen or as off-screen speakers who are heard but not seen, additional personalities give life to a concept and to dialogue.

Testimonials

Getting a current user to talk about his or her experiences with the product or service is priceless. Real people have credibility and are often quite colorful. It can be difficult to work with people not trained to perform on cue, however, so depending on the approach needed, the budget, and/or the time frame, it may prove easier to use real experiences from the public delivered by trained actors. This approach does require the acknowledgment that trained actors are used in lieu of the actual consumers.

Demonstration

Television is great for this show-and-tell approach, which offers several options:

- *Side by side.* If there are distinct differences between the client's product and the competition, consider placing the products side by side and pointing out the differentiating or unique features.
- *Before and after.* There are times when it is better to show how a product solves a problem rather than talk about it. Here, the product is challenged by a problem it quickly solves.

- *Product in use.* This technique shows the product in action while discussing the relevant features and benefits.
- *New and innovative uses.* This type of demonstration is great for reinvented products that have undergone a transformation from one use to another.

Demonstrations must be based on proven results to be credible. If there have been any scientific results or government stamps of approval, or if the product is simply unique, consider showing viewers, rather than telling them, about the product or results.

Torture Tests
If durability is an important product feature, rip it, tear it, and beat it to a pulp. Do not hesitate to show how the product performs under adverse conditions.

Visual Images
Images are windows to opening the viewer's imagination. If the strategy is to develop an image campaign for the product, consider using visuals to set the scene. What kinds of images, real or imagined, does the product bring to mind? Can some of these visual solutions be combined or perhaps create new associations or ideas? Images should present the message both visually and verbally.

Metaphors
If the product can be compared to something not usually associated with it, like skunks to litter boxes, showing it can attract attention and prove a point more quickly than thirty seconds of copy.

Creative Comparisons
Comparing the product to a great work of art or a famous piece of music creates status and indicates quality.

Vignette
A vignette is a series of short stories that are tied together to highlight the product's key consumer benefit. These stories may have a repeated character or feature a variety of characters who routinely use the product to solve a problem.

Expert Presenters
An expert in a relevant field—such as a scientist, engineer, or CEO—lends credibility to product claims. A celebrity can also be used to represent status or class or just to define the essence of cool by using or wearing the product.

The Length of a Commercial Message
Length depends on budget, but the most common television spot is thirty seconds. It is not uncommon for advertisers to purchase a thirty-second spot and then break the commercial time in half, producing two related fifteen-second commercials. This allows the advertised message to deliver two separate points in succession, building awareness one feature

or benefit at a time. If the dual messages are mutually dependent, this technique is called **piggybacking.** If the budget allows, a sixty-second spot offers more time to drive the key consumer benefit home.

Who Is Going to Talk the Talk and React to the Sounds We Hear?

There are many sounds in a television commercial, whether spoken, created, or musically based. Let's take a short look at each one.

Talent

Talent refers to the individuals who will be seen on camera speaking the copy or dialogue; it also includes any off-screen announcers who will be heard delivering the copy. It is important that the talent visually and/or verbally represent the product and target image.

Voice-Over

When an announcer is heard reading the dialogue but is not seen on camera, this is known as a voice-over. A voice-over can be used to deliver all the dialogue or just the closing. This is often a good time to consider using a recognizable celebrity voice. Using a celebrity in a television commercial is less expensive when the celebrity is only heard and not seen.

Announcer

An announcer is both seen and heard on camera delivering the dialogue. This is a great way to associate, introduce, or use a character representative or spokesperson as the voice and face of the brand.

Music

Music is used to set a mood. Imagine a movie without the soundtrack; we wouldn't know how to react or what to expect when the action finally takes place. Music can be used to replace words, represent an emotion, or assist in placing the viewer in the proper emotional state. Volume can also be used to set a mood. Music should be used in the same way talent and dialogue are used to tell the story.

Sound Effects

SFX replicate reality. Almost everyone can relate to the headache caused by the slamming of a door, the tension associated with screaming babies, or the calming sound of the ocean. SFX should support the message, not get in the way of it.

The Preparation of Television Scripts and Storyboards

A script is laid out in three columns. Column 1 is used to label the frames, column 2 is for labeling instructions, and column 3 is for dialogue, music, SFX, and any special instructions. Be sure each label lines up with the corresponding information. Labels must be set in all caps; instructions should be enclosed in parentheses. All dialogue should be typed in caps and lowercase and enclosed in quotation marks. Be sure to double-space the script, place half an inch to one inch of space between columns, and use one-inch margins on all four sides.

There are many ways to lay out or set up a script; the following is just one possible approach. Let's take a look at each script item in the order in which it should appear. Depending on the action happening in the script, placement of SFX, music, or dialogue can be altered. Any information concerning **camera instructions**, camera shots, or **frame transitions** must be consistent from frame to frame, no matter the content or concept. When preparing copy for a television shoot, nothing can be assumed or taken for granted. Television is expensive, and there are too many people involved to safely use generalities. When in doubt about an instruction, write it out.

Opening Frame

Each storyboard must be opened. The first, or opening, frame must describe what will be seen when the commercial begins. OPEN: (on grocery store checkout), followed immediately by the camera shot. OPEN is used only in frame 1. All additional frames will use the frame transition, or the last instruction in the frame, to tell us what we will see next in each additional frame.

Camera Shots

Camera shots are the first thing to appear in every frame except frame 1, where an opening description of the scene appears. Camera shots tell the cameraperson how close or how far away to be from an image or scene. Refer to the human figure depicted in figure 12.2 to see what the camera is focusing on. Adapt this example to the product; the visual cue would be the same if the camera were shooting an apple, a car, or a dirty dish.

The following is a list of possible camera shots for use in a script:

ECU (extreme close-up):	Chin to top of the head would appear in the shot
MCU (medium close-up):	Throat to top of the head
FCU (full close-up):	Neck to top of the head
WCU (wide close-up):	Collarbone area to top of the head
CU (close-up):	Chest area to top of the head
MCS (medium close shot):	Waist to top of the head
MS (medium shot):	Stomach to top of the head
MFS (medium full shot):	Knees to top of the head
FS (full shot):	Bottom of the feet to top of the head

No instructions appear beside a camera shot. The camera shot tells only the position of the camera, not what the camera will be looking at. When writing a script, there is no need to spell any of the camera shots out; use only the abbreviations, and place in all caps.

Camera Instructions

Camera instructions tell the camera what to do or how to move in a shot. Camera instructions can appear anywhere in a frame, depending on when the camera needs to move. If each shot will be a stationary or STILL shot, it needs only to be mentioned in frame 1, following the camera shot. If the camera instruction begins as a STILL shot but moves to a PAN in frame 3, for instance, the script must state that camera instruction in frame 3. If it

Camera Shot Frames

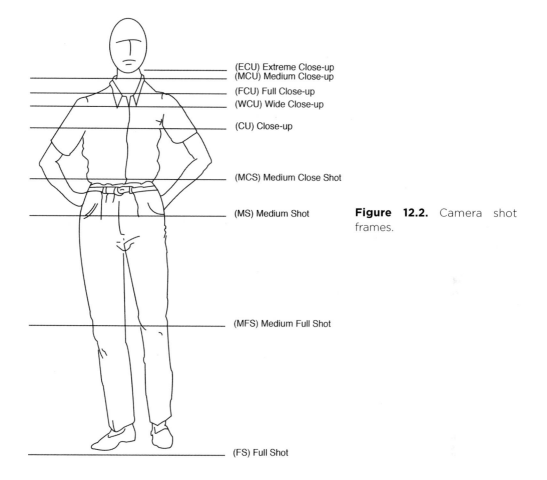

Figure 12.2. Camera shot frames.

is not mentioned, the camera will not be there, set up and ready to go when needed. If the camera goes back to a STILL in frame 4, it must be stated in frame 4. Camera instructions follow camera shots in a frame.

The following is a list of possible camera instructions for use in a script. See box 12.1 for example use of camera shots and instructions.

STILL SHOT:	Instruction for camera to hold on the shot, no movement at all.
PAN SHOT:	This instruction tells the camera to move horizontally left or right from a fixed point. It is important to tell the camera which way the pan should go, PAN LEFT or PAN RIGHT.
TILT SHOT:	This instruction tells the camera to move up or down from a fixed point. Again, be sure to tell the camera which way to go, TILT UP or TILT DOWN.
ZOOM SHOT:	This instruction tells the camera to move in for a rapid close-up or away to a distance shot, ZOOM IN or ZOOM OUT.

BOX 12.1. Camera Shot and Instruction Examples

Frame 1:	OPEN:	(Open onto a grocery store checkout line full of people.)
	MCS:	
	CAMERA:	STILL.
	SFX IN and UNDER:	SFX IN (A lot of people complaining and mumbling in background) UNDER.
	WOMAN 1:	"Why don't they get some more help around here?"
	SFX OUT:	SFX (Of people complaining and mumbling in background) OUT.
	CUT TO:	(Another grocery store where another woman is checking out her own groceries.)
Frame 2:	MFS:	
	CAMERA:	PAN (grocery store, notice all the available checkout lanes) LEFT AND RIGHT.
	CAMERA:	STILL.
	WOMAN 1:	"Grocery shopping is always fast and easy."
	MUSIC IN and UNDER:	MUSIC IN ("A Hot Time in the Old Town Tonight") UNDER.
	ANN:	"At So So Bees, you will never have to stand in line. Open 24 hours, for your convenience."
	MUSIC OUT:	MUSIC ("A Hot Time in the Old Town Tonight") OUT.
	SUPER:	(Logo on parking lot, with grocery store in the background.)

DOLLY SHOT: This instruction tells the entire camera to move forward or backward more slowly than a zoom shot, DOLLY BACK or DOLLY FORWARD.

BOOM SHOT: This instruction tells the camera the shot needs to come from above, from either a boom or a crane. Used for overhead views.

TRUCK SHOT: This instruction tells the camera to shoot alongside a moving subject. Again, be sure to tell the camera where to be and what to do, TRUCK SHOT (along the right side and slightly to the back of the runner).

Audio Instructions

Audio instructions can appear before or after a character speaks in a frame. The placement depends on when the listener will hear the noise or music.

The following is a list of possible audio instructions for use in a script.

SFX: Use SFX alone when a noise is brief and immediately over: SFX (one hand clap).

SFX IN:	This instruction signals the sound to begin and continue: SFX (the clattering of pots and pans) IN.
SFX OUT:	Instruction to end the sound effect: SFX (the clattering of pots and pans) OUT.
SFX UP:	This instruction asks for the volume to increase: SFX (of clapping hands) UP.
SFX DOWN:	This instruction asks for the volume to decrease: SFX (of clapping hands) DOWN.
SFX UNDER:	This instruction asks for the volume to go under or to decrease in volume enough that dialogue can be spoken over it: SFX IN (of clapping hands) UNDER.
MUSIC UP:	This instruction asks for the volume to increase: MUSIC ("Old MacDonald Had a Farm") UP.
MUSIC DOWN:	This instruction asks for the volume to decrease: MUSIC ("Old MacDonald Had a Farm") DOWN.
MUSIC UNDER:	This instruction asks for the volume to go under or to decrease enough that dialogue can be spoken over it: MUSIC IN ("Old MacDonald Had a Farm") UNDER.
SEGUE:	This instruction signals there is more than one piece of music being used. A segue is a musical transition from one song to another, often used to indicate a change in time, place, or mood: SEGUE ("Old MacDonald Had a Farm" to "Row, Row, Row Your Boat").
FADE:	This instruction indicates that the noise or music needs to fade out or away.

Note: *Both SFX and music can continue from frame to frame or go in, out, or under from frame to frame as needed. Use music to set a mood or pace, and use SFX only if they move the commercial along and help make a point. Too many noises can be annoying and can distract from the message.*

Dialogue

Dialogue includes anything spoken by the talent, on- or off-screen, and can appear before or after SFX or camera instructions. All dialogue should be typed in caps/lowercase and enclosed in quotes. See box 12.2 for example frames with dialogue and SFX.

VO:	(Voice-over) This instruction indicates that the speaker will be heard but not seen on air.
ANN:	(Announcer) This instruction indicates that the speaker will be seen and heard on air.
RUSS:	If you are creating a recurring character whose name will be used within the commercial, label the part appropriately.
WOMAN or MAN:	If more than one person will be speaking in the commercial, label their parts separately. If they are not recurring characters and no

---

BOX 12.2. A Sample Frame Showing Dialogue and Sound Effects

If more than one person will be speaking in the commercial, label their parts separately. If they are not recurring characters and no names are used in the dialogue, there is no reason to assign specific names.

WOMAN 1:	"Hey, what's for dinner?"
SFX IN and UNDER:	SFX IN (rattling of pots and pans) UNDER.
WOMAN 2:	"Kraft Macaroni and Cheese."
MAN 1:	"Yummy."
SFX OUT:	SFX (rattling of pots and pans) OUT.

---

names are used in the dialogue, there is no reason to assign specific names.

Frame Transitions

Frame transitions tell the director and postproduction editors how to get out of one frame and into the next. They also indicate what will be seen in the next frame.

Frame transitions appear in the bottom of every frame except the last one. The final frame does not need a transition because the network or cable station will control the move from one commercial to another or from commercial back to programming.

The following is a list of possible frame transitions for use in a script.

CUT:	This instruction indicates that the picture will change instantly or in the blink of an eye; CUT: (To CU of victim).
DISSOLVE:	This instruction indicates the transition will fade out of one picture and into another; a good way to show the passage of time. Dissolves do take a lot of time to evolve, so use them sparingly; DISSOLVE: (Show aging from youth to adult).
WIPE:	This instruction indicates the transition will physically push one picture off the screen in order to reveal another. Great for showing a rapid transition from one activity or one location to another; WIPE: (CU of wound to CU of a healed wound).
SUPER:	Use this instruction when one image will sit on top of another image, color, or pattern. The top image is then superimposed on top of the bottom image. Often, the top visual is reversed out (prints white) over the background image. Supers usually appear in the last frame and are used most often when the logo is placed on top of a background image; SUPER: (Note logo placed on top of the lake).

TEMPLATE 12.1

Example Storyboard and Script: Viravac

A script is laid out in three columns. Column 1 is used to label the frames, column 2 is for labeling instructions, and column 3 is for dialogue, music and sound effects, or any special instructions. Be sure each label lines up to the corresponding information. All labels must be set in all caps; any instructions should be enclosed in parentheses. All dialogue should be typed in caps/lowercase and enclosed in quotation marks. Be sure to double-space the script. Place one-half inch to one inch of space between columns, and use one-inch margins on all four sides.

Frame 1:	OPEN:	OPEN (on soybean field ravaged by weeds and grasses).
	MS:	
	CAMERA:	STILL.
	VO:	"You don't need a field choked with unwanted weeds."
	CUT TO:	(Shot of 50 lb. bags of Viravac.)
Frame 2:	CU:	
	VO:	"What you do need is Viravac."
	CUT TO:	(Farmer pouring bag into a field cultivator.)
Frame 3:	MS:	
	SFX IN and UNDER:	SFX IN (Sound of contents of bag being poured into the field cultivator) UNDER.
	VO:	"Simply add the correct amount of Viravac to your field cultivator or disc and let the machine do the work."
	SFX OUT:	SFX (Sound of contents of bag being poured into the field cultivator) OUT.
	CUT TO:	(Diagram of soil, weeds, and Viravac pellets.)
Frame 4:	MS:	
	VO:	"The Viravac Pellets are mixed into the top 2–3 inches of soil, where they go to work immediately to kill germinating grasses and weeds."
	CUT TO:	(Soybean field thriving without weeds or grasses.)
Frame 5:	FS:	
	CAMERA:	PAN (soybean field) LEFT AND RIGHT.
	VO:	"The results are cleaner fields; a faster, more efficient harvest; and happy farmers."
	CUT TO:	SUPER (White Viravac logo on a black screen.)
Frame 6:	CU:	
	CAMERA:	STILL.
	VO:	"Call your agricultural chemical dealer today and ask for Viravac Herbicide by name, or visit our website at www.viravac.com."

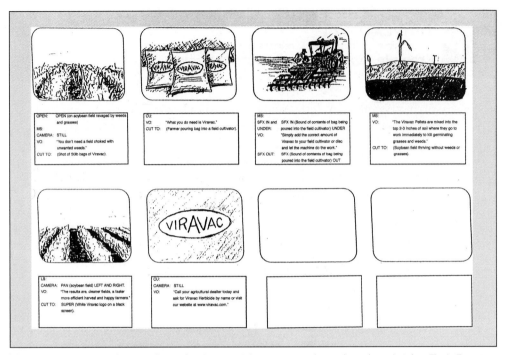

Figure 12.3. Example storyboard: Viravac. Viravac storyboard and script by T. J. Bonner, West Virginia University.

Television has a great amount of influence on who we are both as individuals and as consumers. Although consumers are watching less television, it is still a great choice when launching a new product, maintaining or reinventing an existing product, building or maintaining awareness, or developing both a product and a consumer image. Although expensive to use, television advertising can be highly targeted; with the right message, the use of sight, sound, and motion can attract and hold the target's attention long enough to make a message or image impact. If television is appropriate as part of the media mix, make it entertaining, and be sure to make it interactive by asking the target to do something.

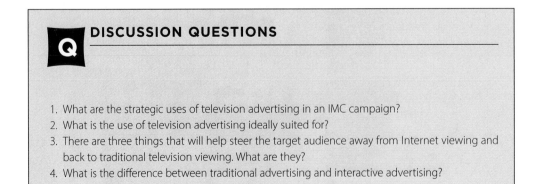

Q DISCUSSION QUESTIONS

1. What are the strategic uses of television advertising in an IMC campaign?
2. What is the use of television advertising ideally suited for?
3. There are three things that will help steer the target audience away from Internet viewing and back to traditional television viewing. What are they?
4. What is the difference between traditional advertising and interactive advertising?

5. Define an infomercial and explain the differences between an infomercial and a traditional television advertisement.
6. How does television advertising help IMC be more consumer focused?
7. What needs to be considered when deciding to use television advertising in an IMC campaign to ensure a cohesive visual and verbal message?
8. How can television be successfully integrated into the media mix?
9. What are the pros and cons of using television in an IMC campaign?
10. What is the strategy behind using television in an IMC campaign?
11. How do scripts and storyboards work together to produce a television ad?
12. What are the tones used in television advertising? Define each.
13. Explain the different types of speakers and sounds used in television commercials?
14. There are six steps that must be considered when developing a script. What are they and how are they used?
15. What types of brands can best employ television advertising?

Out-of-Home
and Transit Advertising

The Strategic Use of Out-of-Home in IMC

Any advertising seen outside the home, with few exceptions, is known as **out-of-home**. Considered a mass medium, it is one of the least expensive media vehicles and typically includes more than thirty different types of outdoor and transit vehicles, shelters, stations, and terminals.

"Minimalist" is the best way to describe the look of out-of-home advertising. Although this medium is blessed with an unusual variety of shapes and sizes, copy is limited to five to seven words, and viewing time is often restricted to only a few minutes or even a few seconds. As a media and creative device used in IMC, out-of-home must present a visual/verbal relationship that relates to and supports any other pieces used in the campaign.

Although it seems to be everywhere, out-of-home advertising is not as dominant as it may seem, amounting to less than 1 percent of all advertising in the United States. But it is growing. Overall growth can be attributed to increased creative options and to media vehicles that stand out and step up the viewing experience in order to deliver what it takes to attract today's distracted, uninvolved audience. Out-of-home is one of the few media vehicles that do not need to compete for audience attention. In many cases, viewers are a captive audience for the duration of the traffic light or the trip to or from work; consumers can't turn the ad off, throw it in the trash, change the channel, or hit the mute button.

Outdoor boards represent out-of-home's largest voice, and transit is its most mobile. Combined, their job is to reach consumers while they move through their day.

Carefully placed out-of-home advertising can be found in urban and suburban areas of large and midsize cities, in small towns, in or on public transportation, and along interstate highways nationwide. Personalized or generic messages can be developed for products sold locally, regionally, or nationally; but most of out-of-home concentrates specifically on local businesses and products.

In an IMC campaign, out-of-home vehicles work as great support media and are an excellent way to build or maintain awareness and reinforce other IMC media. See case study 11 for a look at the Metropolitan Museum of Art Out-of-Home Campaign.

The Diversity of the Out-of-Home Voice

In keeping with its role as a supplemental or support medium for other, more traditional media, out-of-home works best when used to introduce new products, as reminder advertising, or to maintain a product or service's brand image. The best way to do this is to show rather than tell. To do this effectively, advertising efforts must have three elements picked up from other vehicles in the IMC campaign: a bold visual, a short message, and a logo and package used as an identifier.

Out-of-home media vehicles do not have enough room or time to tell a product or service's full story. Their main job is to remind the public about a product or service. Copy should be simple so that the message can be absorbed easily. Bright colors will attract attention; bold visuals will help remind consumers about a product or service's story. The best copy includes a strong key consumer benefit and a slogan or tagline that can tie out-of-home to other media vehicles used in the campaign. Sometimes it will take a combination of several elements to help with product recognition and/or brand image.

Outdoor Boards

Once known as billboards, outdoor boards are one of the oldest forms of advertising. They can be traced back to the Romans, who used wall signs to direct travelers to rooms for rent and local taverns.

The Highway Beautification Act of 1965, enacted to regulate placement of outdoor advertising on interstate highways, was a direct consequence of complaints by consumers that outdoor advertising was visually polluting the environment. It didn't help that alcohol and cigarette advertising and poor creative execution dominated the ads.

Regulation and the granting of any necessary permits at the state level is controlled by each state's department of transportation. The Institute of Outdoor Advertising works continually to push for improved designs and to ensure that signs are placed in locations that do not offend people or impede the view.

Since the 1990s, creative ingenuity, along with improved technology, has greatly improved the image of outdoor advertising. Today's consumers believe that outdoor boards offer helpful travel and business information, and they enjoy the creative options.

Today's big, bold, often technology-based "in-your-face" form of advertising is creative and attractively done, and it's placed into a diverse array of public places—such as office buildings, subways, buses, airport terminals, and shopping malls. It is becoming more attrac-

CASE STUDY 11

C

IMC Out-of-Home and Transit Advertising: The Metropolitan Museum of Art

Background

The Metropolitan Museum of Art is one of the world's largest encyclopedic art museums, with artworks spanning more than 5,000 years from all corners of the globe.

Target

The multicultural richness of the collection positions the Met as a truly global museum; it is a must-see museum for tourists and a source of enormous pride for New Yorkers. Now the Met is spreading this message to tourists and locals alike through an institutional advertising campaign.

Inspiration

Inspired by the diversity of the Met's own collection and of its visitors, New York City ad agency LaPlaca Cohen approached the campaign with a dual focus: The Met brings cultures together, and the art itself transports visitors to various worlds throughout space and time.

Objective

To get people excited about how far they can "travel"—right here in New York—just by visiting the Met. The notion of the Met as a passport a visitor can use to travel around the world and throughout time is a message the Met can own uniquely.

Campaign Strategy

The headline "One Met. Many Worlds" conveys the notion of a journey. LaPlaca Cohen joined the headline with a series of bold art pairings from the museum's collection to show vastly different cultures with a visual connection or similarity. "Where will the Met take you?" was added to inspire excitement and wonder, and invite audiences to engage whether in person or online. The headline was translated into different languages as a supplemental campaign element to speak to international visitors and position the Met as a truly global museum.

   The campaign features extensive use of outdoor media channels seen by both tourists and New Yorkers. Placements include city bus sides, tourist double-decker bus wraps, subway platform posters, and a banner at JFK Airport's Terminal 1. Unique placements, such as painted building walls along the High Line in Chelsea, generated online buzz via social media channels. Online placements on expedia.com reached international tourists as they planned trips to New York City. The campaign also became the basis of the design for the Met's signature shopping bags and the plaza construction site.

Results

The Met continues to remain a market leader both nationally and internationally, with 6.2 million people visiting the Met in the past fiscal year. Of these, 36 percent were international visitors, making the Met the largest tourist attraction in New York City and the greatest attended art museum in America. In addition to the on-site visits, the Met had forty million website visits over the same period. According to a recent survey, the Met remains one of the most recognized institutions in America, with an awareness rating of 85 percent from the general US population and one of the most reputable organizations as well, with 70 percent of the US population viewing the museum favorably.

Source: "One Met. Many Worlds," aef.com, http://www.aef.com/wp-content/uploads/2016/10/met_museum-1.pdf.

tive to marketers, who feel the public isn't paying attention to more traditional advertising efforts. Because of the availability of diverse locations, this mass-media vehicle can be highly targetable. Based on where the boards are placed, they can focus on specific neighborhoods or ethnic groups.

As a vehicle that must both entertain and educate to capture attention, an outdoor board has only about six to eight seconds to deliver its intended message (unless it's located near an intersection where traffic lights help hold the driver's attention a bit longer). Because the message must be brief in order to be read quickly, it must be memorable.

The fun of out-of-home advertising is its diversity of size, form, and location. Design options are limited only by budget and the creative team's imagination. Outdoor boards come in two different varieties: the more traditional painted bulletins and poster panels, and the newer and more creative electronic LED boards.

Painted Bulletin Outdoor Boards

Painted bulletins are large hand-painted boards. Painted boards have evolved into vinyl-coated or single-fabric sheets that are stretched across the board. This new technique has greatly improved image quality, rivaling that found in magazines.

These mega-boards are easy to see when prominently placed on interstate highways or heavily traveled routes. It is not unusual for bulletins to have extensions or three-dimensional additions. Each of these options operates as part of the design, extending it beyond the edges of the board. Some boards use the existing landscape as a part of the design. For example, Bic leaned a large three-dimensional razor against a board in an open field where a strip the width of the razor had been mowed. Nationwide Insurance illustrated how "life comes at you fast" when it used visuals of paint cans spilling paint down the side of a building onto a car covered in the paint in the parking lot below.

This type of board is usually purchased for a longer period, often on a one- to three-year basis, making it more permanent and more expensive than posters.

Moving the Image onto Poster Panels

Posters are created using sheets of preprinted images that are glued directly to the board. They are smaller in size than painted bulletins and are created in sections, or "sheets," rather than painted on-site. These types of boards are usually rented by the month and will most often be found in heavy-traffic areas and along highways. Overall cost is based on the amount of time the board will be used, the size, whether the design has bleed or is illuminated, and the location. Boards purchased for more than thirty days can be purchased at a discount.

Poster panels are preprinted in the shop on paper or vinyl sheets, transferred to the board's location, and mounted. The most common poster panels are thirty-sheet posters, measuring 10 feet, 5 inches × 22 feet, 8 inches. The name "thirty-sheet poster panels" is a relic: Before printing techniques improved, it used to take thirty sheets of paper to create a board; today that number has been reduced to eight or ten sheets of paper, or one full sheet of vinyl.

Smaller, eight-sheet posters known as location signage are often used to mark the location of a business or promote a product near the point of purchase—increasing both reach and frequency, as well as building brand awareness and/or reminding consumers about a product or service. Visual/verbal messages include at least a logo and perhaps a graphic or visual and a short message along with the logo.

LED Boards

Even outdoor boards can't escape the long arm of technology. Lighted and computer-controlled LED boards (figure 13.1) host several different advertising messages that rotate every

Figure 13.1. This electronic billboard changes several times per minute, catching consumer attention. Robyn Blakeman.

eight seconds, holding the commuter's attention. A single board can deliver several different messages for a single product or service, like a campaign, or can advertise multiple products. Both attractive and entertaining, movable boards have made outdoor advertising one of the fastest-growing media vehicles—second only to the Internet, according to the Outdoor Advertising Association of America.

A computer can easily change signs in minutes, compared to the forty-five minutes and labor required to change traditional boards. On a smaller scale, taxicabs can be fitted with global positioning hardware so that this type of sign can change based on a cab's location within a city. This allows local advertisers to promote their messages close to their business locations.

BOX 13.1. Sizes of Outdoor Boards

Outdoor boards come in the following sizes:
30-sheet posters (10 ft. 5 in. × 22 ft. 8 in.)
30-sheet bleed poster (color or visual goes to the edge of the board, leaving no white border; 9 ft. 7 in. × 21 ft. 7 in.)
8-sheet small (5 ft. 11 in. sheets)
Painted bulletins or LED boards (three standard sizes: 14 ft. × 48 ft., 20 ft. × 50 ft., and 20 ft. × 60 ft.)

Large and bright, these boards can often be seen from quite a distance on interstate highways. However, most boards are placed in low-speed, high-traffic locations that feature a four-way intersection, where drivers are stopped long enough to see a board's full rotation.

As an IMC device, marketers can use several boards that show the same or different messages in varied locations throughout a city, ensuring that vehicles along the route will see an integrated stream of messages.

LED boards are creative, attractive, and colorful. They don't fade or tear after prolonged exposure to the elements, and they are easy to change. The only downside is that several cities have banned the boards as too bright and as posing a driving hazard because drivers lock onto the boards' continually moving messages.

Digital boards offer diverse creative opportunities and make outdoor advertising more targetable toward varied demographic groups than ever before.

Whether a brand is using more traditional or technology-based boards, each design should sport a bold visual and be short, sweet, and to the point, using no more than five to seven words. Because of this, outdoor boards are often considered to have a limited creative palette. However, that is untrue: The medium's sheer size and flexibility and its suitability to bold colors add up to a broad range of creative options, which only expand further with the use of extensions or three-dimensional designs.

Wall Murals

Wall murals are outdoor boards that are painted on the sides of older buildings, usually located in urban areas. Wall murals offer a larger canvas and are more permanent than any other type of out-of-home media vehicle.

CHAPTER 13

Transit Advertising Keeps the Message Moving

Transit advertising, another form of out-of-home, targets the millions of urbanites who use public transportation or see public vehicles while they're on foot—or from their motor vehicles, bicycles, or office windows. The diversity of shapes, sizes, and canvases offers an abundance of creative opportunities and challenges. Public transit includes taxis, buses, trains, elevated trains, and subway and airport terminals. Canvases include buses (both interior and exterior, as well as entire bus wraps) and exterior taxi signs. Additional options include stations, platforms, bus shelters, benches, and three-dimensional kiosks. Basically, if there is a flat surface on any moving vehicle or room where the vehicle arrives and departs, it's ripe for transit advertising. Transit, like outdoor, has limited advertising space and thus requires a short message—making it another great support vehicle. Since most public transportation is located in cities, advertising is targeted to middle- and working-class urban consumers.

Frequency is the reason to choose transit as a media option. Riders travel back and forth to work on a daily basis. The fact that these consumers are "trapped" for a set period allows messages to be read repeatedly. Because space constraints keep advertising clutter to a minimum, memorability is increased. Let's take a closer look at some of these diverse vehicles.

Exterior Bus Advertising

Sheer size makes bus advertising like a moving billboard, reaching people who are walking and in their cars. Design should be bold and entertaining to attract commuters' attention.

Exterior bus displays come in three categories: king- and queen-size posters and full bus wraps. The type of display chosen is based in part on a bus's route.

King-size posters display the advertised message on both the curb and street sides of the bus. Queen-size posters appear on the curb side only.

Full-size bus wraps are giant wraps that can creatively carry a story line around the bus, making use of the front, back, side panels, and windows. Designs will almost always make use of the windows, so care must be taken to ensure that riders' views are not blocked by the design. Most wraps are airbrushed directly onto the bus's surface. Creative teams using a wrap should do so only if the design is visually creative and can make use of the entire bus.

Bus Shelters and Benches

Transit shelters are the places where riders wait for the bus. They offer a very creative canvas, which can often be lit from behind by the sun or artificially by strategically placed lighting. They attract the attention of not only riders but also those passing by on foot, in cars, on bicycles, or in public transportation vehicles.

Shelter ads are large (usually 4 × 6 feet) four-color panels. Like most out-of-home advertising, they use a visual, a logo, and perhaps a slogan or tagline to introduce the public to, or remind them about, a local product or service. Many are interactive, requiring the target to take a picture, pop or look under something, or use holographic images. Some shelters also have a bench that can be used to support other, more traditional media vehicles.

However, bench advertising need not be confined solely to bus shelters. Usable bench surfaces can be found in local parks, restaurants, malls, subways, bus and airport waiting areas, and college campuses. Popular and effective, they are usually located in locations with a large amount of pedestrian traffic.

It is important to point out that brands that use city property for advertising are often responsible for not only the upkeep and sometimes even the construction of the vehicles but also of restoring the vehicles to their original states after the campaign is over.

Interior Handhold Bus or Subway Advertising

Creative ideas are not confined to the outside surfaces of public transportation. Riders who must spend their time standing can hold onto an advertised message rather than a simple bar or fabric loop. These engaging and creative messages can turn a simple horizontal bar into barbells or a vertical pole into stacked beer cans. No pole to hold onto? How about hanging a hand attached to an arm that pushes hand lotion?

Interior and Exterior Bus, Taxi, Train, and Subway Cards

These varied vehicles often offer space for little more than a few words and perhaps a small visual. Often these cards are printed on both sides so that the message can be changed out from time to time. It can also be a great direct-response vehicle when offering tear-off pads of applications or order cards, known as car-cards. Passengers can use the car-cards at a later time to request more information, place an order, or apply a discount toward a purchase. Interior vehicle cards come in a number of different sizes and are placed in frames above the vehicle's windows.

Vehicle Advertising

Advertising on vehicles—whether cars, taxis, or buses—can be creative, appearing both inside and outside of these constantly moving vehicles. Exterior messages can appear on the roof, trunk, windows, and doors (figure 13.2). More elaborate designs can be digitally driven, wrap around the vehicle, or support three-dimensional visual enhancements. Because this moving canvas can cover a lot of ground and be seen by thousands of people a day, it has a very broad reach. Vehicles fitted with GPS can feature messages that change out, based on the taxi's location, to highlight nearby restaurants and shopping venues, making it a great way for big and small businesses alike to promote their product or service close to their place of business. Other digital options can be displayed on three- and four-sided roof tents that show videos and even holograms. As a support vehicle, taxi advertising is best used as a branding, reminder, or promotional vehicle.

Interior advertising appears on video screens placed on the back of the front seat. The video typically runs both advertising and promotional information on local events such as concerts, movies, or current theater productions.

Subway, Airline, and Train Terminal Posters

Terminal posters are large, usually local ads located in bus, train, subway, or airline terminals. Many of these posters are illuminated for greater impact. These posters often advertise local products that visitors can enjoy while visiting a city or that locals can find near the stop or station. Often the station posters can be coordinated to match smaller advertisements found inside the transportation vehicles. Many designs feature QR codes that travelers can shoot with their smartphones for more information on the advertised brand or to receive coupons.

Figure 13.2. Advertising on vehicles can be digitally driven, wrap around the vehicle, or support three-dimensional visual enhancements. Robyn Blakeman.

Glass floor displays are also common; these are known as **kiosks** and are used when showing the product itself will make a greater impact than a photograph would.

When ingenuity is added to traditional advertising techniques, it will always catch people's attention. For example, BART, the San Francisco transit system, showcased "mini movies" as a part of an advertising campaign in downtown tunnels. The "movie" used a flipbook technique that relies on a series of strategically spaced posters that are "activated" as the train passes them, making the images look as though they are moving.

Moving Billboards

One of the newest forms of outdoor advertising appears on the backs and sides of semitrailer trucks. The trucks are hired to drive up and down the highway and streets during rush hour, when the audience is virtually a captive one. Designs can appear on either side or on the back of the vehicle and can be either static or digitally enhanced, allowing more than one brand to be shown during the truck's daily route.

How Does Out-of-Home
Advertising Help IMC Be Consumer Focused?

Like all the mass-media vehicles we've talked about, out-of-home is not consumer focused but a monologue that talks *at* the consumer. Because of this, it must be more creative, more targeted, and more flexible than two-way media vehicles.

As a support vehicle, out-of-home will not build a relationship or encourage brand loyalty, but it will keep the product or service front and center in the target's mind. The more creatively delivered the message, the more favorable the image.

Seen every day as consumers travel, out-of-home is a friendly but persistent reminder that the product makes a great lunch or dinner choice, entertainment stop, investment, gift, or news-program choice.

Aside from promoting car purchases, it is not a canvas for image-based products. But it can entertain and grab attention. Outdoor works especially well for teaser advertising before a new product launch, and transit is ideal for long-term maintenance advertising. Transit is particularly effective when tied to a direct-response campaign.

Since all products can be purchased locally, out-of-home can always direct the consumer to the next step in the buying process by including an address.

As a supportive part of the promotional mix, out-of-home can help support both public relations efforts and messages placed in traditional media outlets. Many forms are not especially effective at displaying bold logos or smaller web addresses or hashtags for any social media vehicles used through the campaign, while others can be very engaging and interactive. No matter where it appears, however, out-of-home's single visual/verbal voice is the key consumer benefit.

Incorporating mobile with out-of-home is both engaging and interactive and a great way to deliver a promotional device.

Paired with alternative media, the possibilities are endless. Terminal or shelter ads in particular can push QR codes, use scents, or distribute samples. Many outdoor boards use solar power for illumination; still others use the surrounding landscape as an extended canvas.

Incentives and Deterrents of Out-of-Home and Transit Advertising

To decide whether out-of-home and transit advertising is right for an IMC campaign, let's look at some of the incentives and deterrents associated with them.

What Makes Out-of-Home and Transit Advertising So Great?

The more notable incentives associated with out-of-home and transit advertising include:

- *Availability*. Out-of-home and transit messages are there all day, every day.
- *Reach*. Depending on location, large numbers of people can be exposed to the messages on a twenty-four-hour basis.
- *Frequency*. Since most consumers will see the advertised message while traveling to and from work, the message will be seen on a regular basis, increasing memorability.
- *Demographic diversity*. Since out-of-home and transit are not as highly targeted as some other media vehicles, generic products can reach all age, gender, income, and education levels.
- *Visual impact*. Size and creative options can make out-of-home and transit advertising very attractive and visually stimulating.

- *Creative potential.* Creative options are boundless, limited only by the budget and the creative team's imagination.
- *Location.* Since most boards are placed in high-traffic areas and transit moves about the city, the message is sure to be seen.

Is There Anything Wrong with Out-of-Home and Transit Advertising?

The more notable deterrents associated with out-of-home and transit advertising include:

- *Fleeting.* Outdoor boards and transit vehicles have a very short amount of time to get the message to a mobile and often distracted public.
- *Visual and environmental contamination.* Even the most creative pieces can be seen as a blight on city streets and the landscape.
- *Memorability.* Although large numbers see the visual/verbal message, it is difficult to determine how many read and remember the message.
- *Maintenance affects brand image.* Media buyers cannot inspect each board or transit vehicle for condition. A dirty appearance or signs of disrepair can reflect poorly on the brand.
- *Poor targetability.* Out-of-home and transit are mass media that are constantly in motion or seen while in motion, making it impossible to reach a highly selective audience.
- *Clutter.* Cities are full of advertising messages, both stationary and moving, that bombard the consumer. It is difficult for a single message to be noticed among the advertising noise.
- *Message brevity.* With only five to seven words, messages not only must get to the point—they must be simple. Out-of-home and transit can do little more than repeat a headline, slogan or tagline, and logo.

The Strategy behind Out-of-Home and Transit Advertising

The choice to use out-of-home or transit is based on the need to provide supplemental support for other major media vehicles such as broadcast or print. Strategically, out-of-home and transit vehicles are great for new product launches or to maintain or reinforce existing advertising efforts for mature products or services.

All out-of-home and transit vehicles are meant to build awareness and remind the public about a product or service or persuade them to do something like come into a brick-and-mortar store or visit a web or social media site. Companies that use these vehicles most often include local restaurants, media companies, retail stores, travel-related businesses, entertainment providers, and providers of packaged goods.

As part of the promotional mix, out-of-home and transit can do little more than creatively highlight the key consumer benefit (covered in greater detail in chapters discussing other vehicles within the IMC campaign) with a bold visual and minimal copy. Properly placed, these media can be highly targetable because consumers employ repetitive travel patterns. Reach and frequency are maximized if the advertising is placed in diverse locations.

When working with supplemental vehicles, many questions need to be addressed. For instance, will supplemental vehicles help accomplish objectives? Does the target live in a major city or travel often? Does the target take public transportation or use other means of exposure, such as walking or riding a bike to and from work? What types of boards or transit signs do various city officials allow? Is the ad placed in a location the target is sure to see? Is some kind of interactive device required, such as car-cards or revolving outdoor boards? Will mobile alerts be available? Where is dialogue taking place? Do advertising efforts need to support that dialogue or introduce something new?

Possible out-of-home and transit objectives might be to fortify a current campaign, reacquaint the target with or introduce her to a brand or service, give directions on how to get more information, or reinforce an image.

The choice of strategy of course depends on what is happening elsewhere in the campaign, but the easiest to employ is a product-oriented approach. If the overall campaign features powerful visuals, a consumer approach could come across strongly. The most effective product-oriented approaches would be generic claim, product feature, or unique selling proposition. The best consumer approach would be lifestyle. Because of the limited visual/verbal space, the best appeal would be rational, focusing on a product feature or on the brand's news value. Strategies using an emotional appeal are rare but not unheard of, focusing on personal pleasure rather than image.

The best rational tones for out-of-home are factual, testimonial, news or educational, reminder, or teaser. Useful emotional tones might include humor, animation, or fear.

The Look of Out-of-Home and Transit Advertising

Even though out-of-home and transit play a supportive media role, they offer almost unlimited creative options due to their size and visual impact.

Most out-of-home vehicles are simply but boldly designed. The vehicle should be able to visually and verbally tie back to other media efforts used in the campaign. It should strongly push the key consumer benefit, be brightly colored and creative, use preferably a single bold visual, and, if applicable, showcase a spokesperson or character representative, a headline, a package design, and a slogan or tagline. Messages should get to the point in no more than five to seven words. Copy should be set in a typeface that is easy to read from distances of up to 500 feet. Spacing between letters should be slightly exaggerated; "all caps" and decorative typefaces should be avoided to increase legibility.

Bold, colorful images attract attention. Beyond a powerful color photograph, additional image choices might include high-contrast black-and-white photographs, illustrations, animation, or graphic images.

Choice of image is important: One eye-catching and memorable visual can say more than a page of copy, so make sure the visual chosen speaks for the key consumer benefit, strategy, and overall tone.

It is also important to remember that images need not be confined to the surface of an outdoor board. Extensions, 3-D images, and use of the surrounding landscape are word-of-mouth catalysts.

Interactive boards are both visual and memorable. Some are no longer stationary and can pop up anywhere. Canon used trucks outfitted with digital screens to give photography tips based on varied conditions such as location and weather. Other interactive boards are drinkable or edible. Coke Zero created a 4,500-foot straw that dispensed the bubbly drink from a billboard that debuted at the 2015 NCAA men's Final Four. In London, Carlsberg beer also used a billboard to dispense a cold one to people passing by—IDs required to be served. Another British brand, Mr. Kipling, used its culinary talents to distribute pieces of their billboard, made entirely of cake and icing, to passersby.

Color choice should not overpower the type or overwhelm the visual. Pop is good, but it should not negatively affect readability and legibility. It is also important to ensure that color choices do not blend into the surrounding area; for example, using green on boards appearing near an area of heavy foliage.

If the design and statement are unique, the ad will stand out from the clutter of other out-of-home efforts in the area, as well as (hopefully) meet with less resistance from opponents of outdoor advertising.

As in magazine and newspaper advertising, cooperative opportunities are available for local companies and national brands to team up and share the cost of advertising.

Let's take a look at some of the more creative options.

Mobile

The combination of mobile and out-of-home is opening several engagement opportunities, such as sending a text message to an interactive board that reacts in some visual way to the message. Some boards in pedestrian locations can take a passerby's picture. Once it's displayed on the outdoor board, the target can download the image to his phone along with varied images, video, and music. Other creative options ask pedestrians to take a picture of their board and take it to the nearest brick-and-mortar location to receive a coupon. Still another engaging board asks viewers a question they can answer via text message.

Three-Dimensional Boards

Attaching 3-D images to outdoor boards gives a static board a more realistic and creative appearance. In these boards the visual takes center stage. They are an anomaly in a world full of out-of-home advertising that often recedes into the background of what is going on around it. Whether using 3-D elements or any other interactive device, these very creative and diverse vehicles offer myriad ways to successfully pitch a product or service.

Many outdoor boards enlarge the canvas to include the surrounding landscape. Three-dimensional items placed on the ground create eye flow as the viewer follows the visual to its resting place, creating engagement. Many boards incorporate electrical wires or scaffolding from surrounding buildings or place a 3-D image in front of or below the board. Other 3-D items, perhaps of cows, coffee cups, or logos, can be placed on top of skyscrapers, easily viewable when consumers are sitting in traffic on the way to and from work.

Human Billboards

Don't like any of the canvases talked about so far? How about using the human body as a walking, talking, very interactive out-of-home vehicle? This buzz-building surface can display temporary tattoos and carry messages on clothing or in the hair or beard. Humans can recite memorized messages or give spontaneous and unscripted responses to passerby questions or based on their reactions. They are also an excellent vehicle for handing out promotional devices such as T-shirts, caps, water, and samples.

Sign spinners, also known as sign twirlers, human arrows, and human directional, are also a great way to attract attention to a specific business, event, or sale. Strategically placed outside a business or event, usually near a busy intersection or pedestrian-heavy area, these colorful signs can display both a short message and an identifying logo. Often, their human companion might be dressed in costume, further drawing attention to the signage. Not only are they eye-catching, mobile, and adaptable, they are a great way to create brand awareness and attract impulse buyers.

No matter where we see them, out-of-home advertising messages are no longer easy to ignore—their colorful images and interactive and engaging options can creatively incorporate the landscape or use the target's location to tell a brief but often interactive story.

 DISCUSSION QUESTIONS

1. What are the strategic uses of out-of- home and transit advertising in an IMC campaign?
2. Why is out-of-home considered a mass medium?
3. Why is out-of-home growing?
4. Explain why out-of-home does not need to compete for audience attention.
5. Define the role of out-of-home vehicles.
6. Define support media. As a support medium, when does out-of-home work best?
7. What is the most effective way for out-of-home to both show and tell the advertised message? How can this be done most effectively?
8. Why is it particularly important for many out-of-home vehicles to be memorable?
9. How do LED boards work? How do they compare/contrast visually and verbally with traditional outdoor boards?
10. What are some of the most common transit vehicles?
11. How does out-of-home advertising help an IMC campaign be more consumer focused?
12. What are the pros and cons associated with out-of-home advertising?
13. What is the strategy behind using out-of-home in an IMC campaign?
14. Out-of-home is used primarily as a support medium; it has an abundance of visual and verbal options. How can a medium that says little be seamlessly tied to other media options?
15. What are ways to make out-of-home vehicles both interactive and engaging?

14

Direct Marketing

The Strategic Use of Direct Marketing in IMC

Direct marketing is considered both advertising and a promotional tool. You may be wondering what the difference is between advertising and promotion. Advertising is all about educating the consumer about a product's features and benefits to encourage purchase. Promotion, on the other hand, makes a proposition by offering packaged deals to induce immediate purchase.

When you know exactly who the target audience is and want to talk to the target one-on-one, consider direct marketing as an alternative to traditional advertising vehicles.

Direct marketing is all about creating a dialogue between buyer and seller. Communication is coordinated and individualized through the use of multiple media vehicles and databases. The information collected in databases allows direct marketing to reach targets based on their past buying history, demographics, psychographics, behavioristics, and geographics.

Knowledge about the consumer allows the creative team to create a more personalized message, eliminating the more generic mass-media messages delivered through traditional advertising methods. This more intimate environment makes reaching and talking to the target in a language he can relate to and about a topic he is interested in easier and more effective. The result is development of an interpersonal relationship between the client or marketer, the product or service, and the target. This relationship is one of the foundations needed to build and maintain brand loyalty. The availability of toll-free numbers and access to the Internet and social media carry this interpersonal relationship a step further by allowing the target to communicate directly with the advertiser.

Traditional advertising is where advertisers and their agencies have historically turned to build brand awareness, accomplish repositioning, and eventually build brand loyalty. Today, the cost of advertising—especially on television—and the fractionalization of media and target audiences are changing the way consumers receive messages. Advertising simply doesn't reach the target as well as it used to. The interactive and more personalized nature of direct marketing makes it a better alternative to build a brand's image.

Direct marketing is everything traditional advertising efforts are not. As a mass-media vehicle, advertising delivers a message to thousands—often millions—of readers, listeners, or viewers, most of whom are not part of the targeted audience. Direct marketing can personalize its message on an individual basis, addressing the target by name.

Traditional advertising requires more time to entice the target to action. Its impersonal format requires more frequent messages to reach, educate, and then remind consumers to purchase the next time they are at the grocery store or the mall. Direct marketing eliminates the middleman. To receive a quick response, direct marketing often employs the use of sales promotion devices such as coupons, contests and sweepstakes, samples, giveaways, and rebates, to name a few.

Because traditional advertising offers few interactive opportunities before purchase, the target remains anonymous, and it is difficult, if not impossible, to know where his exposure to the message took place. The highly targetable and interactive nature of direct marketing makes sales efforts easier to measure, especially if advertising efforts use an identifying marketing code, often a combination of letters and/or numbers, that pinpoints the medium from which the order or inquiry originated. Most importantly, since direct marketing is sent to a specific person, it is easy to track who responded to the message and who did not. Ultimately, this information will be used to help determine whether the proper media mix was employed.

Because it is so individualized, reaching the target audience through direct marketing is much more expensive than advertising. However, because it targets one individual whom research has deemed most likely to buy the product or use the service advertised, the overall interest and purchase rate also tend to be higher than in advertising.

Trust in direct marketing has grown steadily over the years, mainly because advertisers have delivered reliable products, included guarantees, and made purchases and returns easy. Additional perks promoted in direct-marketing efforts might include some of the lowest prices anywhere, the opportunity to be the first to own, exposure to limited-time offers, and additional incentives, such as free gifts or rebates and/or refunds, just for buying from the televised or direct-mail message.

The goal of both advertising and promotion is to elicit a sale. However, when direct marketing is part of the IMC promotional mix, its role may not be to generate an immediate sale. Sometimes it is used to generate interest or to encourage information gathering through requests for more information. Additional pre-purchase research on the target's part may require an appointment with a salesperson, a trip to the retailer or brick-and-mortar location, or a test drive. See case study 12 for a look at Auburn University's use of direct marketing.

A Word about Databases

Before looking at the diverse list of media voices direct marketing employs, it is important to look at why it can personalize a sales message, what makes it a relationship-building tool, and what makes it a successful alternative to mass-media advertising. The answers lie in direct marketing's use of database information.

Databases begin life as a short, internally or corporately created list of names, addresses, and phone numbers. Database marketing as an IMC tool requires several years of data collection. Individual customer data is culled from previous interactions with a company, such as purchases or requests for more information. By developing their own database, marketers can save money and aid in customizing future communications while continuing to build customer loyalty. More extensive lists can be purchased from external sources based on the target's demographic or psychographic information. Additionally, names might be culled from telephone directories, the US Census, warranty cards, UPC scanners at the grocery store, credit cards, and professional organizations.

Database information ultimately helps marketers develop messages that are tailor made for the target audience based on their likes, needs, and lifestyles.

A more controversial form of tracking, and one that has involved the Federal Trade Commission (FTC) over the past few years, is cookies. According to the book *Nontraditional Media in Marketing and Advertising* by Robyn Blakeman:

> These covert forms of data collection leave an electronic trail behind that marketers use to track consumer movement online. Oftentimes, consumers do not know that they are being tracked, which results in consumer anger, as many consider these collection techniques an invasion of privacy. Consumer outrage caught the attention of the Federal Trade Commission (FTC) when, in February 2009, it addressed the issue of consumer privacy on the Internet, calling for an official "Do Not Track" system in its most recent report.
>
> The Boucher-Stearns bill, a congressional bill sponsored by the House Energy and Commerce Communications Subcommittee, is pushing to have all websites post how they collect and use a visitor's private information. Additionally, the FTC proposed that websites add "Do Not Track" technology that would allow visitors a choice to opt-out of having their actions and information on the site recorded.
>
> Not surprisingly, the advertising industry does not look on the "Do Not Track" proposal favorably. The Interactive Advertising Bureau believes the proposal will "require a re-engineering of the Internet's architecture," and limit what type of content can be offered for free, say author Jessica E. Vascellaro and her colleagues in a 2011 *Wall Street Journal* online article entitled "The Year Ahead for Media: Digital or Die."
>
> Additionally, the FTC is currently scrutinizing any product promotions being made digitally through blogs or tweets. The new guidelines state that bloggers, including celebrity endorsers, must disclose any compensation they might have received for writing about a product.

Privacy is an ongoing concern for consumers, and the ease with which marketers can gather and sell private information without their knowledge or permission is becoming an unacceptable way of doing business. Many corporations and services are refusing to sell their customer lists in order to protect their targets' privacy. The newest tool in the marketing arsenal to help combat privacy issues is known as **permission-based marketing**. Permission-based marketing lets consumers decide whether they want to receive advertised material. By "opting in," they give the marketer permission to contact them, usually by e-mail or mobile text, about upcoming and often exclusive sales or promotions.

The Diversity of the Direct-Marketing Voice

Direct marketing uses a diverse array of contact vehicles, including mass media, the mail, social media, mobile, the telephone, and personal contact. The most typical forms of direct marketing include:

- Catalogs
- Direct mail
- Infomercials
- E-mail or mobile texts
- Direct response
- Telemarketing
- The Internet and social media

Catalogs

Catalogs, even when they arrive unsolicited, are often opened, read, and lingered over. Like magazines, catalogs are often saved for later use or shared with friends or colleagues, extending the catalog's life and reach. Ordering is made easy, using toll-free numbers, the mail, tablet or mobile options, or the Internet; guarantees allow most, if not all, items to be returned for a full refund if the consumer is not entirely satisfied.

Many of the larger catalog companies create what are known as specialty catalogs. These are smaller versions of a larger catalog, and the specialized content reflects those products the target is most likely to buy based on past purchase history.

Direct Mail

Direct-mail pieces are like bills; they find their way into the consumers' mailboxes unsolicited and eventually into their hands unwanted. Direct mail isn't hated as much as most people would think. Consumers respond to the personalized messages because such messages specifically address their interests and lifestyles.

Direct mail, also known as **database marketing**, is a highly targetable, personal, and measurable form of direct response. The consumer can respond to an advertised message by sending in an order form or logging onto a website to place an order, receive more information, or provide feedback about the product or service. A toll-free number can also be used to speak directly to a customer service representative about colors or sizes, shipping, and guarantees, or to place an order. A typical direct-mail kit can arrive in almost any shape or form, but basic pieces include an outside envelope, a personalized pitch letter, an infor-

C CASE STUDY 12

IMC Direct Marketing: Auburn University

The Challenge

Auburn Alumni Association tried countless marketing campaigns, from the efforts of simple post-cards to complex and expensive packages. What they found was that regardless of their campaign, the membership conversion never got beyond 1.9 percent. This conversion rate correlated with a decrease in membership base, decline in its programs and benefits, and a dismal financial position.

Objectives

1. Increase membership conversion.
2. Drive quantifiable traffic to the alumni website.

Strategy

Create a plan using Variable Data Printing (VDP) [a one-to-one marketing strategy] for direct mail plus e-mail for alumni whose membership had lapsed, as well as a larger list of past alumni.

    To achieve these goals, the campaign focused on reaching alumni on a personal level and offering them a promotional photograph showing their name spelled out on the Auburn field by the marching band. The mailing package included a personalized letter with a perforated membership form, a return envelope, and the photograph. The Auburn Alumni Association also decided to offer a 20 percent discount for additional photos purchased through the portal by a certain date. Along with the mailing list, an e-mail campaign was launched to a list of 29,153 addresses offering online enrollment as well as a link to purchase the personalized photograph.

Results

Once the e-mails and packets were sent out, the association received multiple calls a day in support of the campaign. The association received three to five membership pledges a day generated from the e-mails alone. During the first thirty days of the campaign, response conversion rose to 2.3 percent.

Source: "Auburn University Sees Alumni Association Enrollment Conversion Escalate by 21%," DME, https://dmedelivers.com/case-studies/.

---

mational brochure, an order form or business reply card for ordering, and a return envelope for mail orders.

    As an informational tool, direct mail can be used as an announcement device, a brand-building tool, an incentive to entice nonusers to switch or try a new or existing product or service, or to reward loyal long-term users.

    As an involvement tool, a multipiece mailer requires the target's attention to sort through and read the various pieces, play with the movable parts, or scratch off a game piece. The more time the consumer spends involved with the piece, the more memorable it will be.

A good direct-mail response rate is around 2 percent of the total mailings. For direct mail to succeed, it must be mailed to the right audience and present the right message. Too often, names are duplicated, wasting money and annoying targets.

As a media option, direct mail is very diverse. It can be used as a sales or promotional device or as a primary or secondary media vehicle for almost any product or service. Currently, the heaviest users of direct mail are insurance companies, auto dealers, financial service firms, and department stores.

BOX 14.1. Tips for Working with Direct Mail

- If something can be given away, do it. The word "free" is an attention getter, but it's not really enticing if that's all the brand has to offer.
- If the direct-mail piece is for charity, use black-and-white photography and a lower grade of paper so as not to appear wasteful.
- All additional pieces that appear with a direct-mail letter should be of different sizes and, if possible, varied colors. It is helpful to reuse the graphics or colors from the envelope on the inside pieces.
- Guarantees, limited-time offers, quantity limits, coupons, free gifts, and other offers will increase the number of responses or orders.
- The tone of the message should match the image of the product or service. Personalize the letter, but remember that as a business document, it must make a sale.
- A creative tone works well, but humor belongs in another medium.
- Stick to what the product can do and/or offer; stay away from comparisons with competitors.
- There is a lot of room to make a point; use it wisely.
- Back up facts and benefits with testimonials whenever possible.
- Make the piece appealing; surprise the target with diverse inserts or copy

---

Direct mail needs time to work, so don't make the mistake of thinking the first mailing will be the only mailing. A few gentle nudges may be needed to get the target moving.

Additional forms of direct marketing include statement stuffers, magalogs, and polypaks. A **statement stuffer** is advertising that hitches a ride with a credit card bill, financial notice, or anything else a consumer might receive on a regular or monthly basis.

A magalog deals with a single product, but instead of using a letter, brochure, or circular, it features a layout more like a magazine and presents information in the form of articles. Purchase options and order forms are identical to those used in a direct-mail kit.

A polypak is a series of small index cards, often 3 × 5, used to advertise a variety of products, which are bundled together and delivered through the mail. Often in color and double-sided, each card has about enough room for a picture and headline on one side and the order form on the other. These are often used to generate interest in a product, asking the consumer to call, mail in, or log on to receive additional information.

Infomercials

Infomercials are thirty- to sixty-minute-long television commercials that allow the consumer to order immediately, using information provided on the television screen. Infomercials use the sight, sound, and motion of television to demonstrate a product, to educate, and to entice a consumer to buy. Infomercials take the time to create interest in a product by using testimonials from current users and/or endorsements from celebrity users or technical advisers. Consumers are offered purchasing options with varied guarantees or return policies. A successful infomercial should:

- Place facts into a storyline that speaks to the target's special interests.
- Break down potentially complicated information into easy, demonstrable steps.
- Use a celebrity or expert to talk about uses or key features and benefits.
- Summarize key features and benefits and then repeat them regularly throughout the program.
- Repeatedly tell the target what he or she needs to do.
- Make ordering easy by showing a toll-free number and credit cards that are accepted.
- Outline the guarantee or return policy.

E-mail or Mobile Texts

Two of the most inexpensive ways to deliver direct mail are via text message and e-mail. Personalized messages can be delivered to a target's e-mail address more quickly, more often, and for a lot less money than traditional direct mail. Text messages, although shorter, will include an accompanying link that will get the target to the same web location but with less personalization. Technology makes interaction between brand and consumer faster, less expensive, and more frequent. Alternative media options such as coupons, augmented reality, and games can keep the interaction just as engaging as if the recipient held a direct-mail piece in his hands. Because of this, it will not be long before many smaller direct-mail marketers totally abandon traditionally delivered handheld offers and permanently embrace the use of e-mail, mobile, and/or social media outlets as an alternative way to deliver their offers.

E-mail marketing services such as Constant Contact, MailChimp, and Infusionsoft can help ensure that permission-based e-mails get through as well as help create e-mail lists and professional-looking newsletters. Additionally, these e-mail services offer a diverse assortment of templates, the ability to easily upload data, good analytic metrics to track responses, integration with **customer relationship management** (CRM) applications, or the ability to manage a company's interaction with current and future customers, e-mail delivery, and affordable pricing.

Direct Response

Direct marketing often employs the use of mass-media vehicles such as newspapers, magazines, radio, and television, where the consumer can directly respond to the message via telephone, mail, or the Internet.

Newspapers

Newspapers bring news value to direct-marketing efforts and can be used to target specific geographic areas. If a standard ad is not appropriate, consider using newspaper inserts, which are often full-color and can range from a one-page FSI with perforated coupons to a multipage booklet. Samples, quick response (QR) codes, and web and social media sites can also be used.

Magazines

Magazines might employ multipage inserts bound into the magazine or a bound-in reply card, appearing beside the ad, that can be torn out and used to order, as well as coupons, samples, or multifaceted digital options.

Radio

Radio's biggest contribution to direct marketing is its ability to direct targets to a specific location where they can pick up literature or a sample or talk directly to a brand representative.

Television

Direct marketing uses television to make a sale, create leads, or build awareness; it also works well as a support vehicle or companion piece for direct-response advertising appearing in other media.

Today, interactive television allows the target to order a product directly from the television screen. Although the technology is already available, few programs have employed it.

Telemarketing

Telemarketing uses the telephone as a media device and a salesperson to deliver the message personally to select members of the target audience. This is known as **outbound** telemarketing. Databases are used to identify and contact members of the target audience who have a known interest in the product or service or who are seen as potential buyers based on past purchase history. When a customer initiates contact with a company for any reason, usually through the use of a toll-free telephone number, this is known as **inbound** telemarketing.

The Internet and Social Media

The Internet is an important player in direct marketing. Full of information, the Internet allows consumers to search out the answers to questions, read reviews, and compare products in order to make an educated buying decision. A web page can highlight sale products or suggest accompanying purchases without sales pressure, making purchasing fast and hassle free.

Businesses that take advantage of the Internet for sales and ordering might also find it profitable to offer a catalog or create a direct-mail kit, initiating additional contact points and offering customers a choice of shopping venues.

Combining social media with direct marketing, often referred to as **social media marketing**, creates engagement. Once direct-marketing initiatives invite the targets to join the brand's network, social media is a great way to personally welcome them. Direct marketing can also use social media as an announcement device, letting the target know when new information is being announced. Finally, they are a great combination for ensuring quality customer service initiatives.

Most importantly when using social media as a direct-marketing tool, remember that the consumer did not join the brand's social network to be bombarded with advertising; she joined to have a conversation. Social media is personal and thus requires a more personal touch in order to receive valuable feedback more quickly than most direct-marketing channels can achieve.

As this list illustrates, direct marketing has grown beyond just direct mail. Some of the biggest changes, such as use of the Internet and social media sites, text messaging, and infomercials, have come about because of product reliability and quality, the availability of credit cards and toll-free phone numbers, and guarantees or easy return policies that lower the risk of buying what can't be touched or smelled.

How Does Direct Marketing Help IMC Be Consumer Focused?

Direct marketing brings customer service and personalized messages to the IMC table. Consumers will no longer accept generalized messages as incentive to buy; they want informative, personalized service, and they want their purchases to be adaptable to meet their needs. If they have a problem or need help, they want to be able to talk to someone quickly and easily. Today, brand loyalty is built not only on the quality of the product but also on the quality of the interactivity.

The Internet allows today's savvy, educated consumers to shop from their homes, allowing them to instantly compare products and receive feedback from other users. The need for additional information and research plays a particularly important role when larger, more expensive purchases are under consideration. Advertising that includes a website address, social media hashtag, or toll-free number encourages interaction and can be used as a great response device for requesting a catalog, brochure, or price list; a free consultation; a sales promotion package; coupons; feedback; or even a limited-time discount offer.

There is little differentiation between brands in most product categories, so the creative team must find a way to make the client's product stand out from the competition. One way is the creative message. Strategies and any promotional efforts must be unique and offer more than the competing brands by knowing what the target finds important, useful, and necessary. If the creative is very good, it will successfully grab and hold the target's attention and introduce him to a brand-new product or service he didn't even know he needed. But the most lasting way to create product differentiation is through development of a long-term relationship based on knowledgeable, courteous, and reliable customer service or technical assistance that is available twenty-four hours a day, seven days a week.

Once the team identifies the available options, the next step is to determine the message and the best media vehicle or combination of media vehicles needed to reach the target and accomplish the objectives.

Internal public relations efforts are critical to the success of direct marketing. The dialogue initiated between the target and customer or technical service representatives must be easy, informative, and satisfying to the target. Customer service representatives need to be familiar with any current promotions, such as sales or coupons, to knowledgeably assist the consumer and support existing advertising efforts. Good public relations efforts must be employed at all times when talking to consumers over the phone or responding to e-mail or social media inquiries.

When print ads are used as a direct-marketing device, they can be simple and direct and make the ordering process easy by including an order form, toll-free number, or a website or social media address.

Newspapers are a great place to find coupon inserts such as freestanding inserts or larger product or retail booklets. Newspapers are also a great vehicle for encouraging a visit or a trial, or as a last-minute event reminder. Magazines are great for setting the product's image and use in the target's mind. Direct marketing can be used as a follow-up to encourage immediate purchase.

Television is ideally suited as a direct-response vehicle because its ability to demonstrate allows the target to see the product in use, often in the setting in which it will be used. Because of cost, direct-response television is usually found on cable networks. Its highly specialized programming is also better for reaching special-interest groups.

Internet sites and social networks are a great place for marketers to engage in conversation with consumers and gain valuable feedback about their product or service. Once a relationship is established, consumers can opt in to receive a more informative, marketing-driven sales message delivered through e-mail or a traditionally delivered direct-mail kit.

Interactive elements are critical to engagement efforts. As previously mentioned, digital options like websites, e-mail, and social media are great at holding the target's attention when content is both informative and compelling. If employing traditional methods, be sure the target can interact with the piece(s); perhaps it makes noise, pops up, can be used as a VR device, or can be displayed on a shelf or in a frame. The more unusual and/or creative the piece is, the more time the target will spend with it, and the more sharable it becomes, extending message life.

Incentives and Deterrents of Direct Marketing

To decide whether direct marketing is right for an IMC campaign, let's look at some of the incentives and deterrents associated with it.

What Makes Direct Marketing So Great?

The more notable incentives associated with direct marketing include:

- *Personalization*. Direct marketing can personalize communications to speak to individual members of the target market by name.
- *Measurable*. Using a marketing code placed on direct marketing pieces, the marketer can tell which medium the inquiry came from.

- *Database Use*. Databases provide target information. This information allows direct marketing pieces to address specific individuals and their unique needs.
- *Customer Response*. Direct marketing builds relationships by offering two-way communication between the marketer and the target. It also allows the customer to give feedback that might affect any current or future changes in the product or service.
- *Attention Getter*. Having the right database to target the right individuals is the first step to ensuring your target will open and read your direct mail piece. A piece that is both attractively designed and personally and correctly addressed creates interest and encourages investigation. Once opened, the piece must hold the target's interest through entertaining and informative copy. This might be the trickiest step of all—you do not want the piece to end up in the trash unread.

Is There Anything Wrong with Direct Marketing?

The more notable disasters associated with direct marketing include:

- *Cost*. One of the biggest advantages to direct marketing is also one of its biggest drawbacks. The personalization of each message makes direct marketing expensive compared to other forms of advertising. Additionally, a company that does not have its own database of names will have to purchase a list.
- *Annoyance Clutter*. If targets are not interested in the message, they can deal with direct marketing messages the same way they deal with other annoying media: Turn off the television, throw away the junk mail, or screen telemarketers' calls.
- *Limited Reach*. The highly personalized nature of direct marketing limits the number of consumers that can be reached with any one message.
- *Time Constraints*. Depending on the numbers required and whether the piece is a traditional letter or a more involved mailer, direct marketing can take a great deal of production time. Add the additional time needed for basic folding, stapling, envelope stuffing, and mailing, and you have months invested into pre- and postproduction.

The Strategy behind Direct Marketing

As we now know, mass-message advertising is no longer the only way to differentiate a product or service from its competition. This is where IMC comes in. IMC understands that, properly combined, the efforts of the promotional mix—public relations, advertising, direct marketing, sales promotion, the Internet, out-of-home, mobile, and alternative media—not only will help meet objectives but also assist with positioning, creating brand awareness, and building brand image and brand loyalty more efficiently and effectively than any one medium ever could.

When deciding what promotional mix will best reach the target and accomplish the objectives, IMC uses two different techniques: advertising, which entices the target into a sale or gets the target thinking about purchase, and promotion, which solicits immediate purchase of a packaged offer. Together, advertising and promotion can be used as building blocks in an IMC campaign; one can inform while the other encourages purchase.

Like advertising, direct marketing efforts may target both a primary and secondary target audience. Determining the need for a secondary audience will depend on the target's overall knowledge of, or history with, the product or service and whether it can, or would, be purchased by a family member, friend, or professional associate. Additional factors affecting both the promotional mix and the strategy include how far each audience is from trial, repeat purchase, and brand loyalty.

Effective communication objectives that lend themselves to direct marketing as a viable medium include generating sales, building consumer loyalty, enhancing a corporate or brand image, or encouraging an inquiry or product trial.

Strategically, either a product or a consumer approach will work in direct marketing. Any of the three consumer-based approaches—brand image, lifestyle, or attitude—can flesh out the features and benefits of the product or service. Product strategies that can hammer home the product's appeal and its overall usefulness in the target's life include product feature, USP, and positioning.

The decision to use an emotional or a rational tone depends on the product and the consumer's knowledge of the product. An emotion-based appeal allows the use of such approaches as humor and animation, fear, or slice of life. Rational appeals are considered a hard-sell style, so care should be taken not to go over the top and get too personal. The personal, interactive style of direct marketing walks a fine line between talking to the target like an old friend and getting too personal and inadvertently offending the target. It's important to remember that direct marketing is still a business relationship; it should inform first and build a relationship second.

Finally, the ability to tie the key consumer benefit to the target's lifestyle is crucial in direct marketing because it helps personalize the message.

Effectiveness

Using direct mail to launch an IMC campaign can be very effective. Consider using it as a teaser or announcement device. Teasing the target about a top-secret new product launch or grand opening can build curiosity. Direct marketing can also be used as a status device, delivering invitations to grand openings or private sales.

Once a campaign is launched and interest begins to build, direct marketing can effectively support other media efforts and can make buying the product from home easy. Detailed information can be supplied through copy and/or demonstrations, allowing any direct marketing vehicle to close the sale quickly and conveniently from the target's home or office.

The type of strategy chosen will depend on whether the focus is to reward the consumer for purchase or loyalty or to promote the product. A strong product approach works on any level, as do the consumer approach options. A rational appeal is best if the execution technique employed is a competitive, product or service popularity, or news appeal. Depending on the product's life-cycle stage, a good alternative emotional appeal is the reminder. If it's important to make a quick sale and increase profits for a limited time, the addition of a strong sales promotion device is strategically a good choice.

The Many Documents That Make Up a Direct-Mail Kit

Direct mail consists of any advertising material sent by mail to a targeted consumer to solicit a sale or further inquiry. The personality of direct mail reflects a variety of diverse faces, shapes, and sizes. It is not unusual for simple direct-mail kits to employ a mixture of letter formats or informally handwritten notes, postcards, scratch-off cards, die-cuts, pocketed folders, brochures, price lists, CDs, calendars, key chains, or menus.

More creative direct-mail pieces could include three-dimensional designs that use pop-ups or pop-outs (figure 14.1), employ moving parts or sound, even AR or VR components, but that can become expensive. Most direct-mail campaigns are functional, with a strictly business appearance.

Figure 14.1. An illustrative example of a direct-mail pop-up with coupons. Robyn Blakeman.

Almost 50 percent of all direct mail, known better by the derogatory term "**junk mail**," is never opened because it does not create interest or curiosity. It's considered junk for two reasons: It comes unwanted into the target's home, and the overall design is junk. You can't change the former, but you can change the latter—and that's what will get the piece opened. A typical mailer contains five basic pieces: an outside envelope, a pitch letter, a brochure, an order form or business reply card, and a return envelope for mail orders.

A **direct-mail** kit is a design whole. One piece should not stand out alone; every piece in the kit must work together to create one visual/verbal message. The kit should reflect the key consumer benefit and strategy as defined in the creative brief and use the same tone of voice and reflect the same overall appearance as the other pieces in the IMC campaign of which it is a part. A direct-mail kit most often includes multiple pieces that must be tied together by headline or type style, color, layout, or the use of a spokesperson or animated character. An overview of concept and creative devices will help the designer decide how to tie the kit to the rest of the campaign.

The Outside Envelope

Use color on the outside of the envelope. If possible, use an oddly shaped envelope or one with a die-cut.

Copy placed on the outer envelope of a direct-mail kit is known as **teaser copy.** The job of teaser copy is to engage the reader's interest and attention long enough to open the piece. The envelope should include the logo and, if available, a slogan or tagline. The teaser should contain the key consumer benefit or the *What's in it for me?* factor. The answer to that question is more likely to motivate the target to open and read the piece more quickly than a witty headline that says nothing of value ever could.

If the envelope is perceived as an intriguing piece of eye candy, the target's attention will be held. Use the envelope like a print ad: Feature a large, benefit-based headline that continues building interest after the color, photograph, or graphic image has grabbed the target's attention (figure 14.2). The goal is to create enough curiosity that the target can't wait to see what's on the inside.

Figure 14.2. The outside envelope of an effective direct-mail piece will hook your target into reading more by conveying key consumer benefit. Image courtesy of Leanne Silverman.

Promotional Devices

If working with a tight budget, design a bright, colorful message and consider including a scratch-off card as a promotional device. If the money's there, create some kind of stimulating mental toy associated with the message inside. Design a pop-up or other three-dimensional image that raises up when the piece is opened, such as the spokesperson or a picture of a satisfied customer who goes on to give a testimonial in the copy. Consider movable pieces that reveal one part of the message at a time, allowing the reader to spin a wheel or open a window or door. If there's even more money, include an image the reader can hold up to her webcam to see an augmented reality (AR) image, or use QR codes or mobile apps to help bring reality or fun to the message.

Keep in mind that three-dimensional interactive devices can increase the time a target will spend with the piece, but they don't make the sale—they support it. Take away the bells and whistles, and you're left with the need for a strong visual/verbal message tailored to the target's specific needs.

The Pitch or Business Letter

The direct-mail letter should continue the same tone of voice used in other pieces within the IMC campaign. Open by introducing the product, the key consumer benefit, and the answer to the question *What's in it for me?* The middle section should include features, uses, additional benefits, and any endorsements, testimonials, or studies. Do not be afraid to mention price; it's important to the consumer, so don't hide it until the end.

A direct-mail piece opens the sale, gives a complete and detailed sales pitch, and closes the sale. The only thing the target has to do is drop the order form in the mail, pick up the phone, tap an app, or boot up the computer.

Once the envelope is opened, the entire sale rests with the copy. If you've got the target this far, continue to hold her attention by providing additional benefit(s) associated with the key consumer benefit. Be specific. Copy must answer who, what, when, where, why, and how—creatively and informatively—and should help alleviate any fears or skepticism the target may have. If it does not, the target's hard-won initial interest, created when she first opened the envelope or viewed the cover, will fade.

Copywriters must be able to take an ordinary feature and give it a personality, a new use, or a unique twist for an old use. Direct mail is a "sell the sizzle, not the steak" kind of conversation with the target.

Copy must be believable, not unimaginable. Advertising that appears in print alongside editorial matter, as in newspaper or magazines, appears credible by association. The unsolicited arrival of direct mail affords it no such advantage unless the brand or marketer name is well known and respected.

Long copy can be both intimidating to the eye and boring to the reader. This is especially true with direct-marketing e-mails, where content should be short, concise, and useful to the reader. Messages should focus on no more than three to four items. Leave the biggest array of eye-catching graphics and hard-sell tactics to print. This is where the theme developed throughout the IMC campaign can shine and entertain. A well-written plot or feature/benefit-driven copy that a reader finds intriguing will be read no matter its length and will initiate an inquiry or produce an order. Be sure to use multiple subheads to break up copy, stimulate interest, and make reading easier.

Be sure to close the sale. If this final step is skipped, the target will not know what kind of action he is supposed to take. Make ordering or attaining more information as easy as possible. It is important to reference the enclosed order form and provide information about how to contact customer service for more information by including a toll-free phone number and/or a website address. One way to enhance the response rate is to limit quantities or the time the target has to purchase.

How personal should the copy get? The answer will lie in the overall price and type of product being advertised. If the product is whimsical and reasonably priced, keep the copy light and airy. If the product is expensive or a limited collector's item, the copy should be more formal in tone. Copy should sound like a letter to a friend, so use the second-person pronoun "you" to refer to the target. Whatever tone the copy takes, be sure to give the target as much information as possible, from how the product is made, designed, priced, and sized to the varied color and credit card options.

Don't use too many different point sizes in the letter. This is the first mistake most direct-mail pieces make, creating an environment rich in tacky and low in class. Use a lot of white space to make the letter appear more formal. If there is a lot of copy, consider using an opening key consumer benefit headline, using the same style as on other print pieces, and multiple subheads to break up long blocks of copy. Use bullets to make specific points and create even more white space. Be sure to list the ordering options; let readers know whether they have to use the enclosed order form or can order online or over the phone. Let them know that there are operators standing by to answer any questions they may have. Direct mail has a lot of available space just waiting for the message—in fact, more space than any other medium besides web pages available to creative teams. Use it to sell the product clearly, informatively, and without a lot of flash.

Circulars or Brochures

Many direct-mail kits include circulars or brochures. Circulars can lower the quality of the kit because of their photocopy-like appearance, so design them like a poster: Use the visuals to say something, and use color to create a mood. The copy should include only the key points the target should take away from the kit, such as colors, sizes, prices, and guarantees.

Because of their use of color photography, illustrations, and/or graphics, brochures bring a lot of class to the direct-mail kit. Brochure copy can be more creative, bringing a business letter alive with descriptive copy and visuals.

The design of a brochure is influenced by how it will be folded and eventually used. Brochures can open like a book, with panels opening from both the left and right sides, or folded like a fan. Panels can have small, diagonal die-cuts to hold business cards or come complete with pockets to hold additional printed material that can be removed. However the brochure folds and whatever additional information it may hold, it must be functional and reflect the overall design of the direct-mail kit. The choice of size, number of colors, photographic images or graphics, and whether any samples or interactive devices are included will depend on the budget and overall design.

Reply Cards and Order Forms

The reply card or order form should continue to reflect the kit and campaign design, perhaps through color and/or typeface, style, or layout. Use a headline to announce the offer and a few lines of copy to remind the consumer about the offer and any additional options. It is important to include space for the consumer's name, address, city, state, zip code, day and evening phone numbers, and an e-mail address. Provide the proper boxes or lines if the consumer needs to make a color or size choice. Be sure the form has enough room to fill in the blanks and uses a type size that is easy to read. Repeat credit card information here, as well as the company's contact information.

BOX 14.2. Sizes and Types of Brochures

There are many different sizes and types of brochures, but the three most popular types are tri-folds, fan folds, and double parallel brochures.

A **tri-fold** is the most common type of brochure used in direct mail and is created from a single sheet of paper. It can be either letter size (8½ × 11) or legal size (8½ × 14) that is folded two times, creating six usable panels, folding to around 3⅝ × 8½ (letter) or 4⅝ × 8½ (legal).

Fan folds, also known as accordion folds because the panels do not close into each other but fold in and out like a fan, can be either letter or legal size, folding to 3⅝ × 8½ (letter) or 4 × 8½ (legal).

A **double-parallel** brochure, also known as a double-fold, is larger and more elaborate. This brochure design, also available in either letter or legal size, is created by first folding the paper in half and then in half once again, creating eight usable panels. The final folded size of the brochure is 2¾ × 8½ (letter) or 3½ × 8½ (legal).

Order forms, whether digital or printed, require the consumer to fill out a structured form to make a purchase, receive a free sample, or request additional information. The key is to make it both easy to read and easy to fill out. No consumer wants anything so badly that he will voluntarily struggle with a poorly designed form.

The size of the response or reply card and whether it is single- or double-sided will vary, depending on the number of items the consumer has to choose from and product details such as size or color choices. Don't forget to code the order form so that the marketer knows where the sale originated.

The Return Envelope

Whether the target uses it or not, every direct-mail kit should include a preaddressed, postage-paid envelope. The return envelope should be nice and plain and should have the return address and mailing address preprinted, along with postage bar codes and a statement in the stamp area that states, "No Postage Needed If Mailed in the United States." Make sure the reply card fits inside the envelope without excessive folding or scrunching.

In the end, direct mail gets a bad name because it's usually poorly thought out and often even more poorly designed. By following the principles outlined above, it is easy to design a direct-mail kit that stands out from the crowd.

Bottom Line

As a member of the promotional mix, direct marketing talks directly to the target and initiates a two-way dialogue—an IMC must. Messages are personalized and address the target's known interests based on past purchasing behavior. Direct marketing is less intrusive than any of the other media we have looked at so far, allowing the target to decide what message to respond to, when to respond to it, and where to make further inquiries or purchase decisions.

If the goal is to speak directly to the target with a message he or she is interested in and is sure to open, any form of direct response device is sure to catch the target's eye. If the goal is to introduce a new or reinvented product, employ efforts to remind or encourage retrial, or update the consumer on product changes or additions, direct marketing will reach the target in a shorter amount of time and more effectively than traditional advertising efforts.

To ensure engagement and, most importantly, entice targets to action, be sure to include trial offers, gifts, games, or some other type of enticement that gets them calling, logging in, or visiting a brick-and-mortar location.

Q DISCUSSION QUESTIONS

1. What are the strategic uses of direct marketing in an IMC campaign?
2. Define and explain the difference between advertising and promotion.
3. Why is direct marketing considered a medium that encourages a two-way dialogue between the brand and the target?
4. Why is a more personalized dialogue considered more important in today's advertising methods than a one-way monologue?
5. How are direct marketing methods different from traditional advertising methods?
6. Why are direct marketing methods more expensive than traditional methods but still considered a viable media choice?
7. When used in an IMC campaign, direct marketing's goal may not be to make a sale. So what role(s) might it play?
8. How are databases used in direct marketing? What is their importance?
9. Databases track varied forms of consumer data. How is this considered a privacy issue?
10. Direct marketing has a very diverse array of contact vehicles. What are some of the most commonly used, and how can they each help to visually and verbally express the key consumer benefit?
11. Why is direct mail often referred to as "junk mail," and how can that perception be turned around?
12. What are the differences/similarities between infomercials and traditional advertising?
13. Why are the Internet and social media important aspects of direct marketing?
14. How does direct marketing help an IMC campaign be more consumer focused?
15. What is the role of the visual and verbal message throughout the varied media vehicles in an IMC campaign?
16. What are the pros and cons associated with direct marketing?
17. What is the strategy behind using direct marketing in an IMC campaign?

Sales Promotion

The Strategic Use of Sales Promotion in IMC

Sales promotion is often used in conjunction with other media, especially direct marketing, giving the consumer some type of gift or incentive to prompt an inquiry or encourage purchase. Sales promotions are intended to quickly increase sales or interest through discount pricing or other motivational devices available for a limited time.

Sales promotion differs from advertising in its approach. Advertising influences attitudes and tells consumers why they should buy; sales promotion gives the target an incentive to react quickly to the advertised message.

Incentives can take many different forms. Some of the most commonly used include coupons, premiums, sampling, contests and sweepstakes, in-store displays, refunds and rebates, and percent- or cents-off promotions. The choice of sales promotion vehicle should reinforce the advertised message, reflecting the strategy and both the target and product image.

When advertising and sales promotion are coordinated in an IMC campaign, it's known as **integrated brand promotion (IBP)**. IBP takes place when the brand's image (advertising) is integrated into the promotion (sales promotion). To do this effectively, the brand-building message of advertising must coordinate with sales promotion's incentive to buy. For example, coupons arriving in the mail or appearing in a newspaper send a mixed message if the advertising message is elegance and sophistication. Instead, advertising efforts might direct the target to a web or social media site or toll-free number for more information or to set up an appointment. On the other hand, if the message is young and upbeat, promotional items may be distributed at concerts or at the mall.

The most distinctive characteristic of sales promotion is its intent. While public relations, advertising, and direct marketing bring a product and message to the target, sales promotion sidesteps the message and brings the target to the product. See case study 13 for a look at Pepsi's use of sales promotion.

BOX 15.1. What Is Integrated Brand Communication?

Integrated brand communication (IBC) is a direct result of the success of integrated marketing communication. IMC concentrates on one organized message that is heard across varied media; IBC concentrates on creating the tie that binds the consumer and the brand. In short, IMC creates a position, while IBC works with what is already there. IBC is about positioning: What does the consumer feel about the brand? This feeling becomes the brand and defines the corporation. This feeling then dominates all advertising efforts throughout all media, consistent with IMC efforts.

IMC is one message delivered through multiple and varied media. IBC takes an existing symbol, image, and overall brand performance and makes it the message. Creating a more distinctive position further strengthens this image.

Traditionally, a brand's image was built over time based on quality, reliability, and a product's desired features and overall benefits. IBC is the calculated creation of an image for a product rather than the development of an image by the consumer. Because it is more consumer focused, IBC uses more Internet-based or interactive media choices in order to interact directly with the consumer. This interaction strengthens the brand image.

The basic premise behind sales promotion is to give the target something for purchasing a product or service or for remaining a brand-loyal customer. The job of sales promotion is to attract first-time buyers, stimulate impulse buys, and entice users of a competitor's product to switch brands. It's also an effective tool for raising brand awareness through "try me" promotions and increasing product demand through limited-time offers. This is important to IMC efforts, because initiating trial is the first step on the long road to obtaining brand loyalty.

The use of sales promotion has grown steadily over the past several years due to the overwhelming number of often indistinguishable products available to consumers in any one category. By spotlighting one product, sales promotion can help consumers with a purchase decision by offering an incentive to try the product or use the service.

The Diversity of the Sales Promotion Voice

The success of all communication efforts rises and falls with the economy. Sales promotion can also be used as an incentive to purchase when a poor economy causes consumers to purchase conservatively. However, side effects are numerous, and it's easy for marketers and their products to get caught in the vicious cycle of promotion, finding it hard to get even loyal users to buy when there is no current promotion—consumers will simply wait for the next one.

CASE STUDY 13

C

IMC Sales Promotion: Pepsi

When Pepsi Cola North America decided to design a promotion to increase awareness and sales this summer, they looked to their agency, TLP, and SCA Promotions. Together, SCA, TLP, and Pepsi designed a summer-long promotion that would offer one lucky consumer the opportunity to become the world's next billionaire. Only SCA, could make it happen . . . coverage for $1 billion.

Objectives

1. Boost Pepsi product sales and increase brand awareness with consumers.
2. Capture consumers' interest by offering the largest cash prize in promotion history for a national brand: $1 billion.
3. Gain sponsor support by partnering with the WB Network, Marriott Hotels, and United Airlines.

Strategies

- Offer the billion-dollar prize on a bottle cap promotion that culminates with a live game show on the WB.
- Invite consumers to visit www.billionsweeps.com and enter a unique sweepstakes entry code found on specially marked products.
- Randomly select 1,000 contestants to play a game of chance on the WB's live show for a guaranteed $1 million and a chance to take home $1 billion.
- Have each of the 1,000 selected contestants choose a six-digit number on the day of the game show. The ten contestants whose number was closest to or exactly matched the one selected by Kendall the chimpanzee (aka "Mr. Moneybags") advanced to the elimination round.
- Play a suspenseful game of elimination to determine the final player. In return for forfeiting their chance at the billion dollars, players were offered an increasing cash prize during each round.
- Award other great prizes during the game show to continue the excitement.
- Coordinate additional coverage for the one million $15 instant-win bottle caps. SCA's coverage protected Pepsi from an unexpectedly high rate of redemption. SCA estimated the redemption rate and covered the cost of redemptions over that amount, keeping Pepsi on budget and risk-free.

Results

- Four million consumers submitted more than twenty million game entries. Pepsi captured important demographic information for future marketing efforts.
- Richard Bay, a graphic design teacher from Princeton, West Virginia, was the final contestant and won the guaranteed $1 million. To win the billion, his six-digit number would have had to exactly match Kendall's. He was only two digits away from an exact match.
- United Airlines presented two around-the-world trips, Marriott gave a lifelong time-share membership, and three Mitsubishi cars were awarded.

Source: SCA Promotions, http://www.scapromotions.com.

Other side effects include devaluation of the brand in the mind of the consumer, overall expense, and an end-of-promotion drop in sales. Excessive or unnecessary use of sales promotions can lead to the erosion of brand loyalty, brand image, and eventually brand equity.

When deciding whether sales promotions should play a part in an IMC strategy, it's important to determine whether inducing an immediate sale is a prerequisite to accomplishing the objectives. Can awareness or loyalty be built without using a form of bribery? In the end, that's what sales promotion is, and overusing it can tarnish the brand's image.

Although sales promotion can do a lot of things, it cannot stand alone to build brand loyalty, cover for a poorly promoted or poorly made product, or save the life of an aging brand. These objectives will require the additional and combined efforts of other media in the promotional mix to promote, educate, or reinvent a product or service's image.

There are a lot of options available when deciding on a promotional device. Some are creative, some are functional—but all are consumer motivated. Sales promotions can be broken down into two basic types: in-store and out-of-store promotions. A distinct few fall into both categories. Let's look at some of the most popular.

In-store promotions include:

- Coupons
- Bonus packs
- Price-off offers
- Specialty packaging
- Sampling
- Point-of-purchase (POP)
- Loyalty programs

Out-of-store promotions include:

- Refunds and rebates
- Continuity programs
- Trial offers
- Special events
- Product warranties or guarantees

Promotions that can be either in-store or out-of-store include:

- Contests and sweepstakes
- Premiums
- Giveaways

In-Store Promotions

In-store promotions are a marketer's last shot at influencing the target prior to purchase. The sales promotion devices employed are most often determined by price and purchase location.

Coupons

Coupons come with many different offers, such as cents-off discounts and two-for-one opportunities, also known as buy-one-get-one-free offers. Other offers, often for higher-priced items, might offer a percentage-off option. Whatever the offer, coupons initiate action and account for almost 70 percent of all consumer sales promotions.

Coupons can be found just about anywhere, but one of the most common places is within the Sunday newspaper, where **freestanding inserts** (FSIs) are found. These perforated, usually four-color, 8½ × 11-inch pages offer numerous coupons for one brand of products. Coupons can also be found within newspaper and magazine ads, in the mail as a part of a direct-mail kit or polypak, and as bounce-back coupons on the outside of a product or placed inside packaging. Most coupons can be used immediately and are known as **instant-redemption coupons**. Others, like those used in an FSI, might be valid over several days or weeks to encourage return visits.

Coupons can also be found on the Internet, on social media sites, and in text messages, where distribution is tracked and usually limited on a per-person basis, so it is unlikely the target will print coupons directly off a web or social media site. Instead, coupons are usually sent to the target by e-mail or via mobile text. A request for coupons directly from the consumer, either by toll-free number or through a web or social media site, creates an interaction between buyer and seller. The more time consumers spend actively thinking about the product or service, the more likely the product is to move from their short-term memory to their long-term memory, assisting with recall when they shop.

Technology at the checkout counter is also an important part of coupon distribution. One of the most commonly used coupon systems is Catalina Marketing's checkout coupon. This form of coupon is distributed with grocery receipts. Which coupons are distributed is determined based on current purchases; they are often not for the same brand but for other products in the same brand category. These checkout coupons cannot be used immediately but may be used on the consumer's next visit. If consumers remember to bring the coupons on their next shopping visit, this is a good way to encourage trial.

Crossruffing is another coupon opportunity. Here, two compatible products team up to share one promotion. For example, a coupon for Pillsbury cookie dough might be placed on a package of Nestlé chocolate chips.

Bonus Packs

Bonus packs are very popular, giving the consumer more product for the price of the original size or including a related bonus product in a "try me" size.

Price-Off Offers

"Price-off offer" is a fancy term for a sale. Unlike coupons, price-off deals often appear on the packaging or are announced by shelf signage. A sale can be anything from a cents-off offer to several dollars or even several hundred dollars off, depending on the product.

Specialty Packaging

Used to raise awareness and to attract attention, specialty packaging is often used when a product has been reinvented or repackaged. These offers are most common during holidays

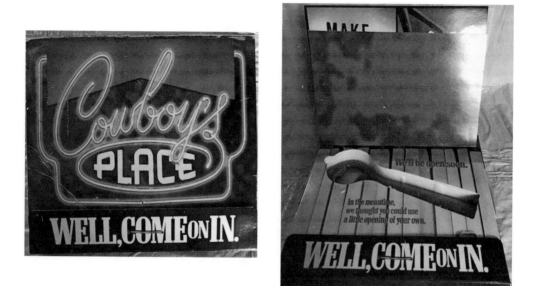

Figure 15.1. This is an example of a give away at the opening of a local club and restaurant. The inside of the promotional piece used accordion folds with four-color images and little copy to entice the viewer down to the bottle opener hidden at the bottom of the piece. Robyn Blakeman.

or in conjunction with a promotional event, such as a movie premiere popular with the target audience, a celebrity endorsement, or a sponsored event (see figure 15.1).

Sampling

Sampling is just what the name implies: The product is available for consumers to try at the point of purchase. If the goal is to entice consumers to try the product, particularly if it is new or repositioned, put it in their hands; let them feel the quality, weight, or texture. Better yet, if it smells good, let the consumer sample its scent at no charge. Samples can also be distributed through the mail as a part of direct-mail kits, bound up in the Sunday newspaper, distributed at events, or sent in response to consumer requests.

Point-of-Purchase (POP)

This is all the advertising seen while shopping, such as store posters, signage inside and outside the store, promotional kiosks that prominently display products either in the aisle or on the endcaps, and shopping-cart signs. Shelf dispensers are a popular way to distribute POP coupons that can be redeemed immediately.

Loyalty Programs

Loyalty programs give something back to customers who repeatedly purchase a product or use a service; such incentives include free products, priority service, and first-to-own opportunities. The goal is to retain and reward brand-loyal users in order to build a new and/or strengthen an existing relationship between the brand and the target user. It is a great way to make a brand with few differentiating features stand out among competitors.

Box 15.2. What Gets a Coupon Redeemed?

The better the offer, the more likely it will be redeemed. Consumers are also influenced by the origin of the coupon. On the negative side, in-store coupons require time-consuming decisions and extend the shopping experience. Other offers, such as bounce-backs or checkout coupons, cannot be used until a future visit. Polypak coupons are the least attractive because of the time required to sort through the stack of cards. On the positive side, coupons that arrive via e-mail or text or that land on the target's front doorstep in the Sunday paper are successful because they can be looked at and organized at the target's leisure. Coupons that arrive at the point of purchase with the target are more likely to be redeemed.

Coupons never go out of fashion; they just hit their stride. Most sales or promotions occur before and during a product's peak season. It is not unusual to see a summer promotion for barbecue grills or a winter promotion for hats, coats, and gloves. This might seem a little strange, because the products would most likely sell even without additional incentives. But remember, the whole point is to get consumers moving now in order to increase short-term sales within a specific time frame rather than waiting for them to get around to a last-minute purchase.

Believe it or not, most coupons are never redeemed, and many that are cause another problem: misredemption. This is when a coupon is accepted for the wrong product or used after the expiration date. Additionally, coupons do not always attract or reach new users and are often redeemed by consumers who are already loyal to the brand.

Out-of-Store Promotions

Out-of-store promotions can be used to reward consumers for their loyalty or for purchase or to draw attention to a brand or service.

Refunds and Rebates

Both refunds and rebates give cash back to the consumer. In the case of a refund, it's possible for the entire purchase price to be refunded, with or without the original sales receipt. Rebates often require the buyer to fill out lengthy forms and supply product information that can be either mailed in or submitted via the brand's website. The target's willingness to give detailed personal and purchasing information in return for an incentive is a great database-building tool.

Continuity Programs

One lesser-known type of sales promotion is the continuity program. Every time consumers use the program and/or make a purchase, they earn points toward a reward or free gift, usually associated with the program's sponsor. Most often used by restaurants, hotels, and airlines, this is a great way to encourage repeat purchase and build brand loyalty.

Trial Offers

Trial offers, most often used for expensive items such as beds, larger lawn and garden tools, and exercise equipment, allow consumers to try the product in their home on a trial basis for a specified time, often thirty to ninety days, before buying.

Special Events

When a product or service attaches its name to an event, it is called a special-events promotion. Sponsors whose products are a good fit with the event and its target audience will experience a high degree of product awareness and recall.

Product Warranties or Guarantees

One of the best ways to generate trust or goodwill in a product or service is to offer a product warranty or guarantee. A **warranty** guarantees that if the consumer is not 100 percent satisfied, the purchase price will be refunded in its entirety. Price **guarantees** ensure consumers that they will not find the product at a lower price anywhere; if they do, the marketer will honor the lower price, refunding the difference.

In-Store or Out-of-Store Promotions

Some promotions can be used whether the target visits a store location or purchases from a website or over the phone.

Contests and Sweepstakes

Of all the promotions we have discussed, contests and sweepstakes are one of the few that do not necessarily require a purchase in order to participate. Consumers love the interactive participation of games of chance. The decision to use a contest or a sweepstakes depends on the type of promotion and the desired outcome. **Contests** are games of skill that require participants to meet a certain set of standards in order to win. A **sweepstakes,** on the other hand, is based entirely on chance. Both can be used to build a database list; information from entry forms can be stored and used for future promotions.

Premiums

Premiums are wearable or usable gifts that are often given away at out-of-store sponsored events, through personal selling, or attached to an in-store product. Usually emblazoned with a company or product logo and/or tagline or slogan, these usable items include T-shirts, pens, calendars, coffee cups, and baseball caps—basically, anything that can display a logo. Not all premiums are free; some require a few proof-of-purchase seals and a little cash to cover shipping.

Giveaways

A giveaway can take place in or out of a store. Although similar to sampling, giveaways rarely give the actual product or service away. Instead, a giveaway is often something that complements the product or service. For example, a DVD player might come with an offer of free DVDs with purchase.

How Does Sales Promotion Help IMC Be Consumer Focused?

Sales promotion brings customer contact to an IMC campaign. It can be used to reinforce an existing campaign message, stimulate trial or repeat purchase, or launch a new product.

A promotion is an interactive direct-response vehicle that often initiates a one-on-one dialogue with the consumer. Products can often be tested and tried on-site, creating immediate feedback between buyer and seller. Most sales promotions are personal.

Because sales promotion, like direct marketing, is so consumer focused, it is more expensive to use than either public relations or advertising mass-media approaches. Cost is also dependent on the size and length of the promotion and the number of prizes or premiums needed. Sales promotion runs the risk of generating big losses if participation is low.

Every buyer likes a bargain, but not all consumers will respond to a bargain. Consumers who are loyal to a product will not be tempted by sales or giveaways; others live only for the next promotion, with brand playing little or no role in their purchase decision. In between these two extremes lie the switchers, those who may be successfully tempted into switching from a preferred brand to a new brand. This is the group most influenced by sales promotion efforts.

Promotions are most often used in an IMC campaign to round out and reinforce the other advertising efforts that make up the promotional mix. The type of promotion used should be chosen based on the product and where it is in its life cycle. New product launches often use coupons, sampling, bonus packs, or contests and sweepstakes to encourage trial purchase. A product in its maintenance stage relies on advertising and requires little promotional assistance. The use of sales promotion is a great way to reawaken interest in a mature brand and might be used to remind the consumer of its value with crossruffing coupons, in- or on-pack offers, or flashy POP displays.

Enticing consumers to take advantage of offers is not always successful, so sales promotion cannot be relied on as the sole way to generate interest and increase traffic or short-term sales.

Incentives and Deterrents of Sales Promotion

To decide whether sales promotion is right for an IMC campaign, let's look at some of the incentives and deterrents associated with it.

What Makes Sales Promotion So Great?

The more notable incentives associated with sales promotion include:

- *Time Limit.* Sales promotions increase a company's cash flow, since consumers are more likely to buy when they are offered an extra incentive on a short-term basis, ensuring an influx of cash for a set period. Any kind of promotion is good for consumers, since it gives something to, or back to, them. As soon as the sale or additional incentive is over, sales will drop or return to pre-promotional levels.
- *Trackable.* After a coupon is redeemed or a contest winner is found, results are easily tracked. The volume of sales made during the promotion will also determine success.
- *Product Visibility.* A good promotion can entice the consumer to try the product. When a product is supported by a promotion, it can increase awareness by making the product temporarily stand out from a competing brand, initiating a trial purchase.

Promotions can be directly responsible for convincing consumers loyal to a competing brand to switch brands based on an initial trial.

Is There Anything Wrong with Sales Promotion?

The more notable deterrents associated with sales promotion include:

- *Negative Sales Effect.* Once a promotion has ended, sales often drop as consumers move on to another product promotion. This is an unfortunate side effect of using sales promotion. To quickly increase sales again, another promotion will be needed.
- *Damaged Brand Image.* Overuse of promotions can damage a product's image in the mind of the consumer by cheapening its appeal. This directly affects the need to build and maintain brand loyalty. A product's image is the voice of advertising efforts, and excessive promotions can quickly erode the message, destroying consumer confidence in the brand.
- *Equity Depletion.* Excessive use of sales promotions can negatively affect the way the target views the product's image or worth, effectively depleting a brand's equity over time.
- *Cost.* Sales promotion is expensive. A relatively small number of consumers will be reached compared to other approaches, and inventory to cover prizes or premiums can be high when compared to the actual number of sales.

The Strategy behind Sales Promotion

Sales promotion works great as a secondary medium for public relations, advertising, and/or direct marketing, social media, mobile, and/or alternative media to induce trial during small or inexpensive product launches. It is a useful tool for any product where a particular feature can be proved at the point of purchase, such as taste or softness. Products in highly competitive categories with little or no product differentiation can benefit from the use of coupons, bonus packs, price-off offers, or sampling opportunities.

So how does sales promotion fit into the promotional mix? A mature product that is being repositioned might lead off with public relations, using the media to announce a new face to an old friend; advertising will then begin building awareness and introduce the new image. A coupon could be placed in almost any print or digital medium, but would most likely be found in newspapers, magazines, and direct mail, on mobile devices, in e-mail, or on websites.

Direct marketing might use sales promotion in a direct mail kit by directing the public to a store location, a website, or a toll-free number to receive a free sample or participate in a trial offer. Incentives such as samples, coupons, point-of-purchase displays, or trial offers can be used to build brand awareness for a new product or to reintroduce the target to a reinvented product.

Like advertising, promotional efforts may target both a primary and secondary target audience. Determining the need for a secondary audience will depend on the target's overall knowledge of, or history with, the product or service and whether it can, or would, be purchased by a family member, friend, or professional associate. Additional factors affecting both the promotional mix and the strategy include how far each audience is from trial, repeat purchase, and brand loyalty.

Key consumer benefits have nothing to say in sales promotion—but they have everything to show. The message should be your guide, along with strategy, overall objectives, and target audience as to what the image of the promotion has to do with the image of the product and target. Sales promotion efforts should be avoided for products with a strong brand image, with the possible exception of event sponsorships or continuity programs.

Effective sales promotion objectives might include encouraging trial or product switching by nonusers, supporting a new product launch, offsetting competitor promotions, gaining a larger market share, and increasing short-term profits.

The type of strategy chosen will depend on whether advertising efforts are focusing on the consumer to reward purchase or loyalty, or to promote the product. A strong product approach works on any level, as do the consumer approach options. A rational appeal is best if the tone or execution technique employed is comparison, price, or news driven. Depending on the product's life-cycle stage, a good alternative emotional appeal is the reminder. If it's important to make a quick sale and increase profits for a limited time, sales promotion is a strategically good choice.

The Look of Sales Promotion

Sales promotion must be an extension of the brand's image and the advertising message. The closer the visual/verbal relationship, the easier it is to excite consumer interest.

It is important to carry the visual/verbal message created elsewhere in the promotional mix through all sales promotion efforts. This is often easier said than done because of the eclectic shape, texture, and size of promotional materials.

Depending on the amount of available surface space, promotional devices such as special packaging, premiums, contest and sweepstakes announcements and/or game boards, POP displays, coupons and freestanding inserts, and special event materials should take their cue from print or direct-marketing materials. Consider adapting unique headline styles, color combinations, typeface and type style, a spokesperson or character representative, and logo and slogan or tagline for use in sales promotions. POP advertising that reflects the overall visual/verbal appearance of the other IMC components can assist with product recognition should the target forget the product name while shopping.

The job of this very consumer-focused approach is to get the product into the target's hands and push for an initial inquiry, a request for follow-up information, or purchase. Sales promotion is a great way to introduce or create excitement about a new product or to reintroduce an old one.

Q DISCUSSION QUESTIONS

1. What are the strategic uses of sales promotion in an IMC campaign?
2. What is sales promotion and how is it used in conjunction with direct marketing?
3. What is the difference between sales promotion and advertising?
4. What are some of the most common incentives used in direct marketing?
5. What is the most distinctive characteristic of sales promotion compared to public relations, advertising, and direct marketing?
6. Like direct marketing, sales promotion has a very diverse array of contact vehicles. What are some of the most common and how can they each help to visually and verbally express the key consumer benefit?
7. What is the difference between in-store and out-of-store promotions? What are some of the most common types of vehicles and how can they be promoted and tied to an IMC campaign?
8. Only a small number of coupons are ever redeemed. What can the visual and verbal message say/do to ensure their use? Explain.
9. How does sales promotion help an IMC campaign to be more consumer focused?
10. What are the pros and cons associated with sales promotion?
11. What is the strategy behind using sales promotion in an IMC campaign?
12. Why is sales promotion a great pairing with multiple vehicles in an IMC campaign?
13. What must sales promotion do both visually and verbally to be successful within an IMC campaign?
14. What is the difference between IMC, advertising, and integrated brand communication (IBC)?

Internet Marketing and Social Media

The Strategic Use of Internet Marketing in IMC

The Internet has changed the way corporations conduct business and connect with customers. Through the Internet, advertising that once spoke to the targeted buyer can now actively interact with that buyer. Consumers can ask questions, get help or technical assistance, and make a purchase without ever leaving their home or office. The Internet allows consumers to decide when, where, and for how long they will view a message. The ease with which information can be gathered makes comparison shopping easier, faster, and more convenient, so when consumers elect to buy, they are much better educated on product use, quality, price, competitor brands, and/or guarantee or return policies than ever before.

When consumers visit websites, it is important that the sites open quickly and are easy to navigate. When consumers initiate contact, they should encounter courteous and knowledgeable customer service or technical representatives who can answer questions quickly and professionally. Often, this is the only thing that separates one product in a category from another. The quality of this interaction is often transferred to the brand or service.

The role of the Internet is still evolving. Its growth as an advertising or direct-selling tool will ultimately depend on how and why consumers use it. Use as a primary vehicle requires the target to initiate contact based on a personal need that begins and ends with a search for information. In the Internet's current role as a secondary or support media source, the target is directed to a website based on exposure in a traditional advertising or promotional media vehicle.

Used together, traditional advertising and **Internet marketing**, also called **cybermarketing**, are effective at building brand awareness, initiating interactive opportunities, and educating consumers about a product or service. As an educational and informational tool, the Internet is a great place to direct the target for information on current promotions, news articles, testimonials, tests or medical results, and advice or tips from relevant experts. Many websites also sponsor social media sites, chat rooms, and/or blogs where consumers can talk to and exchange information with other product users.

After advertising, a website is often the consumer's first concentrated impression of a brand or corporation. The consumer's initial website visit is like stepping into a brick-and-mortar store for the first time: The consumer will take notice of the furnishings, how the floor plan is laid out, and how products are displayed. A messy or haphazard appearance is a turnoff and reflects low budget and quality; a lot of white space and a clean atmosphere gives the illusion of quality and exclusivity. As we have learned, advertising in any medium is all about presentation and the way the visual/verbal message is delivered. Internet marketing introduces yet another dimension: interactivity.

Interactive media focuses on creating dialogue and building relationships between buyer and seller by providing multiple channels of communication to encourage consumer interaction and/or feedback. The successful use of interactive media is an important component to developing an effective IMC approach.

The Diversity of the Internet Marketing Voice

The Internet is interactive, requiring the consumer to participate in the message by scrolling or clicking to retrieve information. This participation should take little thought, and, like any other medium we have discussed, it should lead the consumer on an informative but structured journey. Interactive advertising vehicles can be as uncomplicated as a banner ad or as multifaceted as an entire website.

Advertising as we know it in print does exist on the Internet in the form of pop-ups and banners, and some Internet service providers sell message space at the bottom of each viewable screen. This type of message is more reminder than hard sell and can be targeted to match the demographic and psychographic characteristics of the viewer based on previous searches. This personalization helps brands reach out to those consumers most likely to buy with an offer they will be interested in.

Internet use is popular among consumers, and advertisers are still learning the ins and outs of how to deliver an advertised message that is not overtly intrusive. Making advertising interactive or participatory, rather than just visually and verbally interesting, is a new challenge. To creative teams, interactive means creating an attention-getting activity that can also inform. To marketers, it is a means of creating an informational vehicle for two-way communication with the target audience.

Advertising on the Internet is less expensive than traditional advertising methods, is easier to revise, and is much more targetable and less intrusive to consumers, since they choose when, where, and for how long they will visit a site.

Internet advertising and promotional efforts at their simplest can take many diverse forms, such as banner ads and pop-ups, floating ads, personalized e-mail, and opportunities to enter a contest or sweepstakes or pick up a coupon or two. More sophisticated options might include streaming audio and video, webisodes, augmented reality, games, search, pay-per-click advertising, interactive television, and destination or informational websites.

Banner Ads

With a click of the mouse, a banner can transport a viewer to the sponsored web page. Banner ads are mass media Internet vehicles usually found at the top of web pages. In its simplest form, a banner is nothing more than a brightly colored rectangular bar featuring a logo and a small amount of type. Vertical banners known as **skyscrapers** are another option, although they are not used as often. More complex banners can use moving or blinking images to attract attention. It is important not to get so caught up in what can be done with the technology that basic design principles are ignored. It is not a big leap from animated to tacky and annoying, so take care when deciding how consumers should think about the client's product the first time they see the banner.

Like traditional advertising methods, these often unpopular and intrusive ads are paid for by the advertiser and placed strategically throughout the Internet, usually on very active or highly visited sites. These interactive advertising messages have little type; they briefly present the key consumer benefit and/or a slogan or tagline with an accompanying logo.

When used as a more selective targeting vehicle, banners can be placed on sites that focus on a specific market. For example, a site on dental health might have a banner for a tooth whitening system. This option allows for less waste and creates more interest.

Pop-Up Ads

Pop-up ads are separate windows that pop up on top of a web page. Much like banner ads, these mass-media ads link the viewer to another site. Pop-up ads were originally conceived as a vehicle to drive consumers to the desired website; instead, consumers often consider them an annoyance, making them equally as unpopular as banner ads. Consumers are taking advantage of pop-up blockers offered by their service providers to keep pop-up windows from opening.

For now, banners and pop-up ads make up the limited palette from which Internet advertisers can choose to deliver their message. Advertisers and marketers alike are asking: What is the look of Internet advertising? Is it more like print or broadcast? Banner and pop-up ads currently have more print characteristics than broadcast—and all the annoyance of both. Marketers are constantly working to come up with new and less intrusive ways to catch and direct the target's attention to their websites. The Internet's visual/verbal growing pains are much like television ads were in their infancy. Long and boring, they sounded more like radio ads than the creative, informative productions we see today. As knowledge of what the Internet can and cannot do and how the consumer will interact with and react to Internet advertising develops, creative teams will be better able to define what good advertising on the Internet will look and sound like and how motion should be employed.

Floating Ads

These ads appear when a website opens and "float" or land on top of the page, blocking the site beneath. Each message can last anywhere from five to thirty seconds and can take over a viewer's mouse for as long as it is viewable. These attention-getting but often annoying ads will often try to overcome their intrusive presence by featuring animation and/or sound.

E-mail Marketing

E-mail marketing is another way to reach the target electronically. E-mail makes printed copies and lengthy printing delays a thing of the past, and is an inexpensive and dependable means of reaching the target. As an effective customer service device, e-mail can be used to thank customers by name for their purchase and reinforce ways to contact the marketer with questions or comments. E-mail can also be used to verify the receipt of an order, alleviating concerns that it might somehow have been lost in cyberspace. It is also an excellent way to send a follow-up customer comment sheet, allowing buyers to comment on service, product quality, and so forth.

Like other forms of Internet advertising, e-mail marketing gets mixed reactions. When consumers elect to receive e-mail messages, it's known as **permission or opt-in marketing.** Elective e-mails might come from local retailers announcing sales or from airlines or hotel chains advertising discount fares or room rates. E-mail messages sent without permission are known as **spam**.

Streaming Audio and Video

Streaming audio and video is the Internet version of radio and television advertising. A static image or link can be clicked on and played back, creating an opportunity to use demonstration or testimonial techniques or to give the spokesperson or animated character a role in the website. It takes a fast Internet connection to run streaming audio and video combinations, and because of technology limitations and variables, it is most commonly used not as a straight advertising tool but as an **interactive supplement.**

Webisodes

A webisode is a short original episodic web program that uses sight, sound, and motion to engage the viewer with branded storytelling content. They are often used to promote products or services, introduce music, or publicize news events.

These very engaging forms of **branded content** keep the target engaged and thus coming back for more. The goal beyond an attention-getting device is to encourage the viewer to visit related YouTube channels, Facebook pages, or any other related touch points associated with the brand.

Webisodes are inexpensive to produce compared to traditional television and are a very successful, unobtrusive way to tell the brand's story. A few examples of brands currently and successfully using webisodes are Kraft, Ikea, and Procter & Gamble. The most successful webisodes offer something unique to the viewer, something not found in other media outlets.

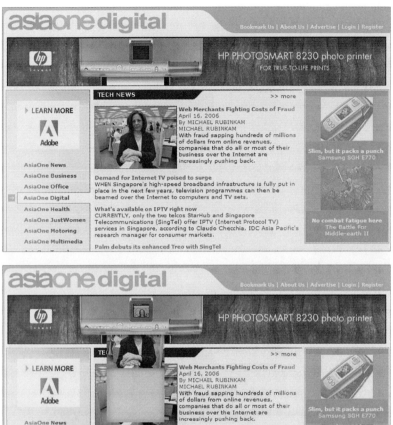

Figure 16.1. The "True-to-Life Prints" online banner ad was designed to demonstrate to home printer users the realistic quality of the prints from the HP Photosmart 8230 Photo Printer. Created by Robin Tan, Jae Soh, and Justine Lee from Saatchi & Saatchi Singapore for Hewlett-Packard Asia Pacific. Images courtesy of Saatchi & Saatchi.

Augmented Reality

Augmented reality (AR) places digitally created images over real-world images to create a three-dimensional holographic image. Largely a promotional tool, its main goal is to engage the viewer, extending the amount of time she spends with a brand. To use, the target must download a software application or browser plug-in and have a built-in webcam.

AR can also be used in traditional advertising and packaging and on mobile devices. Thanks to Pokémon Go raising awareness about augmented reality, consumers are likely to see it used to sell furniture, apparel, makeup, jewelry, and other products. Being able to see something in your home or on your body before buying can help to simplify purchasing decisions. Other uses might include navigation, search, or even the ability to scan someone's face to find out more information about them, similar to scanning a QR code for additional content. But for now, AR in its most common and simplest form can be regularly seen during football games when the first-down yellow line is displayed on the screen.

Technology like AR has everything needed to capture and hold the attention of a distracted, advertising-avoidant target. It is engaging, interactive, memorable, and worthy of being passed on to friends and family members.

Games

There are many gaming opportunities for those who enjoy playing. In-game advertising (IGA), or **advergaming**, is advertising placed inside video games that can be purchased or played for free on computers, tablets, and televisions or via mobile devices.

Some games, like Candy Crush Saga and Angry Birds, can be played for free on Facebook; others distribute games as promotional devices for a particular brand. Popular video games can also display advertising. Most brand placement is simple and game appropriate; in other words, you won't see a Pepsi can in a game featuring dinosaurs. However, that same can may be held by a character in a game that takes place in a present-day or futuristic setting. Other placements might appear on billboards, clothing, transit vehicles, or packaging.

Search Engine Marketing

When brands pay a search engine company such as Google or Bing to place their websites first or toward the top in keyword searches, it is known as **search engine marketing (SEM)**. This top placement increases the chance the site will be clicked on. Sites that employ **search engine optimization (SEO)** include relevant links to other sites to increase engagement. Search engine marketing is very effective because it is based on the target's specific interests.

Pay-per-Click Advertising

Pay-per-click advertising uses short text-only ads that are placed on multiple popular websites. Its only job is to encourage viewers to click on the ad, where they will be quickly transported to the sponsoring website.

Interactive Television

Interactive television is a mixture of computers, television, and the Internet. Television advertising that features a link allows consumers to directly respond to a commercial message viewed on their television screen by clicking on the link using their remote or with a remote control or a keyboard. Satellite television has offered interactive technology for years, allowing viewers to order movies using their remotes. The technology required to make television viable as a two-way media device is currently available and is gaining in popularity.

Destination or Informational Websites

The job of a website is to provide company background and/or product details. There are two basic types of content sites: destination websites and informational websites.

Destination websites are the place for surfers to be. This type of site actively engages viewers, using some form of entertaining activity with the goal of building brand awareness and encouraging return visits. The ever-changing destination website can intrigue, entertain, and interact with visitors as a means of introducing a product and building brand awareness. This type of approach works great for products generally purchased more spontaneously or products that are not technical in nature and need little explanation as to use.

The goal for marketers and advertisers alike is finding out what makes a surfer return to a site. A return visit requires initial interest, but the site must change constantly so that every visit is unique. Easy methods to keep a website fresh include using promotional options, such as contests and sweepstakes; more sophisticated options, such as augmented reality, webisodes, or games; or news and weather updates or stock quotes. The key is to find a way to make visitors bookmark the site.

Since most surfers are on the go from site to site, they like sites that load quickly and can be viewed as easily as possible. A simple visual/verbal format will be read more often than a time-intensive multimedia message. Webisodes and streaming audio and video are great if consumers want to take the time to watch or listen, but even in this popular medium, simple and traditional approaches work best.

An informational website's primary job is to educate rather than entertain. This type of site showcases products or services, offers advice or promotional devices, and provides customer service or technical support. A typical page features descriptive copy with an accompanying visual. Although informational sites are not flashy, interactive opportunities exist through promotional efforts such as free gifts, additional information requests, contests, and "click-and-print" coupon offers.

The Internet of Things

The Internet of Things (IoT), very basically, connects everyday objects like refrigerators to the Internet, allowing for interaction from anywhere at any time. Marketers are using the IoT to connect with their target in very diverse ways. Disney, for example, uses connected wristbands that can be used to enter the park, unlock hotel doors, and purchase food and souvenirs. Brands like Frito-Lay Tostitos are using embedded sensors on a smaller, more temporary basis. As part of a Super Bowl promotion, Tostitos partnered with Mothers Against Drunk Driving and Uber to remind partygoers not to drink and drive. The specially designed bag included an alcohol sensor that could "smell" if you had been drinking. The highly creative "how to" packaging showed a steering wheel that lit up after the sensor at the top of the bag was blown into, showing either a green light, indicating you were OK to drive, or a red light, indicating alcohol was present and you needed to use the $10-off Uber coupon to get a ride home.

The Strategic Use of Social Media in IMC

The Internet is no longer just one surfer individually looking for information; it has become a place to be entertained and to network socially, with sites like Facebook, Twitter, Pinterest, Instagram, and YouTube.

Social sites are a pop culture phenomenon that affects viewers both socially and culturally. These popular networking sites offer participants the opportunity to post personal profiles, including photographs; participate in blogs and chat rooms; post messages on bulletin boards; and listen to music or view videos. Consumers' love of anything technical is boosting revenues on these varied social sites.

Social media, also known as **user-generated content (UGC)** or consumer-generated media (CGM), is the visual/verbal sharing of thoughts and ideas on the Internet between brand users. (See case study 14 on Gatorade's use of social media.)

From a business perspective, since the target generates social media content, it creates a relationship by creating a two-way dialogue between buyer and seller. Businesses that invest in social media can improve or regulate customer relationships, generate promotions or sales, and reduce advertising costs.

The interactive environment created through social media outlets eliminates advertising that talks at the consumer through content that is mass focused for an individually targeted discussion. Advertising appearing on social media sites is more promotional and requires brand representatives to be part of an ongoing conversation with the target rather than delivering a scripted response to inquiries that attempt to control the direction of the discussions by minimizing concerns or selling the brand's virtues. By taking an active role in social media discussions, brand representatives can quickly address any negative comments or rumors or even use consumer feedback in future product upgrades or advertising efforts.

It is important that the strategy employed match the one used throughout the campaign to keep the message relevant and as a way to reinforce claims made elsewhere. When the media mix is synergistic, it can continue to educate and inform, no matter where the advertised message is encountered, and ultimately strengthen loyalty and build or reinforce equity.

To take social media efforts one step further, consider adding some type of video. Gaining in popularity on sites like Twitter, these sponsored videos allow customers to see the product in use. Visual cues help the target remember the brand at the time of purchase as well as help build loyalty.

Social media sites may also include:

1. Trial or other types of promotional offers
2. Opinion posts

CASE STUDY 14

C

IMC Social Media: Gatorade Dunk

For the past thirty years, Gatorade has crowned the champions of the Super Bowl with the iconic dunk at the end of the game. Although it has been seen by millions of broadcast viewers, it has only been experienced by a select few individuals since its inception.

Challenge

How could the brand allow its fans on social media to take part in the celebration?

Idea

The Snapchat Gatorade dunk went live the day of the Super Bowl and featured a 3-D representation of the iconic Gatorade cooler seen on every NFL sideline. Through Snapchat's facial recognition technology, users could select the Gatorade lens to activate an interactive augmented reality Gatorade cooler to splash over their head, giving the impression that the user had just experienced a true Gatorade dunk.

The Gatorade dunk—or "shower" or "bath," depending on the TV announcer—is a Super Bowl tradition. And the sports drink is playing that up for its Big Game ad campaign on Snapchat, showing an animated GIF of tennis star Serena Williams getting doused virtually.

Gatorade is utilizing its ongoing sponsorship of Williams, who dons football-style eye black in the ad. The PepsiCo-owned brand has partnered with Snapchat and purchased a sponsored lens on the mobile-social platform for an undisclosed amount. (*Adweek* reports that the four-month-old branded lens costs $350,000 on non–Super Bowl days.)

The marketer's lens employs animation powered by object-recognition technology to trigger the Gatorade cooler and subsequent dunk. In other words, it's an optical illusion that Williams is getting drenched.

Snapchat users will be able to save the animation and share it. Consumers can personalize the Gatorade lens by pressing down on the app and holding their—or a friend's—face in front of the camera in Snapchat. Filtering options will then appear at the bottom of the screen. The lens will be available through Monday.

Snapchat has become integral to major marketers' attempts to reach millennial consumers, and it's going to be interesting to see how brands do with it during the Super Bowl.

Results

More than 165 million platform views and 8 million unique user-generated videos helped create an increase in brand favorability and purchase intent.

Sources: "How an Iconic Moment for a Few Became an Immersive Experience for Everyone," VML.com, http://www.vml.com/our-work/gatorade.

"Check Out Gatorade's Super Bowl Snapchat Ad with Serena Williams," *Adweek,* http://www.adweek.com/digital/check-out-gatorades-super-bowl-snapchat-ad-serena-williams-169474/.

3. How-to ideas
4. Humorous or motivational stories
5. Imaginative/creative product ideas
6. Q&A
7. Real-time posts
8. Debatable or controversial content
9. Influencer posts

Like in Internet marketing, brands using social media often compile a database of brand-loyal users who, as a reward for their loyalty, are the first to hear about upcoming promotions or are sought out for feedback on new or existing brands and current promotions. Along with social media, many brands may also include within their media mix other digital options such as Internet websites, permission marketing, search, and varied mobile options such as GPS location, texting, and mobile apps, as well as traditional outlets to reach the target.

It is important to remember that all social media sites are networking sites. They are not the arena for pushy sales tactics, hard-sell advertising techniques, or trashing competitor brands.

Brands that incorporate social media into their promotional mix need to be cognizant of the fact that they cannot control content, but they can ensure they always talk *to* visitors, not *at* visitors. By being a part of the conversation, brands can ensure they help accentuate the positive, counter any negative chatter with current facts, dispel rumors, and outline future actions that will be undertaken if applicable.

Social media is a unique promotional vehicle because it allows users to honestly post or write about their personal experiences with a brand. It is the first widely used media outlet where advertisers do not control the message. Because of this, before posting, many sites require visitors to honor a standard conduct agreement prohibiting the use of profanity, defamation, or any other form of inappropriate behavior. Sites should also let visitors know they are legally responsible for any content they post to the site. To ensure compliance, many sites have someone who monitors content and has the authority to remove anything believed to be in violation of this agreement.

It is impossible for any advertised brand to reasonably expect that all posts will express positive experiences or rave reviews, but the brand can reasonably assume posts will express an honest appraisal of users' interactions with the brand.

Postings on social media sites are often the foundation for a new or reinvented brand's success or failure in the marketplace, often overriding anything said in traditional advertising. It has redefined customer service initiatives and how companies create a two-way dialogue between buyer and seller.

The Diversity of the Social Media Voice

Social media encourages word-of-mouth discussions about a brand, conveniently delivers promotions, and is a great source for feedback. Unfortunately, marketers still want more out

---

BOX 16.1. Before Adding Social Media . . .

Before adding social media to any media mix:

- Know what role the site is intended to play in the brand's continued development.
- Know how the target will be initially directed to the site—traditional media, website, e-mail alerts.
- Know what the target wants out of a social media site.
- Know who will monitor the site and when, and know whether they are authorized to respond to all messages, both positive and negative.
- Be sure all internal and external messages are integrated and that all employees are made aware of the current advertising messages and promotions being seen by the target.

---

of social media for their individual brands and are attempting to reinvent and strengthen its role in the promotional mix by finding a term more suitable to its use in their brand's promotional efforts. To more effectively define use, brands have adopted more functional terms for social media, such as social marketing, social buzz, social influence marketing, and social response management, to name just a few new labels.

Social media, unlike most forms of advertising and promotion, is not thrust upon consumers but is used by choice. It is not a venue devoid of advertising but relies most heavily on user-generated content to reinforce the brand's message. Consumers have many choices when it comes to social media, such as Facebook, Twitter, blogs, YouTube, Snapchat, Pinterest, Tumblr, Instagram, Google+, and LinkedIn. Let's take a brief look at what each one has to offer.

Facebook

The best reasons for having a presence on Facebook include ongoing conversations with brand-loyal consumers, building brand awareness, the ability to promote new products, getting feedback on current brands, and providing a convenient outlet for dispensing diverse forms of sales promotions that promote word-of-mouth and viral sharing, as well as purchase or repurchase of the brand.

Traditional advertising, according to research, is the most effective way to promote brand pages, followed by personal recommendations and individualized web searches. To encourage repeat visits, consumers loyal to the brand want their visits to be less about coupons and more about being part of something exclusive and meaningful. They want to access elite content, get insider information, and be the first to learn about opportunities on upcoming product launches and/or play a meaningful role in providing recommendations on improving product performance.

As an engagement, viral, and promotional tool, Facebook offers a location-based, or check-in, feature called Facebook Places, where users can share their location with friends and in return receive some type of incentive. This is also a great viral tool for participating marketers because Facebook alerts their friends with news feeds every time they check in.

Consumers who join a brand's fan page do so because they like and use the product or service at least occasionally, and they use the discounts provided there regularly. To encourage repeat visits, it's important to update the page often with information on the brand or promotions the targets find relevant to their lifestyle. Like a web page, the main reason fans do not return to a brand's page is that content offers nothing new.

To begin with, be sure to make the page more about the brand and its importance to the target's lifestyle and less about promotions. Rules for ensuring engagement include:

- Not posting anything that does not positively promote both the brand and the brand's image.
- Making sure all posts close by telling the target what you want her to do, such as "like" the page or give feedback.
- Engaging the target in a conversation. Start by asking questions or making suggestions. It is important to remember that a social media site is not the place to actively sell the product or service; it's the place to build loyalty and community around the brand.
- Posting comments or articles from outside sources not associated with the brand, such as newspaper articles.

Facebook, like other social media outlets, is constantly changing the way ads are purchased and the types of ads brands can purchase for use. Once boasting more than twenty-seven different types of ad formats, Facebook is cutting out more than half. Instead of a standard format buy, brands can now pick a format based on what they want to accomplish, such as building brand awareness, app download, or driving consumers to brick-and-mortar stores or websites. Facebook will use this information to determine the best format to employ, such as mobile app install ads, or ads designed specifically for mobile, and in-store offers that advertise in-store promotions.

Facebook is constantly changing out and updating ad formats. Some of the more prominent ad formats include Link-Click, carousel, lead generation, dynamic product, canvas, collection, video, and slideshow.

All Facebook ads now have some type of social aspect built in. Not only will this build relationships, but it is a great way to drive both traffic and sales. This is good news for consumers; they will now have to see only one standardized form of brand advertising on the platform, and brands will no longer have to create separate ads to accommodate the various formats. Thanks to the new changes, these social devices can be seamlessly threaded throughout all ad formats, whether appearing in news feeds or in domain ads that are seen along the right-hand side of the page.

As it grows, Facebook is getting better at targeting according to demographics, social connections, interests, and lifestyle.

Twitter

Twitter isn't about lengthy discussions between a brand and its target; it's about making a comment or criticism in 280 or fewer characters. Its ease of use makes it a popular vehicle for promoting more in-depth word-of-mouth discussions. Something said in a few words can be easily misunderstood, so marketers must constantly monitor postings to clear up negative comments, clarify messages, or add to positive ones. Its most important attribute to marketers is the insight into public opinion. Information found here can be used to update a brand's taste, performance, color, ease of use, and so on.

Twitter can be employed to improve and maintain relationships, to create an ongoing two-way dialogue between buyer and seller, or to promote a product. Its main focus is on interaction and building a brand's current target audience; initiating, building, or maintaining brand awareness; and encouraging the target to visit a website or brick-and-mortar location.

Its concise messages can capture attention, keep up an ongoing dialogue with the target, offer immediate feedback on not only the brand but competitors' brands, and often introduce unique uses and engaging promotions.

Consumers who follow brands on Twitter want pre-promotion updates on brands before the launch; to be kept up to date with new technology or innovations; to get coupons, freebies, or trial offers; and to get advance notice of upcoming sale offers.

Twitter is a popular social networking site because it's fast and easy. Its lack of bells and whistles is great for consumers but is often considered limiting and frustrating to marketers. So instead of using it as an advertising outlet, most brands use it as a promotional or interactive vehicle. It is not necessary for all advertising and promotional outlets to tell a lengthy story about a brand; there are other vehicles more suitable for that. A short, creative message is often more memorable, one that focuses on a single feature and benefit, directly addresses lifestyle, and has all the focus one message needs to deliver and create the desired action, such as a visit to a website or brick-and-mortar store to purchase or seek out more information.

Postings on Twitter are known as "tweets" and are a great way to focus attention on a public relations event or add a viral or word-of-mouth component. Twitter is an important member of the media mix because it offers a buyer and seller a forum for exchanging ideas and delivering promotional opportunities. As a public relations device, Twitter can reach or react to client postings quickly; and as a promotional device, it can inexpensively dispense coupons, promote contests and sweepstakes, and offer sample opportunities. As an advertising vehicle, advertising can be placed on Twitter using promoted tweets, promoted trends, and promoted accounts.

Relatively new to Twitter is Periscope, a live content–creation app. Periscope allows users to use their phone to shoot live content. Content can include mobile notifications and location options, work as a social media outlet, and incorporate real-time discussion and feedback.

So, who uses Facebook versus Twitter? According to researchers, Twitter users tend to be influencers, while Facebook users tend to reflect the average consumer. Users of Facebook choose to become a brand fan because they are often already users.

Blogs

If the target is looking for a forum where in-depth conversations between buyers and sellers and numerous unrelated consumers can take place, she can visit a blog. These chatty, opinionated sites are a great place for brand-loyal consumers to gather, often to talk about a niche brand. These outspoken loyalists—or naysayers—often offer valuable feedback on new product launches, product upgrades, or the reintroduction or reinvention of mature brands.

Often visitors have access to customer or technical service advisers or management-level executives.

Blogs are often promoted on search engines or websites, or via a link that takes the viewer to related and relevant content. To ensure participation, each outlet should inform the viewer why he will find the blog helpful, educational, or informational. For example, if a new use has been found for the brand, brand users should be diverted to that site for more information.

Blogs are not as popular as they once were for many Internet surfers. Their decline is due mostly to younger people preferring to use Twitter or Facebook as their public forum. Blog sites, however, have not been abandoned by middle-age adults, who regularly use the Internet as a business or research tool, or by brand-loyal niche enthusiasts. These types of users are looking to engage in more comprehensive, in-depth discussions that offer value-based and usable content.

Visitors who participate in an ongoing blog expect to find honest, valuable, and straightforward discussions. Any misleading or inaccurate information posted there will result in negative publicity.

YouTube

No longer just an outlet for home videos, YouTube hosts name-brand videos by companies such as Kellogg's, McDonald's, and Ford, to name just a few companies that are using this site to premiere professional and hopefully viral messages to their brand's media mix.

YouTube is a popular destination site that has survived and grown almost entirely due to word of mouth on the creative content found there. As an advertising vehicle, YouTube is a relatively inexpensive way, outside of initial production costs, to repeatedly entertain and educate consumers, often without hard-sell advertising techniques. Many spots let the viewer know in an unobtrusive way who is sponsoring the video. This type of content is known as native, or branded, content. The goal of branded content is to tell a story the target can relate to that is not only useful but also assists in building a relationship between the brand and the target. **Native advertising** allows marketers to place branded content within an editorial environment. "Native ads," Chris Rooke, SVP of strategy and operations at native advertising platform Nativo, tells us, "enable the very same experience that a user has come to expect from editorial content. It drives authentic discovery."

An interactive addition is YouTube 360, which allows users to view videos from different angles by either scrolling over or moving their phone.

The ultimate goal when using YouTube as an advertising outlet is to have the video go viral when viewers tell their friends about the creative content. There is no way to ensure that any video will have the power to go viral, but to help its chances, it must first and foremost not contain an advertising sales pitch but instead be creative, entertaining, funny, and/or so unusual and engaging that viewers share it with others within their social network.

Snapchat

Another popular video option is Snapchat, a mobile app that allows users to shoot temporary ten-second videos and photographs that disappear a few seconds after viewing. Brands can use Snapchat to initiate augmented reality options, produce scripted series, and for pro-motional purposes—anything where interactive properties can be included. For example, during the 2016 Super Bowl, Gatorade used an animated Snapchat filter that let users pour a virtual cooler of Gatorade over video selfies. Snapchat also offers a Sponsored Lens option that allows users to lay varied types of graphics over videos and photographs. Newest to the Snapchat arsenal is Sponsored World Lenses, an option that allows the addition of digital objects.

Pinterest

One of the fastest-growing social networking sites, Pinterest is a place to "pin up photo-graphs." This very visual and targetable bookmarking site allows viewers to share personal images or videos of images found online. As an advertising tool, it is a great way to show uses, options, or sponsored events. Pinterest's terms-of-use policy specifies that the site not be used in promotional efforts, but many brands have found creative ways around the bla-tant self-promotion clause. Like Facebook, visitors can "like" a pin or follow or comment on a pin. To be successful, these mini virtual showrooms must either solve a problem for the target or entertain the target. New to Pinterest is Cinematic Pins, videos that play only when viewers scroll.

Tumblr

Tumblr is very simply a mix that is part microblogging site and part social networking site. This diverse site lets the visitor post pretty much everything from text and photographs to music and videos. Adaptable to all commonly used digital platforms, content can be posted from a desktop, mobile phone, or browser. As an advertising tool, content must be visually unique and a fast read. Typical content might include reposting a blog about the brand, "lik-ing" a brand, or commenting on information posted. The goal is to give creative and useful content so that the more people follow the brand on Tumblr, like any other social network-ing site, the more the brand will increase its exposure. Brands like Adidas, for example, have used Tumblr to promote and launch a soccer blog. Users can connect any posted blogs to their Twitter and/or Facebook accounts.

Instagram

This mobile photo-sharing app lets users share both videos and photographs either publicly or privately. Instead of posting a boring cell phone picture on Twitter, Facebook, or Tumblr, Instagram allows the photographer to apply one of many digital filters, transforming the image into something memorable and visually unique. Video options allow brands to post thirty to sixty seconds of advertised material. To deliver more informed options, Instagram is now offering ad carousels, a mobile optimized slideshow that can be seen alongside video options. These carousels allow viewers to view five photographs of material highlighted in the video. Best used as a promotional tool, Instagram can positively position a company as a great place to work while at the same time increasing consumer trust in new and existing brands. For small business owners, products shown on the site can increase chatter and sales leads. It is also a great place for brands to employ user-generated content through photo contests. For example, one restaurant in New York asked diners to snap pictures of their dinner plates and post them on Instagram so that others could share in the varied culinary delights.

Video is the newest tool driving social media engagement. Brands are incorporating short animated GIFs, six- to ten-second disappearing options, longer, more traditional thirty- to sixty-second spots, and livestreaming options. Although more interesting than the static photograph, the video option just adds more clutter the target needs to wade through. Like television, to ensure viewer interaction, brands have only three to five seconds to engage the target. In a 2015 *Adweek* article entitled "These Are the Top 6 Trends Shaping Video Content Today," Stacy Minero cited a recent Twitter study showing that "videos that feature people in the opening moments are up to two times as likely to drive consumers to view" the video. So, like all other advertising content, get to the point quickly.

Social videos are adaptive, easy to use, and multifunctional. They typically play automatically without sound until activated by the viewer. This silent delivery is a great way to cut down on advertising's intrusiveness. However, intrusive behavior is what drives engagement and recall. So, with or without a stunning opening visual, to ensure interaction, it is also important to add visual cues or text overlays to attract attention.

Options for use are still being shaped by marketers and consumers alike. Video formats like GIFs are sharable; user-generated content from influencers is an effective way to deliver creative content and connect with the target. Brand involvement in **cause-related marketing (CRM)**, or the mutual collaboration between a for-profit business and a nonprofit business or organization, can be spotlighted, as can "how to" or instructional information that focuses on assembly or use, and livestreaming options that can bring the target and the brand into contact in very new and creative ways.

Google+

Google+ is Google's contribution to media networking sites. Loaded with many features similar to Facebook and Twitter, what sets it apart is its ability to tie Google's most popular products together, such as search, Gmail, and YouTube. Google's goal is to create a single identity for every person who logs on by allowing him or her to do everything in one place.

For example, Circles organizes and personalizes a user's social circles around such things as work or personal interests. Huddle privately organizes texts from ongoing group discussions in one convenient place. Hangouts focus on instant messaging, and video discussions allow users to share content between phone, tablets, and desktops, while Sparks deals with search. Additional features include an app for phones and a check-in feature.

LinkedIn

LinkedIn is a professional networking site, so as an advertising outlet it is best used by brands that sell to businesses. Located along the sidebar, these small ads typically feature a visual, headline, a small amount of copy (seventy-five characters), and a website address. Brands that want to reach the target personally and immediately can use the lead collection feature, which allows interested users to request you to contact them directly. For larger budgets, LinkedIn offers MPU (mid-page unit) ads, which appear at the top of the LinkedIn home page, profile, company, and group pages, and LinkedIn Today. Skyscraper ads are seen on member inboxes and message pages, and leaderboards are seen before users leave a page.

When using social media, it's all about engagement beyond a simple post or promotion. Some of the more popular devices include widgets, brand profile pages, and branded wrappers. Let's take a quick look at each one.

Widgets

Widgets, also known as gadgets, badges, or applets, are applications that contain a small amount of usually boxed-in content that features the weather, news reports, slideshows, videos, music, or horoscopes, to name just a few examples. Brands that include downloadable widgets on their sites create engagement by giving the target something to do that prolongs her stay on the site or take a piece of the site with her. Widgets can be downloaded to personal profile pages, blogs, and websites or placed on desktops.

Brand Profile Pages

Brand profile pages are a regularly used form of promotion on social media sites. Created by the advertiser for a specific brand, these educational and often entertaining pages often include demonstrations or games or offer downloadable graphics and/or widgets. The more creative and/or interactive the pages, the more viral the experience becomes as users share their experiences with others.

Branded Wrappers

Guaranteed to be seen, a branded wrapper is a single ad that dominates the home or opening page of a social media site. Like widgets, this image, or "skin," can be transferred to the visitor's own pages, creating additional exposure. Because wrappers allow viewers to quickly proceed to their destination, those who do not wish to interact with the message will not find them intrusive in the same way as a floating ad or pre-roll.

Viral and Word of Mouth

Finally, we cannot finish up the discussion on social media without talking about viral and word-of-mouth content.

Viral marketing and **word of mouth** are the most sought-after and difficult to achieve forms of user-generated content. The difference between the two is how they are delivered and their overall length. Viral messages, because they are delivered via the web, have a longer life span than word-of-mouth messages, which are delivered face to face.

Viral Marketing

Viral marketing uses social media to pass along advertising messages to friends and family members within the target's social circle. Today, a campaign's life span can be extended if the message is creative or memorable enough for readers or viewers to pass on a link or verbally share the experience with others in their social circle. Consumers who spread viral content are doing more than just purchasing a product; they are enthusiastically promoting that product to others. Messages or experiences with a brand delivered by a trusted friend or family member are much more believable than any corporate-sponsored piece of advertised material.

It is not easy to define or pinpoint what traits make a message or video go viral, but it is safe to say it must capture the audience's attention, induce curiosity, and be humorous or educational enough for viewers to not only interact with it but pass it along, via e-mail or through social media sites like Twitter, Facebook, or Tumblr. Creative aspects beyond message content that can increase a campaign's chance of going viral might include slogans that can be incorporated into everyday conversations or introduction of a character that becomes the image of a brand.

Advertising with some type of viral component will increase not only brand loyalty but website traffic as well. Conversely, poorly executed viral messages can affect brand image and annoy and alienate brand-loyal consumers.

Unfortunately, creative teams cannot make a message go viral. Success depends largely on its reaching influencers such as bloggers or its appearance on popular media sites. No matter how many of these tactical steps are in place, it still takes a lot of luck to get influencers to talk about the video or post. The goal is to get viewers to talk about the message and build curiosity. Once their curiosity is aroused, the next step is viewing, so it is important to choose the most descriptive keywords possible to make the target's search faster and easier. Once the target is engaged, the discussion widens, increasing the message's stickiness or memorability.

Word of Mouth

Word-of-mouth advertising is all about one person sharing his or her experience with the brand with others. This free-form type of advertising is the best advertising money can't buy. When discussions about a brand are positive, it is a great way to increase awareness, build image, and build or maintain loyalty among new and existing customers. If discussions are negative, however, nothing kills a brand's momentum or negates advertising's claims faster. Understanding what excites and promotes discussion is the first step in creating a successful word-of-mouth campaign.

Advertising appearing on social media sites has been experimental at best, made up mainly of sponsorships, ad placements, or brand applications that have shown little or no measurable return on investment and have not always been well received by social media enthusiasts.

How Do Internet Marketing and Social Media Help IMC Be Consumer Focused?

Internet marketing is a relatively new addition to the advertising promotional mix and is one of the few media voluntarily used by consumers to gather information, find entertainment, and make the occasional purchase. But most importantly, it creates interaction between the buyer and the seller—an interaction that can be taken to the next level through social media.

The Internet is as consumer focused as marketing gets without resorting to personal selling. Electronic media has brought the company to the consumer and made the consumer an active participant in marketing decisions. Marketers have moved a step beyond one-way communication (the message) to two-way communication (target response). This give-and-take creates a relationship between company and target (awareness) and target and brand (loyalty).

The Internet is a great niche-marketing tool. Databases and e-mail make it easy to personally reach those most likely to be interested in a product. Advertising on niche sites is more likely to attract members of the target audience.

Because Internet users are actively engaged in seeking information, consumer attitude is positive. Buyers choose to look at, or look for, messages; since the messages are not thrust upon them, Internet consumers are less apathetic. If, when visiting a website, their attention is drawn elsewhere, they can choose a convenient time to return to the site and finish gathering information or complete an order. The Internet offers a no-muss, no-fuss shopping experience.

Internet users can also decide what they want to look at and how long they want to look at it. A poorly designed site that is confusing or difficult to navigate or read can be removed from the screen with the click of a button.

If the client's website has interactive capabilities, as it should, it is important that the target be asked to do something, such as call or e-mail for more information or a free sample. And don't forget that offering coupons is still a great way to encourage trial or repeat purchase. Most importantly, encourage the consumer to make a purchase or ask for assistance from a customer service representative or technical adviser. Interactive dialogue is the goal of Internet marketing.

Customer Service Is a Must

For an IMC program that is trying to develop or maintain loyalty, customer service is critical. Customer service begins when the website launches; continues with informative messages and visuals, feedback, and ordering; and moves on to delivery, follow-up e-mails, and periodical reminder notes. Customer service and brand-building messages are the Internet's keys to success.

It is important to give the consumer a way to make contact. Once a consumer clicks on a customer service button, he needs to get a response. Knowledge is power; let the consumer know how long it will take to get a response. Whether a reply is almost instantaneous or takes twenty-four hours, let the consumer know. This helps create an environment built on trust and reliability rather than negativity and distrust.

There are two types of customer service: active interaction and passive interaction. **Active interaction** is live, via instant messaging, the telephone, blogs, social media sites, and message boards. Traditional e-mail works great for follow-up or reminder notices, order confirmations, and thank-you initiatives.

Immediate e-mail responses keep an impatient consumer happy. Consumers want their questions answered now, so it is important that the Internet portion of the IMC campaign incorporate contact e-mail links that will immediately connect them with a customer service or technical representative.

Toll-free telephone numbers make contact easy and familiar. Specific questions can be asked and answered with little or no effort. Many consumers are still concerned about making financial transactions on the Internet, so it is important to offer phone, fax, or mail order as options when encouraging purchases.

Having a social media presence allows users with similar interests to interact and share information. Many companies also sponsor chat rooms, message boards, or blogs dedicated to users of their products.

Passive interaction involves a delayed response to questions from customer service representatives, such as receipt of a sample in the mail or a follow-up or confirmation e-mail response.

Incentives and Deterrents
of Internet Marketing and Social Media

To decide whether Internet marketing and social media are right for an IMC campaign, let's look at some of the incentives and deterrents associated with them.

What Makes Internet Marketing and Social Media So Great?

The more notable incentives associated with Internet marketing and social media include:

- *Consumer-centric.* Both forms of electronic delivery are great public relations tools as well as great outlets for building or reinforcing brand loyalty.
- *Flexibility.* Online messages offer convenient accessibility twenty-four hours a day.
- *Interactive.* Internet marketing and social media allow for direct communication between the buyer and seller.
- *Simple integration.* Both the website address and social media hashtags can easily be promoted in other IMC advertising efforts.
- *Engaging.* Consumers look at both the Internet and social media as communication tools more favorably because they choose when to be exposed to its messages.

Is There Anything Wrong with Internet Marketing or Social Media?

The more notable deterrents associated with Internet marketing and social media include:

- *Clutter.* There is a lot of information out there, so finding a way to make a site stand out is important. Traditional advertising methods are still useful to attract readers or viewers, so the web and social media site addresses or hashtags should appear on all advertising materials, but don't litter the page or screen with them. The site itself should also be well organized and easy to navigate; social media links should be used only if they add value and offer sharable information.
- *Word of mouth.* Sites where consumers are allowed to comment can lead to negative word of mouth and rampant rumors. Dedicated customer service people must constantly monitor and be prepared to comment on any issues posted or received.

- *Time intensive.* The upkeep and monitoring associated with both the Internet and social media are very time intensive.
- *Promotional efforts.* Social media vehicles and websites do not work in conjunction to promote the brand. For example, often promotional offers are not mentioned on both a web page and social media site.
- *Buttons.* Many companies do not incorporate social media buttons into their websites.

The Strategy behind Internet Marketing

Internet marketing is an extension of traditional advertising tactics. Websites can be used to help build brand awareness, increase equity, create loyalty, and deliver an informational message. At its core, a website is no different than a brochure or direct-mail kit; what makes the Internet unique is that it allows the seller to interact with the customer, creating valuable dialogue through feedback. The website represents the product through overall appearance, ease of use, and customer service options, replacing retail outlets and salespeople.

Other media used as a part of the IMC campaign should feature the web and social media site addresses to encourage visitation and build interest. A company, product, or service cannot survive on Internet marketing alone. It is still necessary to use traditional media vehicles to get the word out about the site.

Internet marketing efforts should reflect other advertising efforts, both visually and verbally. It is important to know how the Internet fits into the promotional mix: Will it play a supporting role as an informational tool, or will it be the primary location for picking up a coupon before buying or the only location to place an order?

Promotion is a big part of Internet-based advertising. Consumers must be able to reach a customer service representative, order samples, download coupons, and enter contests or sweepstakes on the website.

In public relations, the Internet can be a very effective communications tool. Timely information can be delivered to all levels of the target audience and stakeholders to announce job openings, provide information about sponsored events, or even link to other relevant sites.

Internet marketing combines elements and advantages of newspaper, magazine, and television advertising, catalogs, and sales promotion vehicles and direct-mail kits, making it among the most versatile of all media vehicles. The Internet can use the strengths of each of these media vehicles to engage the viewer and successfully deliver the key consumer benefit. Print requires a visually or verbally dominant element, broadcast entertains, catalogs prominently highlight product features, sales promotion entices with a gift, and direct mail must be eye catching to attract and hold the reader's or viewer's attention. Electronic media use each of these attributes to make information gathering easy and informative, visually/verbally stimulating, and entertaining to keep a viewer from leaving the site and going elsewhere.

Media choices depend on the objectives to be met and the strategy to be used. The Internet is a good choice for building brand awareness, delivering information, and building loyal customers through interactive activities.

Effective communication objectives include developing two-way communication, making sales, building loyalty, encouraging inquiry, developing a relationship, encouraging product trial, and informing or educating.

The strategic approach can be either product or consumer based. Consumer-based approaches work well because the Internet can be used as a relationship builder. Product-based approaches should tie the product or service's features and benefits back to the consumer's self-image, lifestyle, and/or attitude. To educate and inform, the overall style or appeal of an informational site should be rational. Rational appeals to consider might include feature or news stories.

Destination websites are consumer oriented. An image, lifestyle, or attitude approach is especially well suited to this type of site. Emotional appeals based on personal styles or feelings might include stimulation, excitement, happiness, and pleasure. Additional emotional appeals based on social feelings might include approval, belonging, involvement, and status. Choice of appeal used will depend on the product or service and the target.

Possible execution techniques for an informational site include testimonials, the product as a star, straight fact, technical information, science, or news. Possible execution techniques for a destination site might include humor, animation, or fantasy.

The Design of Internet Marketing

A typical website should tell the story of a company, product, or service. It must take consumers on a visually and verbally stimulating trip that creatively informs and educates them about the benefits of the product or service. Accessed through an address called a URL, each page of the site is like a section of a map that can be used to find product information.

Although the Internet can work like television, featuring sight, sound, and motion, it is also important to lay pages out in the same way as a print ad. It is just as important to keep the connection speed of the end user in mind when designing a website. Not everyone has a high-end computer system or fast Internet access, so it is important to design for both the low-end and high-end viewer. Nothing is more annoying than having to wait for a site to load. Remember, a company's website is its online storefront; it is the first impression many consumers will have of the product or company. Graphic-heavy sites take longer to load than copy-heavy sites. Features such as streaming video and webisodes are great for demonstrations and entertainment but should be kept short and have a point. Both formats take more time to load and view than the consumer may want to invest, so make it an option. Don't waste the target's time with creative executions that do not hammer home an answer to the question *What's in it for me?*

At the top of a basic web page is a page header that includes the company logo, site, and/or page name. A page footer, located at the bottom of the page, may have copyright information or numbers for page jumps. The sidebar, usually located on the left side, displays the table of contents or navigational toolbars for the site.

Following the basic design used in print advertising, a website should have a headline, subhead(s), visuals, copy, and a consistently viewable logo. A headline can be used to shout the key consumer benefit; the message can be interspersed with visuals that demonstrate use and/or act as links the target can click on to access AR options, streaming audio and video, or an appropriate webisode. The website should reflect the same tone of voice and visual cues as the other pieces in the IMC campaign. To improve readability and legibility, a site with a lot of copy will need a lot of white space and increased leading, or the amount of white space that appears between lines of text.

Good websites are current and ever changing, recognizing that news is old at the end of every day. Every website should pique and maintain the target's initial interest, build excitement, create need, and encourage action.

Designing for a New Medium

From a design standpoint, the Internet is part print, part television. At its simplest, it is pure text with visual accents; at its most complex, it is sight, sound, and motion. However, the Internet is neither print nor television; it has its own set of rules that must be followed to effectively accomplish the objectives and strategically highlight the key consumer benefit. Keep it simple, keep it clean, make it interactive, and think of the page layout as print and the delivery of information as television.

Like print, web design requires a lot of white space to be readable. It also requires the use of typefaces that are easy to read at a glance, increased leading, lines of text no longer than six inches, varied sentence length, and numerous short paragraphs. Copy should be informative, creative, and intermittently interspersed with subheadings and visual images, whether traditional photographs, illustrations or graphics, or some type of video option is used.

Don't get caught up in what can be done electronically; do what should be done to inform consumers. They are visiting the website, first and foremost, for information; they will not click away to another site once they are engaged. Engagement can successfully lead them to making an inquiry or purchase.

The Creative Website Options

This discussion will concentrate on the section known as the main text, or message, area, where the key consumer benefit will first be featured. The key consumer benefit and visual and verbal elements should reflect the other pieces in the IMC creative series. To brainstorm ideas about how the website should look, the creative team needs to know the purpose of the site. Will it be a destination or informational site? Will any customer service or technical representatives be available? Will consumers be able to order from the site, or can they request additional information only? Will they be introduced to promotional opportunities? Will there be social media access, a chat room, a survey, or a customer feedback area? What about follow-up e-mails? Will there be a way to send information quickly? The marketer needs to commit to these devices by having sufficient staff to manage any service or technical sites twenty-four hours a day, every day. If the service is provided, it must be done well and to the customer's satisfaction to build brand loyalty and ultimately brand equity.

Storyboard thumbs are used to work out the overall look of the pages before the final, full-size storyboard rough is completed. The goal is to keep each page consistent throughout the site.

Each site will require specific categories or subject heads where topical information will be placed. These categories will vary from site to site, depending on the function of the site and the role it will play in the IMC process. However, most sites include the following categories:

- Home page
- Navigational aids
- Menu options
- Links
- Main menu links
- Text-only format options
- Press releases or relevant news articles
- Frequently asked questions (FAQ)
- Banners
- Contact or customer service options
- Back button
- Printer-friendly option

Home Page

Every website has a home page, or the main page of the site. The home page is a corporation's résumé; it should introduce the business and its philosophy and reiterate or strengthen its brand identity. The design should reflect this identity or philosophy. This page is the first impression the viewer will receive about a product or corporation. It should creatively deliver information about a product or service. It is important when developing a website that the home page highlight the key consumer benefit and visually and verbally reflect IMC efforts used elsewhere within the campaign. It is important the side panel or navigational system be consistent from page to page. Organize the site into logical sections that match the menu options. Consider adding visuals to the remaining pages; anyone who gets past the home page is interested and will read the copy while waiting for the visuals to open.

The overall layout should follow print principles. Announce the key consumer benefit in a headline. Use subheads to break up longer blocks of copy. Keep copy light and relatively short, and keep visuals to a minimum to help the site open quickly; any delays could cause viewers to "click out" to another site. Consider using larger headlines to announce different areas within the site. Bold headlines, as in newspaper design, work as an announcement and capture attention. All text should be the same face and/or style used in other pieces within the IMC campaign when possible.

If product steps or a list of product attributes or features must be given, consider using bullets to attract attention and break up the page rather than listing them in sentence form. Another option would be to place them in a graphic box.

The target is at the site for one of two reasons: to gather information or to place an order. Potential orders depend on the consumer knowing how much something costs, including tax and any charges for shipping and handling. Do not be afraid to list prices prominently. Consider making them bold or including them as a part of the page design, as in newspaper ads. However prices are handled, eventual purchase requires they not be hidden.

Color use should also reflect other IMC pieces and/or packaging. Use color as an accent, for headlines, or on top or side banners. If using a colored background, make sure it's light and the type large enough to read over it. Most sites use too much color, giving them a garish or circus appearance. Keep print in mind here; the proper placement of color can call attention to an area or topic, but if too much is used, nothing stands out.

Visuals of varying size interspersed within or around copy are a great way to break up a gray page and draw a viewer's attention. Consider using a rebus-style approach to the page. Visuals that show the product or the product in use or in a setting are critical to informational websites. However, if they're not relevant to what's being said, don't include them. Streaming video is a great way to demonstrate a product or present testimonials from current users or professionals such as engineers or scientists.

Writing for the Internet is often handled as if it were a business document, full of facts and little else. This style completely ignores the fact that the targets must be both visually and verbally stimulated if their attention is to be held.

Creatively written copy can tell the story of the product or service and clearly give the facts, but in a more memorable and attention-grabbing way. Remember the discussion on direct mail; readers will read long copy as long as it's interesting.

Navigational Aids

A website needs to be easy to get around in. Navigational tools can be either text or graphics that allow the viewer to move around the site with ease. When working with large amounts of text or with multiple pages, the bottom of each page should include a footer with page numbers the viewer can click on to jump to another page. These helpful links appear in the same place on every page. The most common navigational tools are buttons labeled "home," "next," "previous," and "help." Consumers do not want to waste their time scrolling through a site to find topics or answers, so it is critical to include navigation buttons that allow the viewer to jump quickly around the site.

Menu Options

Think of the menu options as a table of contents that will logically lead the reader to specific sections within the site. Menu options, also known as site maps, are navigational tools that take the viewer to specific sections within the site. These links are most often graphic bars located on the left side of the screen or on tabs stretching across the top of the page that can be clicked on to move to a specific topic or section. Be sure there are enough menu options to make getting around the site quick and easy so that the viewer doesn't have to scroll to find information.

Links

A website should offer links to help the viewer quickly find additional information such as social media sites, chat rooms, product testimonials, endorsements, surveys, tests, customer service, frequently asked questions, or ordering information.

Main Menu Links

At the top and bottom of each page there should be a link for viewers to click on to quickly and easily return to the main menu.

Text-Only Option

Some consumers may not have the technology to open image-heavy pages, webisodes, or streaming audio or video quickly. No one wants to wait for a site to open, so offer a text-only option. If the target decides to open a visual by clicking on it, the creatively written copy will hold her attention while she waits for the visual to load.

Press Releases or Relevant News Articles

A website is a great place to find information about a company, product, or service. Any events, sponsorships, informative news or feature articles, testimonials, awards, or new product releases should be announced on the website.

Frequently Asked Questions (FAQ)

Consumers often have similar questions and concerns. If the answers are posted in one place, consumers can easily find the answers they need to make an informed buying decision.

Banners

Nothing is more annoying than having something flashing or moving in your peripheral vision while you're trying to concentrate. Banners that move should be avoided. If a site must use them, place them at the bottom of the page, where they can be hidden below the viewable frame.

Contact or Customer Service Options

Offer as many ways as possible for consumers to contact customer service or technical representatives, including instant messaging, e-mail, toll-free numbers, fax numbers, or traditional mail.

Back Button

Many times, when searching for information, a viewer will want to jump back to the previous page. Make it easy by including a back button.

Printer-Friendly Option

Make sure the site is easy to print. Many consumers still like to read from hard copies. If the site uses a lot of color or images, be sure to include a printer-friendly option so that the consumer can print a page that contains only the relevant information.

A website is only the first interactive step a brand can take to initiate dialogue between the brand and the target; the second is social media. Let's take a look at the strategies behind this new interactive step.

The Strategy behind Social Media

Social media is personalized; it creates a two-way conversation between buyer and seller, an IMC must. These social sites can increase brand awareness, encourage interaction between brand users, give feedback, distribute promotional items such as coupons, and promote repeat visits to both web and social media sites. They are great brand-building tools, outlets for idea generation, and means of identifying brand influencers.

Basically, social media is technology's answer to personal selling. Any questions or concerns can be answered immediately either in an open forum or privately. A social site represents a brand by providing customer reactions, promotional opportunities, and interaction between users of the brand or buyer and seller.

Other media used in the IMC campaign should feature logos and appropriate hashtags. Social media will never be a brand's primary advertising vehicle; but as a support vehicle, it is a great way to create or maintain relationships and engage visitors beyond brand performance or selling points.

Visual/verbal efforts seen elsewhere in a campaign will have less importance in social media efforts. Its job is to ensure that claims made elsewhere are open for discussion or to deliver the promotion promised. Because of this, it is important to understand how social media fits into the promotional mix: Will it offer some type of interactive tool or be the only location to find a coupon or sign up for a contest or sweepstakes?

Interaction is the primary advantage social media brings to an IMC campaign. Will visitors have access to people who can effectively answer questions or make decisions without delay? What about the handling of customer service or technical issues? Its secondary advantage is the delivery of promotional vehicles. Is it easy to download coupons, enter contests, or request a free sample?

As a public relations device, social media is critical to answering questions, handling problems, or dispelling rumors quickly, efficiently, and in real time. Social sites that are not the primary destination site for in-depth product information or promotions can be used to direct the target to a website.

Social media, unlike traditional media outlets, encourages a two-way dialogue between buyer and seller and among consumers. It has greater reach, is interacted with more frequently, and is more immediate and permanent. Traditional and alternative media outlets can showcase varied social media logos, as can mobile.

Strategically, the best social media can do is push the key consumer benefit and support what is said in other vehicles used in the media mix.

The use of social media when it is not integrated solidly into the promotional mix can confuse the target and produce negative or incorrect assumptions. A seamless integration ensures that the visual/verbal voice used elsewhere in the campaign will not only produce thoughtful insight and feedback but also increase engagement.

Communication objectives typically involve building or maintaining loyalty, fostering two-way communication, building relationships, and encouraging trial or repurchase through promotional options.

Because of social media's ties to the Internet, the best objectives and strategic choices will mirror those used in Internet marketing.

Bottom Line

Digital options like Internet marketing and social networking connect the target, the product, other users, and the seller through information and dialogue. They are the only members of the promotional mix the target actually seeks out for information on a product or service. It is important that this contact, whether initial or ongoing, be a positive one and be considered meaningful and productive to the target. This type of one-on-one contact with customer service or technology representatives is great for building loyalty beyond knowledge of the product. Site design should reflect the product's image both visually and verbally; offer interactive activity such as AR, instant messaging, order forms, or coupons; and continue the overall message reflected in other IMC pieces. Social media sites that are engaging and create viral or word-of-mouth chatter are an effective way to promote a brand or initiate a promotion and/or build expectations for an upcoming event.

Q DISCUSSION QUESTIONS

1. What are the strategic uses of Internet marketing in an IMC campaign?
2. How has the Internet changed the way brands do business?
3. Why is the Internet considered a direct selling tool?
4. What role does the Internet play as a primary and secondary advertising/promotional vehicle?
5. When is Internet advertising best used in an IMC campaign?
6. Internet marketing adds another dimension to advertising efforts. What is it?
7. What does interactive media focus on?
8. Internet marketing, like other vehicles we have looked at, has a diverse array of advertising options. What are some of the most common, and how can they each help to visually and verbally express the key consumer benefit?
9. What makes the Internet interactive?
10. What does interactive mean to creative teams versus marketers?
11. What are the strategic uses of social media in an IMC campaign?
12. Hoes does social media create a relationship between buyer and seller?
13. How does social media differentiate itself from mass media advertising vehicles?
14. Why is it important for the strategy employed elsewhere in the IMC campaign to remain consistent across multiple vehicles?
15. What is typically shown/seen on social media sites?
16. How are databases employed in social media?
17. Why is it important that social media efforts talk to, rather than at, the target audience?
18. What makes social media unique?
19. How can social media influence and/or encourage a two-way dialogue between buyer and seller?
20. What do creative teams need to know before adding social media to an IMC campaign?
21. Social media has a diverse array of promotional vehicles. What are some of the most common, and how can each help promote the key consumer benefit?
22. What are the differences between viral marketing and word of mouth? Define when it is best to use each.
23. Discuss the pros and cons to a brand of a message going viral.
24. What can help make a message go viral?

25. Why is word of mouth more powerful than an advertised message?
26. How does Internet marketing and social media help an IMC campaign be more consumer focused?
27. Why might the Internet be considered a great niche-marketing tool?
28. Why is customer service considered a must for an IMC campaign?
29. What are the pros and cons of Internet and social media marketing?
30. What is the strategy behind using Internet marketing in an IMC campaign?
31. Why is Internet marketing considered an extension of traditional tactics?
32. What do creative teams need to know about designing for the Internet?
33. What is the strategy behind using social media in an IMC campaign?
34. Why is social media considered technology's answer to personal selling?
35. How does a social media site represent a brand?
36. What role does social media play as a support vehicle?

CHAPTER

17

Mobile Media Marketing

The Strategic Use of Mobile Media in IMC

It is not surprising that many consumers view mobile media marketing as just another vehicle that electronically collects data and displays advertising. However, the truth is that advertising on mobile devices has slowly grown from a one-way communication between a brand and its targeted audience to an interactive and engaging experience for consumers. The variety of experiences available to consumers is more about brands giving something back to their target. The Mobile Marketing Association (MMA) defines mobile marketing as "a set of practices that enables organizations to communicate and engage with their audience in an interactive and relevant manner through any mobile device or network."

The MMA definition goes on to say:

Mobile media is a "set of practices" that includes activities, institutions, processes, industry players, standards, advertising and media, direct response, promotions, relationship management, CRM [customer relationship management], customer services, loyalty, social marketing, and the many faces and facets of marketing. Mobile media that "engages," works to start relationships, acquire, generate activity, stimulate social interaction with organization and community members, and be present at the time of the consumer's expressed need. Furthermore, engagement can be initiated by the consumer ("Pull" in the form of a click or response) or by the marketer ("Push").

Whether a brand's mobile media advertising uses an ad that features all copy, visuals, or video, it is important to push the key consumer benefit to ensure that an integrated message will effectively exploit mobile's highly targetable reach, making it more attractive and cost-efficient than traditional advertising. Because many messages are short and sweet and can be relevant to shoppers in real time, research has shown that text messages are read more quickly than those delivered through e-mail and that consumers are more receptive to ads delivered via their mobile phone.

Location-based features have helped mobile advertising reach consumers near the point of purchase, alerting them to local sales and promotions. This real-time advertising is an asset that makes interaction more likely, making mobile advertising an attractive medium.

Targeted consumers who have downloaded an app or opted in to receive advertising are reachable wherever they are to seek more information or interact with a message that interests them. Because of its flexibility, mobile can deliver a diverse assortment of advertising, promotional, and entertainment options. Consumers can use search wherever they are or be reached by text messaging and through banners, audio and video, animation, interstitials, coupons, GPS and mapping capabilities, and **accelerometers**—an interactive device that allows the phone to detect movement when shaken. It is not only a great way to capture the user's attention but also an important accessory for many games and for controlling the direction of mapping. See case study 15 for a look at IKEA's use of mobile marketing.

Rising advertising costs and an uncertain economy are the catalysts helping new and alternative advertising vehicles such as mobile grow. Advertising practices directed to smaller niche markets that avoid the use of more traditional vehicles allow advertisers to employ less-expensive alternative and often more creative and engaging media options. Mobile options on the rise include mobile in-game advertising, or advergaming; mobile video; and, most prominently, mobile search.

This targetable, location-based, real-time, relatively inexpensive, and measurable vehicle can reach the targeted audience with advertising or promotions for restaurants, shopping, special events, and movie trailers. Very diverse, mobile can send, receive, educate, and personalize a message. Messages delivered to the target are direct, timely, and often immediately useful, making the advertised message appear to mimic a brand loyalty reward rather than junk mail or spam.

A promotional mix that includes mobile creates more opportunities for a product or service to be cross-promoted, strengthening the reach of the key consumer benefit. Mobile's ability to reach those who have opted in to receive messages gives it the ability to reach targets with messages they are interested in.

Brands that want to create opportunities to build or strengthen brand loyalty or encourage interaction will find mobile a great promotional choice. According to Robyn Blakeman in the book *Nontraditional Media in Marketing and Advertising*, mobile also delivers:

- Greater recall and response rates
- Increased brand awareness
- Increased consumer loyalty
- An opportunity to reach high-income professionals
- A highly targeted "opt-in" consumer market
- Increased Internet traffic
- Real-time promotions
- A way to track where the target originally saw the message using multiple keywords

- Easy-to-change-out messages
- The ability to make a purchase or visit a sponsoring website

The Diversity of the Mobile Media Marketing Voice

The diverse types of advertising that can be employed in mobile marketing include mobile web banners and text links, mobile web marketing, short message service (SMS) ads, multimedia messaging service (MMS) ads, mobile video, quick response (QR) codes, augmented reality (AR), short codes, mobile coupons, mobile applications, and in-application ads. Let's take a quick look at each one.

Mobile Web Banners and Text Links

Mobile banners with accompanying text links were the first type of mobile advertising and are still the most common. Not all banners need to have accompanying text links; those that do should take the viewer to a mobile website. Very small and rectangular in shape, banners usually appear on the bottom of the screen and will have little to say. To encourage interaction, copy should have a strong, simply stated call to action. Banners that do not include a link will usually appear either below the banner or as a stand-alone link that can be used like a clickable banner. Although considered by most to be crude and annoying, banners are both inexpensive and simplistic, making them a popular choice for marketers. It is important to remember that mobile advertising must be interactive, so offer recipes, coupons, games, or a contest or sweepstakes to hold attention longer.

Mobile Web Marketing

Very simply, mobile web marketing is advertising created specifically for mobile devices. Since most mobile phones do not have a comprehensive browser to view web pages, mobile web marketing tactics help brands to create websites that can be easily viewed in the browsers of mobile devices. This customization ensures that advertising viewed on mobile phones is easy to load and see.

Short Message Service (SMS)

This very common and simple form of mobile marketing sends ads and promotions through text messages that can reach the target at or near the point of purchase. SMS messages often include a link to a sponsoring website where the target can learn about specials or reward loyalty with incentives or coupons that can be used immediately. Brands that use this simple form of reminder advertising will find it flexible, measurable, convenient, and affordable.

Multimedia Messaging Service (MMS)

Sent only to users who have opted in to receive information, MMS adds to the simple text message by including visual images such as audio/video and photographs that can often be sent in real time.

CASE STUDY 15

C | IMC Mobile: IKEA

Overview

The 2014 IKEA catalog came to life this year, taking the customer experience further with extended digital content. This case study looks at how the furniture brand used augmented reality technology to add a new dimension to the shopping experience, and garnered 8.5 million downloads in the process.

To unlock fifty pages of digital content, including videos, furnishing tips, and room designs, users needed to download the IKEA catalog app and scan the "plus" logo in the catalog with their smart-phone or tablet. One of the features was an augmented-reality capability that allowed customers to view and place selected 3-D virtual IKEA products in their own rooms.

Objective

Create an interactive mobile app that consumers can use to make product selection and purchasing easier.

Strategy

The app allows users to experience new furniture to scale in their room. Going to an IKEA store may be difficult for many customers; enabling them to see virtual images of products will help customers make purchase decisions and buy online.

The service works by users scanning selected pages in the 2014 printed IKEA catalog with the IKEA catalog app (available for iOS and Android) or by browsing the pages in the digital 2014 IKEA catalog on a smartphone or tablet.

After selecting a piece of furniture, users put the catalog itself on the floor, where it acts as a sort of anchor for the 3-D image of the chair or table. If the furniture needs to be rotated, the user simply rotates the catalog.

Marketers should look at every brand touch point as an opportunity to engage digitally, and this app is a perfect example of a brand adding entirely new value to an old medium with digital technology.

Results

According to company reports, the app was downloaded 8.5 million times.

Speaking to the trade journal *Mobile Commerce Daily*, Marty Marston, product public relations manager at IKEA US, said: "Some people are afraid that they're going to make the wrong color choice or the style might not look good with the other styles that they're trying to mix and match it with or just not look good in that space, so they may not buy it, and that's unfortunate because maybe it's exactly what they need. So, we think that this augmented reality feature may be a solution for some people to really help them with that buying decision in the process."

Source: "IKEA Augmented Reality Catalogue," Digital Training Academy, http://www.digitaltrainingacademy. com/casestudies/2014/11/ikea_augmented_reality_catalogue.php.

Mobile Video

The Mobile Marketing Association mobile video committee defines mobile video advertising as "an ad whereby the primary unit consists of delivery of a video advertisement to mobile devices. Different from display, the ad unit delivers video to create consumer demand and engagement, and the video ad delivery is the primary value proposition for the advertiser. During or after the video, it may have rich media features as overlays."

The quality of these sight, sound, and motion ads has improved significantly over the past few years. Content can be either passive or informative in nature, offering no interactive capabilities. Active videos, on the other hand, allow viewers to click buttons on overlays and video player frames. Interactivity can be further enhanced when videos use click-to-call or share-with-a-friend text options.

Quick Response (QR) Codes

Barcodes have been a part of the consumer shopping experience for decades. Every time we pick up an item at the local grocery or drugstore, the purchase price is recorded when the cashier scans the code at checkout. **Quick response (QR) codes**, also known as QR barcodes, are used to engage, inform, and entertain targets through their mobile phones. Simple to use, all consumers need to do is use their smartphone to photograph the black-and-white or colored graphic square to receive a text message; be transported to a web, mobile, or social media site; view photographs, videos, or even webisodes; find clues or play a game; receive coupons; view recipes or additional nutritional information; sign up for contests or sweepstakes; or receive samples (figure 17.1).

To be worthwhile to consumers, QR codes must present relevant information that cannot be found at the point of purchase, such as purchase options, product reviews, product performance, height, weight, and range of colors, or alternative uses. This very diverse symbol can appear anywhere and on a variety of vehicles, such as magazines, newspapers, direct mail, packaging, cups, napkins, and posters, as well as on innumerable types of out-of-home and nontraditional vehicles. This makes them adaptable to almost any type of product, service, or promotion, no matter whether advertising efforts are directed to consumers or businesses.

These interactive barcodes have introduced a new and unique way of reaching the intended target: **context-sensitive marketing (CSM)**, or virtual impulse buying. Their ability to educate and inform makes the decision to purchase easier and faster.

Still a novelty to many, most consumers are curious about the content confined within the QR code's graphic shape. Because they decide whether to scan the code, this activity is not considered an intrusion. When available, one of its most valuable assets is the ability to immediately and effortlessly download a manual or how-to video to a tablet or mobile device.

As the use of QR codes continues to mature, consumers will see more and more repeatedly purchased items with a scannable QR code that directs them to "scan to reorder" conveniently printed on the label. To ensure growth, consumers who scan the code should receive some type of coupon or other relevant incentive.

As with all advertising, the continued success of QR codes will depend on whether the interaction was creative, entertaining, and informative. Like e-mail marketing, if the brand

Figure 17.1. Quick response (QR) codes allow consumers to interact with a brand through their smartphones, accessing information, coupons, and webinars. Robyn Blakeman.

has nothing of value to say or offer the target, the code should not be sent. Advertising must be worth the target's time to ensure he repeatedly chooses to interact with the code. If it isn't creative and engaging or doesn't enhance the target's lifestyle in some meaningful way, leave it out of the media mix.

Mobile Augmented Reality (AR)

Unlike that found on websites, mobile augmented reality is used less often as an entertainment device and more as an informative one. Its job is to engage and create a memorable interactive experience that is associated with a particular brand.

AR on smartphones and tablets uses the built-in camera to overlay copy and/or advertising content over real-world objects or makes images appear to come alive. AR adds to an image with illustrated computer-generated images, making the advertising or educational experience interactive and thus realistic, usable, and memorable.

Brands that include AR in the media mix provide a unique and creative experience that can be shared virally or through word of mouth, extending the brand's message.

Short Codes

One of the least expensive ways to engage consumers is to use a short-code promotion. This simple and easy-to-use promotional device asks consumers to enter a series of numbers into their mobile phones to win a predetermined prize. Short codes are often cross-promoted in traditional advertising vehicles and direct mail or as part of an event promotion. Brands that employ radio advertising, for example, may announce a 30 percent savings on patio furniture if the listener texts a specific short code. In return, the listener will receive a coupon or promotional code that can be used at a participating retailer. Short-code promotions, although relatively common, are very effective and are seen most notably as a way of voting on reality shows and to receive promotional items at sporting or entertainment events. Because these codes can be used at the local, national, and international level, they are a great engagement device for all types of products and services.

Mobile Coupons

To receive a mobile coupon, users do not necessarily have to download an app or opt in to anything. All they need to do is use their phones to go to a brand's website and download the coupon. Easily trackable, these instantly redeemable coupons are automatically deleted after use.

Mobile Applications and In-Application Ads

Mobile application refers to those apps that are native to the device. There are two types of mobile applications: branded and sponsored. Advertisers can employ **branded mobile applications** that push the key consumer benefit and offer some type of utility, entertainment, information, or promotional device. **Sponsored mobile applications** are where a particular brand owns the use of the app for a specified period. The overall format of the advertised message is often customized in some way for the brand (figure 17.2).

 Natural Pet Supply only carries the best products so you can bring out the best in your pet.

Figure 17.2. This is a great example of a colorful mobile banner. Image courtesy of Jordan Vandergriff, University of Tennessee.

Virtual Reality

The use of virtual reality (VR) is on the rise. An ever-rising number of brands are experimenting with its immersive storytelling qualities. To get more engaged eyes, brands that insert VR into the shopping experience offer customers unique interactions with products that cannot be encountered in any other way. Marketers who consider incorporating VR into their media mix can enhance customer engagement. "VR enables the three E's unlike any other channel (Engagement, Experience, and Entertainment)," says Michael Dub, a partner at DXagency, in Alex Samuely's 2016 article entitled "How VR Commerce Could

Figure 17.3. This mobile ad not only lets the reader know about the types of food the brand carries but also makes purchase easy with a simple click. Image courtesy of Jordan Vandergriff, University of Tennessee.

Transform Bricks-and-Mortar Retail." The interactive experiences available through this form of **experiential marketing** are more memorable and sharable than simple words and pictures on a page.

In-Application Advertising

This form of mobile advertising uses an app to distribute content. Some require a paid subscription; others, supported by advertising, are free to users. In-app advertising options include banner and rich media.

In-app banners are very similar to those found on the mobile web and are the most common form of advertising seen in apps. Users who click on the banner can be taken to a mobile website, be taken to a separate site within the app itself, or be able to make a call or send a text.

Rich media advertising options are interactive and unique to each brand. This type of advertising covers location-based, product carousels, mapping and lookbooks, in-game, and interstitials, to name a few such options.

Location-Based Services

This type of mobile advertising uses a phone's GPS to send out advertising messages to target members who have opted in to receive them, based on their current location.

Product Carousels

Product carousels use Flash to create a slideshow that showcases several rotating brands that can be seen on both mobile devices and tablets. Targeted consumers can interact with an ever-changing number of products, usually within the same product category. Each visual can be accompanied by descriptive copy as well as display contact numbers for sending a text or contacting a customer service or technical service representative or include an e-mail link.

Mapping

Mapping helps users find a specific location and check traffic conditions. Ads can appear on or off the map and typically allow viewers to download a relevant app for their location. Each ad has a logo, a small amount of copy, buttons for downloading the app, and a navigation button for directions or a close option. Other mapping options include something called **pushpins**, or geo-targeted messaging, that when moused over contain many rich media and other interactive properties along with location information and a logo.

Lookbooks

Lookbooks allow consumers to browse both products and promotions before they leave their current location. Shopkick has created an app that interested browsers can use to save the information and then remind them of the advertised product when they enter the store. Like product carousels, lookbooks allow consumers to browse must-have products by store location or brand. All consumers need to do to set up a reminder is simply drag and tag the item.

In-Game Marketing

This subtle form of advertising is gaining popularity. Like games found in social media vehicles, mobile games would also have relevant advertisements that match the games' premise. The goal is to have the advertised message not interfere with the game. Another form of in-game marketing includes the sponsorship of an event within a game, such as a car race. In an August 30, 2012, online *Mobile Commerce Daily* article by Chantal Tode entitled "Best Buy, Disney Team Up on Mobile Game Promotion for Back-to-School Push," Michael Burke, cofounder and president of Adtivity by Appssavvy New York, tells us, "Mobile gaming is definitely growing. Gaming is huge on desktops and a lot of those games are now moving to mobile and because of that, advertisers want to follow where the people are." He goes on to say, "There are opportunities in mobile gaming to reach consumers who are on the go, with many playing while they are commuting to work or while waiting for something. Advertisers can also leverage check-ins . . . or do things with photos or adding stuff to a calendar that you really can't do on the Web."

Interstitials

An **interstitial** ad is a full-page rich media ad that loads between page views on a site; a **prestitial** ad pops up before the home page opens. Their job is to encourage the viewer to download the site's native app. Most display for no longer than ten seconds, and almost all include a skip or close button. Because they can be considered annoying, sites should typically use no more than one per session.

Other advertising outlets include search; and as mobile screens get larger, some brands are trying out "takeovers" that temporarily fill all or most of a device's screen. But like any ad that gets in the way of what the target is doing, they can be annoying and so should be used sparingly and offer the target something relevant, unique, and time sensitive that cannot be found anywhere else.

Mobile promotional devices like coupons and short codes are interactive, trackable, memorable, and more likely to be acted upon than traditional advertising. A promotional mix that combines mobile, the Internet, and social media options keeps information timely and engaging. Ads that include links can deliver stronger visual/verbal content than a simple text message. Ads that include rich media allow the target to see the product in action and hear about its features and benefits. Interactive ads that include a link can whisk the viewer away to a website for a coupon or more information, and a call-through link can instantly connect the target to a customer or technical service representative.

Once technology advanced and consumers jumped on the smartphone bandwagon, advertising creative teams began to creatively ignite this "third screen" that includes mobile phones and tablets, using techniques perfected on television and the web and introducing a few new ones.

More and more consumers are using small screens to view movies and television programming and play games. The fact that these small screens can go everywhere with consumers creates both challenges and opportunities for brands that employ them. They must:

- Create relevant, engaging content that encourages the target to opt in;
- Deliver advertising, promotional, and entertainment options that can be employed across multiple platforms;
- Find ways for branded entertainment to engage and educate.

How Does Mobile Media Marketing Help IMC Be Consumer Focused?

A study by application company Tapjoy and market research firm Interpret found that adults twenty-five to thirty-four years old are not only more engaged with advertising on mobile devices but also remember more ads while using mobile apps, especially those using video or fully sponsored/branded apps. This group also had the largest percentage of app click-through rates and stood out from other general app users on the types of rewards they wanted to receive. Most look for cash and gift cards, but the twenty-five- to thirty-four-year-old age group was more interested in premium content, game credits, and new apps.

Consumers who use apps do so for many diverse reasons and in many diverse ways. The study breaks down app users into four specific categories: premium essentials, researcher purchases, gratis only, and freemium users. Premium essential users are willing to pay for an app. When considering purchase, they rely on word of mouth, and when browsing the app store, they do not rely on advertising or promotions. Researcher purchasers use social networking and recommendations to find apps. This group will rely on television ads and promotions to learn about apps for new games and movies and often have the most paid-for apps. The gratis-only group will typically download a free app and never upgrade to a paid version. They typically find ad-supported apps intrusive but are not willing to have the messages removed by paying. Freemium users download many apps but are price conscious when deciding which apps to purchase.

The Tapjoy article concludes by defining premium essential and freemium users as having the best recall for advertising seen in apps. However, those falling within the research purchaser group were more likely to click on an app than any other group. Finally, the premium essentials and freemium users were the most likely to download an app to receive a promotional incentive.

A research study reported in a January 12, 2017, online Pew Research Center article by Aaron Smith entitled "Record Shares of Americans Now Own Smartphones, Have Home Broadband" tells us that "roughly three-quarters of Americans (77%) now own a smartphone." In a 2012 online Open Forum article entitled "Mobile Apps: The New Big Tech Trend," Timo Platt identifies the three most important characteristics marketers can isolate as inherent to smartphones that no other advertising vehicle has: "*They are always on, always near and always dear.*"

This marriage of mobile and social media is known as SoLoMo, or social-local-mobile. Basically, it combines location-based properties with social media to more effectively engage the target. Its origins can be traced to three social media adaptations:

- Facebook advertising that encourages personal engagement through social media.
- Brands that began sending out coupons based on the target's location. These types of promotions used local-mobile or (LoMo) apps such as Shopkick and Gowalla.
- Apps such as Foursquare used a combination of the above that encouraged social interaction to promote the local and mobile components.

SoLoMo is initiated every time the target uses any of these apps to check in and then share the experience with her social networking circle. It is also activated when she uses apps to solicit a recommendation through social media contacts before purchasing.

Platt recommends the following ways to engage the target using SoLoMo:

- "Delivering brand messaging and other promotions to consumers near a local store through hyper-local advertising and promotions.
- "Collecting referrals and recommendations from friends and other trusted influencers, which affect what customers buy at the point of purchase.
- "Offering one-to-one sales guidance, closing and support. Some of these apps include access to a trained off-site salesperson to help close the sale of a premium product.
- "Staying in touch post-purchase without customers having to give up contact data. The merchant can enhance customer satisfaction and service, offer new promotions and drive brand loyalty."

The growth of mobile advertising can in part be traced to its many **location-based** capabilities that allow a brand to target consumers with personalized text messages. This real-time permission-based form of advertising can notify consumers about a sale they are near and/or deliver coupons by sending an alert that includes the brand name, location where it can be found, and a link for a coupon or additional information.

Very simply, it works like a motion detector. Anytime the target walks or drives by a location such as a paint store, she activates a locator device that sends an ad and/or a coupon letting the target in on the current sale on a specific brand of paint or accessories.

This type of immediate advertising makes mobile marketing a great direct-response and point-of-sale medium that encourages impulse or unplanned purchases. A media mix that employs location-based mobile advertising is both engaging and interactive as well as a great way to build an ongoing, one-on-one relationship with the target. To maintain loyalty, it is important that messages be on target, be time sensitive, offer the target something of value, and be easy to opt in and out of.

Advertising appearing on mobile devices, like e-mail advertising, must be correctly targeted. Brands employing it must be sure to collect the type of information that will ensure the right message is sent at the right time for the right target and place.

Brands that employ mobile advertising want to increase awareness, build or maintain loyalty, encourage some type of action such as downloading a coupon or making a purchase, and offer rewards that cannot be found anywhere else. Cross-promotional use in direct mail, broadcast, print, and out-of-home, along with the Internet and through any other alternative media vehicle, should help direct the target to additional information and prolong the life of the message.

Anytime an ad causes the target to act, he is both engaged and interacting with the product or service and the message. Creatively, whether using text only or more complicated rich media devices, to be effective mobile must:

- Have relevance to the target;
- Ask the target to do something, such as download a game;
- Strategically push the key consumer benefit and accomplish the objectives;
- Be simple and easy to do.

As new and exciting technological advances arrive, mobile, like the Internet, offers more and more bells and whistles. The use of apps is now commonplace and choices are numerous, but even more technologically advanced options are available, such as being able to view programming once confined to a television screen on both tablets and smartphones. Also growing in popularity are paying for purchases via mobile devices and varied types of remote management. Consumers can now turn on lights, lock doors, and adjust thermostats via a web-enabled mobile phone while they're away from home.

Incentives and Deterrents of Mobile Media Marketing

To decide whether mobile media marketing is right for an IMC campaign, let's look at some of the incentives and deterrents associated with it.

What Makes Mobile Media Marketing So Great?

The more notable incentives associated with mobile media marketing include:

- *Popularity*. More than three-quarters of the US population own a mobile phone.
- *Search*. Mobile web searches are expected to exceed those done on a personal computer.

- *Cost.* Mobile ads are a less expensive way to reach the target than traditional methods.
- *Geo-targeting.* The target can be reached anywhere at any time with pertinent coupons or promotional devices.
- *Engagement.* Devices that hold the target's attention will be more likely to encourage a response to the message, keeping the target on the site longer.
- *Database development.* Consumers who opt in to receive information build target lists.
- *Buzz building.* Messages that can reach the target while shopping can potentially generate buzz or word-of-mouth opportunities as messages are discussed or forwarded to friends or family.

Is There Anything Wrong with Mobile Media Marketing?

The more notable deterrents associated with mobile media marketing include:

- *Intrusive.* Not everyone wants to receive texts or other types of advertised messages on his phone, nor be slowed down by them.
- *Message length.* Elaborate messages are prohibitive; content must be short but informative.
- *Message type.* Brands using mobile are still test-driving the best ways to reach the target with the best message.
- *Opt-out.* It is easy for consumers to delete or block messages.
- *Technology.* Like computers, consumers encounter mobile advertising that is affected by the capabilities available on their mobile device.
- *Reach.* Marketers are still working on how to reach consumers with a relevant message while searching or shopping.

The Strategy behind Mobile Media Marketing

Research has shown that mobile ads are more engaging than display ads viewed on a desktop computer. There are many advertising and marketing executives, however, who believe it has more to do with novelty than with pure interest in the brand advertised.

Mobile's rise to prominence in the promotional mix can be traced not only to the popularity of smartphones but to the fact that consumers take this direct-response tool with them everywhere. Mobile can be used to research a product, make a call for more information, or make a purchase, no matter where consumers are.

When determining the overall campaign strategy, it is important that mobile be included in the promotional mix and strongly promote the key consumer benefit. The type of advertised message employed will depend on the brand's overall image, whether it is an emotional or rational purchase, and price. As a support vehicle, the best strategic approach will depend on whether the focus will be on the product or the consumer and whether some type of incentive or additional link will accompany the ad. Campaigns using a product approach can use banners, SMS, or more elaborate visual options such as video, lookbooks, or QR codes. Those focusing on the consumer should employ more creative visual and verbal options as well as AR and video to help seamlessly weave the brand into the target's overall lifestyle. The strongest product-oriented strategies for mobile include generic claim, product feature, or unique selling proposition. A strategy that focuses on the consumer can employ any of the consumer-oriented choices.

Choice of appeal like the execution technique will depend on the complexity of the message and what is being said and shown in other vehicles within the campaign. With that said, some of the more expressive emotional appeal choices might include lifestyle or social, while more rational appeals may include feature, price, or news. Rational appeals work best if the execution technique is a straight sell, testimonial, news, reminder, or teaser. Good emotional execution techniques might include humor, animation, and sex.

If mobile is being used as a primary vehicle to launch or tease, video works well. To ensure targets are reached and the message has captured their attention, be sure to run multiple ads with some type of engagement device such as a game, QR code, augmented reality, or a coupon.

High-end emotional purchases might consider using QR codes, video, or lookbooks to maintain or further reinforce image. Brands falling within the rational category can also use texts, QR codes, or more elaborate augmented reality options, display ads, or coupons. All mobile strategic categories should invest in search, since most consumers will begin the purchase process by seeking out information or looking for promotional offers.

Using public relations to advertise a brand's website in ways that are tied to newsworthy topics and creative story lines that align with the visual/verbal messages found elsewhere in the IMC campaign is memorable, as is developing a separate campaign or a joint promotion where a portion of a firm's sales is donated to a charity that is tied to a contest or other notable incentive.

Mobile is a great match with traditional vehicles that showcase QR codes.

To bring more consumer-focused properties to mobile, brands that consider pairing mobile with social media, as previously discussed, will find it a great way to encourage word-of-mouth activities and deliver coupons.

Mobile ads that include a link to the brand's website or that include location-based properties can increase engagement between buyer and seller, deliver promotions, encourage purchase, and educate the target.

Apps that include informative content, have games, or use augmented reality will help create interactive opportunities and build or maintain awareness and set up word-of-mouth or viral exchanges.

Strategically, mobile advertising is an efficient way to not only reach the target but also engage the target. Objectives best suited to mobile use might include selling the brand through e-commerce efforts only, building a database, increasing awareness, announcing a promotion, or using the medium as a teaser or reminder vehicle.

Brands that strategically choose to include mobile media marketing in their promotional mix will find it to be targetable both demographically and behavioristically, as well as useful for locating where the target is in relationship to the brand. Other advantages include interactivity, 24/7 availability, and the ability to develop an imaginative and engaging experience for the target.

The Look of Mobile Media Marketing

Design aesthetics for both mobile phones and tablets rely on the same principles as those introduced in chapter 16 and will not be reexamined here. Design features for these mobile devices rely heavily on how and where the device is used, connectivity issues, smaller screen sizes, overall device features, and their limitations. Consumers use their mobile phones for many things beyond making calls, such as texting, e-mailing, and playing games. The most frequently employed advanced features beyond search include jumping on the mobile web. Let's take a quick look at some of its unique properties.

BOX 17.1. Mobile Marketing Facts

Here are the top ten mobile marketing facts, according to "50 Amazing Facts about Mobile Marketing," a June 29, 2012, online slideshow by Jeanne Hopkins and Jamie Turner seen on HubSpot.

- Mobile ads perform four to five times better than traditional online ads in key metrics such as brand favorability, awareness, and purchase intent.
- Mobile coupons have a redemption rate ten times higher than that of print coupons.
- Seventy-four percent of smartphone users use their phones for shopping; of that, 79 percent make a purchase as a result of using their phones.
- Brands using SMS to reach customers connect with 95 percent of all smartphone and non-smartphone users.
- Seventy percent of mobile online searches lead to an action within an hour; 70 percent of desktop online searches lead to an action within a month.
- Eighty-one percent of smartphone users have done product research via their smartphone, and 50 percent have made a purchase with one.
- Seventy-three percent of smartphone users said they use the mobile web rather than an app to shop.
- Fifty percent of smartphone users have scanned QR codes, 18 percent of whom have made a purchase afterward.
- Of the smartphone users asked why they would scan a QR code, 87 percent said to get a coupon, discount, or deal.
- Fifty percent of smartphone users have purchased a product using their phone.

The Mobile Web

The term "mobile web" can be defined as gaining access to the Internet through sites specifically designed for the small screens found on handheld mobile devices. Although broad, the definition covers everything from traditional browser use to the designing of a brand-specific app. As a descriptive term for information found on the web, the "mobile web" label is often frowned upon. It infers there are multiple webs. There is only one web; the only differences are access and content. In 2010 the late Apple cofounder Steve Jobs stated that "mobile advertising really sucks." That was then; today, mobile advertising is creative, innovative, and interactive. Capitalizing on what mobile can do, advertisers can employ location-based applications, create ads that double as games, or distribute incentives or information of value to consumers. What consumers do not respond to are repetitively used web ads recycled as mobile advertising.

The first thing to consider when designing a mobile website is knowing what type of device the target will use to view the site. Additionally, it is important to know how the target uses her phone and the type of Internet connection she uses or will typically have available. The connection is especially important, for example, if the brand will be including rich media devices or be asking the target to fill out forms using the mobile device.

Understanding how the target will use the site is also important. Most users will surf the mobile web when they are killing time. Design decisions should start with the idea that mobile search is being used in the same way most desktop searches are done.

The creative team must also understand how the target will view the mobile site. This places an enormous emphasis on context. If the target uses his device on the go, then speed will be a priority, as will the need for designing a graphic yet straightforward and stripped-down site that focuses on a streamlined experience. A target more likely to use his device in front of the TV or during lunch will spend more time with content, giving it a more important role.

The successful design of a mobile website involves never losing sight of the type of content that will be displayed, how it will be used across devices, and its small viewable size. How much content to bring over from a brand's traditional website will depend on how the target will use the site. Understand why the target will visit the site, such as making reservations, viewing a menu, or seeing a map. Design the space to ensure that information is easy to find, and limit the number of taps the consumer will have to make to no more than three.

Context is as important as content in mobile web design. Context is all about the environment in which content is viewed. Lighting may be poor, the viewer could be distracted or multitasking, or he may be in motion, whether walking or riding the bus, and the type of connectivity available may change.

When determining content, the creative team needs to consider why the target will visit a mobile site. What features are important to targets when they're on the go? What do they find frustrating when using mobile websites? And what type of device do they use when accessing the mobile web? Answers to these primary questions will help determine what needs to be included on a site and what can be left out.

Because there are so many different types of mobile phones out there, to save money and time it is important to start out with a design and advertising format that can work on as many different devices as possible. To avoid confusion, it is important to keep content and overall look similar to what the target would find on a desktop.

Apps are the way to go when looking for a more focused and personal experience. Whether the product or service needs an app will depend on how the target will arrive on the site. If most of the target audience will go to the site directly and repeatedly, an app would be appropriate. If they arrive at a site via a shared link, an app would be redundant, since visitors will be able to visit the site whether they have installed the app or not. Brands using apps might consider a native app like Instagram that will work with the most diverse number of devices. Like traditional Internet sites, designers must take into consideration that not all visitors will be using the newest operating systems.

The choice of typeface should match that found on the brand's traditional website when possible. Avoid serif fonts, choosing instead clean, easily readable, and legible sans serif fonts.

Something rarely considered is battery life. Both smartphones and tablets have smaller battery life and ramped-up processors, so the more the processor needs to work, the shorter the battery's life span. Big drainers include location-based features, animation, and other varied rich media enhancements.

Why have a specially designed mobile website when a traditional one already exists? First, and most obvious, is the smaller screen size and the slower performance of mobile devices. With that said, many smartphone users can view most traditional desktop websites, but asking them to pinch and zoom in on tiny links and copy has lost its novelty. The major difference between a mobile web user and a traditional desktop user is location. A mobile user is out and about, whereas the traditional desktop user is at home, surrounded by fewer distractions and with a dedicated time allowance.

Designing for the Newest Digital Medium

Design for mobile devices will closely follow the steps and principles used in traditional desktop website design. The major differences that must be taken into consideration are the small screen size, download time, and the fact that the viewer is out and about.

Basically, most web designs start out as sketches that are refined in wireframes. A **wireframe** is the visual/verbal layout of a website. Using simple line drawings, it helps the designers and web developers present and envision how each proposed function, any graphic elements, and the overall structure and content of a website will look.

To decrease download times, avoid background images. Depending on lighting conditions when viewed, readability can become an issue. Additionally, it is important to keep the design simple; avoid using unnecessary visuals and graphics when possible.

Creating a user-friendly experience is critical when designing for mobile. Users expect pages to match the integrity, quality, and performance the brand projects elsewhere. Consumers use their mobile phones on the go to enhance their shopping experience, get them to their destination fast, and offer useful hints and tips as well as offer rewards and an overall pleasant experience. A rewarding customer experience begins with how an app performs. It can look great, but apps that open slowly or crash are frustrating and can affect brand image. Apps that do not perform up to consumer standards compared to other brand applications will receive poor reviews both virally and via word of mouth, affecting adoption, image, and equity.

Before design of an app begins, the creative team members should ask themselves: What does this app need to do differently from competitors to stand out? What can it do better? Once these questions are answered, designers can come up with an app that not only enhances the target's lifestyle but either does something no other competing app does or does it better.

With that said, it is important to remember that design choices affect features, content, interactivity, graphics, and thus overall performance.

Consumers associate acceptable performance with quick download times, how a page behaves when loading, transitions between pages, rich media performance, a low number and type of errors, and waiting time between transitions. Creative teams should always seek to design usable, cutting-edge, memorable, and high-performing sites.

Sites that require viewers to fill out forms need to use a more simplified version than those found on a traditional website. Consider using radio buttons and lists that can be tapped to pick preselected options. Be sure any data entered or page screen viewed is savable for use in later visits or readable at a later time by the target.

Navigation

Do not forget about navigation devices; they should be easy to find and intuitive to use. Be sure to put all navigational and search devices at the top of the site. Use increased amounts of white space around them, since fingers often get in the way of click points spaced too close together. Additionally, the use of increased white space projects elegance and makes the site easier to use.

One simple but important navigation device to keep in mind is how viewers will move around using their fingers. Consider the following possibilities or think up your own: tap, double tap, drag, swipe to scroll, pinch to zoom in or out, and press and hold. When determining a type of navigation device, remember that keeping things straightforward is usually best to avoid making users learn new and often unnecessary techniques. Tap size of any link (width and height) needs to be at least thirty pixels. In its *User Experience Guidelines* concerning navigation, Apple explains that anything tappable should be the size of a fingertip, which translates to around forty-four points wide × forty-four points tall and top out at fifty-seven pixels square. A much smaller text link may measure only fourteen pixels high.

Placement of navigation devices is relatively diverse and will depend on content. More complex sites may place a menu link at the top and navigation buttons on the bottom of the screen so that users do not have to scroll back to the top to continue their search. Still others partially hide the menu until the user taps on it to save valuable viewing space.

To keep design simple, place multiple text links on the opening page to make navigation fast and easy between points. Links can be text only or appear with an accompanying visual. If users must scroll, make sure it is in one direction, usually vertical.

When incorporating video into advertising efforts, it is important to ensure that ads are easy to view. "Horizontal ads," according to a 2016 *Mobile Marketing Daily* article by Ben Frederick, "are more effective at generating purchase intent and increasing familiarity." The article goes on to say that it is strategically important to adjust the tone depending on the "intended outcome: Comedic tones familiarize them with the brand, dramatic and emotional ads appeal to them, and informational ads make them more likely to purchase."

Emojis

Emojis are mobile royalty. According to a 2016 *New York Times* article entitled "Picture This: Marketers Let Emojis Do the Talking" by Robert D. Hof, "92 percent of the online population now use emojis." An emoji is not an emoticon. An **emoticon** is a smiley face :) or a wink ;). An **emoji** is a simple graphic image. Able to communicate both thoughts and emotions, these very communicative and attention-getting little images reimagine how a picture is worth a thousand words. Brands that incorporate emojis into their advertising create a unique way to engage with their target that does not use a hard-sell approach.

Brands like Oreo, Coke, Taco Bell, Dove, and Burger King, to name a few, that want to develop their own branded emojis must first create their own app or work with a messaging app like WhatsApp or Facebook Messenger. Twitter also will create customized emojis, triggered when a specific hashtag is used, that marketers can incorporate into their advertising efforts.

Since many symbols need little translation, emojis are an excellent visual and verbal tool when used in international campaigns. To reach consumers in China, Oreo launched a mobile campaign that asked parents to paste family photos onto dancing emojis. This very successful campaign "generated nearly 100 million emojis," according to a 2015 article in *The Guardian* entitled "The Rise of the Emoji for Brand Marketing" by Michael Brenner.

Tablet Design

Designing for a tablet is not that much different from designing for a smartphone; it must be easy to use, relevant to use, be a problem solver, and be both visually and verbally enticing and informative. Simple is better; battery time is limited. If a brand can incorporate native apps into its site, such as GPS features, calendars, or contact lists, use is less complicated.

Another important consideration is that, unlike smartphones, tablets may be used by multiple members of the family, so simple ways of logging in and out are important, as is displaying who is currently logged in.

Magazines viewed on tablets often allow users to move between articles by horizontally scrolling and use vertical scrolling for viewing and navigating an article.

To make browsing easier and less frustrating, provide a home page. Viewers are used to them and appreciate them.

Consumers will use smartphone, desktop, and tablet interfaces differently, so overall design must reflect that. Research has shown that tablet users, unlike desktop and smartphone users, have an overwhelming tendency to swipe horizontally.

Generally, there are four basic differences to consider between designing for desktop and smartphones and designing for tablets: Size is still a problem. A tablet is not as small as a smartphone or as big as a desktop or laptop, screen resolution varies by device, and options to view content in portrait and landscape must be considered, along with touch interfaces and no mouse but more room for fingers to swipe or tap than in smartphones. And, like smartphones, processing and battery life are limited, so many rich media–enhanced options, unlike those favored on desktops, can be challenging for both tablets and smartphones.

A tablet can be used for in-depth research of a product or service or for quick bouts of surfing for phone numbers or addresses.

All digital design is affected by resolution, screen size, and speed, so a one-size-fits-all space does not apply. As we previously described, mobile sites are trimmed-down versions of a brand's traditional website. A tablet user wants a full version of the site but does not want to spend a lot of time zooming and pinching to see content.

Tablet design should use simple, clean user interfaces with large, well-spaced, easily recognizable navigation devices. Copy or visuals set up in horizontal columns are preferred over vertical ones.

Tablet users tend to read more and for longer periods of time about products they are interested in while in a more relaxed state of mind than desktop or smartphone users.

Tablets blend print and digital qualities together. "Our goal," said David Ho, team leader for the *Wall Street Journal* iPad app, in "The State of the Art in Designing Content," a May 14, 2012, online Newspaper Association of America article by Dena Levitz, "was to blend the best lessons of print with the power and immediacy of the Web to create something new and special."

Ho found that users wanted to be able to turn pages, have copy appear in horizontal columns for easy reading, have a designated final page, and be able to see several, not all, stories at once.

Digital aspects allow readers to be updated in real time, use multimedia features, and share any visual/verbal aspects with others through e-mail or social media. Many newspapers and magazines that are available on tablets also offer video options.

These small differences from traditional online sources give tablet use not only immediacy but also incorporate social aspects into the interactive activity.

Advertising on tablets that offers some type of interactive device is more likely to be clicked on. Chase, for example, used a full-screen interactive ad that allowed users to interact with the graphic elements. When moved, different benefits of card usage were revealed. By turning the tablet different ways, viewers could see a different reward ooze out of the main visual of a large credit card.

Mobile's importance to the overall promotional mix has taken a giant step forward in a very short time. Growth has taken a simple communication device to one that organizes, educates, and entertains consumers. Brands that employ the multilevel creative options available to mobile advertising will not only engage consumers but also get them talking. As an advertising vehicle, mobile is still in its infancy, with marketers still testing how much advertising versus promotional material the target will tolerate and/or interact with.

Q DISCUSSION QUESTIONS

1. What are the strategic uses of mobile media marketing in an IMC campaign?
2. How has mobile grown from a one-way communication between the brand and target to one that is both interactive and engaging?
3. How do consumers use mobile?
4. What does mobile add to the promotional mix?
5. When should brands employ mobile advertising?
6. Mobile has a diverse array of advertising options. What are some of the most popular, and how can each help visually and verbally express the key consumer benefit?

7. How are quick response (QR) codes employed in mobile advertising?
8. How does mobile media marketing help an IMC campaign be more consumer focused?
9. There are four categories of app users. Define each.
10. The marriage of mobile and social is known as SoLoMo. Define what it is and how it is used.
11. How does mobile employ location-based capabilities?
12. Location-based capabilities bring what additional advertising opportunities to the promotional mix?
13. What do brands want to accomplish with mobile media?
14. To be effective and relevant to the target, mobile must do what?
15. What are the pros and cons of using mobile media marketing?
16. What is the strategy behind using mobile media marketing in an IMC campaign?
17. What is cause marketing, and why is it important to have it be a part of an IMC campaign?
18. What is important when writing and designing for mobile?
19. What are the major differences between designing for mobile and tablets?

CHAPTER

18

Alternative Media Advertising

The Strategic Use of Alternative Media in IMC

Alternative media, also known as ambient, emerging, new, or nontraditional media, is defined as creative, shocking, or surprising advertising that appears on unconventional surfaces that can be found anywhere inside or outside that do not fit into the standard or traditional media categories of broadcast, print, or out-of-home.

The term "alternative media" refers to the fact that creative teams are no longer tied to a limited palette of surfaces that are considered static or passive like traditionally delivered print (newspaper and magazine) and broadcast (radio and television) vehicles. These "traditional" media categories, however, can have added or alternative properties. Broadcast media, for example, can incorporate web addresses, QR codes, or social media; print can also incorporate the web, QR codes, augmented reality (AR), or social media into the design, while out-of-home may employ mobile or digital as well as project three-dimensional images. This unique partnership between traditional and alternative vehicles injects a new level of creativity into traditional vehicles never seen before that includes engagement, surprise, and interactive options.

Never boring, visually or verbally, alternative media can be an engaging and interactive facet of the promotional mix on its own. The rich, assorted palette of often atypical vehicles and surfaces makes it a lot easier to reach the target with a memorable message wherever they are. These surfaces, according to Robyn Blakeman in her book *Strategic Uses of Alternative Media*, can be any "large, small, round, flat, stationary or moving, edible or nonedible surface that will hold a message and ensure the targeted consumer will come in contact with it. Often placed in unusual or unconventional places, these highly targeted, creative, and sometimes interactive vehicles are excellent at delivering both a meaningful and memorable ad more effectively than traditional media vehicles. And, unlike most other vehicles, they cannot be clicked out of, turned off, or deleted."

Adoption of these unique surfaces can reach the target with a creative, tantalizing, and sometimes shocking visual/verbal message that is often worth sharing with others, effectively extending the life of the advertised message. (See case study 16 for details on Allstate's use of alternative media.)

Designs may be big or small, colorful or monochromatic; use a dominant visual or rely on copy only to deliver the message. Some may incorporate technology, but all will have creative and inventive visual/verbal ideas that reach targets where they are in unique and inventive ways. Many depend on some type of interactive or engagement device; others stun visually and/or verbally to capture attention. This seemingly limitless category of vehicles has been labeled the *"creative economy"* by countless advertisers because many vehicles are inexpensive, and all are meant to create a memorable experience.

In today's world of overstimulated consumers, finding a memorable visual/verbal solution for a brand's message is difficult. Creative teams have found that messages delivered in an unexpected way can leave a lasting impression on consumers. Marketers, on the other hand, have been less impressed with this new visual/verbal voice of advertising and have been slow to adopt some of the more unusual forms of alternative media. As brands search for more consumer-focused, stimulating, and unusual ways to break through the clutter with an advertised message that not only attracts their target's attention but holds it, adoption rates have substantially increased as alternative vehicles have repeatedly delivered the desired return on investment (ROI). Other market influencers behind the growth of alternative media include audience fragmentation and the younger, more desirable target audience's continued avoidance of traditional advertising vehicles as well as their interest in digital media options such as mobile, gaming, and the Internet.

Success rates have marketers turning less often to traditional advertising vehicles to build brand awareness, create or maintain brand image, or launch a new or reinvented product. To reach a media-blitzed, fractionalized target audience today, an IMC campaign will often incorporate one or more types of alternative media vehicles into the media mix.

Any vehicle or combination of vehicles employed must include some type of engagement device or sharable idea that can grab attention, deliver a memorable encounter, and visually and verbally speak to the target in thought-provoking ways. Some messages might awe, others tantalize or titillate, and still others shock, but all reactions should excite, engage, build curiosity or provoke, remind, drive traffic to a website or brick-and-mortar store, encourage sales or contributions, engage the hard-to-reach eighteen- to thirty-four-year-old target, and show a measurable ROI both on- and offline, no small task.

Brands that are looking for new ways to create buzz and interact with their target will find alternative media vehicles a great option. Small advertisers with small budgets will find it easier to pin down and reach their target, while purveyors of larger mass-produced goods and services will find it a creatively engaging way to utilize the many diverse vehicles to reach multicultural audiences across the globe.

Whether to use alternative vehicles as a primary or secondary media source will depend on the brand, overall creative message, life cycle, budget, and target. When used as a support vehicle, alternative media is highly effective at reinforcing a brand's message or image or as

CASE STUDY 16

IMC Alternative Media: Allstate

Background

Headquartered in Northbrook, Illinois, the Allstate Corporation is the third-largest personal lines insurer in the United States behind State Farm (1, 6). Founded in 1931 by insurance broker Carl Odell, Allstate began as an auto insurance provider and extension of the Sears retail company (1). Currently, Allstate offers a variety of services within the property and casualty insurance categories, including but not limited to auto, homeowners, fire, marine, and life insurance policies, programs, and products (1). In 2008 Allstate purchased the Partnership Marketing Group to expand Allstate's roadside assistance services and, in doing so, also appropriated PMG's legal service benefit plans to Allstate's US membership base (1). In the fourth quarter of 2011, Allstate accrued $31.4 billion in total revenue and $928 million in net income (1).

Problem

In 2006 Allstate sought a way in which it could both promote sales and generate a higher level of consumer interest in its products and services (2). In addition to this, the emergence of DVRs and other entertainment options, such as Netflix, were rendering television commercial viewership obsolete (3). Advertisers and businesses alike scrambled for new ideas and ways to engage consumers.

Solution

That same year, multimedia corporation Destination Media took advantage of then-recent technological innovations and created Gas Station TV, a network aired through most major gas retailers via a small, twenty-inch digital television screen installed at the pump (2, 3). GSTV's quick, cyclical programming now includes news, entertainment, sports, and weather updates, original content, and, more importantly, advertising (3, 4). Upon learning of the new program in 2006 through its media-planning company, Allstate immediately began an advertising campaign tailored specifically to GSTV (2).

Alternative/Emerging Media

Allstate enlisted the help of actor Dennis Haysbert to narrate and bring the familiarity of a recognizable persona to its commercials. At first Allstate's commercial content was focused on a more dramatic approach, showing many of life's unexpected difficulties and the services specific to Allstate in providing protection and insurance for its customers (5). In 2010 Allstate built an overarching advertising campaign for all media, including Gas Station TV, that was based around a persona known as "Mayhem." This more humorous approach personified many of the accidents people can face in their home or automobile.

Results

As a result of both the advertising on Gas Station TV and the Haysbert campaign, Allstate experienced an almost $1 billion increase in sales from 2006 to 2007 (1). Since then, Allstate has suffered major losses in revenue (12.5 percent in 2008) due to economic instability. In 2010, before the "Mayhem" campaign reached popularity, Allstate's revenue fell another 1.9 percent (6). This year, however, revenue increased by 0.9 percent as Allstate's "Mayhem" campaign led to heightened brand recognition, most of which can be attributed to GSTV's 89 percent active viewer engagement statistic, 80 percent positive audience reaction, and twenty-seven million monthly viewer statistics, resulting in Allstate's 5.2 percent market share (3, 4, 6). These numbers are not only indicative of an effective ad campaign but also consistent with the effective communication through GSTV.

Conclusion

Although Allstate experienced a decline in revenue from 2008 to 2010, this was mostly due to the now four-year economic recession in the United States; State Farm also experienced negative percentages during this time. Liberty Mutual's gains throughout this period can be attributed to their overseas business. If Allstate's growth between 2006 and 2007, as well as 2010 and 2011, are indicative of anything, it is that their overarching advertising campaign effectively communicated their message to a large consumer base through Allstate's use of alternative media via Gas Station TV.

Sources: (1) LexisNexis Academic, http://www.lexisnexis.com/hottopics/lnacademic. (2) Becky Yerak, "Allstate Hopes to Fuel Interest in Idle Motorists with Ads," *Chicago Tribune*, June 9, 2006, http://articles. chicagotribune.com/2006-06-09/business/0606090179_1_allstate-media-llc-gas-pumps. (3) "Gas Station TV Drives One Billion Viewers in Just Five Years," Gas Station TV press release, July 19, 2011, http://www. gstv.com/newsitems/gas-station-tv-drives-one-billion-viewers-in-just-five-years. (4) Gas Station TV website, www.gstv.com. (5) "Dennis Haysbert Allstate Commercial," video posted at YouTube by ThatsAll statesStand, 0:31, http://www.youtube.com/watch?v=VBAwXN8lS88. (6) https://clients.ibisworld.com/ industryus/Majorcompanies.aspx?indid=1325. (7) Tim Nudd, "Ad of the Day: State Farm—Are You and Your Family Safe from Giant Marauding Alien Robots?" *Adweek*, August 17, 2011, http://www.adweek.com/ news/advertising-branding/ad-day-state-farm-134187. (8) "Liberty Mutual 'Doing the Right Thing,'" *Adweek*, March 24, 2011, video, 1:01, http://www.youtube.com/watch?v+DJIHBuma4ZE.

a way to demonstrate brand features. Its flexibility and diverse array of shapes and sizes make it an effective choice for small businesses, large corporations, or charities. Use as a primary vehicle makes it a great choice for any brand targeting smaller niche markets or those not easily reached through traditional means. Focus on a smaller number of brand-loyal consumers sets up a great opportunity to take a more consumer-focused message directly to those most likely to purchase the product or service. For example, the best way to reach an advertising-avoidant target is to put the brand directly in his hands. To launch its new phone and reach its tech-savvy consumer, HTC took the product to where its target is instead of waiting for the target to come to the brand. Promotional efforts used pop-up stores and kiosks in malls, set up "BoomSound Lounges" to showcase the phone's speakers, sponsored concerts, and used cinema display ads and lobby demonstrations to create an interactive hands-on experience where the target could actually use the phone. The overall objective was to create a one-on-one experience between the brand and the target that encouraged feedback and heightened interest by allowing those most likely to purchase the product to interact with it.

Creative teams that creatively exploit a vehicle's shape, use, location, and size can capture the target's imagination with a meaningful visual and informative voice. There is not a surface that consumers encounter that cannot or has not been used as a delivery device. These hundreds, perhaps even thousands, of unique surfaces can be turned into a promotional device for any event, product, or service (figure 18.1). The very best create viral opportunities as consumers talk about and post photographs of the advertising or event.

Figure 18.1. Alternative marketing is about capturing the target's imagination or attention, something this Red Bull car wrap with 3-D product display does well. Robyn Blakeman.

Like traditional media before them, alternative media vehicles have carved out a place in our fast-paced, instant-messaging lives; they have become a social, political, and economic force within our culture, helping us communicate and sell locally, nationally, and internationally. Each media vehicle offers marketers, creative teams, and consumers variety, convenience, flexibility, and personalization.

The Diversity of the Alternative Media Voice

These very distinct vehicles cannot deliver an integrated message alone. To be remembered and thus acted upon, the visual/verbal message must be cross-promoted elsewhere. Diverse does not always mean unusual. Many vehicles that fall under the umbrella label of "alternative" can be used daily by the target, such as mobile, e-mail marketing, blogs, and social media. These chatty vehicles are the exception to the less-is-more copy rule seen in most alternative designs. Due to the multitude of divergent sizes and shapes, most vehicles must rely solely on powerful visuals that are supported by a logo and possibly a slogan or tagline. The brand's visual/verbal voice is all about image. Strategically, most alternative vehicles cannot successfully deliver the key consumer benefit, so visual focus must be placed on character representatives, spokespersons, logos, or graphics used elsewhere throughout the IMC campaign. Not all vehicles are measurable, so care must be taken when determining which vehicles to employ and their overall role in the campaign. For example, is the goal to engage, awe, create interactive opportunities, and build or maintain awareness, or just to remind or tease?

Many vehicles are integrated into the target's life as part of a shopping or dining experience, such as coffee cups, doggie bags, table tents, packaging, or shopping bags. Others pop up in unusual places to a captive audience, such as with restroom advertising or on airline seatback trays. These often very targetable and hopefully repeatedly seen ads are great at keeping the brand name in front of the target, but they are not always a good choice if the goal is to reinforce image or build a relationship with the target. Regularly viewed cinema ads, product placement in movies or television programming, or ads seen in video games are also great reminder vehicles, but they can easily annoy the viewer or player if they interrupt the experience. Some of the best engagement devices include QR codes, augmented reality, contests or sweepstakes, or some type of promotional device. Creative designs and unusual placement are unique to alternative vehicles and are what helps capture and hold the target's attention.

Placement of vehicles should complement the brand; for example, placing car insurance ads in parking garages or soda ads on scoreboards. Parking meters or empty storefronts might advertise local shopping and eating establishments within walking distance, bowling balls may sport a popular beer label, and fruit and vegetable stickers may push a chain of local gyms, to name a few ideas.

Many of these oddball vehicles are often creatively edgier and/or rely on technology to get the message out. They can surprise, be taken as a keepsake, or just generally garner some type of response from the consumer. Let's take a look at some of the more commonly seen vehicles.

Product Placement

When a brand logo is seen, talked about, or used in a movie, television show, or game, it's known as product placement. Once a free form of publicity, advertisers now must pay a hefty price to see their brand's logo on-screen. This subtle form of advertising can pack a more powerful punch if it can be associated with a main character or overall storyline, not only making it more memorable but also helping to create interest and build awareness and image. Brands that are incorporated into the storyline and get talked about are worth their weight in gold and often become a sort of mini-commercial that reminds without being intrusive. It is important that any product placement avoid in-your-face messages that scream brand attributes; instead, the goal is to quietly reach a captive audience and tie product use to the character's image.

Success depends on relevant placement. A brand that does not fit seamlessly into the scene or overall environment in which it is placed will not only affect image but also receive negative word of mouth.

As we learned in chapter 12, viewers who wish to avoid watching advertising can get a sandwich; zip, zap, graze; or record programs to skip commercials. Brands that incorporate product placement into their media mix become part of a scenario that cannot be skipped or ignored by the target or create additional clutter, apathy, or ill will.

Pump-Top TV

Almost everybody these days still needs to regularly gas up. Why not reach this captive audience with video advertising placed on the pump? Nineteen-inch LCD screens can deliver one or more messages, complete with sight, sound, and motion, lasting fifteen, thirty, or a full sixty seconds.

Advertisers with less to say may want to consider the gas pump nozzles. Although small, they can clearly display a logo, slogan, or tagline that can successfully remind this stationary audience that she may want to pick up a cup of coffee, a soda, or a candy bar before she drives off. Some of the more innovative nozzles play an advertised message when the nozzle is placed in the car's fuel tank.

ATMs

While the target is stopping to get cash, he may as well get an advertising message too. Busy ATMs are a great way to promote local businesses or services near the machines' location. The ad can appear not only on the LCD screen but also on the receipt, often accompanied by a coupon.

Street and Sidewalk Graphics and Stickers

Always creative, street graphics and stickers can be found on roads, sidewalks, or parking lots. Before using any form of street graphic, also known as **street graffiti**, it is important that the brand get permission from local officials. Folgers coffee used stickers and manhole covers to reach its target. This creative idea took advantage of the steam that rises out of the covers by placing a sticker of a "steaming" hot cup of coffee, as seen from above, on top of the cover with copy that reads, "Hey, City That Never Sleeps. Wake up. Folgers." Brightly colored stickers strategically placed can lead the target to a specific location or deliver the message in stages to hold attention. Street graphics are often incredibly detailed works of art done in multiple media. Some of the most creative are often produced for movie premieres or charities, and often those with the most power to awe are 3-D images that use the sidewalk or a building as a canvas.

Exercise Equipment

Advertisers look for surfaces that are close to targets or that hold them captive by what they are doing. Exercise equipment fits that purpose, fitted with branded touch screens attached to the equipment with which the target can watch TV, surf the web, or visit a social media site—all while working up a sweat.

Cinema Advertising

Until recently, many brands found cinema advertising or advertising seen before the movie trailers too expensive, too time-consuming to produce, and not sufficiently targetable. Now this bigger-than-life, in-your-face vehicle is considered a great way to reach not only a captive audience but also that desirable eighteen- to thirty-four-year-old target group. When choosing this vehicle, care needs to be taken not to alienate the audience with a hard-sell message; instead use one that entertains. If going big is not a desirable or affordable option, theater lobbies hold many highly visible surfaces such as kiosks, posters, drink cups, popcorn tubs, and ticket stubs that can be used alone or to extend the message seen inside the theater or elsewhere in the lobby. Most are clearly marked with logos big and small. Some include social media hashtags and/or QR codes; others may be interactive, incorporating augmented reality, or they may deliver a short message when activated as someone passes by. Few of these vehicles are considered intrusive.

Coffee Cups and Sleeves

These everyday surfaces have great potential to hold not only the drinker's attention but also that of others who are exposed to the target as he carries the cup through his day. This versatile multisurfaced vehicle can employ both the rounded outside surface and the inside bottom of the cup to display a message; the outside bottom can showcase a message to others every time the holder sips his drink. Lids might inform the drinker that there is a surprise message on the inside bottom of the cup, such as a giveaway, contest information, or even a game piece.

Serving more than one purpose, cup sleeves have also been used as very creative surfaces. Some might reveal a hidden message when the hot drink activates the heat-sensitive ink, others may transform into carriers, while still others might plump up into various shapes when liquid is added.

Not unexpectedly, many of these unconventional design options can be very expensive. The limited space on sleeves limits copy to little more than a logo, slogan, or tagline. More elaborate options might include four-color graphics and additional interactive options. To give the designs additional meaning and exposure, consider expanding the design to napkins and/or wrappers for sandwiches and desserts.

Shopping Bags

These surfaces, like cups and sleeves, can be very expensive to produce, but the amount of exposure the brand name will receive as the shopper moves about her day is priceless. Shopping bags that say volumes beyond the logo are usually colorful and creative, and they often incorporate thought-provoking images that say it all. Some of the more creative options incorporate the handles into the imagery seen on the bag.

Scaffolding

Scaffolding used in construction projects is a common sight in most cities. In a cooperative form of advertising, brands can team up with the builder and use the scaffolding to showcase a relevant message that sits high above the cluttered advertising landscape below.

Branded Hand-Stamp Advertising

If you've ever gone anywhere that has an admission or cover charge, you've likely had your hand stamped. Incorporating a visible surface and having a captive audience are two things advertisers using alternative vehicles can't pass up. A great cooperative advertising surface, hand-stamp advertising might feature the message "Don't Drink and Drive" along with the number for a local cab company. Since the surface is less than perfect, these small, single-color stamps will feature a small amount of copy and/or a single image. Often hand stamps will visually or verbally tie in with promotional material seen elsewhere at the event or locations, such as napkins, glasses, water bottles, T-shirts, and other giveaways, as well as table tents, ticket stubs, or bathroom advertising for a more integrated message.

Milk Carton Advertising

This unusual surface can be used to promote a single brand or as part of a cooperative effort between two compatible brands. A great mass-media surface, milk carton advertising can reach a large audience with a simple but relevant message. To increase ROI, many larger brands may also include a coupon or information about a contest or sweepstakes.

Brands attempting to reach school-age children will find the smaller cartons a great surface on which to place games or advertise a movie or children's television programming. Larger cartons aimed at adults can carry public service announcements (PSAs) or ads for health products, desserts, or cereals.

Some cartons may include interactive elements such as games to bring attention to the message. Cooperative efforts may share a logo or include a paper hang tag that is hung from the neck or perforated and glued directly to the carton. These ads can range from one to four colors and will briefly talk about the tie between the two brands. As always, when space is at a premium, visuals or graphics play a dominant role to capture attention. It is not unusual for these hang tags to have a coupon attached to encourage purchase of the co-op partnered brand.

Grocery Cart Advertising

Grocery cart advertising can be used to influence impulse purchases or as a reminder device. About the size of a license plate, they can either employ a copy-only design or picture a dominant four-color visual with accompanying logo. These ads are not the best choice for small niche brands but are a great choice for large national brands selling mass-consumed products such as soda, candy, cereal, or shampoo.

Parking Meter Advertising

If the brand can be found within walking distance of the meter, then parking meter advertising is an effective reminder surface. Brands that use meters can buy space on the meter or the pole holding the meter. An odd space to work with, the meter may use stickers or fabric, while pole ads are often laminated and three sided and can feature either local or national products or services. Visually dominant, ads can scream out with a single color or sport a four-color image. If copy is present, it is limited to no more than one to three words along with the logo. "Thirsty" and "Hungry," for example, get to the point quickly.

Three-Dimensional Advertising

A very engaging and interactive option, this form of alternative advertising employs both print and technology to hold the target's attention and create a memorable ad. This eye-catching concept can be found not only on television, the web, and smartphones but also in magazines and catalogs. To encourage use, print options will include the glasses necessary to view the message in 3-D as a part of the publication.

Sky Promotions

The sky is a blank canvas, and that makes it a great promotional vehicle—not a new vehicle by any means, but it is an excellent way to reach a mass audience with a mass message. Blimps, small airplanes towing banners, and hot air balloons have been used for decades to promote causes and local businesses. Unfortunately, these unusually large surfaces can promote no more than three to five words and/or a logo to be readable and recognizable from a distance. **Skywriting**, a less used form of air advertising, uses vaporized fluid from a plane's exhaust to spell out cloud-like messages that can be seen from up to fifteen miles away. Each letter is about the size of the Empire State Building, and each message can measure about five miles in length.

No matter what vehicle or combination of vehicles is employed, the decision to use any form of alternative media in an IMC campaign will depend on not only a creative idea but also the presence of the following key attributes:

- Exposure
- Reach
- Creative flexibility
- Size, in conjunction with placement
- Coverage

All forms of alternative media, no matter the size, cost, surface, or location, can help the advertised message reach that important, often hard-to-reach eighteen- to thirty-four-year-old target group. Although few forms of alternative media are capable of reaching a mass audience, those with something to show in a unique and visual way will extend the life of the advertised message by encouraging consumers to share the experience with others within their social circle.

How Does Alternative Media Advertising Help IMC Be Consumer Focused?

Advertising must work harder than ever before to reach the target audience. An oversaturated advertising environment makes it easy for the target to tune out unwanted messages, so it is important that more personalized and relevant messages reach the target where she is. Today's savvy consumers rely on more than one medium for general information and/ or reviews on product performance before purchasing. While watching a television program, they may be texting, e-mailing, or visiting a web or social media site. This reliance on multiple vehicles is known as **media multitasking**, the driving force behind target fractionalization. The ability to reach the correct target with the right message at the most advantageous time is possible with good initial research, message repetition, interactive options that engage, and creative ingenuity.

Once the creative team has solidified the visual/verbal message, it is important that the choice of media vehicles employed effectively showcase the message. Beyond that, choice should match the brand's overall image and use a mix (if budget allows) of traditional, **brand-centric**, vehicles and new, **consumer-centric**, media options. Strategically, visual/verbal messages that uniquely showcase the brand's key consumer benefit and offer some type of interactive device or viral component can successfully combine the use of both.

Vehicles that play a supportive role in an IMC campaign must ensure there are ways to determine their precise ROI. Some **guerrilla marketing** and many alternative vehicles alone are hard to track, so it is important that interactive capabilities be built into the message, such as incorporating a marketing or promotional code, a coupon, a social media mention, and so on. By incorporating interactive devices, the message becomes a more consumer-focused form of advertising that creates ways to initiate dialogue, build or reinforce new or existing relationships, and obtain feedback. Many vehicles can successfully place the brand directly in the target's hands, demonstrate use, and immediately answer questions.

As more brands concentrate on smaller, brand-loyal niche markets, alternative media is being employed more often to launch, reinvent, or remind the target about a brand. This one-on-one continual, often personalized dialogue makes it a very interactive choice when soliciting feedback, posting reviews, or initiating contests.

By ignoring the one-way monologue of traditionally delivered messages, alternative vehicles bring not only creative diversity and memorability to an IMC campaign but also engagement by encouraging a dialogue between buyer and seller as well as among consumers, making it an extremely consumer-focused facet of the promotional mix.

This diverse array of vehicles brings more to an IMC campaign than just a simple visual/verbal message. They often have memorable and interactive traits that can successfully reach the target in ways most other vehicles cannot. It is rarely elective, so messages can engage with surprising gimmicks, visuals, and/or copy that can grab and hold the target's attention for more than just a few minutes.

Additionally, dialogue with and the solicitation of feedback from the target audience instills a sense of ownership in the brand's success as well as being a personalized way to reward loyalty, enhance brand image, and successfully compete against other brands in the market category.

More brands are incorporating alternative media into their promotional mix because it's hard for consumers to avoid it. The sheer number of media vehicles consumers choose to use or encounter during their day has fractionalized or broken up a brand's target audience, making them difficult to reach. Alternative media can hit targets over the head with a memorable message they will talk about after exposure. Its use is on the rise because of its many over-the-top aspects and often in-your-face tactics that have been successful at creating buzz and reaching the ever-evasive eighteen- to thirty-four-year-old target or those with the lowest interaction rates with traditional vehicles.

Incentives and Deterrents of Alternative Media

To decide whether alternative media is right for an IMC campaign, let's look at some of the incentives and deterrents associated with it.

What Makes Alternative Media So Great?

The more notable incentives associated with alternative media include:

- *Exposure.* Many alternative media vehicles are a part of the target's daily landscape when she travels to and from work or shops, while smaller or more personalized vehicles deliver messages that the target has opted in to receive.
- *Creative.* Because of the different surfaces and shapes alternative media can exploit, it makes attracting attention easier and, because of that, is often more memorable.
- *Engaging.* The attention-grabbing creativity creates viral and word-of-mouth opportunities as consumers share the experience with others on social media, blogs, e-mail, or phone.
- *Interactive.* Many alternative options can get the product directly into the hands of the consumer, creating a one-on-one dialogue between buyer and seller.
- *Cost.* Because of the multitude of diverse surfaces and event options, many messages can be produced or delivered inexpensively.
- *Nonintrusive.* Since many alternative media options are permission based or the consumer chooses to opt in to receive advertising material, it is rarely considered intrusive.
- *Distinctive.* The unexpected use of varied surfaces, shapes, and sizes can give an advertised message fresh appeal.
- *Creative.* There are no set rules on how a visual/verbal message is presented on its varied canvases.
- *Niche markets.* Brand-loyal consumers can give feedback on product performance or updates, making them feel a part of the brand's success.

Is There Anything Wrong with Alternative Media Advertising?

The more notable deterrents associated with alternative media include:

- *Clutter.* Consumers see thousands of messages every day, so unless the creative is spectacular or unique, it can blend into its surroundings and be missed.
- *Ethics.* Many question the ethics behind some forms of alternative media techniques such as guerrilla marketing, considering them so covert that consumers do not always realize they are being exposed to advertisements or promotions.
- *Value.* Since many media options and events are often temporary, it is only effective if it is noticed, talked about, and/or the target opts in to receive the message.
- *Duration.* Buzz lasts only as long as consumers are talking about the product.
- *Mass reach.* When used as a reminder vehicle, most are better at reaching a mass audience, eliminating interactive and relationship-building opportunities.

- *ROI.* For many vehicles there is no way to determine whether vehicles were seen or acted upon.
- *Cost.* Many vehicles are produced in small numbers or are either disposable or promotional, making their life span short and printing or production costs high.
- *Limited copy.* Many surfaces are small or unusually shaped, making it difficult for them to hold more than the logo and slogan or tagline.

The Strategy behind Alternative Media Advertising

There is so much product parity in the consumer goods arena that brands strategically use varied forms of advertising in order to stand out from competitors. When brands cannot boast a unique feature or use, the choice to use alternative media will give a product or service a distinctly unique appeal that will gain additional exposure as excited consumers share the experience or message digitally or via word of mouth with their friends and family.

As a member of the promotional mix, alternative media can highlight the key consumer benefit, remind, launch, reinforce existing advertising efforts, deliver a thirty-second commercial in unusual places, or create interest through grand promotional events.

Figure 18.2. Sometimes brands will opt for unique advertising outlets, like this pedicab, to help them stand out from the crowd. Robyn Blakeman.

How alternative media vehicles should be employed in an IMC campaign is not unlike other vehicles we have looked at that will take the brand's image into consideration as well as the objectives to be accomplished, the overall strategy employed, the brand's life-cycle stage, the target, and the visual/verbal components used throughout the campaign.

Strategically, whether used as a primary or secondary vehicle, alternative media is an excellent way to remind, tease, engage, or get the product into the hands of the target.

Because of the diverse surfaces and shapes unique to alternative media vehicles, they can be everywhere the target is, urging impulse purchases, reinforcing brand image, increasing brand awareness, and building a brand connection at the point of purchase.

Possible objectives that favor the use of alternative media might include increasing awareness or image, building or maintaining loyalty, promoting trial, and showcasing product performance and capabilities.

Strategically, the choice of approach will depend heavily on the choice of vehicle. Permission-based vehicles are a good choice for consumer-based approaches such as brand image, lifestyle, and attitude. These can be especially successful when used with many guerrilla marketing vehicles that can get the product into the target's hands. Most vehicle choices will do a great job with a product-oriented approach, such as product feature or unique selling proposition, since many messages are short but visually expressive.

Appeal choices not surprisingly will also depend on the vehicle, but the most effective emotional appeals might include lifestyle and image, while the employment of any of the rational appeals would work well.

The best tone of voice can be either rational or emotional, so the best solution is to look at the tone used elsewhere in the IMC campaign and adopt it to a specific vehicle or combination of vehicles.

When paired with public relations, alternative vehicles are a great way to create buzz. Because of its very creative visual/verbal voice, it is best coupled with other image-based vehicles such as television, magazines, or direct marketing.

Digital vehicles such as mobile or the Internet, including e-mail, blogs, and social media outlets, are great announcement devices as well as a terrific way for consumers to share experiences.

Use as a direct-response device can put products directly into the target's hands as well as put product representatives directly in front of consumers, where they can demonstrate brand characteristics or answer questions.

Traditional vehicles that include QR codes, social media hashtags, augmented reality, scratch-and-sniff cards, or pop-ups, to name a few, can take worn-out traditional advertising vehicles and make them not only more interesting but more engaging and interactive. Radio is a great place to announce clues for scavenger hunts or contests, hold meet and greets with celebrities, or create an old-fashioned radio soap opera where the target can in some way interact with the storyline.

The problems faced by traditional media vehicles such as consumer fractionalization, avoidance, digital print and broadcast replacement options, and the love of all things digital can be overcome with a little creative ingenuity. Creating new and unexpected experiences can make all things new again.

Alternative media can be used as a mass-media vehicle or as a way to interact one-on-one with a specific niche of targeted individuals. Strategically, its interactive capabilities make it a great choice as an advertising vehicle, an attention-getter, a teaser device, or a way to educate or increase traffic to a website or brick-and-mortar store. As an effective advertising and promotional tool, alternative media makes it easier to reach a more fractionalized target audience that no longer relies only on traditional media as a place to find out information on a brand. Because consumers are surrounded by thousands of advertised messages every day, alternative media grabs attention using unique tactics and surfaces that stand out from the clutter surrounding them.

Whether to include alternative media in an IMC campaign and what type of vehicle should be employed will often depend on the brand's life-cycle stage. Brands in their maintenance stage can use alternative media as a reminder vehicle. New product launches or brands that are being reinvented might employ alternative vehicles to educate, build image, disperse promotional devices, and announce first-to-own opportunities to a target base that has opted in to receive advertised messages. It is also a great choice for vehicles and events that can build relationships with the target, get the brand directly into the target's hands, and gain critical feedback. IMC campaigns that employ a mixture of both traditional and alternative vehicles can move from a one-way monologue to a two-way dialogue with the target that will strengthen loyalty among current users and educate and build awareness and image among new users.

The Look of Alternative Media Advertising

The fun and miscellaneous assortment of alternative vehicles make it difficult to outline the typical traits, surfaces, and dimensions designers will likely encounter when working with alternative media. The only absolute is that most vehicles rely on a powerful visual/verbal message, a distinctive and/or unusual placement in an unexpected location, and the ability to creatively incorporate buildings or objects found in the target's surroundings to get the message out. As previously discussed, with few exceptions, most vehicles will have a single dominant visual and a small amount of copy that can do little more than push the key consumer benefit and showcase the logo and slogan or tagline. When size, shape, and budget permit, show character representatives or spokespersons; if audio is available, use the same voice-overs. Additional ties include repeating color combinations, headline styles, typefaces, layout styles, and varied visual styles, such as graphics or illustrations, to repeat and reinforce the IMC campaign's visual/verbal voice seen elsewhere.

Creative teams have innovatively embraced cutting-edge digital options on all surfaces and creatively pushed the envelope through attention-drawing guerrilla marketing events. Old surfaces and media vehicles no longer just sit on the page or screen. When bombarded consumers thought they had seen and heard it all, creative teams used evolving technology to step out of the box with visual/verbal solutions and events that can still "wow" a cynical consumer. The number of alternative canvases available to creative teams allows them to combine thought-provoking and stimulating visuals or events with copy that can accomplish the stated objectives while strategically educating, entertaining, and involving the target audience in the message.

Since surfaces and vehicles are so diverse, it is impossible to outline specific design parameters. All alternative media surfaces fall into at least one of three categories: print, broadcast, or digital. Since we have looked at the design standards for each in preceding chapters, this section will concentrate on examples. There are no rules that define how to design memorable, attention-getting advertising. What is known is that any alternative media pieces or events must mimic the visual/verbal voice seen elsewhere in the IMC campaign.

Let's take a quick look at a few of the more unusual and creative traditional vehicles that have adopted alternative media or included varied aspects of alternative media in the creative idea.

Magazines can do more than just show and talk about a brand. Today's magazine ads can use solar power to charge your cell phone. The Nivea Sun line of skin-care products used a Brazilian magazine that not only showed the products but also included a super-thin solar panel and a phone plug. Along with the magazine ad, consumers can view a video that explains how the ad works. A great engagement device, it's more promotional than practical, but it does provide a novel and memorable way to shake up traditional print vehicles.

Oreo took advantage of a real-time television marketing moment when the lights went out at the 2013 Super Bowl. Using Twitter, Oreo reached out to fans as they waited for the game to resume by sending a short but sweet tweet that displayed the image of a spotlighted Oreo cookie surrounded by blackness. Copy read, "You can still dunk in the dark." Using the blackout as a creative catalyst, the simple and witty message resonated with the waiting fans, which paid Oreo back by retweeting it multiple times and filling varied social media vehicles with ongoing discussions. If you throw in the multitude of press coverage that followed, Oreo not only found a way to increase buzz but also effectively kept the brand name in the public consciousness for days and weeks following the game.

Procter & Gamble has combined newspaper and QR codes to create an interactive call to action. In its "Have you tried this yet?" campaign, P&G focuses on brands such as Gillette, Secret, and Pantene. The goal is to engage with and reach out to a large audience as well as be able to educate and drive the target to P&G's mobile site. Once there, visitors can enter their zip code to find out if any local newspapers have a coupon for the product(s) they are interested in or purchase items directly from the site.

The Fox Hotel in Australia teamed up with a local brewery and PBS radio to host a scavenger hunt. Teams had to use their phones' camera and radio access to decipher clues and complete varied challenges in order to locate "good, rare beer and eclectic music." Now that is engagement.

Let's look at a few more alternative media uses that do not need traditional vehicles to reach their audiences.

The logo for Brazilian telecom Oi focuses not on the masses but on the individual. This very interactive logo design changes shape when either spoken to or touched, creating an individualized appearance for anyone who interacts with it. A very memorable way to experience a branded image.

Fiat decided to go where its target is: to gas pumps. To capture the attention of a distracted but captive audience, Fiat used Gas Station TV to make it appear as though a man were stuck inside the pump. Why is he inside the pump? He wants to catch a glimpse of the new Fiat 500 when it stops for gas. The car, to his chagrin, demonstrated by his rolling eyes and complaints, has not shown up. Tired of waiting, he decides to head off to a dealership but cannot find a way out of the pump. What's the point of using a gas pump? The closing message tells our still-pumping target that the car gets forty miles per gallon highway. In a December 7, 2013, *MediaPost* online article by Karl Greenberg entitled "Fiat GSTV Creative: Man in Pump," Casey Hurbis, head of Fiat brand communications, tells us that "our approach is not to just repurpose content, but to talk to the right consumer, in the right environment, with the right message."

Volvo is introducing an interactive ad in movie theaters that puts audience members in the driver's seat. Content seen is determined by how the audience moves when the ad is shown on theater screens. For example, whether the audience sees a daytime driving scene or a nighttime driving scene is determined by the direction audience members move their arms. Movement also determines how fast the car accelerates, the beat of the music heard, and how the car's interior is explored. Audience participation in any type of interactive storytelling is a memorable one.

If you liked the dancing Evian babies made famous on YouTube, just wait—the innovative bottled water company resurrected them in a video entitled "Baby & Me." The video opens with an adult riding a bus and staring into the reflective glass window. Expecting to see his reflection, he instead sees a baby version of himself reflected back. Upon exiting the bus, he passes a full-length mirror, and again there is the baby, mimicking his movements. One creative movement leads to another, and before you know it, you see his image dancing along with the baby. Drawing a crowd, each passerby sees their own young and old image reflected, and as numbers grow, a choreographed group of dancers moves to the sounds of "Here Comes the Hotstepper." Along with the YouTube video, the global campaign will use outdoor posters placed in train stations and on platforms that show dual headshots showcasing a single individual and his or her baby counterpart facing each other. Additionally, the campaign will employ a facial recognition app people can download that can transform uploaded pictures into a redundant baby version of themselves.

Wondering what to get your dad for Father's Day? How about a personalized bottle of Diageo whiskey? All consumers had to do was use their smartphone to scan the code located on the back of the bottle, which allowed them to personalize a film template with a photo and message. All Dad had to do to view the message was scan the bottle with his smartphone. What a great way to create engagement on both ends.

When it rains on the Chicago Cubs games, Reynolds Wrap will be there to roll out the diamond-protecting silver tarp that, not coincidentally, resembles a sheet of aluminum foil emblazoned with both brands' logos. When not in use, the always visible rolled-up tarp resembles a full roll of foil.

To attract visitors to its "Summer's different here" campaign, the Andy Warhol Museum used startling images to promote the exhibitions of three provocative artists using "shock-vertising," a form of advertising that attracts attention and encourages word-of-mouth discussions by using visuals that shock or provoke. The headline, appearing above a distorted series of summertime images, states, "Must be summer at the Warhol." This bland copy definitely does not steal the thunder of its startling companion images. The first image shows the torso of a shirtless man next to a barbecue grill holding up a loaded shish-kebab skewer that is uncomfortably piercing one of his nipples. Other visuals zero in on a hot dog garnished with worms and mustard, a man wearing a very small swimsuit constructed from firecrackers, feet clad in flip-flops made of barbed wire, a bikini-clad woman sunbathing on a lounger made of nails, and a headshot of a woman with a ball gag decorated to look like a beach ball. Now those are attention-getting, unconventional, discussion-oriented images.

A German agency promoting a local horror channel decided the best way to reach its target was to use bowling balls showcasing the image of a decapitated head.

Security brand Schlussel & Schloss used a direct-response mailer that looked like a crowbar; nothing special there, until its street teams placed them into the front doors of local homes and apartments. As returning homeowners saw the realistic-looking promotional device, they thought someone had tried to break in. Interest in the installation of security systems soared.

McDonald's painted a supersize red package of french fries near crosswalks. The fries that spilled out mimicked crosswalk lines. The only other visual was the trademark golden arches.

Pizza Hut Hong Kong delivers pizza in boxes that can be converted into temporary mobile-driven movie projectors. Each box comes complete with pizza, a lens, and table legs that are used to prop up a smartphone inside the box. The makeshift box then projects the phone's screen onto a wall.

Each box comes with one of four genre options. Horror lovers can choose *Slice of Night*, those needing a science fiction scare can opt for *Anchovy Armageddon*, romance lovers can sigh over *Hot & Ready*, and action lovers can jump on *Fully Loaded*. Each movie can be downloaded via a QR code located on the box.

Hershey used interactive grocery aisle kiosks to read shoppers' emotions. All shoppers had to do was smile at the kiosk to get a free sample. The goal: keep Hershey's top-of-mind when making impulse candy buys.

Finally, Cadbury decided it wanted to launch a free game that used augmented reality to turn its chocolate bars into a game board. Using their smartphones, interested gamers could play the "Qwak Smack" game. Once the app was activated, all the user had to do was point the phone's camera at the Cadbury countline to launch a thirty-second game where animated quacking ducks emerge from the bar and move across the screen. Players who tap the most ducks can submit their scores to be entered into a drawing for prizes.

The Choice to Use Alternative Media

Whether to employ alternative vehicles, like traditional ones, will depend on several factors outside the objectives and strategy employed, such as the ways in which a brand will be differentiated from its competitors, what specific primary and support vehicles will make up the overall media mix, how the key consumer benefit will be visually and verbally promoted, and what type of message will compel the target to try the brand or switch brands. Once these factors are determined, the creative team will have the ammunition needed to reach the target with a message he will see and relate to. Additionally, this valuable information will help the creative team weigh each medium's strengths and weaknesses and correctly determine how the target will react to the message, such as calling, using the Internet, or visiting a local store for more information. To strategically accomplish the campaign's objectives, creative efforts must determine: Is lengthy copy needed to inform and educate, or should it be short to remind? Do efforts require a demonstration, or can testimonials tell the story more effectively? Is the surface big or small, smooth or textured? Will the media used have interactive options? Knowing where the target is and how he uses varied media vehicles will make reaching him with less media waste easier, more cost-effective, and measurable.

Although many of the larger, more personalized and informative alternative vehicles can launch or even relaunch a reinvented brand when targeting smaller niche markets, most are used as support vehicles to more traditional image-building print and broadcast vehicles. Alternative media is still a relatively rare promotional tool, so it is often unexpected, making it more memorable and talked about. Many vehicles are inexpensive to employ and are often near where the consumer is encouraged to make an impulse buy.

None of these vehicles is ever dull; many assault consumers' senses through sight, sound, or smell; and others can be touched and interacted with. Always unique, many can reach a mass audience, while others can interact one-on-one with the targeted audience. Creatively, they can be visually powerful with little to say; others can tell a more detailed story. They do not fit into any type of predetermined pattern or use. That is why they are always fresh and often ingenious.

Guerrilla Marketing Is All about the Innovative Encounter

No discussion on alternative media options would be complete without a look at guerrilla marketing. **Guerrilla marketing**, a term coined in Jay Conrad Levinson's book *Guerrilla Marketing*, is an interactive event used to showcase a product or service, attract attention, and create memorable and often unconventional encounters. The more unexpected or unique the encounter or surprising the location, the more talked about and engaging the experience. Today's fractionalized, advertising-avoidant consumers need a message that is so captivating, it stops them in their tracks. Brands that create stunts or spectaculars like those used in guerrilla marketing are more likely to stand out in the cluttered advertising arena by including the consumer in the experience.

One of guerrilla marketing's biggest strengths is its ability to incorporate unexpected spaces into a nontraditional promotional event, creating situations that engage the target on a one-to-one basis. Because many events can be staged for very little money, success depends on the creative idea, its production, the energy level of promoters, the quality of the relationship-building opportunities, and the overall engagement with the brand.

Guerrilla marketing is more than a meet-and-greet or open house announced through traditional vehicles or social media outlets. Technically, it can be defined as any alternative, high-impact, niche-marketing tactic with a goal of producing maximum results, such as sales and awareness, with a minimal investment of time, resources, and budget.

Guerrilla marketing is active not passive. It can pop up anywhere, use one or multiple senses, and take any shape or form. Creative teams incorporate guerrilla marketing into the media mix to exploit consumers' imaginations with a titillating experience that "wows."

No matter what additional vehicles make up the media mix or key consumer benefit employed, guerrilla marketing is a great choice if the goal is to get the brand into the target's hands or demonstrate use. Events are purposeful, showcasing varied product uses, acquiring feedback on brand performance or use, or being used to give away samples or promote taste tests. Promotions for premieres of movies or television programs might use popular characters to hand out T-shirts, caps, and so on. Charities may also use actors or events to raise money and bring attention to a particular cause. The more surprising or awe-inspiring the tactics, the more consumers will talk about it; the bigger the press coverage, the more powerful and lasting the impact.

Typically, guerrilla marketing is not used to immediately encourage a sale but to encourage dialogue with the target and, most importantly, to ignite word of mouth and viral discussions—the most powerful and least expensive form of advertising.

Unlike almost all other forms of advertising, guerrilla marketing is a onetime event. It does not make a hard sell or passively tell a story. What it does do is create interactive, creative, and engaging ways to actively get attention, educate, get up close and personal with the target, and subtly attempt to change perception by creating a buzzworthy event that may or may not be unexpected.

When paired with traditional media, guerrilla marketing events can successfully support any claims made by setting up scenarios that can actively prove results based on those claims. So it is important that the brand can repeatedly live up to the hype, and it is crucial that any sales or customer service representatives interacting with the target be educated on brand promises to continually reinforce advertising and promotional efforts.

As an active member of an advertising campaign, guerrilla marketing can bring product/service claims to the target in fun and unforgettable ways. Any interactive properties only strengthen the campaign's ability to be a targeted and consumer-focused facet of the media mix.

It is guerrilla marketing's job to find a way to break through to the target, separate the brand from competing brands, and stand out in a meaningful way in an advertising-saturated marketplace.

The Diverse Opportunities to Engage in Dialogue

Guerrilla marketing gained popularity as a unique and low-cost way for small businesses to compete against their larger, deeper-pocketed competitors. It didn't take long, however, for the corporate giants to begin building guerrilla marketing into their ample budgets to create larger, more extravagant events. Let's take a look at a few examples.

It's lunchtime, so you head for the elevator and an hour all to yourself. As you patiently wait for the doors to open, you wonder about where to go. When the elevator finally trudges its way up to your floor, the doors open on a scene of violence. Two men are rolling around on the floor, duking it out. One combatant pulls out a cord and slips it around the other's neck and pulls tight, seemingly attempting to strangle the life out of his opponent. Don't even think about calling 911 or wading in to save the day—the scene is staged to promote the upcoming movie *Dead Man Down*. Both the fight and your reaction are being filmed.

An idea a little less over the top comes to us from 7 Up. To grab pedestrians' attention, 7 Up initiated the "Melting Machine." No technology was required for the attention-getting portion of this event, which placed a vending machine encased in ice on a busy street corner. The goal was to engage with thirsty and curious pedestrians as they move about their day. All they had to do after grabbing a free 7 Up from the melting ice block was guess how long it would take for the ice to melt before the last can could be removed and then tweet their guesses.

The Cheesecake Factory used the target's nose and street teams dressed all in white for a guerrilla marketing event. Each team member carried a bouquet of multicolored balloons, each harboring a unique scent. Depending on color, when the balloon was popped, the scent was released. Curious participants might encounter the mouthwatering aroma of peppermint bark cheesecake, chocolate tuxedo cream cheesecake, or original cheesecake. The challenge: Could the targeted consumer guess the smell? Right or wrong, the target received a coupon hidden inside the balloon that read, "Try a slice on us," which could be redeemed for a free slice of delicious cheesecake at the nearby restaurant.

Beyond hosting large attention-getting events, some other more commonly used forms of guerrilla marketing include stealth marketing, street teams, wild postings, pop-ups, video projection, and event graffiti. Let's take a quick look at each one.

Stealth Marketing

Stealth marketing, also known as word-of-mouth, undercover marketing, buzz, or ambush marketing, uses actors to approach the target and talk about a brand without announcing their affiliation with it. Some approaches are so stealthy or undercover that targeted consumers do not even know they are being exposed to an advertised message. This form of guerrilla marketing is known as **astroturfing**, and many question the ethics behind some of these techniques. Although the tactics may be questionable, a sales pitch in today's oversaturated advertising environment does not necessarily need to be printed or filmed. A very in-your-face encounter could come when you least expect it, or you might not even realize you have just been pitched. For example, while you are sitting and trying on shoes, a lady sits down beside you and comments on your great taste in footwear. During the conversation, she just happens to mention that these great new insoles she recently purchased keep her feet both cool and comfortable all day. Not surprisingly, she is wearing them and whisks them out for you to see, all the while talking about their virtues. As she gets up to leave, she suddenly remembers she has a coupon she is happy to share with you.

Street Teams

This form of guerrilla marketing takes the brand or brand name directly to the streets in order to interact one-on-one with consumers. These clearly recognizable brand ambassadors can be found in areas with a large pedestrian population, such as street corners, parks, malls, or other public places where they can hand out samples or coupons, conduct taste tests, demonstrate use, or hand out educational materials. Although not unconventional or unique, this approach does create an interactive, one-on-one experience with the brand.

Wild Postings

Wild postings are decorative posters placed on the street where targets will see them as they go about their day. Many, known as rip-away wild postings, are often a very graphic and colorful bound set of posters that can be torn off a pad and taken away to be used elsewhere. Choice, like all alternative vehicles, is diverse and will depend on use, but the most commonly seen include street posters, window-cling posters, sidewalk chalk drawings, decals, and door hangers. Like many specialty media options, this form of advertising is quick, easy, and a relatively inexpensive form of out-of-home advertising. Wild postings are a creative way to reach a concentrated niche market in a localized area. Postings can be found on walls and telephone and utility poles, outside local schools, on sidewalks, hung on doors, or handed out throughout shopping areas.

Pop-Ups

Pop-ups are temporary showrooms that "pop up" for a short period of time in public places such as street corners, malls, and public parks; some may even take over empty storefronts for the length of the promotion. These unexpected encounters are another way of extending the brand's traditionally delivered message into a real-life interactive and memorable event. For example, instant coffee maker Nescafé placed a large orange tent that served free coffee in a local park and decorated the inside to look like a coffee bar, complete with barista.

Video Projection

A brand that is looking to go big should consider video projection advertising. Very simply, this form of promotional advertising mixes together the properties associated with outdoor and broadcast by projecting a brand's visual image or logo onto the sides of buildings or cruise ships, on window frontage, or even on water. Often used outside nighttime events, these spectacular displays always attract attention and generate buzz. An integrated use of video projection will also include street teams that move about handing out samples, coupons, or free tickets. Brands that want to say more might consider using projected commercials, also known as **guerrilla video projections**. Using the sides of buildings as a screen, guerrilla video projection brings a brand's thirty-second commercial to areas where large volumes of pedestrian traffic are sure to see them. Projection of simple images such as logos, character representatives, spokespersons, slogans or taglines, or more complicated images featuring sight, sound, and motion not only attract attention but also are great reminder devices. As a reinforcement vehicle and to increase memorability, ads are often projected onto more than one surface and in more than one location at a time. Beyond street teams, other integration vehicles might include location-based texts, video games, social media promotions, and Bluetooth broadcasts.

Event Graffiti Performances

This type of guerrilla marketing event uses graffiti artists to create outdoor murals or street art live at an outdoor event such as a concert, sporting event, or street fair. These time-intensive, one-of-a-kind, often temporary creations require the permission of city officials or building owners, since designs will use sidewalks and/or the sides of local buildings as a canvas.

This is certainly not a comprehensive list of the possible guerrilla marketing tactics available to creative teams. Additional options might include reverse graffiti, postering, demonstrations, flash mobs, lectures, and seminars; the possibilities are limited only by the creative team's imagination, time, and budget.

The ability to combine these unusual and creative tactics with engaging and interactive opportunities allowss a brand to get up close with consumers in a memorable encounter, increasing advertising's reach as consumers share their experience with others. "[Guerrilla marketing] works," Jay Conrad Levinson says, "because it's simple to understand, easy to implement and outrageously inexpensive."

It is important to remember that no matter the vehicle chosen, or event staged, to be a successful member of an IMC campaign, guerrilla marketing must:

- Create buzz, both virally and via word of mouth. When paired with other forms of alternative media, it becomes a strong **presence marketing** vehicle, or a vehicle that is everywhere the target is, such as on web and social media sites, prominently built into movies or television shows the target watches through product placement, or at street events the target encounters as they move about their day.
- Employ **grassroots marketing** techniques that encourage relationship-building opportunities over hard-sell advertising tactics.
- Utilize sales promotion devices to get the product into the target's hands.
- When possible and relevant, use **influence marketing** techniques that use public personalities the target trusts and can relate to, to endorse the brand and event without sounding like an ad. Endorsements from trusted members of the target's business or social circles make their opinions more valuable to the target than an advertised message. The employment of influence marketing can quickly give a brand and its message credibility.

Most **experiential marketing** techniques, or marketing that is not only relevant to the target but also allows them to interact with or use the brand, is attention getting and memorable because it is both unique and unexpected.

Staging a guerrilla marketing event goes beyond the need to creatively stun or titillate. Depending on the event, it is important that creative teams check with local police and city officials to ensure they understand local laws and codes and their responsibilities before, during, and after the launching of the guerrilla aspect of a campaign to avoid any negative publicity that will ultimately affect brand image. It is also important that creative teams understand their target audience's tolerance level for distractions and what they may find annoying or offensive. Events that generate negative word of mouth are not the goal of any team, no matter how creative.

Those who don't clear their events can run into some unpleasant consequences, as one small entrepreneur found out. After his company accomplished several growth and promotional objectives, he decided to advertise his company by placing more than five hundred stickers around town. His sense of accomplishment was short lived, however, when an undercover cop arrested him and his cofounder.

Another disastrous guerrilla marketing event comes from drink maker Snapple. The rule behind an attention-getting event is that it must come off without a hitch, something Snapple had to publicly learn the hard way. Making a big statement was exactly what Snapple did when it tried to erect the world's largest ice pop in Times Square. A great idea, except that the 25-foot-tall, 17.5-ton ice pop made entirely of frozen Snapple started to melt while it was being erected due to the eighty-degree June heat. What resulted was kiwi-strawberry Snapple flooding parts of midtown Manhattan. Firefighters had to be called in to close off streets to clean up the huge mess.

IMC campaigns that integrate guerrilla marketing events into the media mix can further expand the brand's visual/verbal message with an array of interactive events. Some will be unique and unconventional, while others will astound in less invasive ways. Some are expensive multilevel promotional extravaganzas, while others are clever and inexpensive to produce. Those showing the most ROI will be those memorable enough to be given a second and third chance to have the experience shared virally.

Brands that have a unique selling proposition or one that is creatively invented are great candidates for employing alternative media vehicles to promote the product or service. Any IMC campaign that includes one or more of these creative vehicles can not only actively push the key consumer benefit but also get the brand into the hands of the target in an unusual, attention-getting, and thought-provoking way.

Q DISCUSSION QUESTIONS

1. What are the strategic uses of alternative media in an IMC campaign?
2. Define alternative media.
3. What are some of the ways alternative media can be integrated into traditional media vehicles?
4. Why has alternative media often been referred to as the "creative economy"?
5. How do creative teams versus marketers feel about alternative media use?
6. Why is alternative media good for both large and small brands?
7. What needs to be considered before determining whether to use alternative media as a primary or secondary media source?
8. Alternative media vehicles have more diverse options than any other advertising and promotional category. What does the advertised message need to relay visually and verbally to strategically express the key consumer benefit?
9. What are some of the most successful engagement devices used in alternative media?
10. How can the unique visual and verbal solutions often found in alternative media vehicles help extend the life of the advertised message?
11. How does alternative media marketing help an IMC campaign be more consumer focused?
12. What is media multitasking?
13. Define brand-centric vehicles.
14. Why are more brands incorporating alternative media into their promotional mix?
15. What are the pros and cons of using alternative media?
16. What is the strategy behind using alternative media in an IMC campaign?
17. What does alternative media do best when included in a brand's promotional mix?
18. What should be considered before including alternative media in an IMC campaign?

19. Creatively, what is important to alternative media use?
20. What determines the choice to use alternative media in an IMC campaign?
21. Define guerrilla marketing.
22. What is one of guerrilla marketing's biggest strengths?
23. What makes guerrilla marketing an active versus passive form of advertising?
24. What do brands want to accomplish with guerrilla marketing?
25. If guerrilla marketing is not used to immediately encourage a sale or passively tell a story, what is it used for?
26. What are some of the more commonly used forms of guerrilla marketing?
27. To be a successful member of an IMC campaign, guerrilla marketing must accomplish four specific things. What are they? Define and explain each.
28. Define experiential marketing and its use.
29. How can guerrilla marketing ensure return on investment?
30. Define and explain the differences between presence, grassroots, and influence marketing.

Glossary

accelerometer: An interactive device that allows the phone to detect movement when shaken.

active interaction: Digital customer service that is live, via instant messaging, the telephone, blogs, social media sites, and message boards.

advergaming: Advertising placed inside digital games.

advertising: A paid form of nonpersonal mass media in which the sponsor of the advertised message is clearly identified. Advertising uses persuasion to sell, inform, educate, remind, and/or entertain the target about a product or service.

alternative media: The use of any nontraditional, clean, printable surface to deliver a message.

announcer: An individual who is both seen and heard on camera delivering the dialogue.

assorted media mix: An assorted media mix uses more than one medium in a campaign.

astroturfing: A term describing the undercover advertising methods used to sell targets something without their immediate knowledge.

augmented reality (AR): A promotional device that can be used on the Internet or on smartphones that places digitally created images over real-world images to create a three-dimensional holographic image.

banner: An announcement device in the shape of a black or dark-colored bar that is often placed at the top of an ad. Banners can also be used as page dividers and feature either white or light-colored type.

banner ads: Mass-media Internet vehicles usually found at the top of a web page.

behavioristic profile: A profile that breaks down the target audience by looking at how a person buys.

benefit: Informs the target how the product will benefit them personally.

big idea: A creative solution that sets a product/service off from the competition while at the same time solving a client's advertising problem.

body copy: The descriptive copy that works to make a sale or create an image. Body copy focuses on product features such as color, price, and size, and/or features a visual/verbal message.

brainstorming: Also known as conceptual development; the thought process creative teams go through to find multiple solutions to a creative problem.

brand: A name, term, sign, symbol, design, or a combination of these intended to identify the goods and services of one seller or group of sellers and to differentiate them from those of the competition.

brand awareness: How much the target knows about a brand.

brand-centric: A term used to describe traditional advertising vehicles.

brand equity: A company's or product's reputation in the marketplace.

brand image: A brand's personality and status compared with other brands of the same or similar quality in its category.

brand loyalty: The relationship between the brand and the target.

brand value: The sum of every experience the target has with not only the brand but also the company that makes and distributes the brand.

branded content: Any original brand advertising that blurs the distinction between advertising and editorial or entertainment content.

branded mobile applications: Offer some type of utility, entertainment, information, *or promotional device.*

branding: A product's identity and its legacy.

buzz: The generation of hype or discussion about a new product launch or the reintroduction of a revamped older brand.

callout: A small amount of copy that appears alongside or below an individual image to which it is connected by a small line.

camera instructions: Instructions that tell the camera what to do or how to move in a television shot.

campaign uniformity: A campaign's overall look and message are consistent no matter the media outlet used or the final appearance of any creative piece.

cause-related marketing: A campaign or joint promotion that is tied to a contest or other notable incentives where a portion of a firm's sales are donated to charity.

clip art: Publicly available line art drawings that can be used without specific permission.

communication objectives: A set of goals the client needs communication efforts to achieve. Communication objectives should describe what the target should think, feel, and do after exposure to the message.

concentrated media mix: A concentrated media mix places all advertising efforts into one medium.

consumer-centric: A term used to describe new forms of interactive media.

contest: A promotional game of skill that requires participants to meet a certain set of standards in order to win.

context-sensitive marketing (CSM): Also known as virtual impulse buying; mobile-based quick response codes that makes the decision to purchase easier and faster.

cooperative advertising: Two individual but compatible clients pair up to share the cost of advertising and to encourage consumers to use their products or services together.

creative: Describes a unique and individual idea.

creative brief: Also known as a copy platform; a document developed from the marketing plan and creative strategy that defines the big idea or unique selling proposition. The creative brief also looks at the individual features and benefits of the product or service, outlines tactics, and redefines the target audience.

creative concept: An idea that imaginatively solves the client's advertising problem.

creative strategy: The part of the marketing process that outlines the creative approach needed to accomplish marketing goals and/or objectives.

creative team: A team made up of at least a copywriter and an art director that is responsible for developing the creative idea for the IMC campaign.

cropping: The removal of any unnecessary part(s) of a visual, allowing the designer to dispense with information that is not necessary to the design.

customer relationship management: The ability to manage a company's interaction with current and future customers, e-mail delivery, and affordable pricing.

cybermarketing: Use of the Internet as a sales device.

database marketing: Use of a computer to store personal information about individuals and their past purchase history.

databases: Collections of individual customer data that are developed from previous interaction with a company, such as a purchase or a request for more information. Databases help marketers personalize the communication message.

demographics: Defines the target audience in terms of age, income, sex, marital and professional status, education, number of children, and other relevant factors.

detail copy: Small copy that features addresses, phone numbers, store hours, website addresses, credit card information, e-mail addresses, parking, and other relevant information.

die cuts: Cut-outs on print material.

direct mail: Also known as junk mail; a direct-marketing tool that includes an outside envelope, a personalized pitch letter, an informational brochure, an order form, and a return envelope for mail orders.

direct response: Interactive television advertising; involves the target in the message process by asking them to do something.

e-mail marketing: The use of e-mail to communicate directly with the target.

embargo: A news release that is sent in advance to an editor or broadcaster.

emoji: A simple graphic image used on mobile devices.

emoticon: An image created using computer or mobile keys.

endorsement: The announcer or celebrity often does not personally use the product and is being paid for his or her time.

experiential marketing: Memorable, attention-getting advertising techniques that are not only relevant to targets but also allow them to interact with the brand.

feature: A product attribute, such as color or size, found in the creative brief.

focus group: A representative sample of the target, usually ten to twelve people, who gather to talk about or try a product in a controlled environment.

font: A typeface's catalog of upper- and lowercase letters, numbers, and punctuation.

formal surveys: Surveys that include closed-ended questions where participants choose from a predetermined set of responses, such as strongly agree, agree, disagree, and strongly disagree.

frame transitions: Directions that tell the director and postproduction editors of a television shoot how to get out of one frame and into the next.

freestanding insert (FSI): Also known as supplemental advertising; full-color ad that is inserted into the newspaper, usually featuring coupons and/or to announce special sales or promotions.

frequency: The number of times an ad or promotion will be seen.

geographics: Break down the target audience by looking at where a person lives.

graphics: Abstract drawings or illustrations used to represent a logo or character that use bright colors and disjointed geometric shapes to create modern, bold designs. Often chosen for their symbolic meaning.

grassroots marketing: Techniques that encourage relationship-building opportunities over hard-sell advertising tactics.

greeking: A jumbled arrangement of letters, numbers, punctuation, and paragraph breaks used to temporarily represent body copy, helping give the ad a finished appearance.

guarantee: A promotional device that ensures consumers will not find the product at a lower price.

guerrilla marketing: An interactive event used to showcase a product or service, attract attention, and create memorable encounters.

guerrilla video projections: Advertising projected onto large objects like buildings or a body of water.

headline: The largest copy in an ad; focus is on highlighting the ad's USP or big idea.

home page: The first or opening page of a website.

horizontal cooperatives: A form of cooperative newspaper advertising where each sponsor's budget is equally distributed and has equal exposure.

in-app banners: A form of mobile advertising that when clicked can take the user to a mobile website, make a call, or send a text.

inbound telemarketing: When a customer initiates contact with a company for any reason, usually through a toll-free telephone number.

influence marketing: Techniques that use public personalities the target trusts and can relate to, to endorse the brand and event without sounding like an ad.

infomercials: Thirty- to sixty-minute television commercials that allow the target to order immediately from information provided on the television screen.

informal surveys: Surveys that include open-ended questions, allowing participants to give their opinions.

inherent drama: An advertised message that highlights and compares the benefits of owning or using a product or service to the target's lifestyle or overall self-image.

inside-out approach: A tactic used where the seller does no more than deliver a message to the buyer.

instant-redemption coupons: Coupons that can be used immediately.

integrated brand promotion (IBP): An IMC campaign that uses advertising and sales promotion in a coordinated effort.

integrated marketing communication (IMC): Also known as relationship marketing; a marketing method that uses databases to interactively engage a specific individual with a specific message through specific media outlets. The goal of IMC is to build a long-term relationship between buyer and seller by involving the targeted member in an interactive or two-way exchange of information.

integrated marketing communication (IMC) campaign: A campaign that talks to an individual via a two-way dialogue, creating interactive opportunities to connect directly with the targeted individual. IMC campaigns employ more diverse media vehicles than traditional efforts and choose media based on the target's lifestyle and media usage.

interactive media: Focuses on creating dialogue and building relationships between buyer and seller by providing multiple channels of communication to encourage consumer interaction and/or feedback.

interactive supplement: Streaming audio and video added to a website that viewers can choose to click on.

interior advertising: Vehicle advertising that appears on video screens usually found on the back of the front seat.

Internet marketing: Use of the Internet as an interactive medium to allow the target to come to the product or service. Consumers can place an order or talk to a customer service or technical representative from the comfort of their own homes.

Internet of Things (IoT): Connects everyday objects like refrigerators to the virtual world, allowing real-time interaction from anywhere at any time.

interstitial: A full-page digital ad that loads between page views on a website.

junk mail: Unsolicited direct mail that is rarely if ever opened by the intended target.

key consumer benefit: The one product feature/benefit that will be stressed in an IMC campaign.

kiosks: Glass floor displays used in out-of-home advertising when showing the product will make a greater impact than a photograph.

layout styles: The look or layout of an ad's components on the page that projects personality or image. Choices include big type, circus, copy heavy, frame, Mondrian, multipanel, picture window, rebus, and silhouette.

leading: A specific numerical value for the amount of white space that appears between lines of text.

legibility: The ease with which an ad can be easily understood when viewed quickly.

letter spacing: The amount of space between letters.

life-cycle stage: The age or amount of time the brand has been on the market: new, mainstream or mature, and reinvention.

line art: Black-and-white line drawing that has no tonal qualities.

line spacing: The visual amount of white space appearing between lines of text.

location-based features: Helps mobile advertising reach consumers near the point of purchase, alerting them to local sales and promotions.

logo: The symbol of a company or a product.

marketing mix: Also known as the 4-Ps; a brand's marketing plan of action, including product, price, promotion, and distribution, or "place." Each of the 4-Ps plays a vital role in message development.

marketing plan: A client's business plan. The marketing plan outlines the company's strengths and weaknesses as well as the opportunities and threats affecting the product or service. It determines marketing objectives, profiles the marketing strategy, and looks at budget issues and evaluation tactics.

marketing public relations (MPR): The selling of a corporate or brand image to a specifically defined target audience.

media mix: Breaks the promotional mix down to specific media vehicles such as newspaper, magazine, and direct mail.

media multitasking: Today's consumers rely on more than one media source for general information and product reviews; the driving force behind consumer fractionalization.

native advertising: A paid media tactic often used in the form of product placement; used in varied types of programing, eliminating the need for long commercial breaks.

news release: A document that contains the latest news and information about the product or service in the form of a finished news article.

niche marketing: Advertising efforts that concentrate specifically on winning the attention of a small group of mostly affluent consumers loyal to one specific brand.

one-way monologue: Non-personalized advertising message that does not reach a specific targeted individual.

orphan: A short line that appears at the bottom of a page, or a word or part of a word on a line by itself at the end of a paragraph.

out-of-home advertising: Any advertising seen outside the home.

outbound telemarketing: Marketing that uses the telephone to personally deliver a sales message to select members of the target audience.

outside-in approach: A tactic used by marketers where products are designed to meet a consumer's individual needs and wants.

outside influencers: Individuals or groups of individuals trusted by the primary target audience who can therefore influence targets' purchasing decisions.

overline subhead: A subhead that appears above the headline as a teaser or attention getter.

passive interaction: Digital customer service that involves a delayed response to inquiries, such as receipt of a sample in the mail or a follow-up or confirmation e-mail response.

permission or opt-in marketing: Electronically delivered advertising the target has elected to receive.

piggybacking: The breaking of a thirty-second television or radio spot into two fifteen-second spots that run back to back.

planned contact: Outside or external advertising and promotions employed to reach the target.

pop-up ad: Mass-media Internet ad that pops up over a website and contains a link directing the target to another site.

positioning: What the target thinks about and/or how the target rates a product or service against that of the competition.

presence marketing: Advertising vehicles that appear everywhere the target is, such as on the web and social media sites.

prestitial: A digital ad that pops up before the home page opens.

primary data: Data that is gathered through original research from a variety of sources, such as surveys, interviews, focus groups, observations, or experiments.

primary target audience: the most likely prospect based on research to buy the product or use the service.

product features (and benefits): A specific product attribute that is matched to the target's needs and wants.

product placement: A subtle form of advertising used within television, movies, and digital programming.

promotional mix: A promotional mix includes any combination of public relations, advertising, direct marketing and sales promotion, and out-of-home and transit, Internet, and social, mobile, and alternative media.

psychographics: Breaks the target audience down by looking at a person's lifestyle.

pushpins: Also known as geo-targeted messaging; when moused over, contain many rich media and other interactive properties along with location information and a logo.

qualitative data: Information presented in a verbal or narrative way.

quantitative data: Information represented by statistics, numbers, or comparative scales.

quick response (QR) codes: A matrix barcode the target can photograph with a smartphone to access material that is used to engage, inform, and entertain the target.

reach: The number of interested people who will see a message.

readability: The ease with which an ad can be read at a glance.

relationship marketing: See **Integrated Marketing Communication.**

repositioning: A strategy to change the way a product is positioned in the mind of the target.

retail advertising: Another term used for newspaper advertising.

return on investment (ROI): The profit realized after advertising and other costs have been deducted.

rich media: Mobile advertising options that are interactive and unique to each brand.

roughs: Also known as layouts; full-size, hand-produced representations of the final piece, with all elements in place and tightly rendered in black and white or color. Conceptual devices such as headlines, subheads, and visuals are readable and viewable.

sans serif: A typeface that has no feet or appendages to letters.

scenes: The visual aspects of a television commercial.

script: The copy sheet used in radio and television that indicates sound, camera instructions, and any spoken parts.

search engine marketing (SEM): When brands pay a search engine such as Google to place their websites first or toward the top in keyword searches.

search engine optimization (SEO): Sites that include relevant links to other sites to increase engagement.

secondary target audience: Influencers whose opinion the primary target audience member trusts or seeks out for advice.

secondary data: Data that has already been collected and is available from external sources such as the public library, the Internet, trade associations, and the US Census.

serif: A typeface style that features feet or delicate appendages that protrude from the edges of letters.

site map: Menu options that are used as navigational tools to take the viewer to specific sections within the website.

skyscrapers: Vertical digital banners.

skywriting: A form of alternative media that uses vaporized fluid from a plane's exhaust to spell out a cloud-like message.

slogan: A statement that represents the company's philosophy or a product or service's image that is usually placed above or below the logo.

slug: Information placed at the top of the second page of a news release that includes a page number and identifier.

snipes or bursts: A type of print banner often seen in reverse (white type/black background) used to announce a grand opening or sale dates.

social media marketing: The combination of social media and direct marketing that creates engagement.

sound effects (SFX): Noises heard in radio and television ads, such as doors slamming, dogs barking, or babies crying.

spam: E-mail messages sent without the recipient's permission.

spokesperson or character: A representative, either animated or human, who can speak for and represent a product or service, giving the brand a personality or face that should appear on all pieces.

sponsored mobile applications: A particular brand owns the use of the app for a specified period. Overall format of the ad is customized for the brand.

spot advertising: Locally tailored radio messages.

spot color: The use of a spot of color to highlight a detail in a black-and-white photograph.

statement stuffer: Advertising that hitches a ride with a credit card bill, financial notice, or anything else a consumer might receive on a regular or monthly basis.

stock art: Existing photographs of all varieties that can be purchased and used in an ad.

storyboard: An illustration of the visual portion of the commercial and the timing sequence between what is heard and what is seen, one frame at a time.

strategy: A plan or tactic to accomplish a creative idea or concept.

streaming Internet video: Internet television that digitally distributes television content that can be viewed through a television, computer screen, or mobile device.

street graffiti: A form of alternative media found on roads, sidewalks, or in parking lots.

super comprehensives: Also known as super comps; representations of an ad created from the final roughs. Super comprehensives are generated on the computer and include all headlines, subheads, visuals, and a logo—and, for the first time, completed body copy in place, simulating exactly how the design will look and read.

support statement: A feature/benefit combination found on a creative brief that can be used to directly support or advance the key consumer benefit.

sweepstakes: Consumers can enter to win a prize that does not require a prior purchase.

tagline: Placed above or below the logo, the tagline is a sentence or statement that defines the IMC campaign's advertising philosophy.

talent: The individuals who will be seen on camera or heard on radio reading the copy or dialogue.

target audience: Also known as target market; the group of people research has determined is most likely to buy the product or use the service. A target audience can be broken down based on demographics, psychographics, geographics, and behavioristics.

teaser copy: Copy placed on the outer envelope of a direct-mail kit.

testimonial: A celebrity or an average consumer endorses the product by telling of his or her personal experiences with the product.

thumbnails: Small, proportionate drawings that are used to get concept ideas down on paper.

tone: The personality and overall voice or style a message will portray.

two-way dialogue: Interaction between the buyer and seller.

type alignment: The way type is aligned on a page, such as centered or justified.

typeface: The name given to a specific style of type.

type style: The form of typeface used; for example, boldface, italic, roman.

type weight: The thickness or thinness of a typeface's body.

underline subheads: A subhead that appears below the headline and explains in more detail what the headline is saying, elaborates on the statement or comment made, or answers the question posed.

unique selling proposition (USP): A key consumer benefit that is unique to a client's product or service or a commonplace feature promoted as unique.

unplanned contact: Internal, or corporately focused on employees and vendors; the least controllable form of advertising or promotion.

user-generated content (UGC): Also known as consumer-generated media; the visual/verbal sharing of thoughts and ideas by the target on the Internet and social media sites between brand users.

verbal uniformity: A campaign where all creative pieces promote one idea or key consumer benefit.

vertical cooperatives: A form of cooperative advertising where one sponsor pays more and receives a larger, more prominent amount of exposure.

viral marketing: The use of interactive and/or entertaining Internet advertising, often delivered via e-mail or on a web or social media site, to inform and "infect" the receiver with enough interest about a product or service to visit the host website.

visual: A basic design element that can take the form of a photograph, an illustration, line art, or graphic design.

visual uniformity: A campaign where all creative materials have a unique appearance or look.

voice-over: Dialogue read by an announcer who is not seen on camera.

warranty: A promotional device that guarantees that if the consumer is not 100 percent satisfied, the purchase price will be refunded.

widow: A single word or short line of text that appears at the top of a page or at the top of a new column of copy.

wireframe: The visual and verbal layout of a website.

word list: One way the creative team can brainstorm ideas.

word of mouth: Face-to-face discussions about a product or service.

Bibliography

Ackerman, Kristina. 2010. "Buy a Newspaper, Hear an Advertisement." *Editor and Publisher* (Dec. 21). http://www.editorandpublisher.com/printarticle.aspx?ArticleID=63579.

Allen, Gemmy, and Georganna Zaba. 2000. *Internet Resources for Integrated Marketing Communication.* Orlando: Harcourt.

Altstiel, T., and J. Grow. 2006. *Advertising Strategy: Creative Tactics from the Outside/In.* Thousand Oaks, CA: Sage.

———. 2010. *Advertising Creative.* Thousand Oaks, CA: Sage.

American Marketing Association (AMA). 2007. *Marketing Power.* Retrieved from http://www.marketingpower.com/AboutAMA/Pages/Definition-of-marketing.aspx.

Apple. 2013. "Designing for iOS 7." https://developer.apple.com/library/ios/documentation/User-Experience/Conceptual/MobileHIG/index.html#//apple_ref/doc/uid/TP40006556.

Avery, Jim. 2000. *Advertising Campaign Planning.* Chicago: Copy Workshop.

Baar, Aaron. 2013. "HTC Makes Some Noise." *Marketing Daily.* http://www.mediapost.com/publications/article/197471/htc-makes-some-noise.html.

Baker, D. 2010. "The New Social Marketing Paradigm." *EmailInsider* (Oct. 4). http://www.mediapost.com/publications/article/136919/the-new-social-marketing-paradigm.html.

Beltrone, Gabriel. 2012. "Ambient Overload: A Look at Some New and Unusual Ad Placement." *Adweek* (Apr. 4). http://www.adweek.com/news/advertising-branding/ambient-overload-139333.

Bangs, David H. 1998. *The Market Planning Guide.* 5th ed. Chicago: Upstart.

Bendinger, Bruce. 1993. *The Copy Workshop Workbook.* Chicago: Copy Workshop.

Bercovici, Jeff. 2011. "America's Most Loved Spokescharacters." *Forbes* (Mar. 14). http://www.forbes.com/2011/03/11/old-spice-snoopy-m-and-m-most-loved-spokescharacters.html.

Berman, M. 2007. *Street-Smart Advertising: How to Win the Battle of the Buzz.* Lanham, MD: Rowman & Littlefield.

Bernbach, W. 1989. *Bill Bernbach Said . . .* New York: DDB Needham Worldwide.

Bernstein, R. 2010. "Integrate Social Media with Traditional Advertising for Higher Returns." *Social Media Today* (Jan. 20). http://socialmediatoday.com/SMC/167993.

Birgfeld, R. 2010. "Social with a KISS: Keep It Short, Stupid." SmartBlogs.com (Sept. 20). http://smartblogs.com/socialmedia/2010/09/20.

Blake, Gary, and Robert W. Bly. 1997. *The Elements of Copywriting.* New York: Simon & Schuster.

Blakeman, Robyn. 2004. *The Bare Bones of Advertising Print Design.* Boulder, CO: Rowman & Littlefield.

———. 2009. *The Bare Bones Introduction to Integrated Marketing Communication.* Lanham, MD: Rowman & Littlefield.

———. 2011. *Advertising Campaign Design: Just the Essentials.* Armonk, NY: M. E. Sharpe.

———. 2011. *Strategic Uses of Alternative Media: Just the Essentials.* Armonk, NY: M. E. Sharpe.

———. 2013. *Nontraditional Media in Marketing and Advertising.* Thousand Oaks, CA: Sage.

Book, Albert C., and Dennis C. Schick. 1997. *Fundamentals of Copy and Layout.* 3rd ed. Lincolnwood, IL: NTC Contemporary.

Brenner, Michael. 2015. "The Rise of the Emoji for Brand Marketing." *Guardian* (Jan. 26). https://www.theguardian.com/media-network/2015/jan/26/rise-emoji-brand-marketing.

Brogan, C. 2010. "Alternatives to Straight Advertising." *Open Forum* (Nov. 1). https://www.american express.com/us/small-business/openforum/articles/alternatives-to-straight-advertising-1.

Burnett, John, and Sandra Moriarty. 1998. *Introduction to Marketing Communications.* Upper Saddle River, NJ: Prentice Hall.

Burnett, L. 1995. *100 LEO's.* Lincolnwood, IL: NTC Business.

Burton, Philip Ward. 1999. *Advertising Copywriting.* 7th ed. Lincolnwood, IL: NTC Contemporary.

Clow, Kenneth A., and Donald Baack. 2002. *Integrated Advertising, Promotion and Marketing Communications.* Upper Saddle River, NJ: Prentice Hall.

Coyer, K., T. Dowmunt, and A. Fountain. 2008. *The Alternative Media Handbook.* New York: Routledge.

Dalzell, C. 2009. "Building Relationships and Trust Online with E-mail." *Marketing Site.* http://www.themarketingsite.com/live/content.php?Item_ID=1104.

Della Femina, J. 1970. *From the Wonderful Folks Who Gave You Pearl Harbor.* New York: Simon & Schuster.

Duncan, Tom. 2002. *IMC: Using Advertising and Promotion to Build Brands.* Boston: McGraw-Hill.

Elliott, Stuart. 2013. "New Ads for Warhol Museum Offer Different Look at Summer." *New York Times* online (July 15). http://www.nytimes.com/2013/07/15/business/media/new-ads-for-warhol-museum-offer-different-look-at-summer.html.

eMarketer. 2012. "USA Network Brings Advertisers into Its Social TV Journey" (Aug. 17). http://www.eMarketer.com/Article/USA-Network-Brings-Advertisers-its-social-tv-journey/1009271.

Evans, Joel R., and Barry Berman. 1990. *Marketing.* 4th ed. New York: Macmillan.

Frederick, Ben. 2016. "Marketers Struggle with Effective Mobile Ads." *Mobile Marketing Daily* (Apr. 29). http://www.mediapost.com/publications/article/274660/marketers-struggle-with-effective-mobile-ads.

Galin, Michal. 2013. "Magazine Tablet Editions' Top Interactive Ads: How Marketers Got Readers to Get More Info, Open Sites and Download Apps." *Advertising Age* (Mar. 14). http://www.adage.com/print/240326.

Gianatasio, David. 2013. "Prankvertising: Are Outrageous Marketing Stunts Worth the Risks? Liabilities Galore." *Adweek* (Apr. 1). http://www.adweek.com/news/advertising-branding/prankvertising-are-outrageous-marketing-stunts-worth-risks-148238.

Giannini, G. T. 2010. *Marketing Public Relations.* Upper Saddle River, NJ: Pearson.

Gladwell, M. 2002. *The Tipping Point.* New York: Back Bay.

Green, Lucie. 2015. "Move Over Millennials, Here Comes Generation Z." *New York Times* (Sept. 18). https://www.nytimes.com/2015/09/20/fashion/move-over-millennials-here-comes-gen eration-z.html.

Greenberg, Karl. 2012. "Fiat GSTV Creative: Man in Pump." *Marketing Daily* (Dec. 7). http://www.mediapost.com/publications/article/188752/fiat-gstv-creative-man-in-pump.html.

Guth, David W., and Charles Marsh. 2003. *Public Relations: A Values-Driven Approach.* 2nd ed. Boston: Allyn and Bacon.

Hafer, Keith W., and Gordon E. White. 1982. *Advertising Writing.* 2nd ed. St. Paul, MN: West.

Hester, Edward L. 1996. *Successful Marketing Research.* New York: Wiley.

Hof, Robert D. 2016. "Picture This: Marketers Let Emojis Do the Talking." *New York Times* (March 7). http://www.nytimes.com/2016/03/07/business/media/picture-this-marketers-let-emojis-do-the-talking.html.

Hopkins, Jeanne, and Jamie Turner. 2012. "50 Amazing Facts about Mobile Marketing." *HubSpot* (June 29). http://www.slideshare.net/HubSpot/50-mobilefactsdeck62812.

Jaffe, J. 2005. *Life after the 30-Second Spot: Energize Your Brand with a Bold Mix of Alternatives to Traditional Advertising.* New York: Wiley.

Jakacki, Bernard C. 2001. *IMC: An Integrated Marketing Communications Exercise.* Cincinnati: South-Western.

Jay, Ros. 1998. *Marketing on a Budget.* Boston: International Thomson Business.

Jewler, A. Jerome, and Bonnie L. Drewniany. 2005. *Creative Strategy in Advertising.* Belmont, CA: Thomson Wadsworth.

Jones, Susan K. 1998. *Creative Strategy in Direct Marketing.* 2nd ed. Chicago: NTC Business.

Kessler, D. A. 2009. *The End of Overeating.* Emmaus, PA: Rodale.

Kinnard, S. 2001. *Marketing with E-mail.* 3rd ed. Gulf Breeze, FL: Maximum Press.

Klara, Robert. 2016. "5 Reasons Marketers Have Largely Overlooked Generation X." *Adweek* (Apr. 4). http://www.adweek.com/brand-marketing/5-reasons-marketers-have-largely-overlooked-generation-x/170539.

Krugman, Dean M., Leonard N. Reid, S. Watson Dunn, and Arnold M. Barban. 1994. *Advertising: Its Role in Modern Marketing.* 8th ed. Fort Worth, TX: Dryden.

Levinson, J. C. 2001. *Guerrilla Creativity.* New York: Houghton Mifflin.

———. 2007. *Guerrilla Marketing.* 4th ed. New York: Houghton Mifflin.

Levitz, Dena. 2012. "The State of the Art in Designing Content." Newspaper Association of America. http://www.naa.org/~/media/NAACorp/Public%20Files/TopicsAndTools/SenseMakerReports/SenseMaker_May2013.ashx.

Loechner, Jack. 2001. "TV Advertising Most Influential." *Research Brief* (blog, March 23). http://www.mediapost.com/publications/article/147033/tv-advertising-most-influential.html.

Malickson, David L., and John W. Nason. 1977. *Advertising: How to Write the Kind That Works.* New York: Scribner.

McDonald, William J. 1998. *Direct Marketing: An Integrated Approach.* Boston: Irwin/McGraw-Hill.

McLuhan, M. (1964) 1994. *Understanding Media: The Extensions of Man.* Cambridge, MA: MIT Press.

McNeil.-Pearson, Cheryl, and Todd Hale. 2011. "Dissecting Diversity: Understanding the Ethnic Consumer." Nielsen.com (May 15). http://www.nielsen.com/us/en/newswire/2011/dissecting-diversity-understanding-the-ethnic-consumer.html.

Mobile Marketing Association. 2009. "Mobile Marketing." http://www.mmaglobal.com/wiki/mobile-marketing.

———. 2013. "MMA Mobile Video Committee Releases Mobile Video Lexicon to Simplify Communication and Transaction" (May 22). http://www.mmaglobal.com/news/mma-mobile-video-committee-releases-mobile-video-lexicon-simplify-communication-and-transaction.

Monahan, T. 2002. *The Do It Yourself Lobotomy.* New York: Wiley.

Moscardelli, Deborah M. 1999. *Advertising on the Internet.* Upper Saddle River, NJ: Prentice Hall.

Moses, Lucia. 2010. "Death of a Salesman?" *Adweek* (Aug. 22). http://www.adweek.com/news/press/death-salesman-115973.

Nevins, Michael. 2010. "Mobile Display Advertising: Not Just Tiny Banners." *AdExchanger* (Oct. 20). http://www.adexchanger.com/now-serving-mobile/mobile-display-advertising.

Ogden, James R. 1998. *Developing a Creative and Innovative Integrated Marketing Communication Plan: A Working Model.* Upper Saddle River, NJ: Prentice Hall.

Ogilvy, D. 1971. *Confessions of an Advertising Man.* New York: Ballantine.

———. 1985. *Ogilvy on Advertising.* New York: Vintage.

O'Guinn, Thomas C., Chris T. Allen, and Richard J. Semenik. 2003. *Advertising and Integrated Brand Promotion.* 3rd ed. Mason, OH: Thomson South-Western.

O'Toole, J. 1985. *The Trouble with Advertising.* New York: Times Books.

Parente, Donald, Bruce Vanden Bergh, Arnold Barban, and James Marra. 1996. *Advertising Campaign Strategy: A Guide to Marketing Communication Plans.* Orlando: Dryden.

Pavilka, Holly. 2015. "Get Creative with Your Millennial Grocery Shopper." *MediaPost* (Jan. 2). https://www.mediapost.com/publications/article/240997/get-creative-with-your-millennial -grocery-shopper.html/.

Percy, Larry. 1997. *Strategies for Implementing Integrated Marketing Communication.* Chicago: NTC Business Books.

Peterson, Robin T. 1989. *Principles of Marketing.* Orlando: Harcourt Brace Jovanovich.

Platt, Timo. 2012. "Mobile Apps: The Next Big Tech Trend?" *Open Forum* (May 7). https://www. americanexpress.com/us/small-business/openforum/articles/mobile-location-apps-the-next-big-tech-trend.

Raphelson, Samantha. 2014. "From GIs to Gen Z (Or Is It iGen?): How Generations Get Nicknames." *NPR* (Oct. 6). www.npr.org/2014/10/06/349316543/don-t-label-me-origins-of-generational -names-and-why-we-use-them.

Reeves, R. 1981. *Reality in Advertising.* New York: Knopf.

Ries, A., and J. Trout. 2000. *Positioning: The Battle for Your Mind.* New York: McGraw-Hill.

Ross, M. 2010. *Branding Basics for Small Businesses: How to Create an Irresistible Brand on Any Budget.* Bedford, IN: NorLights.

Rothenberg, R. 1994. *Where the Suckers Moon: An Advertising Story.* New York: Knopf.

Samuely, Alex. 2016. "How VR Commerce Could Transform Bricks-and-Mortar Retail." *Mobile Commerce Daily* (May 20). http://www.mobilecommercedaily.com/why-vr-commerce-has-the-potential-to-transform-bricks-and-mortar-retail.

Schultz, D. E. 1996. *Essentials of Advertising Strategy.* 3rd ed. Lincolnwood, IL: NTC Business.

Severn, Steven. 2013. "Guerrilla Cheese Marketing" (blog). www.guerrillacheesemarketing.com.

Shimp, Terence A. 2000. *Advertising Promotion: Supplemental Aspects of Integrated Marketing Communications.* 5th ed. Orlando: Dryden.

Sirgy, Joseph M. 1998. *Integrated Marketing Communication: A Systems Approach.* Upper Saddle River, NJ: Prentice Hall.

Smashing Editorial. 2012. "Guidelines for Mobile Web Development." *Smashing Magazine* (July 2). www.smashingmagazine.com/guidelines-for-mobile-web-development.

Smith, Aaron. 2017. "Record Shares of Americans Now Own Smartphones, Have Home Broadband." Pew Research Center (Jan. 12). http://www.pewresearch.org/fact-tank/2017/01/12/evolution-of-technology/.

Smith, Natasha D. 2016. "The Differences Between Branded Content and Native Advertising." *DMN News* (Apr. 6). https://www.dmnews.com/content-marketing/the-differences-between-branded -content-and-native-advertising/aricle/487434.

Thaler, L. K., and R. Koval. 2003. *Bang! Getting Your Message Heard in a Noisy World.* New York: Doubleday.

Throckmorton, Joan. 1997. *Winning Direct Response Advertising.* 2nd ed. Lincolnwood, IL: NTC Business.

Tode, Chantal. 2013. "Apple Bets Augmented Reality Will Drive Next Wave of Mobile Growth." *Mobile Marketer.com* (March 20). http://www.mobilemarketer.com/cms/news/manufacturers/14996.html.

———. 2012. "Best Buy, Disney Team Up on Mobile Game Promotion for Back-to-School Push." *Mobile Commerce Daily* (Aug. 30). http://www.mobilecommercedaily.com/best-buy-disney-team-up-on-mobile-game-promotion-for-back-to-school-push.

Vascellaro, J. E., S. Schechner, E. Smith, J. A. Trachtenberg, R. Adams, N. Winfield, and E. Steel. 2011. "The Year Ahead for Media: Digital or Die." *Wall Street Journal* (Jan. 4). http://online.wsj.com/news/articles/SB1000142405274870380870457606159179722229.

Vanden Bergh, Bruce, and Helen Katz. 1999. *Advertising Principles.* Lincolnwood, IL: NTC Contemporary.

Vonk, N., and J. Kestin. 2005. *Pick Me: Breaking into Advertising and Staying There.* New York: Wiley.

Walsh, Mark. 2013. "Digital, Alternative Media Revs Forecast to Hit $436B by 2017." *Online Media Daily* (June 19). http://www.mediapost.com/publications/article/202829/#axzz2Xca9KNUo.

Wilcox, Dennis L., Glen T. Cameron, Philip H. Ault, and Warren K. Agee. 2003. *Public Relations Strategies and Tactics.* 7th ed. Boston: Allyn and Bacon.

Index

accelerometers, 290

account executive, 19, 53, 89, 108, 110, 112

active interaction customer service, 278

added price incentives, 191

advertising, 3, 15, 1 8, 34, 134, 138, 145, 149, 159, 165, 177, 198, 230, 231, 238, 240, 241, 244, 248, 249, 256, 257, 260, 261, 267, 270, 272, 277, 289, 290, 298, 300, 307, 314–316, 319, 322, 324, 329

African Americans, 36

alternative media, 10, 16, 24, 225, 236, 240, 257, 286, 290, 300

animation, 227, 263, 305

announcement devices, 238, 241, 323

announcer, 104, 183, 185, 186, 188, 200, 201, 207, 211

appeal, 63, 65, 67, 72, 102, 116, 123, 139, 181, 201, 204, 227, 241, 258, 281, 301, 323

approach, 63, 67, 72, 102, 116, 123, 139, 181, 201, 204, 241, 281, 323

apps, 171, 201, 244, 269, 271, 273, 290, 295, 298, 300, 302, 304, 305, 307, 327

art director, 53, 70, 71, 74, 76, 108

Asian Americans, 37

assorted media mix, 14

astroturfing, 330

audio, 200

audio instructions, 210

augmented reality, 16, 157, 165, 166, 171, 236, 242, 244, 265, 266, 274, 281, 287, 302, 310, 315, 317

Baby Boomers, 37

Baby Busters. *See* Generation X

backgrounder, 145

behavioristic profiles, 16, 34, 56, 230, 302

bellybands, 164

big idea, 60, 61, 70, 122, 183, 204

billboards. *See* outdoor boards

blogs, 261, 267, 272, 278, 279, 315, 323

blow-ins, 166

body copy, 12, 78, 85, 89, 99, 101, 104, 106, 116, 123, 124, 157, 159, 172, 245, 281

bonus packs, 252, 256, 257

bounce-back coupons, 252

bound-in postal reply cards, 166, 237

brainstorming, 69, 71–74, 76, 87, 95–97, 105, 113, 122, 152, 282

brand, 11, 43, 46, 60, 116, 129, 133, 134, 157, 185, 238, 244, 251, 253, 254, 256, 260–263, 267, 269–271, 273, 274, 277, 286, 289, 290, 291, 295, 299, 300, 307, 311, 313, 315, 316, 318, 322, 328, 332, 333

brand attitude, 168, 169

brand awareness, 4, 15–17, 19, 46, 47, 49, 57, 62, 63, 96, 133, 138, 159, 175, 177, 181, 184, 188, 190, 198, 217, 220, 226, 229, 232, 237, 240, 249, 257, 261, 266, 270, 272, 277, 280, 285, 302, 311, 315, 323, 324

brand-centric vehicles, 320

brand equity, 11, 12, 31, 43, 46, 49, 50, 52, 57, 63, 104, 112, 117, 118, 122, 126, 130, 133, 134, 138, 155, 156, 169, 198, 251, 257, 267, 280, 282, 305

brand identity, 46, 96, 97, 122, 123, 129, 166, 283

brand image, 4, 11, 12, 15, 18, 21, 22, 43, 46–48, 51, 62, 67, 71, 85, 89, 97, 98, 102, 104, 110, 112, 116, 118, 121, 123, 129, 133–136, 138, 156, 165–168, 172, 184, 185, 198, 217, 226, 231, 240, 248, 251, 257, 258, 271, 277, 305, 311, 315, 320, 323, 324, 332

brand influencers, 286

brand loyalty, 4, 11, 12, 14, 17, 36, 43, 46, 50, 52, 57, 62, 63, 65, 108, 112, 117–119, 122, 130, 136, 138, 156, 165, 169, 198, 199, 225, 230, 231, 238, 240, 241, 249, 251, 254, 256, 258, 267, 269, 270, 272, 277, 279, 280, 282, 287, 290, 300

brand name, 46, 184, 317

brand name advertising, 151

brand management, 136

About the Author

Robyn Blakeman received her bachelor's degree from the University of Nebraska in 1980 and her master's degree from Southern Methodist University in Dallas, Texas, in 1996.

Professor Blakeman began teaching advertising and graphic design in 1987 with the Art Institutes. As an assistant professor of advertising, she taught both graphic and computer design at Southern Methodist University. As an assistant professor at West Virginia University, she held several positions, including advertising program chair, coordinator of the integrated marketing communication online graduate certificate program, and coordinator of student affairs and curriculum, in addition to developing the creative track in layout and design. She was responsible for designing and developing the first online integrated marketing communication graduate certificate and online integrated marketing communication graduate program in the country.

Professor Blakeman is the author of five other books, including *The Bare Bones of Advertising Print Design*, *The Bare Bones Introduction to Integrated Marketing Communication*, *Strategic Uses of Alternative Media*, *Advertising Campaign Design*, and *Nontraditional Media in Marketing and Advertising* and is coauthor of *The Brains behind Great Ad Campaigns*. She is currently an associate professor at the University of Tennessee, Knoxville, where she teaches advertising design and creative strategy.

Politics and Culture in the Developing World